THE Whole School Library Handbook

EDITED BY
Blanche Woolls
AND
David V. Loertscher

**AMERICAN
LIBRARY
ASSOCIATION**

Chicago   2005

Composition by Priority Publishing using Adobe PageMaker 7.0 on a Windows platform. Selected artwork from ClipArt.com.

Printed on 50-pound white offset, a pH-neutral stock, and bound in 10-point cover stock by McNaughton & Gunn.

The paper used in this publication meets the minimum requirements of American National Standard for Information Sciences—Permanence of Paper for Printed Library Materials, ANSI Z39.48-1992.

Library of Congress Cataloging-in-Publication Data

The whole school library handbook / edited by Blanche Woolls and David V. Loertscher.
    p.   cm.
    Includes bibliographical references and index.
    ISBN 0-8389-0883-7
    1. School libraries—United States—Handbooks, manuals, etc.
I. Woolls, Blanche. II. Loertscher, David V., 1940–
Z675.S3W66 2005
027.8'0973—dc22   2004020198

09   08   07   06   05   5   4   3   2   1

CONTENTS

9 PROGRAM

10 PROMOTION

11 FUNDING

Abbreviations used in this book

AASL	American Association of School Librarians
ADA	Americans with Disabilities Act
ADAAG	Americans with Disabilities Act Accessibility Guidelines
AECT	Association for Educational Communications and Technology
ALISE	Association for Library and Information Science Education
ALSC	Association for Library Service to Children
ASCD	Association for Supervision and Curriculum Development
CEU	Continuing Education Unit
CSAP	Colorado Student Assessment Program
CSD	Children's Services Division (ALA)
DMCA	Digital Millennium Copyright Act
ESEA	Elementary and Secondary Education Act
IASL	International Association of School Librarianship
IFLA	International Federation of Library Associations and Institutions
INTASC	Interstate New Teacher Assessment and Support Consortium
ISTE	International Society for Technology in Education
LIS	Library and Information Science
	Library and Information Student
LM	Library Media
LMC	Library Media Center
LMS	Library Media Specialist
LTA	Library Technical Assistant
NBC	National Board Certification
NBCT	National Board Certified Teacher
NBPTS	National Board for Professional Teaching Standards
NCATE	National Council for Accreditation of Teacher Education
NCES	National Center for Education Statistics
NCREL	North Central Regional Educational Laboratory
NCRTEC	North Central Regional Technology in Education Consortium
NCTE	National Council of Teachers of English
NDEA	National Defense Education Act
NEA	National Education Association
RFP	Request for Proposal
SLMS	School Library Media Specialist
WWW	World Wide Web
YALSA	Young Adult Library Services Association
YASD	Young Adult Services Division

Dedication

This book is dedicated to Elizabeth T. Mahoney, Librarian's Librarian to the faculty and staff in the School of Information Sciences at the University of Pittsburgh, with thanks for introducing Blanche to George Eberhart's first edition of *The Whole Library Handbook*, and to the memory of Margaret I. Rufsvold, who, during our doctoral program at Indiana University, encouraged us to become educators of school librarians, a challenge we continue to enjoy.

A special dedication to the contributors

This book is a collection of articles from books and library journals. It would not exist without the generosity of the authors, editors, and publishers. These professionals have shared their work for the greater good. This is but a small token of appreciation for their contributions here, with a suggestion that this continue in a more concrete way.

Authors, editors, and publishers provide essential information for school librarians. Although it is difficult at any time for large academic libraries serving library and information programs to buy everything needed by school libraries, it is especially important for individual school libraries to obtain copies of professional journals in tough budget times. Journals provide reviews of resources so that librarians can choose the best additions for their collections. Journals provide articles that help justify programs to keep school librarians aware of changes that affect them, such as changes in copyright laws. Journals give information to help librarians understand federal legislation, such as the No Child Left Behind Act. Journals and other publications help librarians keep up with the newest technologies, the newest educational movements, the newest research reports.

The journal publishers and their contact information have been placed at the back of this volume for your convenience in requesting catalogs or in ordering subscriptions.

Preface

The idea for *The Whole School Library Handbook* was borrowed shamelessly from George Eberhart's very creative compilation and distillation of information, facts, hints, and suggestions from the professional world all nicely bound in one volume and used by one of the editors of this book in her Information and Society class.

The reader of this handbook will find articles from school library periodicals filed under a variety of categories roughly related to its parent volume. Here you can meet giants in the school library field, past and present. You will find suggestions for obtaining a school library position in an international setting, creating a rubric for training teachers to use technology, and developing electronic library collections. Suggestions for evaluating your collection and a discussion of the future of e-books are followed by tips for incorporating comic books and graphic novels into your library. Practical solutions abound for the challenges of evaluating your library, using technology, and designing and remodeling your library. Ideas for promoting your library can jump-start your efforts while new perspectives on finding funding could improve your budget. Finally, this volume provides information for school librarians who wish to write for professional publication.

To take yet one more suggestion from George Eberhart, "please keep in mind that many of the selections are only [edited] extracts of longer books or articles. The originals in their full glory are almost always worth seeking out." We hope our choices will please you.

HISTORY

CHAPTER ONE

A new vision

by David V. Loertscher

Twice in this century, school libraries have undergone a major redesign. The first was in the 1960s when book libraries had to be rethought to include a new wave of audiovisual devices and software. The second began in the 1980s with the proliferation of the microcomputer, computer networks, and the Internet. The first redesign required only a shift in contents. The second requires an entire rethinking.

We have usually thought of the library as the "hub of the school," a place where everyone comes to get materials and equipment. Now, however, in the age of technology, the library media center becomes "Network Central," with its tentacles reaching from a single nucleus into every space of the school and into the home. Where we once thought of the library as a single learning laboratory, now the entire school becomes a learning laboratory served by

OLDER LIBRARY CONCEPT

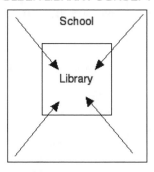

NEWER LIBRARY CONCEPT

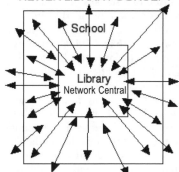

Traditional	New
Print rich	Information rich in every format
Print and AV oriented	Multiple technologies
Centralized (one location)	Centralized/decentralized simultaneously
Rigidly scheduled	Flexibly scheduled
Single-person staff	Professional and technical staff
A quiet, almost empty place	A busy, bustling learning laboratory
Open during school hours	Online services 24 hours/day, 7 days/week

Network Central. It becomes both centralized and decentralized at the same time.

With the advent of high technology and sophisticated networks, many schools have approached technology as if it were separate and distinct from "the library." But after the networks are in and the equipment in place, it soon becomes evident that materials and information merely have new paths to take. The concept of a vast store of materials and information poised to serve teachers and learners remains intact no matter what it is named—the library, the library media center, the information portal, or Network Central.

SOURCE: Adapted from David V. Loertscher, *Reinventing Your School's Library in the Age of Technology*, 2nd ed. (San Jose, Calif.: Hi Willow, 2002), 4. Used with permission.

History of school libraries and library media centers

by Blanche Woolls

The history of the development of libraries and library media centers in schools is relatively short compared with the history of other types of libraries. This program is indeed an educational innovation of the 20th century. The first professionally trained school librarian, Mary Kingsbury, was appointed in 1900.

Prior to 1900, schools built collections of books into libraries to the point that, in 1876, *Public Libraries in the United States of America* reported 826 schools of secondary rank with libraries containing nearly 1 million volumes, or a little over 1,000 volumes per library. Between 1876 and 1900, statistics reported the number of volumes but not the number of high school libraries, so further comparisons are not possible.

Growth in the number of libraries was slow, and growth of the collections was even slower. In 1913, Edward D. Greenman wrote, "Of the 10,000 public high schools in the country at the present time, not more than 250 possess collections containing 3,000 volumes or over." He continued, "The libraries are well managed, and are frequently under the supervision of a trained librarian. The students are given practical training in the use of the library, in cataloging, classification and in the value of reference books."

> PUBLIC LIBRARIES
>
> IN THE
>
> UNITED STATES OF AMERICA
>
> THEIR
>
> HISTORY, CONDITION, AND MANAGEMENT
>
> SPECIAL REPORT
>
> DEPARTMENT OF THE INTERIOR, BUREAU OF EDUCATION
>
> PART I
>
> WASHINGTON
> GOVERNMENT PRINTING OFFICE
> 1876

The condition of school libraries was further described in 1915 by Mary E. Hall, the second person to be appointed a school librarian in the nation when she was named to the Girls' High School in Brooklyn in 1903. She wrote that

> to realize what we mean by a "modern" high school library one must actually see it in action. . . . To have as your visitors each day, from 500 to 700 boys and girls of all nationalities and all stations in life, to see them come eagerly crowding in, 100 or more every 40 minutes, and to

realize that for four of the most important years of their lives it is the opportunity of the library to have a real and lasting influence upon each individual boy and girl, gives the librarian a feeling that her calling is one of high privilege and great responsibility.

The activities were rapidly outgrowing a single reading room, and new facilities were built that included a librarian's office or workroom. At Mary Hall's own school, a library classroom was proposed.

The library classroom adjoins the library reading room and should be fitted up to have as little of the regular classroom atmosphere as possible. It should be made quite as attractive as the reading room and have its interesting pictures on the walls, its growing plants and its library furniture. Chairs with tablet arms on which pupils can take notes, one or more tables around which a small class can gather with their teacher and look over beautiful illustrated editions or pass mounted pictures and postcards from one to another, should surely form a feature of this classroom. . . . For the English work and, indeed for German and French, a Victrola with records which make it possible for students to hear the English and other songs by famous singers, will help them to realize what a lyric poem is. . . . This room will be used by the librarian for all her classes in the use of reference books and library tools, it will constantly service teachers of history, Latin, German, French, and be a boon to the departments of physical and commercial geography. After school it will be a center for club work. Reading clubs can be made more interesting. . . . Classes will be scheduled for a regular class recitation there when a teacher wishes the aid of the room in awakening interest.

She goes on to say that this library had come a long way from "the dreary room with its glass cases and locked doors, its forbidding rows of unbroken sets of standard authors, its rules and regulations calculated to discourage any voluntary reading."

In spite of the enthusiasm of Mary Hall and others, school libraries continued to develop slowly. The impetus to expand secondary school libraries accelerated in the mid-1920s, when regional accrediting agencies specified a high school library with a trained librarian as a requirement for all schools seeking to be accredited by their associations.

Although elementary school library standards were published in 1925, not many elementary schools had libraries or librarians. If monies were allocated for the purchase of library books, these books were kept in individual classroom collections. Size and quality of such collections depended on four criteria. The first two were the budget allocated and the skill of the teacher in selecting suitable books. The third was the stability of the teacher's grade assignment. Many books ordered by a teacher for students in an above-average fourth grade arrived at the end of the school year. In the fall, the teacher's assignment might change to a below-average third grade for whom these selections were inappropriate. The last criterion was the longevity of the teacher in a particular classroom. When teachers left a school, their classroom collections, if not redistributed by the teachers before their departure, were "raided" by other teachers before replacements arrived. The demise of the classroom

---

SCHOOL LIBRARIES FOR
TODAY AND TOMORROW

FUNCTIONS AND STANDARDS

PREPARED BY

The Committees on Post-War Planning

of the

AMERICAN LIBRARY ASSOCIATION

Division of Libraries for Children and Young

People and Its Section

The American Association of School Librarians

MRS. MARY PEACOCK DOUGLAS

Chairman

AMERICAN LIBRARY ASSOCIATION

CHICAGO, 1945

---

collection was a slow and painful process for many teachers who did not wish to lose control over their old favorites.

The Soviet Union's launching of the *Sputnik* satellite in 1957 produced an upheaval in U.S. education and caused the U.S. Congress to provide funds for workshops, special programs, and institutes for training and retraining teachers, and for materials and equipment to supplement classroom textbooks, especially in math, science, and foreign languages. This National Defense Education Act (NDEA) reimbursed school districts 51 cents on each dollar spent, but these materials and equipment were rarely housed in the school library. High school libraries were inadequate in size and staff to add these materials, and elementary schools had no libraries or staff at all.

Several events in the early 1960s had great impact on the expansion of school libraries and the initiation of the concept of elementary school libraries in the United States. The first was the completion of *Standards for School Library Programs*, which updated *School Libraries for Today and Tomorrow*, published in 1945.

Immediately following the publication of the 1960 *Standards*, the American Association of School Librarians (AASL) received a grant from the Knapp Foundation to assist in the development of school libraries. The motion picture *And Something More* was produced to show an excellent example to parents and community members and to encourage support for an elementary school library program. In December 1962, the Knapp Foundation awarded AASL a grant of $1.13 million for a five-year demonstration program to be conducted in phases: pilot programs in five elementary and three secondary schools at locations throughout the United States and library science degree students placed in so-called Knapp Schools to complete their practicum or field experience requirements. When the sites were in full operation, administrators in other school districts were invited to apply for grants to visit the model libraries.

Another event that affected the development of school libraries was publication in 1964 of a report by Mary Helen Mahar and Doris C. Holladay for the U.S. Office of Education showing that fewer than 50% of U.S. elementary schools had libraries. The report attracted the interest of private industry, and additional materials were prepared to bring the plight of school libraries to the attention of the public.

The lobbying efforts of the American Library Association's Washington, D.C., office and the concentrated efforts of key school librarians across the country resulted in passage of the Elementary and Secondary Education Act (ESEA) in 1965. Funds were placed in Title II specifically to purchase library materials. These funds were then combined with local initiatives and volunteer efforts to build school libraries in elementary buildings and to expand libraries in secondary schools.

Nearly 50 years after ESEA Title II, many changes have occurred in school library media centers. Federal funding guidelines were rewritten and categorical restrictions lessened. Library media specialists now competed with other programs, not only for declining federal dollars but also for declining state and local funding. The monies spent for microcomputers further decreased funding for other types of materials and equipment in school libraries, and, in the early 1980s, the school library media picture seemed bleak.

In the late 1980s and early 1990s, site-based management changes meant that many staffs did not include a library media specialist as part of the essential programs for students. In other states, certification requirements came under review, and it was no longer considered necessary for the media center staff person to hold teacher certification.

Mid-decade, the DeWitt Wallace–Reader's Digest Fund provided a $40,000,000 initiative to create model elementary and middle school libraries. This Library Power project, administered by the American Association of School Librarians, included a total of 19 sites, districts which received up to $1.2 million over three years to increase their collections, train staff, and improve facilities. Schools were required to commit to providing full-time library media specialists, maintaining a flexible schedule in the library, and encouraging collaboration between teachers and library media specialists. The funding organization ended this phase in 1998, but was considering alternative projects.

SOURCE: Adapted from Blanche Woolls, *Managing School Library Media Programs* (Englewood, Calif.: Libraries Unlimited, 1999), 2–26. Used with permission.

Pioneers and leaders in library service to young people
by Marilyn L. Miller

These distinguished 20th-century school librarians and their supporters were selected from the *Dictionary of American Library Biography* and its two supplements and from the *Dictionary of Pioneers and Leaders in Library Service to Young People*, all published by Libraries Unlimited in 1978, 1990, 2003, and 2004, respectively.

> These individuals were selected for inclusion in these volumes for their dynamic leadership and contributions to school librarianship. Though now deceased, their vision and contributions at state, regional, and national levels live on in the established school library media programs of today. Through their work in developing school libraries where none existed; through their efforts to develop and implement national and state standards; through their numerous writings, research, teaching, speeches, and endless committee meetings they set extremely high benchmarks for the professionals of today. May it be remembered, however, that those on this list are representatives also of the many in the last century who contributed to the development of what may prove historically to be one of the richest lodes developed for the education of the young.

Eleanor E. Ahlers (1911–1997)

Served as AASL executive secretary during publication of the 1960 *Standards for School Library Programs* and, later, as president of AASL, school library supervisor for the state of Washington, and professor of library science at the University of Washington.

May Hill Arbuthnot (1884–1969)

Universally accepted as an expert on children's literature and valued as a teacher, scholar, writer, lecturer, and advocate for children's reading and quality children's books.

Mildred Leona Batchelder (1901–1998)

Served in both school and public libraries and completed a distinguished career as the first executive secretary of ALA's unit for school and children's services and subsequently as executive director of the Children's Library Association and the Young Adult Services Division.

Lillian Lewis Batchelor (1907–1977)

Charismatic leader of midcentury school library development through work as director of libraries for the School District of Philadelphia and as an early proponent of the instructional materials concept. President of AASL.

Esther Virginia Burrin (1908–1975)

Dynamic director of school libraries for the Indiana Department of Public Instruction; founded the Indiana Association for School Librarians, advocated for professional education, encouraged the development of elementary libraries, and served as president of AASL.

Gladys Louise Cavanagh (1901–1988)

First school library supervisor in Madison, Wisconsin, and pioneer of school library development throughout the state; member of the first governing board of the Children's Cooperative Book Center.

Casper Carl Certain (1885–1940)

A Detroit English teacher respected by school librarians for playing a crucial role in development of the first standards for school libraries: *Standard Library Organization and Equipment for Secondary Schools of Different Sizes* (ALA, 1920).

Margaret Elizabeth Chisholm (1921–1999)

An impressive speaker and writer who worked with great commitment and success in the areas of school librarianship, library education, and higher education administration, concentrating on the future of technology and its applications in librarianship and the need for creative leadership in the profession. President of ALA.

Chisholm

1

Florence Damon Cleary (1896–1982)

Michigan school librarian, university professor, and writer; wrote extensively on reading guidance developed through cooperative relationships between librarians and teachers and on the value of integrating library skills into the curriculum.

Ruby Ethel Cundiff (1870–1972)

Library educator who wrote extensively about the use of multimedia resources in school libraries, the development of programs that meet the reading interests of young readers, and the necessity for cooperation between school librarians and teachers.

Mary Teresa Peacock Douglas (1903–1970)

North Carolina state and school district supervisor of libraries, a legend in her time; a visionary practitioner, evidenced in her work throughout the state and region, and nationally as chair of ALA's School Libraries Section; developer of the 1945 national standards, and author of the internationally accepted *Teacher-Librarian's Handbook* and other publications.

Ruth Marion Ersted (1904–1990)

Dynamic Minnesota state supervisor of school libraries who was a no-nonsense leader and pioneer in AASL activities in the arenas of national standards, planning, and evaluation.

Lucile Foster Fargo (1880–1962)

A "true pioneer" who gave impetus to school library development in the early years of the 20th century, especially the development of high school library service, and whose definitive text *The Library in the School* is yet to be surpassed in school library literature.

Fast

Elizabeth Astrid Trygstad Fast (1931–1977)

An outstanding activist who moved from parent volunteer to professional librarian and dedicated member of ALA and AASL and who used effective committee work to become a "mover and shaker" from the mid-1960s to the mid-1970s.

Phyllis Reid Fenner (1899–1982)

An elementary school librarian noted for excellence but especially remembered for her outstanding publishing career focusing on the role of the elementary school library, suggested selections for children's reading, and anthologies of stories.

Sara Innis Fenwick (1908–1993)

Public children's and school librarian who became professor of library science at the University of Chicago and developed international stature through her publications, coordination of conferences, and presentations on storytelling and cooperation between public and school libraries. President of both ALA's CSD (now ALSC) and AASL.

Ruth Gagliardo (1895–1980)

Although not a librarian, Gagliardo, known as "the Kansas Book Lady" (1942–1966), was a primary leader in the development of library service to children in school and public libraries through her book exhibits, speeches, reviews in print and on the radio, and newspaper and periodical columns on books and libraries and her tireless work outside the state in the national PTA, NEA, and ALA. President of CSD (now ALSC).

Gaver

Mary Virginia Gaver (1906–1992)

School and college librarian, professor of library science, researcher, writer, and leader in all the "direction-setting events" in the school library movement of the mid-1950s and 1960s. President of AASL and ALA.

Inez Mae Graham (1904–1983)

Maryland state supervisor of school libraries midcentury and a true mover and shaker in the era of state and national attention to school library development with standards, statistics, unique development projects, and growth.

Margaret Hayes Grazier (1916–1999)

Incisive and thoughtful writer and speaker whose themes in school librarianship, academe, and professional associations were the importance of professional staff, the curricular work of the professional, and the professional's preparation in the use of a variety of learning resources, including technology.

Mary Evelyn Hall (1874–1956)

Dynamic and committed librarian at Girls' High School, Brooklyn, New York, from 1903 to 1944; worked with C. C. Certain on the 1918 *Standards for High School Libraries*. Major role in founding, and serving as the first chairperson, of ALA's School Libraries Section, which would become AASL.

Alice Sinclair Harrison (1882–1967)

First school librarian in Texas with rank of teacher; by 1921, had developed libraries in all of Austin's schools staffed by at least a half-time teacher-librarian; provided leadership in the state and Southwest region.

1

Frances Stokes Hatfield (1922–1987)

Early proponent of the integration of multimedia resources; developed one of the first facilities for central processing and production of resources and predicted early the powerful impact computers would have on instruction. President of AASL.

Charlotte Irene Hayner (1896–1989)

Michigan school librarian and library educator committed to library service to young adults; served ALA on many committees and was chair of the School Libraries Section (now AASL).

Frances Elizabeth Henne (1906–1985)

Distinguished leader, scholar, inspiring teacher, iconoclast, prophet, dreamer, and commanding speaker. Chaired AASL.

Mary Frances Kennon Johnson (1928–1979)

Visionary activist who led the 1960 School Library Development Project, played a pivotal role in the development of the 1969 and 1975 standards, and developed one of the earliest higher education programs that integrated the instructional materials approach for future school library media specialists.

Johnson

Sarah Lewis Jones (1902–1986)

One of the cadre of dynamic leaders in the Southeast who led school library development in Georgia, in the entire region, and in the nation through her commitment to the implementation of standards and school–public library cooperation.

Margaret Ellen Kalp (1915–1978)

Jones

A distinguished North Carolina library educator who devoted her entire career to school librarianship and the education of school librarians and who still serves as a model for those library educators who wish to become integrated into the life of a university.

Mary A. Kingsbury (1865–1958)

With her appointment to Erasmus High School of Brooklyn, Mary Kingsbury became the first professionally trained librarian to manage a school library in the United States.

Joseph Palmer Knapp (1864–1951)

In December 1962, the Knapp Foundation supported its first major national educational program through a grant of $1,130,000 to ALA that supported

AASL's School Libraries Project, a major force in establishing contemporary school library media programs.

Gladys L. Lees (1902–1986)

A school library director whose career can be reviewed for her administrative acumen, for her work with ALA, AASL, and many educational organizations, and for her prophetic advice about the coming impact of automation.

Hannah Logasa (1879–1967)

A major contributor to school librarianship in the early years of the century who believed that the school library was "not an ornament in the educational process, but a necessity"; compiler of unique and classic bibliographies, several of which are still in print.

Mary Helen Mahar (1913–1998)

A school library leader with great political skill and acumen who served the entire profession well in the critical decades of the 1960s and 1970s from her positions with the U.S. Office of Education.

Franklin K. Mathiews (1872–1950)

First chief scout librarian for the Boy Scouts of America; member of ALA and passionate spokesperson throughout the country on the role good books play in the lives of boys; with Frederick Melcher founded *Children's Book Week*.

McJenkin

Alice Brooks McGuire (1902–1975)

Influential in the field of school librarianship for more than four decades as a practitioner in an experimental school library, as a consultant and speaker, as a leader in professional organizations, and as an author. President of AASL.

Virginia McJenkin (1905–1981)

First city director of media services in the state of Georgia, and one of very few in the nation in 1937, who began early in her career to talk about resource-based teaching, integrated collections, flexible scheduling, and cooperative planning. President of AASL.

Melcher

Frederick Gershom Melcher (1879–1963)

This noted publisher and advocate for librarianship co-founded *Children's Book Week* and was the originator and donor of the Newbery Medal (1922) and the Caldecott Medal (1937).

Margaret E. Nicholsen (1904–1999)

A career librarian dedicated to the profession; active in promoting and advocating for quality school libraries with good multimedia collections, and very involved in various divisions of ALA.

Lucille Nix (1903–1968)

Early experience in school libraries and, later, a broadened career in the field fostered her belief in the necessity for interlibrary cooperation and the strengthening at all levels of support for public and school library service to young people.

Nix

Peggy Leach (Hunley) Pfeiffer (1928–1983)

Widely recognized as a dynamic school library leader in Indiana and nationally; a mentor to young school librarians and an excellent manager who favored the needs of the child over policies, procedures, and rules. President of AASL.

Elnora Marie (Manthei) Portteus (1917–1983)

Recognized for steadfast promotion and development of school library media programs, for her strong commitment to the development of the reading interests of children, and for her opening in 1967 of 117 elementary school libraries in Cleveland, an example of the accomplishments of school library supervisors in large city schools. President of AASL.

Michael L. Printz (1937–1996)

A dynamic and charismatic high school librarian in the latter quarter of the century who crusaded for young adult reading interests through improved and relevant publishing, selection, and reviewing.

Martha Caroline Pritchard (1832–1959)

Pioneer school librarian who served both NEA and NCTE as section president and was one of the organizers of ALA's Normal and High School Librarians Round Table, which became the School Libraries Section (now AASL), which she chaired 1919–1921.

Sara Srygley (1916–1991)

Excellent speaker and storyteller who provided outstanding leadership to the state of Florida as a school librarian, a consultant for school libraries in the state's Department of Education, a university professor, a writer, and a major contributor to AASL during the 1950s and 1960s.

Whitenack

Carolyn Irene Whitenack (1916–1984)

Developed one of the earliest integrated library science/ audiovisual programs for school librarians in higher education; from her position in academe, made notable contributions to the field as teacher, writer, consultant, and speaker. President of AASL.

Marion Bernice Wiese (1905–1977)

Developed a strong city school library program in Baltimore, Maryland, in midcentury; provided outstanding service in her memberships in many professional organizations, including ALA and AASL; was a strong participant in international efforts to develop school libraries throughout the world.

Elizabeth Owen Williams (1897–1988)

Los Angeles city school library director, one of a cadre of midcentury leaders in large cities; supported school library development through a broad array of professional associations, including ALA and AASL. President of AASL.

Williams

Azile May Wofford (1896–1977)

School librarian, academic, and activist in Kentucky and in the nation through her writings on collection development, administration, and the development of policies and procedures through good management and common sense.

Mary Lorraine Woodworth (1926–1986)

Wisconsin school librarian, library school professor, and researcher with a special interest in young adults; provided outstanding national leadership in intellectual freedom issues, especially as they affected young adults. President of YASD (now YALSA).

SOURCE: Created by Marilyn L. Miller, Professor Emerita, School of Education, Department of Library and Information Studies, University of North Carolina at Greensboro.

103 outstanding school librarians

School librarians around the United States were asked to nominate people whom they considered outstanding school librarians. Responses came from participants in the school librarians' list created by Mike Eisenberg and Peter Milbury (LM_NET), and from state association lists. School librarians were asked for names at a variety of professional meetings, including ALA Midwinter. The following list of names includes people who were nominated by more than one individual. In most cases, the wording of the nomination is included. The authors thank those who nominated so many others, although their names have not been placed on this list.

1. **Debbie Abilock** is assistant head of the San Francisco School library, is editor of *Knowledge Quest Online*, and was named in *Library Journal* as a mover and shaker in the Internet world.

2. **Helen Adams**, a high school librarian in Rosholt, Wisconsin, served as president of the Wisconsin Educational Media Association and as president of AASL and writes in the professional literature.

3. **Don Adcock** has served school districts and two professional associations, AASL and IASL, throughout his career. He is an active member who joins the

Abilock

   AASL staff for special projects. He served as treasurer of IASL for many years and continues as chair of the nominating committee.

4. **Susan Ballard** sees a good project and implements it in her Londonderry, New Hampshire, school with a style that should be cloned. It is no surprise that her library won the School Library Media Program of the Year award in 2002.

5. **Dan Barron** is director of the School of Library and Information Science in the College of Mass Communications and Information Studies at the University of South Carolina. He received the South Carolina Association of School Librarians Distinguished Service Award in 2003.

6. **Pamela Barron** is a faculty member at the University of North Carolina at Greensboro and creator of *Jump Over the Moon*, one of the first courses in children's materials prepared for television transmission.

7. **Ruth Bell**, legendary director of school libraries in two districts in Kansas, has led superintendents to provide exemplary school library services for their students.

8. **Priscilla Bennett** has "inspired, enlightened, and educated many library media specialists in Georgia, positively impacting thousands of school media specialists."

9. **Pam Berger**, an experienced school library media specialist, is publisher of *Information Searcher*, a newsletter for integrating technology into the curriculum, and was instrumental in the creation of AASL's National Technology Initiative, ICONnect.

10. **Rebecca Bingham**, for many years in charge of school library services for the Jefferson County (Louisville), Kentucky, schools, most recently served on the U.S. National Commission on Library and Information Services.

11. **Genevieve "Kay" Bishop** is "a fantastic instructor, highly knowledgeable, inspiring, who led both my husband and [me] into pursuing school library media."

12. **Cora Paul Bomar**, a legend in our time, was in the North Carolina State Education agency, and from that venue was responsible, with Mary Helen Mahar and others, for the passage of ESEA Title II in 1965.

13. **Pauletta Bracy** is a professor in North Carolina Central University's School of Library and Information Science and was 2003 president of the

Bishop

   North Carolina Library Association. She is a member of the board of directors of NCATE where she chairs the Finance, Personnel, and Membership Committee.

Gail Bush   Laura Bush

14. **Carolyn Brodie**, at Ohio's Kent State University, is "everything I ever hope to be as a librarian and a human being, and her workshops and classes are extraordinary."

15. **Gail Bush**, high school librarian and, most recently, library educator, is teaching at Dominican University in River Forest, Illinois, and writing for the profession.

16. **Laura Bush**, as First Lady of the United States and former elementary school teacher and school librarian, is in a unique position to strengthen libraries across the country. As the governor's wife in Texas, she initiated programs to honor authors and to foster interest in funding public libraries.

17. **Carolyn Cain** led school library services in her district in Wisconsin while earning national prominence for her work in the American Association of School Librarians and on important ALA Council committees.

18. **Connie Champlin** is a former school librarian, a director of school libraries, an author, and often a consultant to the Indiana Department of Education, developing workshops to provide school librarians with the means to increase student achievement.

19. **L. Anne Clyde**, a native of Australia, is presently professor at the University of Iceland and the creator, designer, and maintainer of the IASL website. She also serves as chair of the School Library Section of IFLA.

20. **Sharon Coatney**, a past president of AASL, was a member of the staff in the Shawnee Mission School District in Kansas. She is currently a consulting editor for Libraries Unlimited.

21. **Barbara Cole**, as head of the Bureau of Library Development in the Pennsylvania State Library, assisted John Emerick, the bureau's school library director, and the librarians of Pennsylvania in securing funding for development and continuation of the Power Libraries project, which provides statewide access to a series of databases and is funded wholly by national and state sources.

22. **Evelyn H. Daniels** is professor and dean emerita, School of Information and Library Science, University of North Carolina at Chapel Hill, where she coordinated the School Library Program. She is a writer, and she has an international reputation as a library educator.

23. **Judie Davie** is media services director for the Guilford County (North Carolina) schools and is the author of articles and books on service to disabled students.

24. **Marvin Davis** for many years before his retirement directed media services in the Heartland Area Education Agency's Media Center, offering exemplary regional services to school librarians and the students in the Des Moines, Iowa, area. His creativity and leadership abilities made this program a model for regional center organizations nationwide.

25. **Doris Epler Dewart**, while director of school library services in the Pennsylvania State Library, initiated and directed the creation of Access

Pennsylvania, a database of library holdings connecting school libraries with all types of libraries and providing a system of local, regional, and state consortia sharing Pennsylvania's resources throughout the Commonwealth.

26. **Gail Dickinson**, assistant professor and coordinator of School Library Media, University of North Carolina at Greensboro, has been a K–12 school librarian in public and private schools, and a district-level library supervisor. She also conducts workshops for school librarians preparing to meet criteria developed by the National Board for Professional Teaching Standards.

27. **Carol Doll**, former school librarian, is now teaching students who wish to become school librarians, and she serves and has served as a mentor to countless students.

28. **Eliza Dresang**, currently professor of Information Studies at Florida State University and formerly the director of Library, Media, and Technology in the Madison (Wisconsin) School District, is a member of the advisory committee of the Laura Bush Foundation for America's Libraries, a foundation granting funds to schools for collection development.

29. **Mike Eisenberg**, cocreator of LM_NET, is well known for his Big Six research skills program designed for student research and critical skills development. He is dean of the Information School at the University of Washington and was, for many years, professor of Information Studies at Syracuse University and director of the Information Institute of Syracuse (including the ERIC Clearinghouse on Information and Technology).

30. **Theresa M. Fredericka**, currently executive director, INFOhio, is responsible for coordinating online data services to schools throughout Ohio. She is an active member of AASL and a proven leader.

31. **Dan Fuller** wears and has worn many hats, including newspaper sportswriter, high school librarian, head of sales for a major software company, bibliophile, and, most recently, professor at San Jose State University.

32. **Carrie Gardner** is on the faculty of the School of Library and Information Science at the Catholic University of America. Formerly a high school librarian at the Hershey School in Hershey, Pennsylvania, she testifies, writes, and speaks on First Amendment issues.

33. **Linda Garrett** is a teacher, elementary school librarian, and high school librarian. She is executive director of Library Media Services in the Dallas (Texas) Independent School District, the 12th-largest school district in the United States, where she has planned 20 new schools and renovated 18, with 18 new schools and 40 renovations in her future. She is an adjunct professor for Texas Woman's University and currently teaches at Texas A&M University–Commerce.

34. **Carolyn Giambra** was librarian in the high school in the Williamsville (New York) Central School District until her recent retirement. She has been active in the New York Library Association and in lobbying for school libraries in New York and Washington, D.C.

35. **Violet Harada** is an incomparable researcher, an LIS educator, and head of the school library certification program at the University of Hawaii at Manoa. She is a creative thinker and a prolific writer.

36. **Frances Jacobson Harris** is librarian at the University Laboratory High School in Urbana, Illinois, where she manages the school collection and the unique relationship between the school library and the university and its library. She has written articles for a range of publications and has presented widely on topics related to young adults, Internet ethics, and digital information.

Harris   Haycock

37. **Ken Haycock**, past president of several associations, including AASL and the Canadian Library Association, was executive director of the International Association of School Librarianship, is a member of the ALA Executive Board, and has held many civic positions in his city.

38. **Dianne McAfee Hopkins**, until recently on the faculty at the University of Wisconsin–Madison, is noted, among other things, for her efforts for intellectual freedom.

39. **Barbara Immroth** left the Central Catholic High School library in Pittsburgh, Pennsylvania, to join the faculty at the University of Texas at Austin. She has served as president of the Texas Library Association.

40. **Barbara Jeffus**, the first school library consultant at the California Department of Education in over two decades, has been a school library media teacher and library program director for a school district and for the Fresno County Office of Education. She has taught library-related courses for Fresno City College, San Jose State University, and Fresno Pacific University.

41. **Doug Johnson**, director of media and technology for the Mankato (Minnesota) public schools, served as an adjunct faculty member at Minnesota State University, Mankato. His teaching experience includes grades K–12 in the United States and in Saudi Arabia, and he is the author of three books and a regular column in *Library Media Connection*.

42. **Deb Kachel**, an adjunct instructor, is, along with others, developing the distance learning program at Mansfield University in Pennsylvania, providing a new online credential program for potential school librarians. She is currently employed by the Ephrata Area (Pennsylvania) School District as a high school media specialist and department chairperson for library media services and was the 2001 recipient of the Pennsylvania School Librarians Association's Outstanding Contributor Award.

43. **Earlene Killeen** is a district-level coordinator of school libraries and is very active in the youth divisions of the American Library Association.

44. **Pam Kramer**, director of educational services at the DuPage Library System in Geneva, Illinois, is responsible for consulting and support to librarians and for the continuing education program. After a long career as an English teacher, building-level

Kramer

media specialist, and district director, she joined AASL as deputy executive director. She is an adjunct faculty member at Marycrest College in Davenport, Iowa, and taught in the LTA program at the College of DuPage. She continues to work diligently toward excellence of school libraries in Illinois.

45. **Ginny Moore Kruse** directed the Cooperative Children's Book Center, a noncirculating library of the School of Education, University of Wisconsin–Madison, and has been honored with ALSC's Distinguished Service Award.

46. **Keith Curry Lance** has been director of the Library Research Service of the Colorado State Library and the University of Denver. He is best known as the lead author of *The Impact of School Library Media Centers on Academic Achievement* (a.k.a., *The Colorado Study*, 1993) and others. In June 2002, he was a featured speaker at the White House Conference on School Libraries.

Lance   Latrobe

47. **Harriet LaPointe** made a major contribution to the development of the concepts of the Library Power project and has provided vision and leadership in AASL. Her vision and her lively personality coupled with a passion for young people have been a shining light for every professional whose life she has touched.

48. **Kathy Latrobe**, library educator and prolific author, continues to provide guidance to school librarians in Oklahoma and nationally.

49. **Kathy LeMaire** has been chief executive of the School Library Association (Great Britain) since 1997. Before taking up her post with the SLA, she was principal librarian with Oxfordshire School Library Service, and LEA (Local Education Authority) advisor for school libraries. She is a member of the executive committee of the International Association of School Librarianship (IASL) where she serves as financial officer, and of the School Libraries and Resource Centers Section of the International Federation of Library Associations and Institutions (IFLA). She was recently elected a Fellow of the Royal Society of Arts.

LeMaire

50. **Deborah Levitov** is coordinator for the Lincoln (Nebraska) Public Schools Library Media Services. She is a doctoral student at the University of Missouri–Columbia and shares responsibilities for practicum placements for the University of Missouri–Columbia.

51. **Karen Lowe**, a former school library media specialist, was an education consultant at the Northwest Regional Educational Service Alliance in Wilkesboro, North Carolina, a consortium of 16 school systems, until she retired. She continues to work with media specialists and beginning teachers on a part-time basis, and she teaches graduate courses in library science at Appalachian State University in Boone, North Carolina.

52. **Jean Lowrie** was dean of the library school at Western Michigan University in Kalamazoo and served as president of ALA and AASL. She organized the International Association of School Librarianship and served as its executive secretary.

53. **Shirley Lukenbill**, a school librarian in Round Rock, Texas, also teaches part-time at the University of Texas at Austin, and, for much of her life, has rescued injured wild animals.

54. **Gloria McClanahan**, when a member of the staff of the Texas Education Agency, led the way for statewide school library services through the development of a test to confirm the competencies of school librarians seeking certification in Texas.

55. **John McGinnis**, one of the most astute and effective lobbyists in the United States, is a junior college librarian in Cerritos, California.

56. **Joy McGregor**, former teacher-librarian, is currently senior lecturer in teacher-librarianship in the School of Information Studies at Charles Sturt University in Wagga Wagga, New South Wales, Australia. Joy taught at Texas Woman's University for nine years before moving to Australia.

57. **Mabel McKissick**, cofounder of the Coretta Scott King Award, is a past president of the Connecticut Educational Media Association.

58. **Carroll Makemson**, coordinator of library media services in the Liberty (Missouri) public schools and writer of the proposal that won her district the National School Library Media Program of the Year award for 2003, is one of the most effective leaders in the school library media field.

59. **Jackie Mancall** is a past president of AASL and received the association's Distinguished Service Award. A professor on the faculty of Drexel University, Jackie has written some of the most provocative articles concerning school librarianship in print today.

60. **Joe Marrone**, a former middle school librarian, is as close to being a Renaissance man as can be found today. His expertise in technology resulted in a multimillion-dollar grant to bring cutting-edge technology to the Quaker Valley School District in Sewickley, Pennsylvania. In this district, every student in grades 3 through 12 has a school-provided computer and wireless connections in the home, the school, and the public library.

61. **Anne Masters**, one of the finest school library supervisors in the country, built the school library program in Norman, Oklahoma. As a result of her leadership, every school library is now served by professional librarians. The collaborative programs built in the district were models for the entire state and the nation.

62. **Peter Milbury**, high school librarian at Chico (California) Senior High School, developed LM_NET. He is also an instructor and coordinator of the Library Media Teacher Service Credential Program in the Department of Education at California State University, Chico.

63. **Andrea Miller**, current director of the library program at Clarion University, worked diligently with the Pennsylvania Department of Education to help create the Pennsylvania Toolkit for school librarians.

64. **Marilyn Miller** is a past president of ALSC, AASL, and ALA and a library educator who coordinated the most recent AASL *Guidelines* process.

65. **Paula Montgomery**, cocreator and coeditor of *School Library Media Activities Monthly*, worked for a time in the Maryland State Department of Education.

66. **Jackie Morris**, a past president of AASL, served on the ALA Council. Upon retiring from her position in the Indiana Department of Public Instruction, she became a public librarian.

67. **Celeste DiCarlo Nalwasky**, formerly the LMS at Peters Township Middle School, McMurray, Pennsylvania, is currently teaching part-time at Clarion State University of Pennsylvania where her energy level is to be coveted and her love for school librarianship is readily apparent.

Montgomery

68. **Toni Negro** is a retired media specialist from the Montgomery County (Maryland) School District. She served in several positions in that district and remains an active member of ALA and AASL.

69. **Dianne Oberg** is professor of teacher-librarianship in the Faculty of Education at the University of Alberta in Canada where she currently serves as chair of the Department of Elementary Education. Before coming to the university, she worked as a classroom teacher and teacher-librarian in the public school system. Dianne is editor of the international journal *School Libraries Worldwide* and is an active member of school library associations at local, national, and international levels.

70. **Marjorie Pappas** came into the school library field with a strong technology and curriculum background. Her expertise affected many national discussions in AASL as the profession concentrated on building impact in national guidelines. Her information literacy model, coauthored with Ann Tepe, has a national following for its vision of what information literacy contributes to learning. Her students have been enriched by her insight and high expectations.

71. **Patsy Perritt**, until she retired from her faculty position at Louisiana State University, maintained the *School Library Journal* biannual reporting of school library certification programs in each state.

72. **Elizabeth Polk** is currently library supervisor in the Austin (Texas) Independent School District where she has participated in the planning and construction of many new buildings as the population of that district continues to grow.

73. **Sandy Schuckett**, middle school librarian, has been an active and effective participant in legislative activities at the local, state, and national levels.

74. **Jan Segerstrom**, district coordinator of media services and library media specialist of the Jackson Hole (Wyoming) High School, Teton County School District #1, is active at the state level.

75. **Carol Simpson**, professor in the School of Library and Information Science at the University of North Texas, places practicum students in Texas and Thailand. She is an expert and prolific writer on copyright.

Schuckett

76. **Bob Skapura**, recently retired as director of Learning and Learning Resources at Los Medanos College, is recognized as a leader in bibliographic instruction and a pioneer in library automation, a technology

guru beginning with the earliest of microcomputers. His early soft-ware package, *Overdue Writer*, helped librarians manage overdue no-tices, and his *Bibliography Writer* helped students create bibliographic citations. He published *The Cover Story Index*, *The AV Catalog Writer*, and *The Skills Factory*.

77. **Paul Spurlock**, retired for some time now, deserves recognition here for his responsibility in furthering school library media services in the Iowa Department of Education. He initiated the development of evaluative studies confirming the excellence of the Iowa Area Education Agency Media Centers and funded workshops to bring school administrators, school librarians, public library administrators, and public librarians to-gether to discuss joint services.

78. **Barbara Stein** is a professor in the School of Library and Information Science at the University of North Texas where she encourages the de-velopment of school librarians for Texas schools.

79. **Jack Alton Strawn**, "a true master of library and information science, engages students with his memorable book talks and demonstrates lim-itless energy that produces brain-based lessons which combine learning and laughter."

Stripling

80. **Barbara Stripling**, past president of AASL, led the Library Power project in the Chattanooga, Tennes-see, schools, returned to Fayetteville, Arkansas, to become the school district library director, and later moved to New York City as director of library pro-grams at New Visions for Public Schools, a local edu-cation fund. An established author of numerous books and articles and a past president of AASL, she cur-rently serves on the ALA Executive Board.

81. **Peggy Sullivan**, past president of ALSC and ALA, has been a faculty member and dean, and was ex-ecutive director of the American Library Association. She was di-rector of the Knapp Project for AASL in the mid-1960s and taught school librarians at the University of Pittsburgh. She also was a member of the faculty at the University of Chicago and at North-ern Illinois University.

82. **Esther Swink** has been a first-grade teacher, a librarian in elementary, middle, and high school libraries, and a director of media services for the Nashville, Tennessee, school system. She joined Trevecca Nazarene University to design and implement a master of library and information science degree program with emphasis on children and youth, and has been named the dean of the School of Education.

83. **Ann Symons**, a former school librarian from Ju-neau, Alaska, is a past president of the American Library Association and a tireless supporter of in-tellectual freedom.

Symons

84. **Marge Tassia**'s professional career was spent in an education program teaching school librarians and observing them in their practicum situations. As president of the Pennsylvania School Librarians Association and a winner of its Outstanding Con-tributor Award, she has been a mentor to many school librarians.

85. **Lucille Thomas**, legendary director of school library services in the New York City schools, initiated that city's storytelling event to encourage children to tell stories, spearheaded the national recognition of School Library Media Month, served on the ALA Council and Executive Board, and continues to serve the library community as president of the board of trustees of the Brooklyn Public Library.

86. **Marge Thomas** took an early retirement from the Fairbanks, Alaska, schools, joined the staff at NewsBank, left there to pursue a doctorate, and is now on the faculty of the School of Library and Information Science at Louisiana State University in Baton Rouge.

87. **Ross Todd**, associate professor in the library and information science program in the School of Communication, Information, and Library Studies at Rutgers, was formerly senior lecturer in the Department of Media Arts, Communication and Information at the University of Technology in Sydney, Australia. He had previously been a secondary teacher in New Zealand and a teacher-librarian in Australia. He is a superb researcher, prolific writer, and sought-after speaker worldwide, and Rutgers is fortunate to have him as a part of its Center for International Scholarship in School Librarianship.

88. **Ruth Toor** and **Hilda K. Weisburg**, coeditors of *School Librarian's Workshop* and coauthors of 11 books, are so closely associated that it is impossible to place them separately in this list. Ruth served as president of AASL and as a member of the ALA Council and was librarian at the Southern Boulevard School in Chatham, New Jersey, while Hilda is a library media specialist in the Morristown (New Jersey) High School.

89. **Phil Turner**, professor and dean in Library and Information Sciences as well as associate vice president for academic affairs for distance education at the University of North Texas, has been a classroom teacher in Florida, a school library media specialist in Wisconsin, and a dean at the University of Alabama.

90. **Phyllis Land Usher** joined the Indiana Department of Education and has been responsible for the steady growth of funding for staff there and for projects increasing excellence of school library service to students in that state.

91. **Joyce Valenza**, director of the library at Springfield Township High School in Erdenheim, Pennsylvania, is also an adjunct instructor at Mansfield University in its Distance Learning master's degree program. Joyce has been a Library of Congress American Memory Fellow as well as author of *Power Tools* (ALA), bringing together all the forms any school librarian could wish to use.

92. **Dawn Vaughn**, director of the Cherry Creek High School library in Greenwood Village, Colorado, and president of AASL, led her school to win the School Library Media Program of the Year award in 2003.

93. **Idella Washington** has been president of her state school library association and her state library association and has served on the AASL board.

94. **Peggy Watson** is currently an elementary school media specialist in South Carolina, but she has been a middle school media specialist, a high school teacher, and a junior college librarian, and was the first female librarian at the Citadel. As a director of a county library, she was responsible for overseeing the planning and construction of the county library headquarters.

95. **Ann Carlson Weeks**, former executive director of ALSC, AASL, and YALSA as well as director of school libraries in the Chicago public schools, is now a member of the faculty at the University of Maryland where she is overseeing a special project to digitize children's literature around the world.

96. **Judy Westerman** is director of school library services in the Pittsburgh public schools where she has developed and maintained exemplary library programs in a district dealing with the problems of older school buildings, inner-city schools, and high administrator turnover.

97. **Merchuria C. Williams** is media services coordinator in the Atlanta (Georgia) public schools. She was president of the Georgia Association of Educators and currently serves on AASL committees.

98. **Terry Young**, school librarian in Crescent City (New Orleans), writes a column for *Knowledge Quest*.

Yucht

99. **Alice Yucht**, librarian at the Heritage Middle School in Livingston, New Jersey, also teaches at Rutgers. Creator of the Flip It! framework for problem solving, she has also taught in the classroom and is a sought-after speaker, writer, and trainer.

100. **Nancy Zimmerman** has school library experience in Alaska, California, and Texas. As a faculty member in Buffalo, New York, she received the SUNY Chancellor's Award for Excellence in Teaching. She is a widely published author and has served as president of the New York Library Association and as treasurer and president of AASL.

School librarians' honor roll

The following individuals have made outstanding contributions to school librarianship through their creativity, gifts, and other contributions to the field:

Hartzell

1. **Gary Hartzell**, honorary school librarian, through his constant support of school libraries and librarians, has provided leadership by constantly showing school librarians the path to success. He is presently professor of education at the University of Nebraska at Omaha. He has been a high school teacher, an assistant principal, and a principal in California. His research in the last few years has concentrated on roles and relationships, particularly among school librarians and their colleagues. He is an internationally known school library advocate and speaker on librarian–principal relationships, and he spoke at the White House Conference on School Libraries in June 2002. He is a member of the Laura Bush Foundation for America's Libraries and a monthly columnist for *School Library Journal.*

2. **Mort Schindel**, founder of Weston Woods, gave children's and school librarians filmstrips, 16 mm films, and videos transforming children's books into audio and visual experiences.

SOURCE: Participants in LM_NET, and state, national, and international library associations.

National School Library Media Program of the Year winners

1

For the past 41 years, a committee of the American Association of School Librarians has honored school districts with exemplary school library programs. In 1984, the award was divided into two categories: large school districts (10,000 and more students) and small school districts (9,999 and fewer). A third category, single school, was added in 1987. The winners receive a cash award and a crystal obelisk at AASL's annual award luncheon.

2004 Northside Independent School District, San Antonio, Texas (Large District)
Boston Arts Academy/Fenway High School, Massachusetts (Single School)
Lois Lenski Elementary School, Littleton, Colorado (Single School)

Boston Arts Academy/Fenway H.S. library

2003 Millard, Kansas City, Kansas (Large District)
Liberty (Missouri) Schools (Small District)
Cherry Creek High School, Greenwood Village, Colorado (Single School)
2002 James River High School, Midlothian, Virginia (Single School)
2001 No awards given
2000 Irving Independent School District, Irving, Texas (Large District)
Londonderry School District #12, Londonderry, New Hampshire (Small District)
New Trier Township High School, Winnetka, Illinois (Single School)
1999 Lincoln Public Schools, Lincoln, Nebraska (Large District)
1998 Hunterdon Central Regional High School, Flemington, New Jersey (Single School)
1997 Gwinnett County Public Schools, Lawrenceville, Georgia (Large District)
Iowa City Community School District, Iowa City, Iowa (Small District)
Timothy Dwight Elementary School, Fairfield, Connecticut (Single School)
1996 Maine Township High School West, Des Plaines, Illinois (Single School)
1995 Southern Bluffs Elementary School, La Crosse, Wisconsin (Single School)
Smoky Hill High School, Aurora, Colorado (Single School)
1994 Duneland School Corporation, Chesterton, Indiana (Small District)
Providence Senior High School, Charlotte, North Carolina (Single School)
Lakeview Elementary School, Neenah, Wisconsin (Single School)
1993 Blue Valley School District USD 229, Shawnee Mission, Kansas (Large District)

Indian Prairie School District 204, Naperville, Illinois (Small
    District)
1992 Fulton County School System, Atlanta, Georgia (Large District)
    Manhattan/Ogden Unified School District 383, Kansas (Small District)
1991 Irving Independent School District, Irving, Texas (Large District)
    Beecher Road School, Woodbridge, Connecticut (Single School)
1990 Greensboro Public Schools, Greensboro, North Carolina (Large
    District)
    Cherry Creek High School, Greenwood Village, Colorado (Single
    School)
1989 Norman Public Schools, Norman, Oklahoma (Large District)
    Middletown Enlarged City School District, New York (Small
    District)
    David A. Hickman High School, Columbia, Missouri (Single School)
1988 West Bloomfield Schools, Michigan (Large District)
    Round Rock Independent School District, Round Rock, Texas (Small
    District)
1987 Independent School District 47, Sauk Rapids, Minnesota (Large
    District)
    Community Consolidated School District 62, Des Plaines, Illinois
    (Small District)
    Monterey Peninsula Unified School District, California (Single
    School)
1986 District 108, Highland Park, Illinois
1985 Shoreham-Wading River School District, New York
1984 Riverside Brookfield Township High School, Riverside, Illinois
    (Large District)
    Richmond School System, Richmond, Virginia (Small District)
1983 No award given
1982 Shaker Heights City School District, Shaker Heights, Ohio
1981 Blue Valley School District USD 229, Shawnee Mission, Kansas
1980 Irvine Unified School District, Irvine, California
1979 Greenwich Public Schools, Greenwich, Connecticut
1978 Cobb County Public Schools, Marietta, Georgia
1977 Los Alamitos School District, Los Alamitos, California
1976 Littleton Public Schools, Littleton, Colorado
1975 Rochester City Schools, Rochester, New York
1974 Cedar Rapids Community Schools, Cedar Rapids, Iowa
1973 Duneland Community Schools, Chesterton, Indiana
1972 Atlanta Public Schools, Atlanta, Georgia
1971 Leflore County Schools, Mississippi
1970 Alhambra School District, Phoenix, Arizona
1969 Iowa City Community Schools, Iowa City, Iowa
1968 San Ramon Valley School District, Danville, California
1967 Cleveland Public Schools, Cleveland, Ohio
1966 Albuquerque Public Schools, Albuquerque, New Mexico
1965 Dade County Public Schools, Florida
1964 Durham County Schools, North Carolina
1963 Anne Arundel County Schools, Maryland

SOURCE: This list was compiled by AASL and Follett Library Resources, sponsor of the
    program.

The *SLJ* spending survey

by Marilyn L. Miller and Marilyn L. Shontz

Media specialists are feeling the effects of the nation's economic downturn, according to *School Library Journal*'s latest survey on spending, resources, and services. Media library spending from all sources, which was $14,047 for 1999–2000, fell to $13,341 in 2001–2002 (see table 1). And while book expenditures per pupil have doubled in the last 12 years—rising by 9% since 1999–2000 to $8.89—the increase is not enough to keep pace with higher book prices and aging collections. Similarly, total median book spending per school has inched up to $6,000, a paltry increase of less than 1% since our last survey. Despite the sluggish figures, there are reasons for guarded optimism in other areas of the profession.

Table 1. Mean and Median Expenditures for All Resources, All Funding Sources

2001–2002	Number Responding	Mean	Median
Funding			
Total all local funds	583	$15,707	$11,236
Total all federal funds	155	5,318	3,000
Total all gift/fund-raising	334	2,492	1,161
Expenditures (all funds)			
Books	577	9,565	7,100
Periodicals	574	1,423	1,000
AV resources/equipment	484	2,647	1,531
Computer resources/equipment	454	6,426	2,800
Total Expenditures	588	18,385	13,341

Library media specialists continue to provide valuable services, using their information acumen to influence the school's purchase of other resources (see table 2). Eighty-six percent of respondents, for example, keep teachers abreast of new resources on the market, and more than two-thirds say they offer information-literacy or computer-literacy skills programs that are integrated with the school curriculum. Fifty-seven percent of those surveyed also assist their school curriculum committees, recommending resources and programs. More media specialists are also providing students and teachers with interlibrary loan services—63% in the present survey, compared to only 57% in 1999–2000. While increases are reported in many library services, two areas have seen a significant decline in activity. Only 36% of librarians help parents understand the importance of showing their children the benefits of lifelong learning and reading, a drop of 13%, and just one-third plan or conduct workshops to help teachers evaluate, select, and use resources, a decrease of 11%.

Since developing quality services and programs involves a great deal of thought, creativity, and planning, the increase in the amount of cooperative planning between librarians and teachers is encouraging (see table 3). Media specialists in elementary, middle, and high schools report a 13% increase in the total number of weekly hours spent planning, from 3.42 hours in 1999–2000 to 3.94 hours in 2001–2002. During the same period, there was also an upturn in total hours spent on formal planning, from .97 hours to 1.24 hours.

Table 2. Services Typically and Currently Offered by LMS

N = 562	Number Offering Service	Percentage Offering Service
Offers a program of information/computer skills instruction integrated with the school curriculum	380	68%
Helps parents realize the importance of assisting their children to understand the benefits of lifelong learning and reading, listening, and viewing for pleasure as well as for information	203	36
Plans or conducts workshops for teachers in the evaluation, selection, and use of resources	186	33
Assists the school curriculum committee by recommending resources and media program activities for units and curriculum topics, transmissions, and related activities in school	312	56
Provides teachers with information about new resources to be considered for purchase	485	86
Provides interlibrary loan service to students and teachers	353	63
Coordinates video production and dissemination activities in school	149	27
Coordinates cable TV, satellite transmissions, distance education, and/or closed-circuit TV	206	37

And school librarians at all levels spent more time in informal planning last year, except in high school media centers, where they spent slightly less time with this activity.

Cooperative planning in elementary schools has increased from 79% in 1999–2000 to 87% in 2001–2002 for those with flexible schedules. However, those with combination fixed and flexible schedules report a drop in planning time from 82% to 52% during the same period. Sixty-seven percent of all elementary library media specialists report formal and informal planning with teachers, an increase from 49% in 1999–2000.

Many library media specialists are also participating in leadership activities, which are essential to increasing their influence on the school's instructional program. Almost all respondents say they informally communicate with their principals each week, and 18% say they formally meet with them once a week. Of the 77% of school librarians who participate in their own profes-

Table 3. LMS/Teacher Instructional Planning: Activity by Grade Level

2001–2002	Mean Hours of Formal Instructional Planning	Mean Hours of Informal Instructional Planning	Mean Hours of Total Planning
Elementary (n = 187)	0.96	2.27	3.23
Jr. High/Middle (n = 170)	1.55	2.82	4.37
High School (n = 181)	1.30	3.20	4.50
K–8 and Other (n = 55)	0.98	2.19	3.17
Total	1.24	2.70	3.94

sional development leadership activities, 63% serve in leadership roles in state, regional, and national associations, and 59% serve on state, district, or school curriculum and/or planning committees. Nearly half of respondents prepare and distribute annual reports for the library media program, up from 44% in 1999–2000. A total of 19% report having established and maintained a library media advisory committee, a key component in collaborating with teachers and cultivating their understanding of the media program.

The growing cooperation between school and public libraries is another noteworthy trend. When asked which, if any, of seven joint public–school library activities they participate in, 25% or more of school librarians say they're involved in five out of seven. Sixty percent of respondents indicate that they promote and support summer reading club activities, and one-half say they maintain ongoing communications with the public library through e-mail messages, phone conversations, or faxes. About one-fourth say they distribute and exchange newsletters and promote visits to the public library.

Although a modest 12% of schools and 6% of media centers currently use wireless technology, 54% of schools and media centers access their online resources via local area networks and 58% through wide area networks. The commitment to finding communications tools and software remains strong; purchases of CD-ROMs and software have increased by $125 to $800 per media center since 1999–2000. Online resources are now nearly ubiquitous at most of our nation's schools: nearly 100% of students have access to state-funded databases and 91% of school librarians say the Internet is available for teaching and learning. Another 87% of media specialists use the Web when searching for references or information. At the same time, 81% say they seek online help with reading and book selection. The use of distance education and videoconferencing has held at a steady 5%, and audiovisual spending rose by only $51 per school. Even cable television has seen an increase, with 45% of media centers and schools using the service to supplement instruction, a 12% hike from 1999–2000. By comparison, local broadcast television use among schools and media centers is down to 27% from 55% in 1999–2000. The biggest drop on the local level, however, was in web product spending, which dipped from $2,000 in 1999–2000 to $1,737 in 2001–2002. Although local building funds for online resources have declined, it is important to note that it is now common for districts to purchase many of these resources for local schools. Some 96% of all students have access to state-funded electronic databases. In addition to these databases, many students also have access to EBSCO, SIRS Researcher/Discoverer, and InfoTrac.

Most money for school library resources comes from local districts. In addition, about half of the 593 media specialists who responded to our survey say their funding is bolstered by gifts or fund-raising projects, which totaled $1,161 per school last year, down from $1,305 in 1999–2000. About 96% use some outside funds to help pay for Internet/telecommunications costs; 70% use some for web products; 31%, AV/computer equipment; and 20%, computer software. Only 25% of respondents receive federal funds for media centers, but that money rose to $3,499, a $400 increase since 1999–2000.

While the number of media specialists working in schools remains relatively unchanged from previous surveys, there has been a modest $2,200, or 5%, median salary increase in the last two years. Elementary school librarians earn an average annual salary of $43,000, while those in middle school and high school earn about $48,000. Indeed, middle and high school library media specialists have fared somewhat better, with high school librarians earning $3,500 more than they did in 1999–2000 and middle school librarians earning $3,000 more. These two school levels earn almost $10,000 more than media specialists listed in our "other" category. Years of teaching experience has dropped to 14 years from 20 years in 1999–2000, probably due to the beginning stages of the baby boomers' retirement phase. During the same period, there was a one-year drop in the experience of school librarians, from 13 to 12 years.

Although the median number of media specialists per school remains the same, there are changes in the size of support staff. Middle and senior high school libraries have fewer student assistants than their elementary school counterparts and the same number of support staff and paid clerks as they reported last survey. However, support staff in elementary schools has increased from half time to full time in the typical school. Although all schools may use adult volunteers to some extent, only elementary and middle schools rely on them.

Conclusion

We are sympathetic with those library media specialists who must wince when they see the length of our present surveys—after all, our first report for 1981–1982 was a much shorter document. We feel, however, that our research provides the profession with a great deal of information about library media specialists and their work. Many librarians write us notes, thanking us, criticizing us (but, thankfully, they've filled out the surveys anyway), and sharing good and bad times. Some tell us about their dismal funding, the loss of clerical staff, and the diminution of media programs as their districts decide to assign one media specialist to a number of elementary school library media centers. Others tell us how great their jobs are, how rewarding it is to be an active, viable part of their school's instructional program, and how good it is to have a job working with young people.

T. S. Eliot noted that he had measured his life in coffee spoons. We have measured a large, rewarding part of our lives for the past 20 years with *SLJ*'s surveys. Thanks to all who have responded.

SOURCE: Adapted from Marilyn L. Miller and Marilyn L. Shontz, "The *SLJ* Spending Survey," *School Library Journal* 49 (October 2003): 52–59.

PROFESSIONALISM
CHAPTER TWO

Information power: What media specialists do

As *teacher*, the library media specialist collaborates with students and other members of the learning community to analyze learning and information needs, to locate and use resources that will meet those needs, and to understand and communicate the information the resources provide. An effective instructor of students, the library media specialist is knowledgeable about current research on teaching and learning and skilled in applying its findings to a variety of situations—particularly those that call upon students to access, evaluate, and use information from multiple sources in order to learn, to think, and to create and apply new knowledge. A curricular leader and a full participant on the instructional team, the library media specialist constantly updates personal skills and knowledge in order to work effectively with teachers, administrators, and other staff—both to expand their general understanding of information issues and to provide them with specific opportunities to develop sophisticated skills in information literacy, including the uses of information technology.

As *instructional partner*, the library media specialist joins with teachers and others to identify links across student information needs, curricular content, learning outcomes, and a wide variety of print, nonprint, and electronic information resources. Working with the entire school community, the library media specialist takes a leading role in developing policies, practices, and curricula that guide students to develop the full range of information and communication abilities. Committed to the process of collaboration, the library media specialist works closely with individual teachers in the critical areas of designing authentic learning tasks and assessments and integrating the information and communication abilities required to meet subject matter standards.

As *information specialist*, the library media specialist provides leadership and expertise in acquiring and evaluating information resources in all formats; in bringing an awareness of information issues into collaborative relationships with teachers, administrators, students, and others; and in modeling for students and others strategies for locating, accessing, and evaluating information within and beyond the library media center. Working in an environment that has been profoundly affected by technology, the library media specialist both masters sophisticated electronic resources and maintains a constant focus on the nature, quality, and ethical uses of information available in these and in more traditional tools.

As *program administrator*, the library media specialist works collaboratively with members of the learning community to define the policies of the library media program and to guide and direct all the activities related to it. Confident of the importance of the effective use of information and information technology to students' personal and economic success in their future lives, the library media specialist is an advocate for the library media program and provides the knowledge, vision, and leadership to steer it creatively and energetically in the 21st century. Proficient in the management of staff, budgets, equipment, and facilities, the library media specialist plans, executes, and evaluates the program to ensure its quality both at a general level and on a day-to-day basis.

SOURCE: Adapted from "The Vision," chapter 1 in *Information Power: Building Partnerships for Learning* (Chicago: American Library Association, 1998), 4–5.

Is the library profession over-organized?

by George S. Bobinski

Some basic facts:

- There are at least 152 library associations in the United States with a total of about 228,000 members.
- Fifty-six of these are national organizations (or international but based here and with many U.S. members) totaling 130,813 members.
- Seven are regional library associations with 5,248 members.
- Fifty are state library associations (plus the District of Columbia, Guam, Puerto Rico, and the U.S. Virgin Islands) with 67,002 members.
- Thirty-five are state library associations limited to school library media members, with 25,237 members.

There are local library organizations and clubs, many active library-school alumni associations, and nearly 20 related professional organizations to which many or a significant number of librarians belong, such as the American Society for Information Science and Technology. Some librarians in the United States are active in international groups, like the International Federation of Library Associations and Institutions, based outside of the country. Finally, there are almost 500 library networks and consortia on the national, regional, state, and local level—often performing many of the functions of professional library associations.

National library associations

From 1876 to 1942 there seems to have been a normal and expected pattern of development as libraries grew and librarians became more specialized. After the establishment of ALA in 1876, the next four library associations established were the Medical Library Association (1898), the American Association of Law Libraries (1906), the Special Libraries Association (1909), and the Association for Library and Information Science Education (1915). Medical, law, and special librarians remain the three largest national groups after ALA. ALISE began as the Association of American Library Schools with only institutional membership until 1947 when it began accepting personal memberships.

ALA itself began to subdivide as the profession became more specialized. Its largest division, the Association of College and Research Libraries, was established in 1889. The American Library Trustee Association (now the Association of Library Trustees and Advocates) was founded in 1890. The year 1900 saw the establishment of an ALA Cataloging and Classification Division, while a Work with Children Section had its origins in 1901. Thus began specialization by type of work as well as the representation of library supporters.

Between the two world wars, another five organizations were established. The Library Public Relations Council was the first example of an independent library association based on type of work within libraries. The Catholic Library Association was the first of many religious library organizations that would be established in the future.

ALA continued to form new divisions as libraries and librarians grew more specialized. In 1930, the Young Adult Services group was established. This was followed by the Public Library Association in 1944 and the American Association of School Librarians in 1951. (AASL had begun as a section of the Division for Children and Young People in 1941.)

Currently ALA is made up of 11 divisions and 19 round tables with a total of 1,220 committees and 55 autonomous geographic chapters. The ALA pattern is similar to other large professional associations.

State library associations

The New Hampshire Library Association was established in 1889 by a group of 50 prominent legislators, lawyers, judges, bankers, manufacturers, and one librarian (the head of the Dartmouth College Library) to promote the usefulness of the state's libraries.

In looking at the chronological listing by founding date, 42 of the 48 states had a library association by 1915. Five more were established in the 1920s, including an association in Hawaii. One additional state library association was established in the 1930s, two in the 1940s, and one in the 1960s. The last was in Alaska, which became a state in 1959.

What does all of this mean?

First of all, it shows we have a rich heritage of professional growth. Since 1876, the profession has developed a well-organized and complex structure of organizations supporting its practitioners.

Are we over-organized? Perhaps we are, in some areas.

One could question the duplication of library associations in the 34 states and the District of Columbia, where one group exists for school library media specialists and another for the remaining types of librarians.

One could also question the structure in New England, where there is a New England Library Association, a New England Educational Media Association, six state library associations, and six school library media state associations.

On the other hand, such diversity is not all that unusual compared to other groups. For example, the legal, nursing, and social-work professions show the same patterns. Each of them has a large national professional association with many divisions, state associations (in some cases also regional and local), and specialized national associations.

Our professional associations are themselves becoming digital and virtual associations, particularly through their web pages and use of the Internet for continuing education. It is truly a new era in professional association development.

SOURCE: Adapted from George S. Bobinski, "Is the Library Profession Over-Organized?" *American Libraries* 31, no. 9 (October 2000): 58–60. Used with permission.

National, state, and local school library organizations

National organizations

American Association of School Librarians (AASL)
　　http://www.ala.org/aasl/
Association for Educational Communications and Technology (AECT)
　　http://www.aect.org/
Association for Library Service to Children (ALSC)
　　http://www.ala.org/alsc/
Association for Supervision and Curriculum Development (ASCD)
　　http://www.ascd.org/

State and local school library organizations

Alabama
Alabama Instructional Media Association
　　http://www.alaima.org/

Alaska
Alaska Association of School Librarians
　　http://www.akla.org/akasl/home.html

Arizona
Arizona Educational Media Association
　　http://www.aema.net/main.htm
Arizona Library Association, Teacher-Librarians Division
　　http://www.azla.affiniscape.com/displaycommon.cfm?an=1&subarticlenbr=7

Arkansas
Arkansas Association of Instructional Media
　　http://aaim.k12.ar.us/

California
California School Library Association
　　http://www.schoolibrary.org

Colorado
Colorado Association of School Libraries
　　http://www.cal-webs.org/casl.html

Connecticut
Connecticut Educational Media Association
   http://www.ctcema.org/

Delaware
Delaware School Library Media Association
   http://www.udel.edu/educ/slms/dslma.html

2

District of Columbia
District of Columbia Library Association—Children,
   Young Adults and School Libraries
   http://www.dcla.org/

Florida
Florida Association for Media in Education
   http://www.floridamedia.org

Georgia
Georgia Association for Instructional Technology
   http://www.gait-inc.org/
Georgia Independent Schools Library Media Group
Georgia Library Association, School Library Media Division
   http://www.library.gsu.edu/gla/divisions/media/
Georgia Library Media Association
   http://www.glma-inc.org/

Hawaii
Hawaii Association of School Librarians (HASL)
   http://kauila.k12.hi.us/~hasl/

Idaho
Idaho Library Association
   http://www.idaholibraries.org/

Illinois
Illinois School Library Media Association
   http://islma.org

Indiana
Association for Indiana Media Educators
   http://www.ilfonline.org/Units/Associations/aime/

Iowa
Iowa Association of School Librarians
   http://www.iema-ia.org

Kansas
Kansas Association for Educational Communications and Technology
   http://skyways.lib.ks.us/kansas/KAECT/AECTR7.html
Kansas Association of School Librarians
   http://skyways.lib.ks.us/kasl/
Kansas Library Association, Children and School Libraries Section
   http://skyways.lib.ks.us/kansas/KLA/divisions/csls/

Kentucky
Kentucky School Media Association
   http://www.kysma.org/

Louisiana
Louisiana Association of School Librarians (LASL)
   http://www.llaonline.org/sig/lasl.php

Maine
Maine Association of School Libraries
   http://www.maslibraries.org/

Maryland
Maryland Educational Media Organization
   http://mdedmedia.org/

Massachusetts
Massachusetts School Library Media Association
   http://www.mslma.org/
New England Educational Media Association
   http://www.neema.org/

Michigan
Michigan Association for Computer Users in Learning (MACUL)
   http://www.macul.org/
Michigan Association for Media in Education
   http://www.mame.gen.mi.us/

Minnesota
Minnesota Educational Media Organization
   http://www.memoweb.org/

Mississippi
Mississippi Library Association, School Library Section
   http://www.misslib.org/org/sections/main.html

Missouri
Missouri Association of School Librarians
   http://www.maslonline.org/

Montana
Montana Library Association, School Media Division
   http://www.mtlib.org/slmd/slmd.html

Nebraska
Nebraska Educational Media Association
   http://nema.k12.ne.us/
Nebraska Library Association, Public Library Section
   http://www.nol.org/home/NLA/PLS/index.html

Nevada
Nevada Library Association, School and Children Librarians' Section
   http://www.nevadalibraries.org/publications/handbook/nscls.html

New Hampshire
New Hampshire Educational Media Association
   http://www.nhema.net/

New Jersey
Educational Media Association of New Jersey
    http://www.emanj.org/

New Mexico
New Mexico Library Association
    http://www.nmla.org/

New York
New York Library Association, School Library Media Section
    http://www.nyla.org/index.php?page_id=52

North Carolina
North Carolina Association of School Librarians
    http://www.nclaonline.org/ncasl/
North Carolina School Library Media Association
    http://www.ncslma.org/

North Dakota
North Dakota Library Association
    http://ndsl.lib.state.nd.us/ndla/

Ohio
Ohio Educational Library Media Association
    http://www.oelma.org/

Oklahoma
Oklahoma Association of School Library Media Specialists
    http://www.oklibs.org/~oaslms/

Oregon
Oregon Educational Media Association
    http://www.oema.net/
Oregon Library Association, Committee on School/Public Library
    Cooperation
    http://www.olaweb.org/org/cosp.shtml

Pennsylvania
Pennsylvania School Librarians Association
    http://www.psla.org/

Rhode Island
Rhode Island Educational Media Association
    http://www.ri.net/RIEMA/index.html

South Carolina
South Carolina Association of School Librarians
    http://www.scasl.net/
South Carolina Library Association, Services for Children and Youth in Schools
    and Public Libraries Section
    http://www.scla.org/docs/cy-section.html

South Dakota
South Dakota Library Association, School Library/Media Section
    http://www.usd.edu/sdla/sections.htm

Tennessee
Tennessee Association of School Librarians
    http://www.korrnet.org/tasl/
Tennessee Library Association, School Libraries Section
    http://www.lib.utk.edu/~tla/

Texas
Texas Association for Educational Technology
    http://www.taet.org/
Texas Association of School Librarians
    http://www.txla.org/groups/tasl/index.html

Utah
Utah Educational Library Media Association
    http://www.uelma.org/
Utah Library Association, School Library Section
    http://www.ula.org/organization/sections/school/school-co.htm

Vermont
Vermont Educational Media Association
    http://www.vema-online.org/

Virginia
Prince William School Librarians' Association
    http://members.aol.com/pwsla/
Virginia Educational Media Association
    http://www.vema.gen.va.us/
Virginia Library Association, School Library Section
    http://www.vla.org/

Washington
Washington Library Media Association
    http://www.wlma.org/

West Virginia
West Virginia Library Association, School Library Division
    http://www.wvla.org/divisions/divisions.htm

Wisconsin
Wisconsin Educational Media Association
    http://www.wemaonline.org/ab.main.cfm
Wisconsin Library Association, Wisconsin Association of School Librarians
    http://www.wla.lib.wi.us/wasl/index.html

Wyoming
Wyoming Library Association, School Library Media Section
    http://www.wyla.org/schools/index.shtml

Preplanning for a library conference

by Blanche Woolls

Here's what I've learned from years of attending library conferences that will help you have a better experience:

1. Send your registration early so you will get the early bird registration fee.
2. Make your hotel reservations early so you get the site and price you need.
3. Find a roommate—perhaps someone you went to college with, but not someone with whom you work as you can see them easily all the time. Adding someone new (and perhaps someone who has already attended a conference) helps you renew old acquaintances and meet new people that they know.
4. Take the preliminary program and scout out the sessions that sound really good to you. You will need to match it to the final program once you arrive, but start thinking now. The program will be overwhelming once you arrive. Here is when you start your daily calendar—with times and places (similar to your plan book at school).
5. Think about what you will wear—consider such things as the weather at the site. Will you need to pack an umbrella?
6. Get a list of things to have in a hotel in case of emergency and pack those, for example, a flashlight in case lights go off.
7. Plan to bring a large enough suitcase (caveat: airlines now limit you to a strict weight allowance and you need to find out what that is) to pack the things you collect—although sometimes a mailing room is available in the exhibits.
8. Get lots of $1 bills for tipping the bellmen and to use for your share of the cab to another hotel.
9. Check with your hotel to see if there is a coffee pot in the room. If so, you can pack instant oatmeal and instant soup to stave off hunger between conference meals.
10. It's good to pack Pepto-Bismol or some other stomach aid. Food at parties and dinners can be heavier than most of us eat in our more regular lives.

When you arrive:

1. Get your conference program immediately and scope the sessions to see if you want to make any switches in what you had planned. June Berry suggests that you tear out the pages of your conference program (when it is as thick as the ALA conference program) so you aren't carrying around all that bulk.
2. Look at the vendor lists and their placement on the exhibit floor so you can go directly to them in a systematic order. Otherwise you'll waste a lot of time going up and down rows and rows of exhibitor booths. You may want to make some appointments *before* you leave. This can often result in an additional invitation to something special—if you are a good customer.
3. Beware of filling six shopping bags with exhibit things. Most people weed out before they pack, making hotel staff empty heavy wastebaskets

of excess catalogs, posters, and other things that seemed irresistible in the exhibits. They are heavy to carry through the exhibits and they don't lose any weight packing to go home.

4. Look at the distances between meetings. Even with taking a cab, it is seldom possible to move from one location to another in less than 20 minutes—you must wait for elevators, stop to talk with friends, and hail cabs—and finding the room is often a challenge even when they put floor plans of hotels and conference centers in the conference program. Go to sessions early or you may find the audience lining the walls and sitting on the floor at the back—if you can even get into the door. Watch for last-minute cancellations so you don't go to a room to find it empty.

5. If you do go with a colleague from home, try to attend different sessions so you can share information, rather than both attending the same session.

6. Take notes of things you see and hear that will be interesting to those you left behind—your school library colleagues, your teachers, and your principal. It never hurts to bring them some of the goodies—and not all of the same thing.

7. Plan to have a worthwhile experience. You certainly will.

8. Make sure you write a letter to your principal and superintendent detailing what the conference meant to your continuing education and how the experience you had will help you help teachers and help raise student achievement.

SOURCE: Adapted from Blanche Woolls, "Preplanning for a Library Conference," *Knowledge Quest* 32, no. 1 (September/October 2003): 12.

ALA youth divisions (AASL/ALSC/YALSA): Staff and contact information

American Library Association
50 East Huron
Chicago, IL 60611-2795
Telephone: (800) 545-2433

American Association of School Librarians (AASL) and
Young Adult Library Services Association (YALSA)
Julie Walker, Executive Director
AASL direct dial: (312) 280-4386
Fax: (312) 664-7459
E-mail: aasl@ala.org
Website: www.ala.org/aasl/
YALSA direct dial: (312) 280-4390
E-mail: yalsa@ala.org
Website: www.ala.org/yalsa/

Young Adult Library
Services Association

Association for Library Service to Children (ALSC)
Malore I. Brown, Executive Director
ALSC direct dial: (312) 944-2163
Fax: (312) 944-7671
E-mail: alsc@ala.org
Website: www.ala.org/alsc/

2

SOURCE: Courtesy of the American Library Association and its divisions: American Association
of School Librarians (AASL), Association for Library Service to Children (ALSC), and
Young Adult Library Services Association (YALSA).

ALA youth division presidents

The three American Library Association youth divisions—American Association of School Librarians (AASL), Association for Library Service to Children (ALSC), and the Young Adult Library Services Association (YALSA)—represent three of ALA's eight divisions. Officers are elected annually.

Year	AASL	ALSC	YASD-YALSA
2005–2006	J. Linda Williams	Ellen G. Fader	Pam Spencer Holley
2004–2005	Dawn P. Vaughn	Gretchen Wronka	David C. Mowery
2003–2004	Frances R. Roscello	Cynthia Richey	Audra Caplan
2002–2003	Nancy Zimmerman	Barbara Genco	Caryn Sipos
2001–2002	Helen R. Adams	Carole Fiore	Bonnie Kunzel
2000–2001	Harriet S. Selverstone	Virginia Walter	Mary Arnold
1999–2000	M. Ellen Jay	Caroline Ward	Jana R. Fine
1998–1999	Sharon Coatney	Leslie E. Holt	Joel Shoemaker
1997–1998	Ken Haycock	Elizabeth Watson	Michael Cart
1996–1997	Barbara Stripling	Stephen Herb	Deborah Taylor
1995–1996	David V. Loertscher	Therese Bigelow	Patricia Muller
1994–1995	Jacqueline Mancall	Virginia McKee	Jennifer J. Gallant
1993–1994	E. Blanche Woolls	Ellen Stepanian	Judith Druse
1992–1993	Ruth Toor	Kathy A. East	Elizabeth M. O'Donnell
1991–1992	Dawn H. Heller	Linda Perkins	Mary E. Wendt
1990–1991	Winona Jones	Barbara Barstow	Christy Tyson
1989–1990	Retta Patrick	Barbara Immroth	Gerald Hodges & Christy Tyson
1988–1989	Jacqueline G. Morris	Marilyn B. Iarusso	Susan Madden
1987–1988	Karen A. Whitney	Mary R. Sommerville	Vivian Wynn

Dawn P. Vaughn, AASL   Gretchen Wronka, ALSC   David C. Mowery, YALSA

Year	AASL	ALSC	YASD-YALSA
1986–1987	Marilyn L. Miller	Jane Botham	Marion Hargrove
1985–1986	Shirley L. Aaron	Gail M. Sage	Joan Atkinson
1984–1985	Elizabeth Day	Margaret Bush	Lydia LaFleur
1983–1984	Judith King	Phyllis Van Orden	Penelope S. Jeffrey
1982–1983	Dorothy Blake	Margaret M. Kimmel	Barbara Newmark-Kruger
1981–1982	Betty Jo Buckingham	Helen M. Mullen	Evie Wilson-Lingbloom
1980–1981	D. Philip Baker	Amy Kellman	Audrey Eaglen
1979–1980	Rebecca Bingham	Marilyn L. Miller	Eleanor Pourron
1978–1979	Anna Mary Lowrey	Lillian Gerhardt	Bruce Daniels
1977–1978	Frances C. Dean	Barbara S. Miller	Rosemary Young
1976–1977	Peggy Pfeiffer	Peggy Sullivan	Mary K. Chelton
1975–1976	Judith G. Letsinger	Spencer Shaw	Helen Kreigh
1974–1975	Helen D. L. Snoke	Barbara Rollock	Carol Starr
1973–1974	Bernard Franckowiak	Priscilla L. Moulton	Marilee Fogelsong
1972–1973	Elnora Portteus	Anne R. Izard	Thomas Alford
1971–1972	Frances Hatfield	Sara I. Fenwick	Jane Manthorne
1970–1971	Roberta Young	Mary E. Ledlie	Mary Ann Hanna
1969–1970	John Rowell	Isabella Jinette	Elaine Simpson
1968–1969	Phyllis Hochstettler	Mae Durham	Julia M. Losinski
1967–1968	Carolyn Whitenack	Augusta Baker	Mary L. Woodworth
1966–1967	Richard L. Darling	Winifred Crossley	Florence M. Sanborn
1965–1966	Eleanor E. Ahlers	Sara H. Wheeler	Opal C. Eagle
1964–1965	Virginia McJenkin	Helen Sattley	Mildred L. Krohn
1963–1964	Jean Lowrie	Ruth Gagliardo	Audrey Biel
1962–1963	Cora P. Bowmar	Barbara S. Moody	Lucile Hatch
1961–1962	Sara I. Fenwick	Jean A. Merrill	Sara L. Siebert
1960–1961	Elizabeth O. Williams	Elizabeth Burr	Hanna Hunt
1959–1960	Esther Burrin	Carolyn Field	Pauline O'Melia
1958–1959	Elenore Alexander	Elizabeth Nesbitt	Pauline Winnick
1957–1958	Mary V. Gaver	Charlemae Rollins	Jane S. McClure
1956–1957	Lillian L. Batchelor	Margaret Scoggin & Marian C. Young	Frances M. Grim
1955–1956	Dilla W. MacBean	Maxine La Bounty	
1954–1955	Nancy J. Day	Alice L. LeFevre	
1953–1954	Alice B. McGuire	Marian C. Young	
1952–1953	Mary Lee Keath	Eleanor Kidder	
1951–1952	Laura K. Martin	Elizabeth Groves	

NCATE/ALA schools

The American Library Association has joined the National Council for the Accreditation of Teacher Education (NCATE) to develop guidelines for higher education programs offering school library media teacher credentials or certification. Members of AASL develop the competencies and write the documents to guide program approval. This specialized certification is also available through programs in many schools of library and information sciences accredited by ALA's Committee on Accreditation (COA). The ALA programs offer courses to prepare students for employment in all types of library and information centers. When ALA's COA has approved a program, NCATE accepts this approval for its programs. However, because school librarian credential or certification programs are also evaluated by individual state departments of education, many school library program directors participate in both reviews.

Alabama
University of Alabama–Tuscaloosa
Arkansas
University of Central Arkansas, College of Education
California
San Jose State University
Delaware
University of Delaware, School of Education
District of Columbia
Catholic University
Florida
Florida State University
University of South Florida
Hawaii
University of Hawaii–Manoa
Illinois
Chicago State University, Department of Reading, Elementary Education,
Library Science/Communications Media (REEL)
Indiana
Indiana University–Bloomington and Indianapolis
Kansas
Emporia State University
Kentucky
University of Kentucky
Western Kentucky University
Louisiana
Louisiana State University
Maryland
Towson University, College of Education
University of Maryland–College Park
Massachusetts
Bridgewater State College, School of Education
Salem State College, School of Education and Allied Studies
Michigan
Central Michigan University, Department of Teacher Education and
Professional Development
Grand Valley State University, School of Education
Mississippi
University of Southern Mississippi
Missouri
Central Missouri State University
New Jersey
Rowan University, College of Education
William Paterson University, College of Education
North Carolina
Appalachian State University, Reich College of Education
East Carolina University, Department of Librarianship, Education, and
Distance Education
North Carolina Central University
University of North Carolina–Chapel Hill
University of North Carolina–Greensboro

2

Ohio
  Kent State University
  Wright State University, College of Education and Human Services
Oklahoma
  Oklahoma State University, College of Education
  University of Oklahoma–Norman
Pennsylvania
  Clarion University of Pennsylvania
  Drexel University
  University of Pittsburgh
Puerto Rico
  University of Puerto Rico
Rhode Island
  University of Rhode Island
South Carolina
  University of South Carolina–Columbia
Tennessee
  University of Tennessee–Knoxville
Texas
  Sam Houston State University, Library Science Department
  University of Houston at Clear Lake, School of Education
  University of North Texas
Utah
  Southern Utah University, College of Education
  Utah State University, College of Education
Virginia
  Longwood University, Department of Education
  Old Dominion University, Darden College of Education
Washington
  University of Washington–Seattle
Wisconsin
  University of Wisconsin–Oshkosh, College of Education and Human
    Services

Departments of Education in the United States

Alabama Department of Education
  http://www.alsde.edu/html/home.asp
  50 North Ripley Street
  P.O. Box 302101
  Montgomery, AL 36104
  Telephone: (334) 242-9700

**Alaska Department of Education
and Early Development**
  http://www.educ.state.ak.us/
  801 West 10th Street, Suite 200

Juneau, AK 99801-1878
Telephone: (907) 465-2800
Fax: (907) 465-3452

Arizona Department of Education
http://www.ade.state.az.us/
1535 W. Jefferson
Phoenix, AZ 85007
Telephone: (602) 542-4361

Arkansas Department of Education
http://arkedu.state.ar.us/
#4 Capitol Mall
Little Rock, AR 72201
Telephone: (501) 682-4475

California Department of Education
http://www.cde.ca.gov/
1430 N Street
Sacramento, CA 95814
Telephone: (916) 319–0800

Colorado Department of Education
http://www.cde.state.co.us/index_home.htm
201 East Colfax Avenue
Denver, CO 80203-1799
Telephone: (303) 866-6600
Fax: (303) 830-0793

Connecticut Department of Education
http://www.state.ct.us/sde/
165 Capitol Avenue
Hartford, CT 06145
Telephone: (860) 713-6548

Delaware Department of Education
http://www.doe.state.de.us/
401 Federal Street
P.O. Box 1402
Dover, DE 19903-1402
Telephone: (302) 739-4601
Fax: (302) 739-4654

District of Columbia Public Schools
http://www.k12.dc.us/dcps/home.html
Main Administration Building
825 North Capitol St. N.E.
Washington, DC 20002
Telephone: (202) 442-5635

Florida Department of Education
http://www.firn.edu/doe/
Turlington Building
325 West Gaines Street
Tallahassee, FL 32399-0400
Telephone: (850) 487-1785

Georgia Department of Education
http://www.doe.k12.ga.us/index.asp
205 Jesse Hills Dr. SE
Atlanta, GA 30334
Telephone: (404) 656-2800; (800) 311-3627

Hawai'i Department of Education
http://doe.k12.hi.us/
P.O. Box 2360
Honolulu, HI 96804
Telephone: (808) 586-3230
Fax: (808) 586-3234

Idaho Department of Education
http://www.sde.state.id.us/Dept/
650 West State Street
P.O. Box 83720
Boise, ID 83720-0027
Telephone: (208) 332-6800

Illinois State Board of Education
http://www.isbe.state.il.us/
100 N. First Street
Springfield, IL 62777
Telephone: (217) 782-4321
TTY: (217) 782-1900

100 W. Randolph, Suite 14-300
Chicago, IL 60601
Telephone: (312) 814-2220
TTY: (312) 814-5821

123 South 10th Street, Suite 200
Mt. Vernon, IL 62864
Telephone: (618) 244-8383

Indiana Department of Education
http://ideanet.doe.state.in.us/
Room 229, State House
Indianapolis, IN 46204-2798
Telephone: (317) 232-0808

Iowa Department of Education
http://www.state.ia.us/educate/

Grimes State Office Building
Des Moines, IA 50319-0146
Telephone: (515) 281-5294
Fax: (515) 242-5988

Kansas State Department of Education
http://www.ksbe.state.ks.us/Welcome.html
120 SE 10th Avenue
Topeka, KS 66612-1182
Telephone: (785) 296-3201
Fax: (785) 296-7933

Kentucky Department of Education
http://www.kde.state.ky.us/
500 Mero Street
Frankfort, KY 40601
Telephone: (502) 564-4770
TTY: (502) 564-4970

Kentucky Department
of Education

Louisiana Department of Education
http://www.doe.state.la.us/DOE/asps/home.asp
P.O. Box 94064
Baton Rouge, LA 70804-9064
Telephone: (225) 342-4411
Fax: (225) 342-0193

Maine State Department of Education
http://www.state.me.us/education/homepage.htm
23 State House Station
Augusta, ME 04333-0023

Maryland State Department of Education
http://www.msde.state.md.us/
200 West Baltimore Street
Baltimore, MD 21201
Telephone: (410) 767-0100

Massachusetts Department of Education
http://www.doe.mass.edu/
350 Main Street
Malden, MA 02148-5023
Telephone: (781) 338-3000
TTY: (800) 439-0183

Michigan Department of Education
http://www.michigan.gov/mde
608 W. Allegan
P.O. Box 30008
Lansing, MI 48909
E-mail: MDEweb@michigan.gov

Minnesota Department of Children, Families and Learning
http://www.education.state.mn.us
1500 Highway 36 West
Roseville, MN 55113
Telephone: (651) 582-8200

Mississippi Department of Education
http://www.mde.k12.ms.us/
Central High School
P.O. Box 771
359 North West Street
Jackson, MS 39205
Telephone: (601) 359-3513

Missouri Department of Elementary and Secondary Education
http://www.dese.state.mo.us/
P.O. Box 480
Jefferson City, MO 65102
Telephone: (573) 751-4212
Fax: (573) 751-8613

Missouri Department of Elementary and Secondary Education

Montana Office of Public Instruction
http://www.opi.state.mt.us/
P.O. Box 202501
Helena, MT 59620-2501
Telephone: (406) 444-3095

Nebraska Department of Education
http://www.nde.state.ne.us/
301 Centennial Mall South
Lincoln, NE 68509
Telephone: (402) 471-2295

Nevada Department of Education
http://www.doe.nv.gov/
700 E. Fifth Street
Carson City, NV 89701
Telephone: (775) 687-9200
Fax: (775) 687-9101

New Hampshire Department of Education
http://www.ed.state.nh.us/
101 Pleasant Street
Concord, NH 03301-3860
Telephone: (603) 271-3494
Fax: (603) 271-1953

New Jersey Department of Education
http://www.state.nj.us/education/
P.O. Box 500
Trenton, NJ 08625
Telephone: (609) 292-4469

New Mexico State Department of Education
http://www.sde.state.nm.us/
300 Don Gaspar
Santa Fe, NM 87501-2786
Telephone: (505) 827-5800

New York State Education Department
http://www.nysed.gov/
Education Building
Albany, NY 12234
Telephone: (518) 474-3852

North Carolina Department of Public Instruction
http://www.dpi.state.nc.us/
301 N. Wilmington St.
Raleigh, NC 27601
Telephone: (919) 807-3300

North Dakota Department of Public Instruction
http://www.dpi.state.nd.us/
600 E. Boulevard Ave., Dept. 201
Floors 9, 10, and 11
Bismarck, ND 58505-0440
Telephone: (701) 328-2260
Fax: (701) 328-2461

Ohio Department of Education
http://www.ode.state.oh.us/
25 South Front Street
Columbus, OH 43215-4183
Telephone: (877) 644-6338

Oklahoma State Department of Education
http://www.sde.state.ok.us/home/defaultie.html
2500 North Lincoln Boulevard
Oklahoma City, OK 73105-4599
Telephone: (405) 521-3301
Fax: (405) 521-6205

Oregon Department of Education
http://www.ode.state.or.us/
255 Capitol Street NE
Salem, OR 97310-0203
Telephone: (503) 378-3569
TDD: (503) 378-2892
Fax: (503) 378-5156

Pennsylvania Department of Education
http://www.pde.state.pa.us/pde_internet/site/default.asp
333 Market Street
Harrisburg, PA 17126
Telephone: (717) 783-6788

Rhode Island Department of Elementary and Secondary Education
http://www.ridoe.net/
255 Westminster Street
Providence, RI 02903
Telephone: (401) 222-4600

South Carolina State Department of Education
http://www.sde.state.sc.us/
1429 Senate Street
Columbia, SC 29201
Telephone: (803) 734-8815
Fax: (803) 734-3389

South Dakota Department of Education
http://www.state.sd.us/deca/
700 Governors Drive
Pierre, SD 57501
Telephone: (605) 773-3218
Fax: (605) 773-3782

Tennessee Department of Education
http://www.state.tn.us/education/
6th Floor, Andrew Johnson Tower
710 James Robertson Parkway
Nashville, TN 37243-0375
Telephone: (615) 741-2731

Texas Education Agency
http://www.tea.state.tx.us/
1701 North Congress Ave.
Austin, TX 78701
Telephone: (512) 463-9734

Utah State Office of Education
http://www.usoe.k12.ut.us/
250 East 500 South
P.O. Box 144200
Salt Lake City, UT 84114-4200
Telephone: (801) 538-7500

Vermont Department of Education
http://www.state.vt.us/educ/
120 State Street
Montpelier, VT 05620-2501
Telephone: (802) 828-3154
E-mail: edinfo@doe.state.vt.us

Virginia Department of Education
http://www.pen.k12.va.us/
P.O. Box 2120
Richmond, VA 23218
Telephone: (800) 292-3820

2

Washington Office of Superintendent of Public Instruction
http://www.k12.wa.us/
Old Capitol Building
P.O. Box 47200
Olympia, WA 98504-7200
Telephone: (360) 725-6000
TTY: (360) 664-3631

West Virginia Department of Education
http://wvde.state.wv.us/
1900 Kanawha Boulevard East
Charleston, WV 25305

Wisconsin Department of Public Instruction
http://www.dpi.state.wi.us/
125 S. Webster St.
P.O. Box 7841
Madison, WI 53707-7841
Telephone: (608) 266-3390

Wyoming Department of Education
http://www.k12.wy.us/
2300 Capitol Avenue
Hathaway Building, 2nd Floor
Cheyenne, WY 82002-0050
Telephone: (307) 777-7673

SOURCE: Excerpted from U.S. Department of Education, "State Education Agency (State Department of Education)," http://www.ed.gov/about/organizations.jsp (accessed April 30, 2003).

International school library organizations

International

International Association of School Librarianship (IASL)
http://www.iasl-slo.org/
PMB 292
1903 W. 8th Street
Erie, PA 16505, USA

P.O. Box 587
Carlton North, Victoria 3054
Australia
E-mail: iasl@netspace.com.au

International Federation of Library Associations and Institutions (IFLA), School Libraries Section
http://www.ifla.org/
IFLA Headquarters
P.O. Box 95312
2509 CH The Hague
Netherlands
Telephone: 011-31-70-314-0884
Fax: 011-31-70-383-4827
E-mail: ifla@ifla.org

International Reading Association Headquarters Office
http://www.reading.org/
800 Barksdale Road
P.O. Box 8139
Newark, DE 19714-8139, USA
Telephone: (302) 731-1600
Fax: (302) 731-1057

Asia/Pacific

Pacific Islands Association of Libraries and Archives (PIALA)
http://www.uog.edu/rfk/piala/piala.html
c/o Pohnpei Public Library
Kolonia, Pohnpei
Federated States of Micronesia

Austria

Österreichischen Schulbibliotheken (in German)
http://www.schulbibliothek.at/
c/o Werner Schöggl
Bibliothek GRG 21
Ödenburgerstraße 74
A-1210 Vienna
Austria

Australia

Australian Library and Information Association, School Library Section
http://hsc.csu.edu.au/pta/members/alia.html
P.O. Box 577
Leichhardt, New South Wales 2040
Australia

Australian School Library Association
http://www.asla.org.au/
P.O. Box 155
Zillmere, Queensland 4034
Australia

2

Australian School Library Association (Australian Capital Territory)
http://www.pa.ash.org.au/aslaact/
c/o Geraldine McNulty
P.O. Box 700
Jamison, Australian Capital Territory 2614
Australia

Australian School Library Association (New South Wales)
http://www.asla.nsw.edu.au/
P.O. Box 1336
Parramatta, New South Wales 2124
Australia

Australian School Library Association (Tasmania)
http://www.asla.neat.tas.edu.au/
P.O. Box 164
Sandy Bay, Tasmania 7006
Australia

School Library Association of the Northern Territory (SLANT)
P.O. Box 3162
Darwin, Northern Territory 0801
Australia

School Library Association of Queensland
http://www.slaq.org.au/
P.O. Box 252
Mt. Gravatt, Queensland 4122
Australia

School Library Association of South Australia
http://www.slasa.asn.au/
P.O. Box 2093
Kent Town, South Australia 5071
Australia

School Library
Association of
South Australia

Resource Centre Teachers' Association
c/o Sheidow Park School
Adams Road
Sheidow Park, South Australia 5158
Australia

School Library Association of Victoria
http://www.slav.schools.net.au/
150 Palmerston Street
Carlton, Victoria 3053
Australia

Western Australia School Library Association
http://www.apea.asn.au/%7Ewasla/
P.O. Box 1272
West Perth, Western Australia 6872
Australia

Botswana

Botswana Library Association (BLA)
http://www.bla.0catch.com/
P.O. Box 1310
Gaborone
Botswana

Canada

Association for Teacher-Librarianship in Canada (ATLC)
http://www.atlc.ca/
P.O. Box 9
Pouch Cove, Newfoundland
Canada A0A 3L0

Association for Media and Technology in Education in Canada
http://www.amtec.ca/
3-1750 The Queensway, Suite 1318
Etobicoke, Ontario
Canada M9C 5H5

Canadian Association for Media Education Organizations
http://interact.uoregon.edu/MediaLit/CAMEO/
c/o Jesuit Communication Project
1804 – 77 St. Clair Avenue East
Toronto, Ontario
Canada M4T 1M5

Canadian School Library Association
http://www.cla.ca/divisions/csla/
328 Frank Street
Ottawa, Ontario
Canada K2P 0X8

British Columbia
British Columbia Teacher-Librarians' Association
http://www.bctf.bc.ca/PSAs/BCTLA/
c/o British Columbia Teachers' Federation
100 – 550 West 6th Avenue
Vancouver, British Columbia
Canada V5Z 4P2

Manitoba
Manitoba School Library Association
http://home.merlin.mb.ca/~msla/

Nova Scotia
The Teacher-Librarians' Association of Nova Scotia
c/o Nova Scotia Teachers Union
3106 Joseph Howe Drive
Halifax, Nova Scotia
Canada B3L 4L7

Ontario
Ontario School Library Association
http://www.accessola.com/osla/
100 Lombard Street, Suite 303
Toronto, Ontario
Canada M5C 1M3

Québec
Association du personnel des services documentaires scolaires
http://rtsq.grics.qc.ca/apsds/
303, rue Blainville Est
Sainte-Thérèse, Québec
Canada J7E 1N3

Saskatchewan
Saskatchewan School Library Association
http://www.stf.sk.ca/prof_growth/ssc/ssla/

China–Hong Kong

Hong Kong Teacher-Librarians' Association
http://hktla.school.net.hk/
Kowloon Central
P.O. Box 74493
Hong Kong

香港學校圖書館主任協會
Hong Kong Teacher-Librarians' Association

Hong Kong Professional Teachers' Union, Teacher-Librarians' Group
http://librarian.school.net.hk/

Denmark

Danmarks Skolebibliotekarforening—Danish Association of School Librarianship (in Danish)
http://www.emu.dk/gsk/skolebib/index.html

Europe

School Libraries in Europe—The European Network for School Libraries and Information Literacy
http://www.eun.org/eun.org2/eun/en/vs-Library_vs/
    content.cfm?lang=en&ov=25745
c/o Lourense Das
Rijksweg 26
6095 NC Baexem
Netherlands

Nordisk Skolebibliotekarforening (Nordic Association of School Librarians) (in Danish)
http://n-s-f.ismennt.is

Finland

School Library Association in Finland (in English)
http://www.suomenkoulukirjastoyhdistys.fi

Germany

LAG Schulbibliotheken in Hessen
http://www.schulbibliotheken.de/
Dahlienweg 17
D-35396 Giessen
Germany

Iceland

Félag Skólasafnskennara (in Icelandic)
http://www.ismennt.is/vefir/skolasafn/

Upplýsing—Félag bókasafns- og upplýsingafraeði / Information—The Icelandic Library and Information Science Association (in Icelandic)
http://www.bokis.is/
Lágmúli 7
108 Reykjavík
Iceland

Japan

Japan School Library Association
http://www.j-sla.or.jp/

Latvia

Latvian School Librarian Association
http://www.liis.lv/lsba/

Netherlands

Landelijke Werkgroep Schoolmediathecarissen Voortgezet Onderwijs (LWSVO) (in Dutch)
http://www.digischool.nl/lwsvo/
c/o Judith de Lange
Treubstraat 163
8072 WG Nunspeet
Netherlands

New Zealand

School Library Association of New Zealand
http://www.slanza.org.nz/
P.O. Box 36-511
Merivale, Christchurch
New Zealand

Norway

Skolebibliotekarforeningen i Norge—The Norwegian Association of School Librarianship (in Norwegian)
http://www.gs.bergen.hl.no/sin/
c/o Inge Hovden
Postboks 71
8455 Stokmarknes
Norway

Portugal

Rede de Bibliotecas Escolares—School Libraries Network
http://www.dapp.min-edu.pt/rbe/index.htm
Trav. Terras de Sant'Ana, 15
1250-269 Lisbon
Portugal

Slovenia

Union of Associations of Slovene Librarians
http://www.zbds-zveza.si/
Turjaška 1, 1000
Ljubljana
Slovenia

United Kingdom

School Libraries Group (SLG–UK)
http://www.cilip.org.uk/groups/slg/slg.html

School Library Association (UK)
http://www.sla.org.uk/
Unit 2, Lotmead Business Village
Lotmead Farm
Wanborough, Swindon
United Kingdom SN4 0UY

SOURCE: Adapted from International Association of
School Librarianship (IASL), "School
Library Associations on the Internet,"
http://www.iasl-slo.org/slibassoc.html
(accessed April 30, 2003).

Principals of success:
Getting the boss's attention is crucial to your effectiveness

by Gary Hartzell

Forgive the pun, but your "principal relationship" at work is your relationship with the principal. You may be the best school librarian to ever grace education, but you won't get the opportunity to prove that unless your principal values what you do. Being ready, willing, and able is only three-quarters of the key to your success. The fourth element is opportunity, and your principal plays a large part in that.

The good news is that research has shown that the librarian is a principal's best source of information about the library's value. There is legitimate hope that you can build a better working relationship, but you must take the initiative in getting your principal's attention—or you'll grow old waiting for him to come to you. Here are three quick suggestions on how you can get started:

1. Find ways to interact with the principal regularly. Arrange a formal meeting each quarter of the year to bring him up-to-date on what's going on in the library. Carefully prepare before each visit, and create a short executive summary that you can leave behind. Emphasize the teachers you've collaborated with and the number of students that were served—not circulation. Circulation doesn't mean anything to a principal, but instruction does. Suggest new projects that involve more interaction with teachers and students.

2. Don't stop with formal exchanges. Try to interact with faculty and students during coffee breaks or at lunchtime. Social psychology research clearly demonstrates that we tend to like people more if we have continuous contact with them (assuming that they're pleasant). But be careful not to overdo it, or the principal may think that you're neglecting your duties.

3. Keep abreast of activities in your school, and find ways to show the principal how you and the library can help deal with challenges and take advantage of opportunities. How often should you do this? Anytime you get the chance. The mountain men used to say that the best time to shoot bears is when bears are around. There is no shortage of bears in schools. Watch for your opportunity, and then seize it.

Pay attention to your colleagues. You're in an ideal position to monitor school events and trends because of your contact with those who use the library. But take it one step further: get out and talk to people. Network with those involved in the school play, dance, or ball game. This not only provides you with better information sources, but it increases your visibility and familiarity with the faculty.

Most importantly, pay attention to what the principal talks about—whether it's information shared at a faculty meeting or a seemingly idle remark made in the hallway. Every topic the principal mentions offers you an opportunity to make an impression.

Take the first chance you have to conduct a quick search for information on that subject. There are dozens of online resources you can tap into. Once you've completed your research, prepare a report (perhaps just a package of some pages you've printed out) and deliver it to the principal as soon as possible. Imagine the impression you'll make if the principal mentions that he is interested in or worried about topic "x," and a half-hour later you put a summary of related research and descriptions of model programs on his desk.

Doing this once, or even a half-dozen times, won't reshape your principal's perceptions of libraries and librarians, but by repeatedly taking the initiative, and coupling that with greater contact and visibility, you'll become a fixture in his thinking—and that is the goal. We all value those who help us become more successful, make our jobs easier, and make us look good.

SOURCE: Adapted from Gary Hartzell, "Building Influence—Principals of Success," *School Library Journal* 48, no. 4 (April 2002): 4. Courtesy of *School Library Journal*, Copyright 2002. To learn more about *School Library Journal*, or how to subscribe, go to http://www.slj.com.

Evolution of education for school librarians

by Anne Riedling

The year is 1974. What was it that one learned specializing in "Educational Media" in 1974? Attempting to recall 25-plus years ago, the following come to mind: threading a 16 mm projector, inserting a filmstrip, using an opaque projector, operating a 35 mm camera, inserting slides properly into a slide carousel, using an 8 mm camera, running an overhead projector, making transparencies (even the "fancy" ones using diazo color from *National Geographic*, *Life*, and *Look* magazines!). Videos were just in their dawning; "the" computer at this university took up the basement floor of the School of Business and required key cards.

Things have changed, and along with those changes has come new education, in the area of library science as well (now renamed Information Science, Educational Media Technology, and other more "fashionable" terms). The role of the educator of school librarians has changed over the past two decades. We have a communications revolution, an information-based society at hand. Our society has shifted from an economy based on capital goods to an economy based on services–information. One could be bold enough to express that virtually every component of educating the prospective school librarian has changed; the entire curriculum has altered.

The major transformation is an emphasis on information access. Every kind of information imaginable is accessible; it is just a matter of knowing where and how to look for it (in addition to evaluation). Technology in all areas is evolving at a rapid pace, fueled by faster, smaller, more powerful, and less expensive components that are easier to use. S. Tickton pointed out that technologies make education more productive and more individual, instruction more powerful, learning more immediate, and access more equal.

A new world

One sees a new world coming into reality within the next few years: libraries available on video-discs; students of all ages learning at home on computers linked by telephone lines; vast educational databases; instant access by satellite to an unlimited variety of televised information. Those who teach and learn will need time and experience to incorporate these new methods of teaching and learning into their individual, social, and economic patterns of behavior. The integration of technology is challenging, frustrating, time-consuming, and expensive. Educators of prospective school librarians have the role of fostering change rapidly, and with as little distress as possible.

The constant in all of this transformation is the need for educators of school librarians to become technology/information literate and to relay that knowledge. Technology has not fundamentally changed the function of libraries, however; it has dramatically changed the role of school librarians. Educators must teach upcoming librarians to educate students (and faculty) to sort, to discriminate, to select, to analyze, and to evaluate the vast array of messages presented. To paraphrase Christine S. Doyle, librarians must learn to access information by recognizing the need for information, recognizing that accurate and complete information is the basis for intelligent decision making, by formulating questions based on information needs, by developing successful search strategies, and by accessing print and technology-based sources of information. Educators must instruct prospective librarians to evaluate information by establishing authority, by determining accuracy and relevance, by recognizing points of view and opinions versus factual knowledge, by rejecting inaccurate and misleading information, and by creating new information to replace inaccurate or missing information. To prepare the school librarians of tomorrow, educators must instruct them to become critical thinkers, intellectually curious observers, creators and users of information. These new school librarians must be able to challenge validity of information and to understand the political, social, and economic agendas of information creation and dissemination. Today, to know means to have access to information. Possession is replaced by access. Educators must teach prospective school librarians to foster a climate in which they see themselves as facilitators of lifelong learning.

An integrated approach

Educators of librarians are in an important position to help create tomorrow's information literate workforce by emphasizing the power of information and by providing opportunities to develop information seeking skills. Educators must teach librarians to move from isolated skill instruction to an integrated approach. This is a crucial step that takes a great deal of time and planning, but is necessary and worth the effort. Educators of prospective school librarians must not only teach a skill, but a new way of thinking in order to derive meaning from learning. They must teach upcoming school librarians when to use online resources, how to access information competently, how to evaluate information as to accuracy and pertinence for each need, and how to use this information to communicate effectively—lifelong skills for the Information Age.

The foundation of school library services remains stable. Information in various formats must still be collected, organized, and preserved; and that information must be identified and located by users. Educators of prospective school librarians must relay that they are no longer experts—masters of a known body of knowledge. School librarians must be—can only be—explorers and pathfinders, navigating unbounded, evolving sources of information to map the way for users who are now fellow searchers. According to D. Barclay, the distinction between experts and laypersons (students, faculty, administrators, parents, community) is dissolving. Educators must stress that school librarians accept learning as a new constant in our profession and *learn how to learn*.

Educators must not only foster changes, but also teach prospective school librarians to believe in what they are doing, or the inertia generated by innovation for its own sake will quickly disappear. Chris Dede lists critical components to assist with this role change:

1. Envision opportunities where technology can make a contribution.
2. Displace cherished notions.
3. Inspire others to act on faith.
4. Demonstrate that the use of technology can improve efficiency and effectiveness of the school library functions (as well as total school functions).

If the school library is to be the instructional heart of the school, school librarians need assistance in coping with new technologies. Educators must communicate to prospective school librarians that no one can ever feel completely up to date with technologies, and an anxious feeling is perfectly normal. The job of a school librarian is not to know everything, but to know how to find information. The challenge can be exciting, but it does require continuing work to keep current with trends and new advances. Educators of upcoming school librarians must teach the "basics" and make it clear that their challenge is to remain current with technologies via conferences, networking, reading, workshops, and other professional development opportunities.

The adult lives of students will be drastically different from the lives of their parents and teachers. The integration of technology into the school library is no longer a luxury: it is a prerequisite to survival in a future that will be driven and supported by technology. Technologies can provide an excellent avenue for student motivation, exploration and instruction in a multisensory, diverse world. Technology, however, is only a tool. The real challenge rests with educators to teach prospective school librarians their new roles and how to cope appropriately and effectively with inevitable changes in our world.

SOURCE: Adapted from Anne Riedling, "Evolution of Education for School Librarians," *School Librarian* 48, no. 2 (Summer 2000): 69–70. Copyright 2000. Used with permission.

Stop the whining

by Ann Carlson Weeks

A popular television commercial features annoyingly cute children complaining sulkily about the food on their dinner plates. A voice-over suggests that if you are experiencing "too much whine with your meals," the solution is a packaged pasta product. Every time I see this commercial, I am reminded that we have much, too much "whine" within the school library media profession. Over the past 25 years, I have heard library media specialists whine that no one understands what we do. They whine that we are not treated as professionals. They whine that our budgets are inadequate.

They whine that we have too much to do. They whine that our libraries are too small or too cavernous, too old or too dark, too hot or too cold.

Whining seems to be an "equal opportunity" activity. I have met whiny librarians in big cities and small towns, in wealthy districts and in impoverished communities, in elementary schools and in high schools. The condition does not seem to be directly related to chronological age or length of service in the profession.

I would never deny that the conditions in many school libraries are sufficient to provoke frustration and dismay. However, whining rarely improves the situation, and often does nothing but create a greater distance between the whiner and somebody who can actually do something to change the conditions.

Since whining has brought about few positive results, I would like to propose that the rallying cry of the school library media profession for the 21st century should be "Stop the Whining!" (Perhaps there also should be bumper stickers and support groups.) The energy formerly used for whining can be redirected into positive action. Rather than complain that "none of the upper grade teachers use the library," spend time becoming more familiar with your school's science or social studies curriculum. Do a collection map to determine how well the current library media resources support and expand the topics. Check to see whether the materials are current, relevant, and appropriate for the ability levels of the students. Be "aggressively helpful" by taking particularly appropriate resources to teachers' classrooms or by planning meetings rather than waiting for the faculty to come to you.

Ask if you can attend departmental meetings if you are not regularly included. Although teachers may be suspicious at first, make it clear that you are not "spying" for the administration, but simply hoping to learn more about what they are teaching so that you can provide better assistance. You may not win over everyone immediately, but in all likelihood, several teachers will be pleasantly surprised by your interest and will welcome your help.

If others in the school community do not understand what it is that we do, explain it to them—without using "libraryese"! Don't talk about collection development policies. Instead, talk about choosing materials that will help the sophomores in your school learn about primary sources, since last year's standardized tests showed that the students were weak in that area.

Don't talk about weeding the collection. Share examples of books that you are discarding because the information is wrong, outdated, biased, or stereotypical. Most faculty and administrators have no idea how old the collections are in many school libraries in this country and can be convinced only through specific examples.

It is difficult to make a compelling argument that the library media budget must be increased when the library's shelves are filled to capacity with books, even if the books are more than 30 years old and completely irrelevant to the current curriculum. Demonstrate why empty shelves are better than shelves filled with books that have outdated, incorrect, and misleading information.

Don't talk about flexible access or flexible scheduling. Talk about giving students and teachers opportunities to use the library's books and computers, and the library media specialist's assistance throughout the school day. Show how the resources provided through the library media program can help students pose questions and discover answers—when they need them.

The "if I whine long enough, someone will give me more money or space or help for my library program" tactic was used without much success during much of the 20th century. It is now time to employ the activist approach. We must take responsibility for documenting the importance of the library media program to student learning. We must then present this evidence in compelling terms that demonstrate the value of the program to our users, rather than merely applaud (or bemoan) the virtue of our work.

SOURCE: Adapted from Ann Carlson Weeks, "Stop the Whining," *School Library Journal* (September 1, 2001): 56–57. Courtesy of *School Library Journal.*

Stepping outside!

by Paul Rux

How do you keep going? How do you keep yourself fresh as a librarian?

Professional reading is one tested way. Continuing education through colleges and conferences, workshops, meetings, and courses are others. Eventually, online, interactive learning technology will pipe much of this kind of educational cornucopia to anyone with access to a phone line, modem, and personal computer.

Five nontraditional ways to develop as a professional are (1) vendors, (2) benchmarking, (3) internships, (4) writing, and (5) travel.

Vendors

Sales representatives are excellent resources for personal and professional growth.

First, salespeople are not apt to talk down to you, unless they want to abort a sale. Salespeople are nonthreatening and share expertise with us as equals.

Second, salespeople must compete to survive. This means they must be on top of their products and expertise as well as those of their competition. If we want handles on trends—present and future—we need to take time to get to know our vendors.

Third, vendors are excellent, informed pipelines to jobs. If we want to know who's coming and going out there with a view to getting a better job, we ought to build a personal rapport with our vendors.

Benchmarking

Benchmarking means creative borrowing. Quality experts in business and industry benchmark regularly. They identify a process in need of improvement in their organization. Then, they see how an organization noted for success in another field handles the same process. The experts compare how the two organizations handle the same process, creatively borrow features from the success story, and apply them to the process in need of improvement. None of us has to be a quality expert in order to do such creative borrowing.

People in the same line of work tend to clone themselves. There's a tendency for them to think alike. The idea in benchmarking is to take a look at problems from fresh vantage points. Go outside your own field in order to creatively borrow and benefit from the "success stories" of others.

Internships

Unfortunately, we tend to see internships as something for students, not practicing professionals. Internships in mid or late career offer exciting avenues for professional development. We ought to treat ourselves to internships—and often!

Writing

Writing has been an important way to keep developing as a professional. In fact, the best professional publications—and most successful—are those which invite articles, reviews, and opinion pieces from practitioners.

Fortunately, most librarians like reading and writing. It's natural and easy, therefore, for many of us to write book reviews. This is a good place to start. Traditionally, reviewers get to keep the review copy of the book. The review itself is usually short, and there's nothing like seeing your name in print at the end of the review as the reviewer! In the process, you also have expanded your professional knowledge.

Typically, the next level of writing is articles or opinion pieces. To put something in writing so somebody else can easily make sense of it means the writer needs to be on top of the subject. This need for subject mastery in writing is a good way to develop professionally.

The nice part of most writing projects is that usually you can do them on your own and at your own rate of speed. In the bargain, they can be good escape from inevitable mundane problems. The point is: there are lots of formats and outlets for writing, from letters to editors, to crafting books. All of us have something to say and share—especially after service in the trenches!

Travel

There's an old saying about how travel can broaden one's outlook. Today, one can purchase library tours as part of some university's formal continuing education program. However, I prefer the informal, impromptu approach. We need to step outside the routine channels of our lines of work to seek out professional development.

SOURCE: Adapted from Paul Rux, "Stepping Outside," *The Book Report* 13 (November/December 1994): 18–19. *The Book Report* is now published as *Library Media Connection*. Used with permission.

How to be an international school librarian

by Sarah Prescott

Hankering to explore new horizons? Here's a how-to guide to becoming an international school librarian.

Always had a yen to travel? Looking for a radical alteration in lifestyle? Well, as you actually have some time to ponder, perhaps you should consider the always-amazing, ever-evolving, nothing-ever-works-quite-right world of international librarianship. Here are some answers as well as some resources where you can go to find more information.

The schools that need to employ school librarians are U.S.-sponsored international schools. They serve American families working abroad, as well as students from the host country. There are approximately 180 such schools, located in 113 different countries, and more are opening every year. The curriculum is American, the instruction is in English, and there are usually English as a Foreign Language classes for students new to the school. The majority of the students will attend college upon graduation.

In addition to these schools, there are the Department of Defense Dependents Schools (DoDDs) for kids whose parents are in the American military. The schools are well established and are often in need of specialists, such as librarians.

An important fact to know: as most of these are independent institutions, they can vary widely in quality. An educational board from the United States must approve them, but there are no unions or organizations ensuring teachers' rights. Most of the schools are reputable and follow the terms stated in their contracts. It is important to remember, however, that it is up to you to research a school before accepting a contract.

The majority of the international schools hire through recruitment agencies. These agencies screen applicants and organize large hiring fairs, which both applicants and school administrators attend. Before going any further, know that most of the agencies charge a fee, both to join and to attend their hiring fair. These fees can range anywhere from $5 to $150, but on average expect to pay $100.

The recruitment fairs, held on both the east and west coasts of the United States, take place in February and March for positions beginning in August or September of that year. Therefore, the time to contact agencies and ask questions is September; the time to complete paperwork is October; the time to make hotel reservations for attending a hiring fair is November; the time to read the agency's job listings is December; and, finally, the time to practice interviewing techniques and shop for a new suit is January.

The hiring fair is a fascinating experience in itself. Imagine a plush hotel filled to the brim with teachers and librarians, some single, many married. A buzz of excitement and talk fills the lounges, hallways, bars, and even the elevators. Everyone is busy greeting old friends, networking, asking questions, and scurrying around organizing paperwork.

Typically, you will arrive at the hotel on a Friday night and register at the fair. You are then handed a name tag and that golden list that tells who is hiring librarians and gives you some contact details. Most people then retire to their rooms to spend the rest of the evening poring over the positions available list and coming up with a strategy for the sign-up session that will be held the following morning from 8 a.m. to 10 a.m. In the sign-up session, every school that is recruiting will have a desk with one or two administrators scheduling educators for interviews. Therefore, it is very important to create a list of schools that interest you, so that you get in their lines early, before all the time slots for interviews are filled.

For librarians, this process is not as competitive as it is for teachers. Why is that? Although there are usually not many library positions—maybe up to 20 at a large fair—my experience has been that there will be only about that number of librarians attending, so the odds of obtaining a position are actually quite good. Also, recruiters will normally sit up and take notice when librarians approach them, as these positions are often hard to fill.

On the downside, some schools will fill a library position with a less-than-qualified person if they have to. Example: the wife of an administrator or the husband of a special education teacher will sometimes be offered a library job. These spouses often have teaching qualifications but no qualifications or experience as a librarian. Also, if you are a media specialist who is certified in more than one area, smaller schools may want to hire you as a part-time librarian and part-time teacher. This may be acceptable to you, but be sure to ask many questions concerning your work schedule before signing a contract.

Interviewing begins promptly after the interview sign-up session and goes all day Saturday and Sunday until 5:00 p.m., at which time the fair officially ends. Interviews are held in recruiters' hotel rooms, where they will usually have a table and chairs set up. If you were organized and fortunate in the sign-up session, you may have as many as eight interviews spread over two days. Therefore, you will spend the weekend interviewing, waiting in hallways with other candidates, and hurrying back to your room for more resumes.

Each interview lasts about 15 to 20 minutes, and you will be expected to be friendly but succinct. I have seen every style of dress and interviewing technique imaginable. Expect anything is all the advice that can be offered. Most recruiters are very nice and are simply trying to do their best to sort out a sea of faces and resumes. Be understanding of this and they will be grateful. Remember, you are a librarian and you will know within five minutes whether they know anything about the library and care about hiring a qualified professional.

Will you get an offer at the fair? More and more often the answer is yes, because as the international school market expands and there is a growing teacher shortage at home, fewer teachers are going overseas. This is especially true for specialists, of which, fortunately, you are one. If you are well qualified, interview well, and can fill a position they absolutely need filled, you may be offered a position during the first interview. But be careful—ask many questions and never accept an offer on the spot. Go away and think about it. You can always arrange to call them later, have another interview, or meet them at the cocktail party.

Yes, there is an informal cocktail party held on Saturday night in the hotel. This is the place to socialize, meet new people, and hobnob with recruiters. Personally, I find the whole thing overwhelming, but I force myself to put in a

half-hour appearance because recruiters have been known to draw people aside and make arrangements for second interviews.

Sunday is normally a calmer day. You will see some people relaxed, dressed in jeans and smiling. This means they have signed a contract and are floating around elated. Those who did not get any interviews or feel they have not done well are sometimes already checking out and leaving. But the majority of attendees are still bustling about looking hopeful, because Sunday is the day when the most contracts are offered. Also, there are many cases where recruiters will go on to other fairs and contact you only after they have attended them all. It is tough to leave a fair without a job after spending all that time, money, and emotional energy, but don't give up hope. There are also hiring fairs held in June, and an agency might contact you as late as August to fill a vacant position.

Most educators are offered a two-year contract, although occasionally some may be offered a one- or three-year contract. Salaries and benefits vary widely, but generally look for:

A salary paid in U.S. dollars or a local currency that is on par with the U.S. dollar;
Free or subsidized housing;
Quality health insurance;
R & R, meaning that you're able to return home once a year, or once every two years;
Free or reduced tuition for your children;
And at least six weeks paid vacation every year.

The important question to ask about salary is not how much you will earn, but how much of that salary will you be able to save. In other words, what is the cost of living and will my salary cover that?

Schools hire single candidates as well as married teaching teams. Those without children stand a better chance than those with, but there are many teaching families overseas. I would be concerned if you have more than two children, which seems to be the acceptable number. If you do, then make sure that you have qualifications that are in demand, a lot of experience, and some great recommendations.

A note for teaching couples: your chances of being successful depend a great deal on how you fit professionally as a couple. If, for example, you are a librarian and your spouse is a music teacher, then technically you will both be sought after—but the odds of finding a school that needs both are quite small. If you are a librarian and your spouse is an elementary school teacher or is certified in a number of areas, then you increase your chances greatly. The recruiting agencies are very helpful in answering questions about this sort of thing. Ring or e-mail them to ask frankly about your chances and they will usually answer quite honestly.

Pets are allowed, depending on the country. But be prepared for lots of paperwork and some stress for you and the animal.

Now that you understand the bare essentials of how the system works, you must delve deep into your psyche and decide whether this rather portable lifestyle is for you. International schools are looking for a weird mix of individual qualities that often have nothing to do with your professional life. The list varies but here are the five basics:

Flexibility/adaptability: Can you read a story loudly enough to drown out a group of chattering monkeys sitting outside in the palm trees?

Resiliency: Can you work without air conditioning for eight hours in the heat of the summer?

Creativity: Can you create bulletin boards with only black paper and dried-out markers?

Risk-taking ability: Can you change a light bulb while standing on an old chair on a rickety table on the crooked floor of the library?

Sense of humor: Can you laugh when your computer goes up in smoke?

I have been an international librarian for four years. Parts of this adventure have been exhilarating and other parts harrowing, but I would not erase a single moment, as each one has helped me to grow in my understanding of people and thus, I believe, has made me a better librarian.

SOURCE: Adapted from Sarah Prescott, "Strangers in Paradise," *School Library Journal* 47, no. 6 (June 2001): 48–51. Courtesy of *School Library Journal.*

MATERIALS
CHAPTER THREE

Information power

Principle 5 of *Information Power* states, "The collections of the library media program are developed and evaluated collaboratively to support the school's curriculum and to meet the diverse learning needs of students."

Goals for the school library media specialist

1. Maintain current and comprehensive knowledge of the curriculum, of students' characteristics and needs, and of instructional and informational resources in the full range of formats and topic areas.
2. Collaborate with teachers and others to develop and publicize policies that govern selection and deselection of resources as well as reconsideration of questioned or challenged resources.
3. Develop and direct a continuous collection development and evaluation process that focuses on regular, collaborative assessment of teaching and diverse learning needs and the formats and resources to meet them.
4. Maintain and use a variety of appropriate, up-to-date tools and techniques—for example, reviewing sources, published evaluations, and selected Internet sites—to locate and select materials.
5. Promote learning resources by maintaining and circulating published evaluations of materials and equipment, by establishing opportunities for teachers and others to preview resources, and by soliciting teachers' and students' regular evaluations of program collections.

SOURCE: Adapted from "Information Access and Delivery," chapter 5 in *Information Power: Building Partnerships for Learning* (Chicago: American Library Association, 1998), 90–91.

Collection development: Our assignment through history
by Blanche Woolls

Choosing materials for school libraries requires more attention now than in the beginning when much less funding was available to purchase items. In the United States, the 1876 report *Public Libraries in the United States of America* described school libraries in one county in Indiana as having 2,066 volumes: taken out during year, 428; added during year, 17. An accompanying note read,

"Each township has a good bookcase and the books are kept tolerably well. In some townships they are not kept as well as in others. They get weak for want of exercise." The slow development of school libraries continued during the early 1900s.

It was not until the mid-1960s that dedicated dollars for school libraries arrived from the U.S. government through President Johnson's Great Society plan in the aftermath of the Russians' launch of *Sputnik* and in the hope that education could become equal to all. Elementary and Secondary Education Act funding allowed school librarians additional money to choose books and media beyond their very limited local dollars. Suddenly we were able to buy more titles than those starred reviews in *School Library Journal* or selections from *Booklist,* allowing us to actively seek teacher recommendations. It was not that easy to encourage teachers to recommend titles for addition to the library collection.

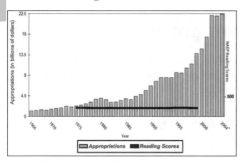

The federal funds stopped, and school district administrators neglected to increase local funding. Lack of success in efforts to include teachers in selection often meant lack of success in including them in other activities within the library. Lack of interest in selecting materials predicted lack of support for school libraries when cuts in funds first reduced materials budgets and then resulted in reassignment of school librarians to classrooms, with their replacement by clerical aides and volunteers.

Funding for school libraries remained stagnant for 10 years. As funds were increased to support education in the mid-1980s, attention turned to providing microcomputer technologies for students rather than supporting information resources in the library. Those school librarians who had weathered the storm now began using computers as online public access catalogs and purchased references on CD-ROM, justifying these as technology expenditures. The work to convert to an online catalog and to purchase the best in CD-ROMs was a professional task, moving the school librarian into an essential role in the area of technology.

While some attention is turning back to adding print reference books as well as fiction and nonfiction, the major thrust still remains with technology. Online access to the Internet sometimes leads the uninformed to believe that library collections are no longer necessary. School librarians who have not made their presence appreciated in the past aren't consulted about the changes or asked what software would be best. Mistakes in the choice of online resources waste limited funds. The inability of students to make the best use of what they locate and to use information wisely means a waste of their education. The importance of an excellent collection of resources managed by a capable information professional is essential on many levels. School librarians are essential for collection building, especially with the inclusion of online resources. Maintaining the collection defines our worth to our school communities, but it isn't all.

Improvement in hardware and software, combined with access to commercial databases, creates problems for all types of librarians who must use steady-

3

state or reduced funds for print materials that continue to increase in price. Publishers dictate the choice between online and print periodicals, or insist on the purchase of both to get one or the other, or they may offer one for a greatly reduced rate if you buy the opposite format. If the publisher does not make the choice for you, how do you decide? Obviously back issues of print require storage, and retrieval and shelving are major considerations. Yet, how will we budget for future increasing charges for online services? When we halt the purchase of an online service, we immediately lose access to past resources as well as present and future access to the resource. Demonstrating and explaining options to administrators and teachers is one way to show your worth to your school community.

The dilemma of what to buy is critical, and with many choices of available databases, it is not an easy task. If we are to build and maintain an adequate collection, especially with limited funding, of the best resources for our students, we must make careful, critical choices. We must choose the best possible sources of information resources with our database choices. You are the expert when it is time to make these choices. If you need some suggestions, check the literature for articles for evaluative summaries and comparisons between companies when selecting databases. Post a note to LM_NET and you will receive more mail than you thought possible. Your ability to choose the best makes you an asset, an essential component in the education of students and the assistance to teachers and administrators as well as students who have questions for which they need relevant and accurate answers.

Negotiating with publishers of databases is difficult for they are striving to make a profit in the midst of strong competition. You are the expert to make sure the choice is the best one for quality and price. You will apply the selection criteria as you have been applying the criteria to other purchases.

In some states in the United States, the department of education or the state library uses state funding to purchase multiple-use licenses to databases, and then all types of libraries may use the state licenses. This model may often be not only the best but, for smaller school districts, the only means for school librarians to reap the benefits of more resources for their available funds. When communities lack access to a "free" system, school librarians organize to share the purchase of a database. With consortium purchases, the shared cost makes it affordable. Your worth to your school district is in knowing with whom to negotiate to save the district funds through a consortium. Indeed, you may be the catalyst to get the consortium started.

Your job doesn't end with finding resources. It takes a competent school librarian to show teachers and students how to use these resources wisely. This begins to address our greatest challenge: survival in a networked world. The opening of the Internet to educational institutions and the expansion of resources available on the World Wide Web have added new dimensions to access to information. These dimensions are little understood by students, teachers, administrators, and parents. In some cases, online resources do replace print, but in others, they do not. Who is going to help students decide when information is inaccurate or irrelevant?

SOURCE: Adapted from Blanche Woolls, "Collection Development: Our Assignment through History," *School Libraries in Canada* 21 (2002): 7–8. Used with permission.

Evaluating your library media center collection

by Arlene Kachka

Fine-tuning the collection is a vital and ongoing part of every library media center program. Every day, we should look at our collection and evaluate if it is meeting the needs of our students and faculty. The following strategies will improve your collection.

Books

With the advent of the Internet, the way we select books has changed. When considering books for purchase, we now ask: Is the same information available on the Internet for free? The availability and quality of reference sources from the Internet means funds may be available to purchase additional fiction, paperback, career, or foreign language titles.

Weeding is an important part of fine-tuning your collection. Discarding outdated and worn books leaves your shelves with the best your library has to offer. The library collection should keep pace with changing social issues. Students need to be informed, and the materials that students check out of your library and bring home communicate directly to parents the quality of library service.

Periodicals

Selecting periodicals becomes easier as you become familiar with the needs and tastes of your students and faculty. Ask your students and faculty which periodicals they would like to see added to the library collection. Students still enjoy reading the issues in hand, rather than on the Internet. Tailor your periodical order to include duplicate issues of magazines that are used for class assignments.

Technology

This is the big one. Evaluating the many resources available for purchase on the Internet can be an overwhelming task. How do you choose the best online resources available for the library? The best advice is to try before you buy. A free trial should be available for any online product being considered for purchase. Here are additional points to consider when selecting online products for preview or purchase:

Does the online product include remote access? Is the number of connections provided to the school limited?

Does the company provide good customer service and technical support?

If you are considering a periodical database, will your students recognize the sources included? Does the database include pictures, multiple search methods, and links to websites on the subject? Can students e-mail the articles to their own accounts?

The bottom line

Keep on top of fine-tuning your collection by making it an ongoing process. Recognize that gaps will occur as curriculum requirements, individual class requirements, and student enrollment change. Record these gaps on a list as they become apparent so you can respond to these changing needs.

In addition to listening to students, you can survey them to determine whether your collection is meeting their needs. Ask your students and faculty what they want and need; they will let you know how your collection stacks up.

3

SOURCE: Adapted from Arlene Kachka, "Evaluating Your Library Media Center Collection," *The Book Report* 19, no. 5 (March/April 2001): 19–20. *The Book Report* is now published as *Library Media Connection.* Used with permission.

Children's freedom to read

by Phyllis J. Van Orden and Kay Bishop

Media specialists continually call on decision-making skills while building a collection. Each decision reflects personal perceptions of the characteristics of collections, views about the responsibilities of a selector, and philosophical positions on issues. For example, the materials selected reflect the media specialist's stance on intellectual freedom and students' rights. The media specialist's position on these and other issues consciously or unconsciously influences decisions about the collection.

These issues are complex and can arise within a variety of contexts: social, ethical, economic, political, religious, psychological, or in regard to pornography. The issues are not new. We constantly scrutinize the opinions of both society and our profession. You, the media specialist, must know yourself. Where do you stand on those issues? Bear in mind the very real possibility that you may one day face situations where you may not wish to select something for the collection because of your beliefs.

Children's rights: First Amendment rights

In the United States, the First Amendment serves as the basis of intellectual rights. A child's intellectual rights can be viewed as legal rights as well as ethical rights. The application of the First Amendment to children generally arises in matters dealing with public education, particularly in court cases concerning censorship. David Moshman, in his *Children's Intellectual Rights: A First Amendment Analysis,* describes the intellectual rights of children as

Legal rights

Free Expression—Government may not control a child's right to form or express ideas.

Freedom of Nonexpression—Government may not require a child to adopt or express belief in a particular idea.

Freedom of Access—Government may not restrict children's access to ideas and sources of information.

Free Exercise of Religion—Government may not restrict children from acting according to their religious beliefs.

Distinction of Child from Adult—Limiting First Amendment rights must be based on compelling reasons by showing that harm would occur because the children in question are less competent than the typical adult.

Moral rights

Free Expression II—A child has the right to form, express, and communicate ideas.

Freedom of Nonexpression II—A child has the right to choose not to adopt or express belief in particular ideas.

Inculcation II—Children have the right not to be indoctrinated and to be subject to inculcation only when there is a legitimate reason.

Freedom of Access II—Individuals responsible for children's development have an obligation to provide access to diverse sources of information and to diverse opinions and perspectives.

Free Exercise of Religion II—Children have a right to act according to their religious beliefs unless such actions would be harmful or illegal.

Distinction of Child from Adult II—Restrictions on children's intellectual rights should be based on the individual child's circumstances and intellectual limitations.

Right to Education—Children have the right to the type of environment that will facilitate their intellectual development to the extent of their intellectual limitations.

Librarians tend to take one of two positions. One position, the protector, assumes that adults know what is best for children, what will harm them, what information they need, and how their needs should be met. Such protectors create barriers. The other position, the advocate, assumes an open stance, perceiving children as capable of defining both their information needs and their resource needs. The first position strives to protect students from themselves, from others, and from ideas. The second strives to help students identify, evaluate, retrieve, and use information.

Selection is a process of choosing among materials. The choices are relative as one item is compared with others. In choosing materials, the media specialist strives to give each item fair consideration and makes a concerted effort to suppress personal biases. In censorship, an individual or a group attempts to impose certain values on others by limiting the availability of one or more items.

Elements of censorship

Censorship can be described in terms of who is doing the questioning, which materials they are questioning and what is being questioned, and how the questions are handled.

The American Library Association's (ALA) Intellectual Freedom Committee (1996) offers the following definitions for various levels of inquiry and challenge to materials in the collection:

Expression of Concern—An inquiry that has judgmental overtones.

Oral Complaint—An oral challenge to the presence and/or appropriateness of specific material.

Written Complaint—A formal, written complaint filed with the institution (library, school, etc.), challenging the presence and/or appropriateness of specific material.

Public Attack—A publicly disseminated statement challenging the value of the materials presented to the media and/or others outside the institutional organization in order to gain public support for further action.

Censorship—A change in the access status of material, based on the content of the work and made by a governing authority or its representatives, including: exclusion, restriction, removal, or age/grade level changes. (American Library Association, 1996, 47–48)

Common objections to materials include sexuality, profanity, obscenity, immorality, witchcraft, nudity, occultism, and violence. Less frequently cited reasons include incest, mental illness, and slavery. Censors state family values and the immaturity of students as reasons for their challenges.

If either freedom of expression or freedom of access to ideas is stifled, then intellectual freedom does not exist. Ironically, commitment to intellectual freedom obligates media specialists to safeguard the rights of censors. On the one hand, media specialists recognize the right to unrestricted access to information; on the other hand, media specialists recognize the right to protest.

Before the 1990s, the majority of censorship challenges dealt with materials that were housed in the school library. However, with the advent of Internet access in school libraries, one of the main targets of censorship has been the use of the Internet.

The Internet is very different from other resources in the school library in that it is made up of a huge number of resources, many of which provide rich research materials for students. However, the Internet also provides access to numerous sites that a school media specialist would not consider useful or appropriate for students' use in the school library. Initially, the choice was an all-or-nothing proposition for school libraries: Either provide access to the Internet or don't provide it. Because of the possibility of accessing inappropriate sites (particularly those that were sexually graphic), many parents, organized groups, and legislators challenged access to the Internet in media centers (or anywhere in the school). It is important that a school have a written Internet policy or an acceptable use policy (AUP) that includes parental consent for the use of the Internet. It is essential that school media specialists be well acquainted with any policies (state, district, or school) that relate to Internet access in their school libraries.

INDEX
LIBRORVM
PROHIBITORVM
ALEXANDRI VII Pontificis Maximi
iussu editus.

SOURCE: Adapted from Phyllis J. Van Orden and Kay Bishop, *The Collection Program in Schools: Concepts, Practices, and Information Sources*, 3rd ed. (Englewood, Colo.: Libraries Unlimited, 2001), 35–45. Used with permission.

School library resources: Jobbers

Books

Baker & Taylor, Inc.
http://www.btol.com/
Baker & Taylor, Inc.
2550 W. Tyvola Road, Suite 300
Charlotte, NC 28217
Telephone: (800) 775-1800; (704) 998-3100

Blackwell
http://www.blackwellpublishing.com/
350 Main Street
Malden, MA 02148
Telephone: (781) 388-8200
Fax: (781) 388-8210

The Book House, Inc.
http://www.thebookhouse.com/
208 West Chicago St.
Jonesville, MI 49250
Telephone: (800) 248-1146; (517) 849-2117
Fax: (800) 858-9716; (517) 849-9716

The Booksource
http://www.booksource.com/
1230 Macklind Avenue
St. Louis, MO 63110
Telephone: (800) 444-0435; (314) 647-0600
Fax: (800) 647-1923

Brodart Co.
http://www.brodart.com/
500 Arch Street
Williamsport, PA 17705
Telephone: (800) 233-8467
Fax: (570) 326-6799

Cook's Books
http://www.cooksbookcompany.com/
246-248 Woodwork Lane
Palatine, IL 60067
Telephone: (800) 232-6244
Fax: (800) 232-3299

Crown West Media
http://crownwestmedia.com/
575 East 1000 South
Orem, UT 84097
Telephone: (800) 658-8516; (801) 224-1455
Fax: (801) 426-5042

Follett Library Resources

http://www.flr.follett.com/
1340 Ridgeview Drive
McHenry, IL 60050
Telephone: (815) 759-1700; (888) 511-5114

Gumdrop Books

http://gumdropbooks.com/
802 N. 41st Street
P.O. Box 505
Bethany, MO 64424
Telephone: (800) 821-7199; (660) 425-7777
Fax: (660) 425-3929

Ingram Book Group

http://www.ingrambookgroup.com/
One Ingram Blvd.
P.O. Box 3006
La Vergne, TN 37086-1986
Telephone: (800) 937-5300

Junior Library Guild

http://www.juniorlibraryguild.com/
7858 Industrial Parkway
Plain City, OH 43064
Telephone: (800) 743-4070
Fax: (800) 827-3080

Knowbuddy Resources

http://www.knowbuddyresources.com/
Post Office Box 37
Collingwood, Ontario
Canada L9Y 3Z7
Telephone: (800) 667-1121
Fax: (705) 444-0274; (800) 561-1763

Library Media Service

http://www.librarymediaservice.com/
112 Nod Road Unit 12
Clinton, CT 06413
Telephone: (800) 222-8663
Fax: (860) 669-9521

Mackin Library Media

http://www.mackin.com/
14300 W. Burnsville Parkway
Burnsville, MN 55306
Telephone: (800) 245-9540
Fax: (800) 369-5490

ainbow Book Company
http://www.rainbowbookcompany.com/
500 East Main Street
Lake Zurich, IL 60047
Telephone: (800) 255-0965; (847) 726-9930
Fax: (847) 726-9935

Regent Book Company
http://www.regentbook.com/
25 Saddle River Road
South Hackensack, NJ 07606
Telephone: (800) 999-9554; (973) 574-7600
Fax: (888) 597-3661

Southeastern Book Company
http://www.sebcobooks.com/
2001 SW 31st Ave.
Pembroke Park, FL 33009
Telephone: (800) 223-3251
Fax: (954) 987-2200

YBP Library Services
http://www.ybp.com/
999 Maple Street
Contoocook, NH 03229
Telephone: (800) 258-3774; (603) 746-3102
Fax: (603) 746-5628

Audiovisual: General

Blackwell
http://www.blackwellpublishing.com/
350 Main Street
Malden, MA 02148
Telephone: (781) 388-8200
Fax: (781) 388-8210

Califone International, Inc.
http://www.califone.com/
21300 Superior Street
Chatsworth, CA 91311
Telephone: (800) 722-0500
Fax: (818) 407-0397

Distribution Video & Audio, Inc. (DVA)
http://www.dva.com/
133 Candy Lane
Palm Harbor, FL 34683
Telephone: (727) 447-4147
Fax: (727) 441-3069

Live Wire Media
http://www.livewiremedia.com/
273 Ninth Street
San Francisco, CA 94103
Telephone: (800) 359-5437; (415) 564-9500

Audiovisual: Software

Ace Video Resources Software
http://www.acemath.com/
11767 South Dixie Highway, Suite 222
Miami, FL 33156
Telephone: (888) 223-6284
Fax: (305) 256-0467

Audiovisual: Video

AEC One Stop Group
http://www.aent.com/
23 Francis J. Clarke Circle
Bethel, CT 06801
Telephone: (800) 329-7664

Distribution Video & Audio, Inc. (DVA)
http://www.dva.com/
133 Candy Lane
Palm Harbor, FL 34683
Telephone: (727) 447-4147
Fax: (727) 441-3069

Library Video Company
http://www.libraryvideo.com/
P.O. Box 580
Wynnewood, PA 19096
Telephone: (800) 843-3620; (610) 645-4000
Fax: (610) 645-4040

Developing electronic library collections

by Diane Kovacs

Librarians invest time and resources in creating reference websites because doing so extends four familiar library service functions into cyberspace:

Selection: Users who can rely on reference websites save significant time by avoiding inefficient, inconclusive web surfing.

Endorsement: Librarians implicitly vouch for the quality of the linked sources—their relevance for solving a given problem, their constant availability, and the accuracy and currency of their content.

Organization: A well-designed website allows users to move rapidly and accurately among a large number of websites, finding a high proportion of relevant resources.

Cooperation: These sites allow experienced librarians to share their knowledge of the Web with each other and with users, at all times of the day and irrespective of distance.

Another analogy we might use is that the Internet is like the shelves that we fill with organized books/information products. The Web is an information product supplier. We must select what we want to organize on our own e-library shelves.

Learning from what other e-builders have already done is the best strategy to follow in planning your own e-library project. At this state in the development of e-libraries there is no need for anyone to recreate the wheel and try to create their e-library from scratch as it were.

Preliminary planning for the web-based e-library

1. Is an Internet-connected computer running web server software already available through your organization?
2. What computer hardware and web server software will need to be purchased or otherwise acquired? What will it cost? How will it be funded?
3. Are personnel available that are knowledgeable enough to produce and maintain an e-library by collecting, evaluating, and selecting resources and incorporating them into a website?
4. How much time do you estimate that responsible individuals will be able to commit to the planning, collecting, evaluating and selecting of Internet resources, construction, and maintenance of the e-library?
5. How many people will be needed to plan, collect, evaluate, and select Internet resources and then maintain the e-library?

Knowledge necessary to evaluate Internet information

1. Nature—Awareness of the nature of Internet information: bad stuff and good stuff on the Internet.
2. Problems—Awareness and understanding of basic problems with information obtained from the Internet.
3. Source Determination—How to acquire the information needed to determine the source. It is useful to remember the mnemonic PAST: Purpose and privacy; Authority and accuracy; Source and security; and Timeliness.

Good stuff on the Internet

1. Personal web pages that offer valuable educational information
2. Commercial pages that offer product support, directory services, tutorials, or other valuable services
3. Government pages that provide government-collected information
4. Educational pages from universities, colleges, schools, museums, and other organizations with educational missions
5. Discussion lists and newsgroups with education, research, or professional intent
6. MUDS, IRC, or web chat or people just talking about matters of interest

Basic problems with Internet information

Some basic problems with information obtained from the Internet, or just about anywhere else for that matter, are listed below in order of their observed frequency on the Web:

1. Typos
2. Factual errors (accidental or deliberate)
3. Opinion stated as fact
4. Out-of-date information
5. Bias
6. Deliberate fraud

3

SOURCE: Adapted from Diane Kovacs, *Building Electronic Library Collections: The Essential Guide to Selection Criteria and Core Subject Collections* (New York: Neal-Schuman, 2000), 17–18, 19–21. Used with permission.

The search is on

by Dawn Dobie, Marilyn Fowler, Kevin Coots, and Adele Bildersee

[*Ed. Note:* Many database names have changed since this article was written. Names of databases have been removed from examples.]

Doing a search on Google, an eighth-grade chemistry class student, exploring the periodic table of elements focusing on the element argon, gets 73,300 hits, many of which are from universities and above her reading level.

To help students avoid wading through a deluge of unreliable Internet sites, more and more school libraries are investing in online periodical databases. These databases are amazing resources, which over the last decade have allowed K–12 school libraries to vastly expand the range and depth of information available to students.

But, with a large number of databases available, and increasingly complex offerings, how does a school figure out which database to buy? To answer that question, we assembled a team of library media specialists and teachers to test-drive and rate the major products. We looked for products geared toward K–12 students and available nationally and then tried to test a typical system that a school might use. In choosing products to review, we used the marketing information on the vendors' Web sites to determine which products were appropriate for each grade level. Some systems are marketed as appropriate for various ages.

We found that these systems have improved significantly in the last few years, especially in the range of resources offered and in their ease of use. While it's not that complicated to put together a large database of periodicals, it is complicated to put together something even a fifth-grader can use. Now, thanks to better graphics and searching innovations that anticipate students' needs, even elementary-school children can perform successful online research.

There are important distinctions among the various systems, but despite these differences, all the databases we looked at are above average in quality—a library might not go wrong buying any of these products. Still, there was simply no database we could call "the best." That's because these products have such varied features that what's best for one school or grade level would not be the best choice for another. A librarian working to choose a database needs to look at his or her curriculum, student reading levels, the kind of technical support they can expect, and of course, price.

The cost of subscriptions to these databases varies significantly. Your library may negotiate different rates, depending on your school population, your membership in a consortium, or prenegotiated state agreements. And, of course, adding or subtracting content or choosing a different package can affect the price you'll pay. Still, while every library does not have a dream budget, we believe that good products can be purchased in all price ranges.

Searchability. In evaluating the databases, one of our key criteria was searchability. We found that all the databases offer the advantage of multiple search methods. In addition, most allow for natural-language searching and provide many limiters within advanced searching. But, we found that the best searching systems also offer subject headings for the articles that come up in a results list. Even a database can give students too much material that's not on their topic—these subject headings help them hone in on the right resources. Another handy feature in some databases is a tool that lets users receive search results classified by category—for instance, magazine articles, encyclopedia articles, maps, or multimedia. Some products also help students narrow their searches by providing general subject headings that become more and more narrow as the students choose among categories.

Types of resources. We found an impressive number and variety of high-quality materials in all the databases we examined. How do database holdings differ? Most provide general interest and current events magazines, but beyond that, some have specialized subject focuses.

Formats included. Another way databases differ is by the types of formats in which they provide information—some offer only magazines and newspapers, while others add images, audio, video, photos, and maps. With students doing more and more multimedia presentations, having both graphics and traditional print is helpful. But, before you sign up for a glitzy product, check your school's bandwidth to make sure you can use it.

Currency. The time span for holdings in the databases we examined varies from 2 years to more than 10. Our view is that with the many topics students research—especially historical and literary ones—an archive that reaches further back in time offers a greater wealth of resources. At the same time, we were impressed with the currency of materials included in most databases. Frequently we ran across articles with publication dates a few days ahead of the current day. Some databases have reviewers choose articles for inclusion. This review process delays articles being posted for about a month (except in the "current events" section). The user trades immediate access for a reviewed and indexed product.

Help. Users who need help learning the ropes of searching can find aids in most of the databases. But in our experience, help sections that are searchable are much quicker to provide answers than those that only offer an index of help topics.

Technical support. In the event of problems with a database, good technical support is essential. Most companies have toll-free telephone support on weekdays.

After using these databases extensively, it was clear to us that any of them can do a good search. But it was also clear that only well-trained students and teachers can search effectively. Even with user-friendly features like natural-language searching, librarians must teach students how to use the powerful tools that today's K–12 databases provide. The subscription is just the first step along that road.

Elementary level

3

Searchability. The introduction of natural-language searching has been a boon for the elementary set. They can simply write in any way that is comfortable and the database will figure out what they are trying to find.

Navigability. Tabs, big buttons, and clearly defined links are all very helpful for younger children. All the databases have good navigation tools.

Help. Some databases use the same "help" language for their elementary-level databases as for the middle and high school levels. This is a problem because in order to be useful for children, help must be clear and simple. Some databases have hot links within the text that can help younger children find quick explanations.

Appearance. Most of the databases have attractive and appropriate interfaces.

Reading level. All the databases use a general grade level in some format, including reading levels.

Speed. All databases loaded quite well. Sometimes loading is a bit slower for graphics, but generally speed is quite acceptable.

Document printing, e-mailing, and saving. We gave the highest score to databases that allow for saving lists, as well as those that provide a variety of print formats. Several of the databases allow printing only through the browser function, which will vary with the version of the browser available to users.

Types and time span of resources. This varies a great deal among databases. Most have some graphics available, with several offering an outstanding array of materials.

Middle schools

Searchability. The databases are generally strong. Students who have become accustomed to "Ask Jeeves" want to use natural language for their searches. They will get better results (or at least we did) with Boolean searching, but the option of natural-language searching sets some databases apart from others. Some list subject headings with articles, which is important for narrowing searches to relevant results. The other databases do not consistently offer subject headings with articles, making for less effective, and sometimes more frustrating, searching.

Navigability. The strongest contenders in this category deliver consistent design, easy maneuvering from one part of the site to another, and icons to help along the way. The other databases are above average in navigability; some are inconsistent, however, about offering the same icons or destination choices throughout the site.

Help. The help sections of most databases are written for the intended audience level and provide examples to aid users.

Appearance. All of the databases have appealing visual qualities. None are crowded or confusing.

Reading level. Many packages reviewed were created specifically for middle school audiences. The reading levels of periodical articles can vary, so we gave a higher ranking to those that clearly display reading level in articles.

Speed. All the databases have above-average speed. At times, pages with high graphic content are slower to load.

Document printing, e-mailing, and saving. E-mailing is easy with all of the databases. Some offer more print formats than others.

Type and time span of resources. Users can find reliable, helpful information in all of these databases. The holdings of the databases vary in terms of time spans.

High schools

Searchability. All of the databases are well above average.

Navigability. Many high school students like to work on their own, so the ability to find what they want without getting lost or frustrated is important.

Help. Most help sections have subject or category divisions of assistance.

Appearance. Bright bold colors, soothing "cool" colors, earth tones, strong visual graphics, or no graphics at all, make each database unique.

Reading level. All of the databases reviewed are designed for high school students. One database allowed users to search by five different reading levels or by all levels. Users can even sort search results by reading level.

Speed. All loaded quickly during our evaluation and are rated excellent.

Printing, e-mailing, and saving. Though all of the databases had most of these functions, none had all of them together.

Type and time span of resources. Six of the products we evaluated hold articles and pictures from mainstream publications—and their offerings can enrich any high school library's collection. The seventh database did not score in the excellent range in any category. This does not mean it is not a worthwhile product. It focuses on diversity in America and includes views not often heard in the mainstream press. If students are researching topics that touch on ethnicity, race, religion, gender, disabilities, youth and age, they can find articles from smaller presses here.

SOURCE: Adapted from Dawn Dobie, Marilyn Fowler, Kevin Coots, and Adele Bildersee, "The Search Is On," *School Library Journal* 47, no. 11 (November 2001): 51–61. Courtesy of *School Library Journal.*

Databases

American National Biography
http://www.anb.org/
c/o Online Subscription Department
Oxford University Press
198 Madison Avenue
New York, NY 10016
Telephone: (800) 334-4249, ext. 6484
E-mail: onlinesubscriptions@oup-usa.org

Britannica Online
http://www.britannica.com/
310 South Michigan Ave.
Chicago, IL 60604
Telephone: (800) 323-1229; (312) 347-7159
Fax: (312) 294-2104

EBSCO Information Services
http://www.ebsco.com/home/
P.O. Box 1943
Birmingham, AL 35201-1943
Telephone: (205) 991-6600
Fax: (205) 995-1518
E-mail: ebsfeedback@ebsco.com

Facts on File
http://www.factsonfile.com/
132 W. 31st Street, 17th Floor
New York, NY 10001
Telephone: (800) 322-8755
Fax: (800) 678-3633

Gale Group
http://www.galegroup.com/
27500 Drake Rd.
Farmington Hills, MI 48331-3535
Telephone: (800) 877-GALE
Fax: (800) 414-5043
E-mail: galeord@thomson.com

HW Wilson
http://www.hwwilson.com/
950 University Avenue
Bronx, NY 10452
Telephone: (800) 367-6770; (718) 588-8400
Fax: (800) 590-1617; (718) 590-1617
E-mail: custserv@hwwilson.com

NewsBank, Inc.
http://www.newsbank.com/
4501 Tamiami Trail North, Suite 316
Naples, FL 34103
Telephone: (800) 762-8182
Fax: (239) 263-3004
E-mail: sales@newsbank.com

ProQuest
http://www.umi.com/
300 North Zeeb Road
P.O. Box 1346
Ann Arbor, MI 48106-1346
Telephone: (800) 521-0600; (734) 761-4700
E-mail: info@il.proquest.com

Scholastic Library Publishing
http://www.scholasticlibrary.com/grolierdocs/home.html
90 Old Sherman Turnpike
Danbury, CT 06816
Telephone: (800) 621-1115
Fax: (203) 797-3657

Online selection tools

by Beth Wrenn-Estes

School librarians have one of the most challenging jobs in education today. They are charged with managing the day-to-day operations of the school library and in many cases are responsible for teaching, too. The effective school librarian is one who collaborates with teachers and administrators to support curriculum and to improve standard testing scores. In order to achieve all the expectations of the school administration and teachers, school librarians must select the proper materials for their libraries and must also be financial wizards who can stretch library book budgets. Maintaining a collection that has the best primary source materials as well as the most current materials in core subject areas is a continual challenge.

Librarians learn to use their time wisely since time is one of their most precious commodities. The ability to use online selection tools helps facilitate selection. With the right electronic selection tools, ordering can be made much easier and less time consuming, and librarians can concentrate on other tasks and goals for the development of their collection.

In my position as the Library Acquisitions and Collection Development Supervisor for Denver Public Schools (DPS), I am responsible for finding tools and systems that help all 115 DPS librarians accomplish their ordering both quickly and effectively. My office provides the electronic selection tool and training and the districtwide, web-based, online catalog, Innovative Interfaces Inc. (III). Our electronic selection tool is "Title Source 2."

Two years ago DPS researched and selected an electronic selection tool and interfacing it with III has allowed us to select and order materials in a one-step process. The librarians select the best and most appropriate materials for their collections and the central staff both places and monitors the actual orders, tracking individual school accounts. Thus, the librarians' time is spent most on the most important aspect, selection.

Old-fashioned paper-based orders and paper catalogs slowed the system down due to the quantity of materials ordered each year. The clerical staff necessary to process all of the paper was costly. The original focus of the investigation of selection tools was financial, but we discovered that an added benefit of using an electronic selection tool was the time saved.

The amazing fact about using an electronic selection tool is that the amount of paper a librarian deals with diminishes substantially as trust in the tool develops. The electronic selection tool allows librarians to do the same process in an electronic environment by using online folders within the computer instead of paper files.

In choosing an electronic selection tool, consideration must be given to all of the different selection tools on the market. DPS found that many electronic selection tools have similar features. Sorting out the differences proved time-consuming and frustrating. A major criterion in choosing any tool is the number of steps required before reaching the desired results. If putting together an electronic list takes as much time as compiling a paper list, then the tool generally lacks the required sophistication.

Some online selection tools must be purchased while others are free of charge. Fee-based systems usually offer more enhancements. It is best to start with a list of desired features. For example, DPS required a custom interface to connect the selection tool to our III system requiring custom programming. However, a free tool may be feasible if requirements are less complex.

Three popular electronic selection tools on the market are Title Source 2 (TS2, Informata in partnership with Baker & Taylor), Bibz.com (Brodart), and TITLEWAVE (Follett). All three selection tools involve multiple steps to create title lists for ordering, TITLEWAVE being the most complicated. All three also allow you to search for Scholastic Reading Count and Accelerated Reader titles. Brodart has centered the Bibz.com tool on their own product line and does not include the features found in TITLEWAVE and TS2. The TS2 tool resembles Amazon.com with sophisticated features including the ability to blow up pictures of jacket covers. A unique feature of the TS2 is the fingertip access to all the current review sources (i.e., *School Library Journal*), on a menu bar that links by selecting the title and then adding it to the cart all in one step. TS2 has a weakness in searching series titles though, while TITLEWAVE excels in finding serial titles.

All three companies mentioned offer free trial periods; simply send an e-mail from their home pages requesting a test password. It is advisable to test several of the tools for at least a week before making a decision. A week allows you to think of all the different subjects and materials you may need to acquire and to actually input data that will be useful later in the decision-making process. DPS has no regrets about utilizing the available technology for collection development, ultimately leaving the paper behind. We recommend an electronic selection tool to anyone wanting more efficiency in school library collection development.

SOURCE: Adapted from Beth Wrenn-Estes, "Online Selection Tools: The Future for Collection Development in Public Schools," *Colorado Libraries* 28, no. 1 (Spring 2002): 14–15. Used with permission.

Race matters: A librarian looks at books about racial identity and relationships

by Ed Sullivan

Race is an issue that few people are comfortable discussing. Teachers want to avoid the controversies that inevitably arise. It's one of those topics, like politics and religion, that my mother always told me are impolite to discuss in public. But if we do not discuss race, how will we ever get past it? Until we are willing to have open and honest dialogue, the ignorance and misunderstanding that is at the root of racial prejudice will continue to divide us.

We still have a long way to go before we can achieve Dr. Martin Luther King Jr.'s dream of a world in which people are judged "not by the color of their skin but by the content of their character." In the last few years, there have been many novels and nonfiction books published that address historical and modern viewpoints on interracial relationships and racial identity, and this article offers an overview of how those works reflect racial realities and conflicts in American society and beyond.

When Tiger Woods became a prominent public figure several years ago, racial identity became a hot topic of discussion in the media. The multiracial Woods refused to categorize himself or to define himself by some societal label. Some outstanding books that address how young people grapple with, identify with, and ultimately define racial identity have recently come on the scene. Gary Nash's *Forbidden Love: The Secret History of Mixed-Race America* (Holt, 1999) offers a fascinating historical overview of mixed-race issues in America from colonial times through the late 20th century. In *What Are You? Voices of Mixed-Race Young People* (Holt, 1999), Pearl Fuyo Gaskins conducted in-depth

interviews with 80 mixed-race teens who spoke candidly about the problems they face with dating and family life, prejudice from whites and other racial groups, and their struggles to find their own place in the world. In *The Color of Our Future* (Morrow, 1999), Farai Chideya tackles a similar topic. She interviewed biracial and multiracial teens from a variety of geographic areas across the country. Her approach, however, is more like that of an investigative journalist.

Racially mixed young people wrestling with identity issues is a prominent theme in many novels with contemporary settings, such as Chris Crutcher's *Whale Talk* (Greenwillow, 2001), Han Nolan's *Born Blue* (Harcourt, 2001), and Marilyn Reynolds's *If You Loved Me* (Morning Glory, 1999). Jacqueline Woodson addresses both the issues of racial identity and interracial relationships in many of her novels, including *The House You Pass on the Way* (Delacorte, 1997) and *If You Come Softly* (Putnam, 1998).

Interracial relationships, whether they are about friendship or romance, always seem to be a source of great conflict, if not outright tragedy, for example, in Mel Glenn's *Foreign Exchange: A Mystery in Poems* (Morrow, 1999). Bruce Brooks depicts the tensions that arise in an interracial friendship with great skill in his Newbery Honor book *The Moves Make the Man* (HarperCollins, 1984). Sports serves as backdrop for similarly themed stories like David Klass's *Danger Zone* (Scholastic, 1996) and Chris Lynch's *Gold Dust* (HarperCollins, 2000).

Historical fiction has provided a perfect vehicle for bringing our sometimes painful past to life for contemporary readers and showing the human side of economic and political struggles as well as emerging social movements, as in Mildred D. Taylor's *The Land* (Penguin Putnam/Phyllis Fogelman, 2001). Katherine Paterson's *Jip: His Story* (Dutton, 1996), a novel set in mid-1800s Vermont, also depicts a young man trapped between two worlds by his mixed race. A female protagonist wrestles with the same identity problems in Sandra Forrester's *Dust from Old Bones* (Morrow, 1999).

The Civil Rights–era South serves as the setting for three novels about interracial friendships and the intense conflicts they cause: Kristi Collier's *Jericho Walls* (Holt, 2002), Diane Les Becquets's *The Stones of Mourning Creek* (Winslow, 2001), and Mildred Barger Herschler's *The Darkest Corner* (Front Street, 2000). A story with a contemporary setting in which the prejudices of parents come between a friendship is Adrian Fogelin's *Crossing Jordan* (Peachtree, 2000).

War comes between friends in Graham Salisbury's *Under the Blood-Red Sun* (Yearling, 1995). A story with a similar theme, but from a Canadian perspective, is Eric Walters's *War of the Eagles* (Orca, 1998). In Garry Disher's *The Divine Wind: Love Story* (Scholastic, 2002), prejudice among family and neighbors surfaces when white Hart Penrose and Japanese Mitsy Sennosuke begin dating in World War II Australia. Two stories in which interracial friendships develop in order to combat racism are Caroline Cooney's *Burning Up* (Delacorte, 1999) and Lorri Hewett's *Lives of Our Own* (Dutton, 1998).

These various books share the message that conflict, whether the inner struggle of a racially mixed individual wrestling with his or her identity or a violent act of prejudice, will always be there as long as we allow race to divide us. The subject may make us uncomfortable but ignoring the issue will not make it go away. Race does matter; it matters very much to many people and for many different reasons. These books can open up opportunities for librarians and teachers to engage readers in discussions about our nation's past and about our contemporary realities. It is only through open and honest dialogue that we can move toward realizing Dr. King's dream.

SOURCE: Adapted from Ed Sullivan, "Race Matters: A Librarian Looks at Books about Racial Identity and Relationships," *School Library Journal* 48, no. 6 (June 2002): 40–41. Courtesy of *School Library Journal.*

Books behind bars

by Melissa Madenski

In 1994, librarian Naomi Angier entered the Donald E. Long Juvenile Correctional Facility in Portland, Oregon, toting some of her favorite books for teens— titles by Stephen King, R. L. Stine, and Walter Dean Myers. She also brought along a bunch of graphic novels: Superman, Green Lantern, and Batman. Prior to Angier's coming, the library consisted of books that nobody else wanted: discarded titles from the nearby Multnomah County Library, magazines that the postal department had found undeliverable, and old books that community members felt like donating. But thanks to a two-year grant through the federal Library Services and Technology Act, which Angier had applied for, she was about to begin a new program with hip, teen-friendly titles for incarcerated young men and women.

"I started with the assumption that I could bring in a wide variety of books," she recalls. At the Long juvenile detention center, she planned to use a tried-and-true strategy for getting kids to read: simply give them the books that they were interested in, the ones that matched their interests. But the correctional facility staff informed Angier that she was not dealing with "normal" teens. Although she acknowledges that these are troubled kids doing time for serious crimes ranging from assault to theft to rape, she asserts that there is not as much difference between imprisoned youth and their "outside" peers as one might think. "Kids at the juvenile center," she says, "may be more needy, wanting more attention and adult response. They don't have the same veneer as teens on the outside, but they love the same stories."

That was the problem. Early on, correctional facility staffers began to criticize the appropriateness of the adult thrillers on Angier's circulation cart, page-turners that included novels by Stephen King and Dean

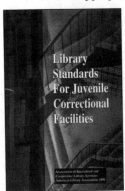

Koontz. The staff's thinking, says Angier, was that since some of the kids were serving time for committing violent crimes, stories with violent scenes would only fuel that kind of anti-social behavior.

Angier soon realized that she had made a major professional gaffe. "My greatest mistake was coming in without a written [book-selection] policy," she now says. She also realized that her new patrons didn't have the same First Amendment rights, the same guaranteed broad access to information, that their peers in the outside world enjoyed.

Before Angier began the program, she expected that its book-selection and intellectual freedom issues would be similar to those she had encountered working as a public librarian. She was wrong. After attending a workshop on juvenile detention center libraries, Angier realized that the boundaries for book selection and First Amendment rights in correctional facilities were all over the map.

Diana Reese, chairperson of the Library Services to Prisoners Forum and regional librarian for the Colorado Department of Corrections, says that when it comes to selecting books, detention centers have their own set of rules. "There's the obvious no's," explains Reese—no books that can aid in escapes, no books that encourage disruption or hatred, no books that are instructive in helping to commit a crime. Beyond those obvious no-brainers, opinions can differ widely on what's appropriate for troubled teens to read.

Angier continued to struggle along for almost two years without a book-selection policy, doing the jobs of five people—purchasing materials, giving book talks, scheduling volunteers, shelving and checking out books. But policy or no policy, Angier could see that she was making some headway with her captive audience. As she pushed the overflowing book cart to the detention center's 10 "pods," or locked units, her young patrons began to point out Angier to newcomers: "The librarian, she's really cool," they'd say. And as Angier met once a week with anywhere from 100 to 150 kids—individually or in small groups—kids began listening to her reading recommendations and began giving her requests of their own.

This is all the more impressive considering the fact that many of these 12-through 18-year-olds had never read an entire book. "This [is] very different than [serving] regular teens," says Angier. "They want books. They're in their rooms a lot. . . . They do not have open access to TVs and computers; they have some, [but] it's very limited, by honor status. Basically, they have nothing to do. And when you put a teenager in a situation where they have nothing to do, they become readers," she says, with a laugh. "It was just a matter of finding books that they were interested in."

As Angier continued to struggle to satisfy the detention center's administration and put good books into kids' hands, the unexpected happened. One day, when the head of the detention center was looking into a complaint about a novel, a formal book-selection policy that had been buried away in the detention center's archives suddenly surfaced. The existing policy specified that books should contain no explicit sex, no extreme violence, no gang literature, no hate literature. The policy also stated that a library book should be looked at as a whole—and not be judged on the basis of isolated passages.

With this policy in hand, Angier formed a library committee, whose members included the detention center's school custody workers, its teachers, and herself. And she went to work, applying the policy to the existing collection on a book-by-book basis. First off, she removed tales about violent crime that many staffers thought glorified crime in the inner city. She pulled two titles that she thought were inappropriate, and left the rest alone. She removed one book because of the adult nature of its sexual humor. And she yanked some comics because of their violent images and scantily clad women. She occasionally snipped out offending pictures from books—like a comic frame of two people having sex. On the other hand, although there were staff complaints about other books, Angier and the committee decided the books were valuable and should remain in circulation.

To satisfy some of the staff's concerns about inappropriate books falling into the hands of younger readers—the 12-, 13-, and 14-year-olds—she's also grouped some books by age appropriateness. In other words, Angier has made a lot of concessions she would never have dreamed of making back in her public library days.

Given the bald fact that Angier works in a center for incarcerated teens—and not in your typical public or school library—means that she routinely deals with challenges most librarians never encounter. Angier takes special care whenever she visits the sexual offenders' unit. Since research has established that there's a link between exposure to sexually explicit visual and written images and crimes of sexual violence, Angier carefully screens each book before checking it out, making sure it doesn't contain any lascivious content.

Complaints wax and wane, says Angier, but clearly the administration believes in her program. For the past two years, the department that oversees the correctional facility has picked up a third of the program's current operating budget: $93,000. The Multnomah County Library, which pays Angier's salary, covers the other two-thirds. In general, says Angier, the detention center staff is now supportive of the library services, even occasionally requesting books themselves.

As for Angier, she's changed, too. "I think when I actually started, I was such a strong, intellectual-freedom, public-librarian type that I had an 'Ahhh-you-can't-do-this type of attitude,'" she says. "What's worked really well—and it's not perfect—but what's worked somewhat well is the fact that I actually went ahead and did take out the most-offending books, did institute the age policy. I showed the people I was listening to them."

SOURCE: Adapted from Melissa Madenski, "Books Behind Bars," *School Library Journal* 47, no. 7 (July 2001): 40–42. Courtesy of *School Library Journal.*

Ability, disability, and picture books

by Linda L. Walling

[*Ed. Note:* This article addresses selecting materials for children with limitations or special strengths in specific learning modes. All books selected for them should meet the same criteria for quality literature as books selected for other children.]

Howard Gardner's *Frames of Mind* (1983) makes a strong case for seven types of intelligence: linguistic, musical, logical-mathematical, spatial, bodily-kinesthetic, and internal and external personal intelligence. Each can be viewed on a continuum from strength to deficit. A child can be strong in one intelligence and have a deficit in another. Christy Brown, with severe motor impairments and strong linguistic and artistic skills, is a well-known example. There is no apparent correlation between or among the intelligences. Nancy Pollette suggests that picture books can support a child's development in all of them. According to Walling and Marilyn Karrenbrock, many children with disabilities need picture books that are carefully selected with attention to their available learning modes.

Disabilities in children are developmental in nature. They interfere with the usual pattern of development and limit ability to adapt in the area of the disability. A child with severe hearing loss cannot easily compensate if the storyteller is at a distance. Some children use adaptive technologies to access picture books and to respond during storytime. Loss of vision most obviously affects use of picture books, but severe hearing impairments, dyslexia, mental retardation, and other disabilities interfere as well. Children who have difficulty using books because of low vision, deafness, or dyslexia are often labeled "print-impaired" or "reading-disabled."

Children who are developmentally advanced in one intelligence may use certain materials at a younger age. Children who are developmentally delayed may use the same materials when they are older than their age-mates.

Linguistic intelligence

Gardner says the "ability to use language to convince other individuals of a course of action, . . . to use [language] to help one remember information, . . . convey basic concepts, [and] . . . reflect upon language" is highly prized in today's society.

For strong linguistic skills. According to Judith W. Halstead, stories should introduce new, fascinating words, respect the child as an intelligent, learning person, and demonstrate "a playful, joyful sense of fun with words."

For linguistic deficits. A child with a linguistic deficit may have difficulty understanding words and/or expressing ideas verbally. The child may be labeled dyslexic, autistic, mentally retarded, brain-injured, or hearing-impaired. Coy Hunsucker

Cock-a-doodle-doo.
My dame has lost her shoe:
My master's lost his fiddlestick,
And knows not what to do.

suggests that visual, auditory, and/or tactile reinforcement can improve understanding. Taking plenty of time also improves understanding. Jed P. Luckow says stories need underlying themes of unity, a oneness of mood, plot, character, and harmony between picture and story or between picture and detail. The book's theme should be apparent on every page. "Colorful, tongue-tickling" phrases stimulate language, although they may lead to perseveration. Rhythmical speech and sound patterns aid understanding. The best stories for these children, according to Luckow, include a hero who is the only main character or part of a group operating as one. Large, simple print with good contrast and only a few words per page is best.

Logical-mathematical intelligence

Beginning with observations and objects, individuals move toward increasingly abstract formal systems. Gardner says these interconnections become matters of logic rather than of empirical observation.

For strong logical-mathematical skills. Books that challenge children at high levels of abstract and logical thinking may fascinate children with strengths in this intelligence.

For deficits in logical-mathematical development. Children with deficits in this area may be labeled learning-disabled, attention-deficit-disordered, autistic, mentally retarded, brain-injured, or hearing-impaired. Their disabilities may involve cognition and/or perception. Picture books for them should be similar to those for children with visual deficits, with some exceptions. If the disability is severe, illustrations must be realistic and have some kind of organization. Luckow's advice that the story have a unifying theme fits here. Rhythmical sound patterns may be less confusing. The best stories include a hero who is the only main character or part of a group that operates as one. The book's paper should be high quality, nonglare. Large print with good contrast and few words per page are needed. Multimedia materials of a concrete nature support observation, thinking skills, and analysis.

Musical (auditory) intelligence

According to Gardner, musical intelligence demands an awareness and understanding that "patterned elements must appear in sounds; and they are finally and firmly put together in certain ways not by virtue of formal consideration, but because they have expressive power and effects." In picture books, musical intelligence becomes important in understanding rhythm, rhyme, and sounds of words.

For strengths in musical (auditory) intelligence. Children with strong skills in musical or auditory intelligence take special pleasure in poetry, riddles, and word plays.

For deficits in musical (auditory) development. Children with musical or auditory deficits may be labeled learning-disabled, attention-deficit-disordered, autistic, brain-injured, or hearing-impaired. Some need muted background noise to focus. Visual and tactile materials reinforce meaning. Some use adaptive technology like amplifiers. Others communicate using speech reading or sign language. Many enjoy rhythms, rhymes, and sounds even if deficits limit their understanding. A child with a severe hearing impairment can enjoy sound vibrations.

Spatial (visual) intelligence

According to Gardner, spatial intelligence demands "the capacities to perceive the visual world accurately, to perform transformations and modifications upon one's initial perceptions, and to be able to re-create aspects of one's visual experience, even in the absence of relevant physical stimuli." Children of the television age are especially attuned to visual information. To understand it, one must look closely, discriminate and communicate visually, classify and compare perspective, size, shape, texture, pattern, color, shadings, light, and points of view. Symbolic awareness, visual and sequential memory, form consistency, and the ability to derive meanings are also critical.

For strong spatial (visual) skills. Illustrations should be vibrant, original, and nonstereotypical. They should complement and enhance the story line and encourage the child to return for repeated looks. Some illustrations should require mental exercise. They might be abstract or provide only some details, requiring the child to use imagination to complete the picture. Children with spatial or visual strengths may seek highly complex visual images, preferring pictures that others would consider cluttered. Some children with dyslexia (as Thomas West notes), autism, and other disabilities have strong visual skills and are attracted to highly complex visual images.

For visual deficits. Children with spatial or visual deficits may be labeled learning-disabled, attention-deficit-disordered, autistic, mentally retarded, brain-injured, visually impaired, or print impaired. They need clearly outlined visual images. Illustrations can be either black and white or colored. They should be uncluttered. They need organization and a unifying theme; and good contrast and bold outlines to distinguish pictures from the background. Unusual perspectives or incomplete pictures may confuse. Backgrounds should contrast without glare. Pages should include only a few pictures and words and have plenty of white space. Auditory and tactile materials reinforce meaning.

Children with visual deficits generally need at least an 18 point typeface. Letter shapes should be simple and easily distinguished, and the print should be bold on a contrasting background. Uncluttered pages with well-defined borders should provide adequate white space between letters and lines. Lines of print should be parallel to the bottom of the page with only a few lines per page. The book's design should include a visually pleasing balance of text and illustration. It should be easy to sort out visual and linguistic details. Paper should be of high quality, without glare.

Bodily-kinesthetic intelligence

Gardner defines bodily-kinesthetic intelligence as "the ability to use one's body in highly differentiated and skilled ways, for expressive as well as goal-directed purposes . . . the capacity to work skillfully with objects, both those that involve the fine motor movements of one's fingers and hands and those that exploit gross motor movements of the body," including nonverbal language, touch, shapes, texture, taste, movement, and dexterity.

For strong bodily-kinesthetic skills or deficits in the skills. Most children delight in materials that involve them physically through touch or movement. Children with deficits in this intelligence may be labeled learning-disabled, attention-deficit-disordered, autistic, brain-injured, or physically disabled. Some may be frightened or confused by certain textures; some use tactile material that is brought to them or touched to their skin. Through adaptive technology, many learn to move and manipulate objects.

Personal intelligence (directed toward others)

Gardner identifies two personal intelligences. One involves "the ability to notice and make distinctions among other individuals and, in particular, among their moods, temperaments, motivations, and intentions." Empathy, friendship, the quality of relationships with others, the ability to work with others, kindness, appreciation of other cultures, and peer acceptance or rejection are all important.

For strengths in personal intelligence (directed toward others). Children with strengths in this area are likely to seek out materials about subtleties of relationships. Halstead believes the story should "depict characters, whether animal or human, who display real emotions, feelings, and relationships the child will recognize."

For deficits in personal intelligence (directed toward others). Children with deficits in this intelligence may be labeled learning-disabled, attention-deficit-disordered, autistic, brain-injured, mentally retarded, or behavior-disordered. Many children with disabilities have deficits in their social skills because they have few opportunities to practice those skills. Children with strengths in any of the various intelligences may have deficits in social skills because they have spent little time with their age-mates. Children with deficits in this intelligence need materials that demonstrate successful and appropriate social interactions in a variety of settings.

Personal intelligence (directed toward self)

Gardner's second personal intelligence focuses on personal worth, honesty, integrity, justice, importance of the individual, dealing with fears, dealing with loss, dealing with disappointment, and dealing with money. He says, "the core capacity at work here is access to one's own feeling life."

For strengths in personal intelligence (directed toward self). Children who are strong in this intelligence may want materials that focus on the subtleties of personal feelings and values.

For deficits in personal intelligence (directed toward self). Children with deficits in this intelligence may be labeled learning-disabled, attention-deficit-disordered, autistic, brain-injured, mentally retarded, or behavior-disordered. They need materials that help them recognize and understand their feelings and the appropriate management of those feelings.

SOURCE: Adapted from Linda L. Walling, "Ability, Disability, and Picture Books," *School Libraries Worldwide* 7, no. 2 (July 2001): 31–38. Used with permission.

Serving special needs students: Criteria for material selection

by Caren L. Wesson and Margaret J. Keefe

Materials should be selected in all types of formats: videos (both signed and closed captioned), audiocassettes, books, kits comprising materials in several formats, toys, games, computer software, puppets, children's and young adult magazines in alternative formats, and the appropriate equipment to make these materials accessible. Children with differing abilities have various learning styles. The school librarian must look for quality in all types of formats just as when selecting any other materials for the collection. He or she should be as practical as possible and think about all the ways an item may be used and the learning needs it will meet.

Manipulative materials

The specific learning need may suggest use of a manipulative item, such as a game, toy, or puppet for development of fine motor skills, for social skills development, or as an aid to self-expression. Items should be safe to use, easily cleaned, and durable enough to withstand a great deal of handling. The number of pieces to track and how the item(s) will be stored, are additional considerations.

Audiovisual materials

Criteria for selecting audiovisual materials include good-quality production with clarity of picture and sound, a reasonable pace of presentation of ideas and information, length, accuracy of content, and appropriateness for various age, interest, and cognitive levels.

Books and magazines

Books should be selected from a wide range of formats to meet a significant need for those with differing abilities. Children with physical disabilities often have to expend so much intellectual, emotional, and physical energy in coping with the disability that their reading skills fall behind. Students with special needs who have difficulty reading will find the most success with books in special formats. High interest–low vocabulary materials, with brief text on a first- to fourth-grade level and many clear illustrations or photographs, are  especially important. Predictable picture books, wordless picture books, picture books in an oversized format ("big" books), large print, signed stories, books on sign language, books on tape, and books in braille are all important formats to consider, both fiction or nonfiction, to meet the varying interests and skill levels of those with differing abilities.

Creativity is a key element. By assessing the existing collection and looking for materials that can be adapted or used in a variety of ways, the school librarian will discover new uses for materials already on hand. For example, predictable books, books with photographs, books with paper architecture built in, captioned videos, and books on tape can be used for a variety of special-needs purposes. Knowing the learning need, the purpose(s) for the item, how it might be used, by whom it will be used, and how often it will be used are important components of selection for children with special needs.

Selecting materials to increase
acceptance of students with disabilities

Faculty and students need to be aware of various disabilities and be sensitive to those with differing abilities. Probably there are many materials in the collection already that can be used to foster awareness and sensitivity. Students with disabilities may also benefit from these materials as they discover ways in which others have managed their disabilities and their abilities.

Criteria for nonfiction about disabilities. Materials should give current, accurate information at an accessible reading level. The writing style should be clear, unsentimental, and use accepted disability terms. Unacceptable terms include using the disability to label a person, such as saying, "Susan, the epileptic," or "John, the paraplegic." Another unacceptable phrase is "confined to a wheelchair." Antiquated terms such as *imbecile, moron, gimp, retard,* and others are also red flags that the material is inappropriate. Illustrations should be accurate and clear and follow the text. The book should help remove stigmas and stereotypes about individuals who are challenged with disabilities.

Criteria for fiction about disabilities. A criterion to consider is quality, just as it would be used in the selection of any type of fiction for young people. The person or persons with disabilities should be portrayed as real people with full personalities. The character's abilities, rather than the disability, should be the focus. It is important to check reviews for literature that has plausible settings and characters with realistic relationships, conflicts, and problem-solving episodes.

SOURCE: Adapted from Caren L. Wesson and Margaret J. Keefe, *Serving Special Needs Students in the School Library Media Center* (Westport, Conn.: Greenwood, 1995), 85–88. Used with permission.

E-books: Flash in the pan
or wave of the future?

by Shelley J. Civkin

As a leader in information technology in libraries, Richmond Public Library (RPL) in British Columbia has long been committed to both traditional print resources and a variety of new and innovative electronic resources, including e-books. E-books were introduced at RPL in December 1999 and we began circulating the SoftBook Reader in January 2000 as a new and exciting format that would help connect our customers with ideas and information in yet another way. RPL has the distinction of being the first Canadian library and the second in North America to introduce e-books for public use in libraries.

We started by acquiring five SoftBook Readers and downloading a dozen bestseller fiction and nonfiction e-titles, which we have since increased to 14 titles and *Time* magazine. These titles include mysteries, legal thrillers, suspense, general fiction, business and self-help books, adventure, and

E-Book Publishers

Antelope Publishing
http://www.antelope-ebooks.com/
1382 NE 10th Ave.
Hillsboro, OR 97124

Atlantic Bridge Publishing
http://www.atlanticbridge.net/
6280 N. Crittenden Ave.
Indianapolis, IN 46220

Book Locker
http://www.booklocker.com/
P.O. Box 2399
Bangor, ME 04402-2399

Book-On-Disc
http://www.book-on-disc.com/
P.O. Box 6028
Palm Harbor, FL 34684-0628

Buffalo Creek Press
http://buffalo-creek-press.com/
P.O. Box 2424
Cleburne, TX 76033

Candlelight Stories
http://www.candlelightstories.com/

DiskUS Publishing
http://www.diskuspublishing.com/

Ebooks on the Net
http://www.ebooksonthe.net/
c/o Write Words, Inc.
2934 Old Route 50
Cambridge, MD 21613

fictionwise
http://www.fictionwise.com/home.html
407 Main St.
Chatham, NJ 07928
Telephone: (973) 701-6771
Fax: (973) 701-6774

Hard Shell Word Factory
http://www.hardshell.com/
P.O. Box 161
8946 Loberg Rd.
Amherst Jct., WI 54407

Hypertech Media, Inc.
http://www.hypertechmedia.com/

Kids' Corner
http://wiredforbooks.org/kids.htm

MightyBook, Inc.
http://www.mightybook.com/
10924 Grant Rd. #225
Houston, TX 77070

Zorba Press
http://www.zorbapress.com/
209 E. Jay Street
Ithaca, NY 14850

biography. There are also free, public domain titles that customers can down-load and read. For the time being, we manage the selection of e-titles for our customers but this could change in the future. There has been limited use by school-age children.

It's anticipated that e-books will become more commonplace in the near future and it's important that the library be able to supply the electronic content for e-book readers to our customers. While it's true that people are spending more and more time in front of computers reading, writing, and sending e-mail, and are accustomed to using digital technology, they have not been that quick to embrace e-book technology. The original novelty of the e-book readers prompted people to borrow them nonstop the first 18 months that RPL offered them, but since that time, their popularity has died down.

Until more publishers of popular material jump on the e-book bandwagon and title selection improves, and until universal standards for formats and software exist, e-books will likely remain on the periphery of information technology in terms of their broad appeal, usage, and acceptance.

To the extent that they are used, our experience has shown us that people typically use e-books for "hard" information, rather than for recreational and fiction reading. For example, e-titles containing research information and literature-based interpretation and critical information seem to be more popular than fiction titles. This suggests that their use is more prevalent with businesspeople and students, and points toward the potential and much anticipated use of e-textbooks for high school and university students.

Our experience so far has been very positive, with no damage, theft, or vandalism of the e-books. Customers who use them are made aware of their value before they borrow them and this likely contributes to their careful handling of them.

The majority of customer comments about the e-books have been positive and enthusiastic. Customers enjoy the convenience, portability, and novelty of e-books. They also like the convenient features of searchable text, customization of font size, the ability to highlight, underline, scribble, mark up, and dog-ear pages. In addition, many people enjoy the interactive reading experience that e-books offer. The only other comments we have received pertain to the limited selection of e-titles.

As for the future of e-books, there is great hope on the part of the big computer companies and retailers that the popularity of e-books will increase. However, this does not seem likely until such time as universal standards are developed that will make them easier to use, more compatible on a variety of computers and handheld devices, less expensive, and able to offer a much broader selection of titles.

There are many controversial issues surrounding e-books that still need to be addressed. These include the "napsterization" of e-books, author payment, copyright issues for older titles, and much more. In the meantime, e-books at the public library are a novelty item that has sparked the interest of a limited group of library users. I believe, however, that ongoing and consistent promotion of e-books to library users of all ages is valuable and will help integrate e-books into the mainstream of library usage.

The bottom line is that Richmond Public Library has no regrets about acquiring e-books regardless of their questionable popularity at the moment. E-books are a new and exciting technology that we feel bound and obligated to offer our customers, in an effort to give them the widest choice possible when it comes to learning and recreation. So the question remains: Are e-books a flash in the pan or the wave of the future? Only time will tell. Stay tuned.

SOURCE: Adapted from Shelley J. Civkin, "E-Books—Flash in the Pan or . . . Wave of the Future?" *Impact* 11, no. 2 (Fall 2002): 16–17. Used with permission.

Comic books and graphic novels in the library

by Gail deVos

"Everywhere, print-only books hold the highest position for literacy achievement; art forms that mix words with stylized pictures in bold colors receive attention primarily as commercial trivia," from Shirley Brice Heath and Vikram Bhagat, "Reading Comics, the Invisible Art," in the *Handbook of Research on Teaching Literacy through the Communicative and Visual Arts* (New York: Macmillan Library Reference, 1997), 586.

Comic books, to a large number of the population in North America, mean one of two things: superhero male fantasy stories or tales aimed at child readers. To be fair, there are an overwhelming number of superhero titles on the market today but there are only a few titles that are aimed at young readers. In actual fact the demographic of today's comic book reader is a male between ages 18 and 24 and attending a post-secondary institution. The themes and genres of comic books are as varied as the themes and genres of mainstream fiction. In other parts of the world, notably Japan and Europe, the perception and appreciation of the comic book format is very different. Comic books are valued as works of literature and art. In Japan, for example, there are as many different types of comic books as there are types of readers, with specific titles for young females, their older counterparts, young males, businessmen, and so on.

Comic books and graphic novels have not been readily accepted as valid reading material in the past by a vast majority of educators, librarians, and parents for a variety of reasons. The purpose of this article is not to revisit these reasons but to move forward given that establishing a graphic novel collection has become an increasingly common focus for many people in the school and public library sectors. This interest is substantiated by the American Library Association's theme for teen reading week during October 2002—"Get graphic @ your library"—and the increasingly active Graphic Novels in Libraries listserv which addresses concerns from shelving problems to censorship issues. According to Ellen Butler Donovan, there has also been a recent reemergence of scholarship on the comic book format and collection development concerns. "Children's literature has set a precedent for analyzing mixed genres by its attention to the picture book, and on that basis, we can also justify scholarly attention to the graphic novel." This type of scholarly attention is long overdue but with the aid of the Internet and a wider readership of graphic novels, help is now available for people struggling with the rationale and challenges of establishing comic book and graphic novel collections.

In her book for parents on how to get children to read, and to keep reading, Mary Leonhardt suggests that comic books should be read at home with preschoolers. "They have short selections and are full of action, perfect for kids always on the run—and gradually see if you can get him/her to start reading some of the parts." She quali-

fies her recommendation by stating that the titles shared by parents and preschoolers should be age-appropriate. She states that comic books usually have plot lines of much greater interest to children than most picture books and they motivate children to try to figure out what happens next from the pictures. Leonhardt maintains that "the value of comic book reading is that it gives this group of readers a jump start on reading skills, which they'll need, because most of the reading in this field is pretty sophisticated." While I endorse her comments, I argue that it may be very difficult to find titles that are truly age-appropriate for the preschool group. However, her argument is as appropriate for older readers, emerging and reluctant, as well as those who are accomplished and gifted, as it is for preschoolers. In our highly visual universe, the comic book format is coming into its own.

An active dialogue revolves around the definitive definition of a comic book. Creators, distributors, and fans are busy establishing a universal definition. The comic book is actually one of the great misnomers in the world of publishing as they are not actually books and are rarely funny. Most of those preferred by contemporary readers have little that is directly humorous. Heath believes they speak to readers about loss of control, struggles with parents and bullies, and the contradictions of women as nurturers and as superheroes.

Graphic novels are as difficult to illuminate as they are frequently not fiction or novels, but may be compilations of single-issue comic book story arcs or short stories. For the purpose of easy clarification,

- comic books are single-issue magazines that may or may not contain a complete story between their covers.
- graphic novels are bound books, fiction and nonfiction, that are created in the comic book format and are issued an ISBN.

How do you go about selecting and purchasing suitable items for your collection? The critical analysis of comics should go beyond comparison with and derivation from other narrative forms, such as the short story or novel, as well as go beyond an evaluation according to graphic and visual arts criteria. This means that a familiarity with the format and its distinctive elements is absolutely essential. Critical questions must be able to be addressed:

- How does one read a comic book?
- What do the different shapes of the word balloons mean to the reader?
- What about the range of fonts used within the same page?
- In what order should the panels on the page be read?
- How is the connection between one panel and the subsequent or preceding one made?
- What of the use of color?
- The lack of color?

These are all questions that increased experience with reading comic books can help answer and that comic book readers almost automatically understand without thought. Thus, those who are building the collection must be familiar and at ease with both the building blocks (the format) and the types of materials (the genres) that make up the building blocks themselves.

But knowledge of the comic book format and the titles themselves is not enough. Once the mechanics of the comic book format are understood and appreciated with some comfort, the following questions evaluate it effectively:

- What is the story or basic plot being imparted and how is it communicated by the text? The illustrations?
- Are the two balanced? If one dominates the other for a series of panels, what effect might be intended by such domination?
- Are there subtextual elements of the story and if so, how are they expressed through recurring words in the text or visual imagery?

Note the very specific elements in the comic: facial expressions, clothing, background details, lettering, and panel composition.

- What do they communicate to the reader?
- How do they help to tell the story? Always ask yourself if the comic achieves its apparent goals (and if those goals seem unusual, what might they be?).
- Are there particular elements that lend to that achievement, or particular elements that hinder the comic?

These questions are similar to the ones that should be contemplated when analyzing the effectiveness of picture books, films, and other visual art.

This may seem like a rather daunting task—becoming familiar with the format, the various titles and publishers, and the inherent problems in establishing a new collection. But you do not have to face this task alone. There are a myriad of available resources that discuss comic books and graphic novels for librarians and teachers. I encourage you to open the pages of a graphic novel and experience for yourself what the format has to offer.

3

Print resources

Will Eisner, *Comics and Sequential Art.* Tamarac, FL: Poorhouse, 1994.

Will Eisner, *Graphic Storytelling.* Tamarac, FL: Poorhouse, 1996.

Scott McCloud, *Understanding Comics: The Invisible Art.* Tamarac, FL: Poorhouse, 1993.

D. Aviva Rothschild, *Graphic Novels: A Bibliographic Guide to Book-Length Comics.* Littleton, CO: Libraries Unlimited, 1995. Updated online at Comics Get Serious, http://www.rationalmagic.com/Comics/Comics.html.

Stephen Weiner, *The 101 Best Graphic Novels.* New York: NBM, 2001.

Online resources

Diamond Bookshelf: http://bookshelf.diamondcomics.com/. This link on the major North American distributor of comic books and graphic novels is aimed at librarians. Included on the web page are articles on "why comics," book reviews, lesson plans, a glossary, and cataloging information.

Friends of Lulu: http://www.friends-lulu.org. Friends of Lulu is a national organization aimed at getting more girls and women involved in comic books. The group's main purpose is to promote and encourage female readership and participation in the comic book industry.

Graphic Novels in Libraries: http://www.angelfire.com/comics/gnlib/index.html. This site not only contains information about the listserv but also contains the archives as well as links to resource sites for librarians interested in comic book collections.

Recommended Graphic Novels for Public Libraries: http://my.voyager.net/~sraiteri/graphicnovels.htm. Features an annotated list of more than 350 recommended titles and links to many other useful graphic novel websites, including several provided by librarians.

SOURCE: Adapted from Gail deVos, "Comic Books and Graphic Novels in the Library," *Impact* 11, no. 3 (Fall 2002): 17–19. Used with permission.

Sex information
by W. Bernard Lukenbill

When parents are asked about sex education for their children, almost all agree that it is needed. However, they often disagree about what values to present, techniques to employ, and materials to use in sex education programs.

Recent research indicates that adolescents want information about the following subjects (from Kathy McCoy and Charles Wibbelsman's *The Teenage Body Book*):

birth control
homosexuality
abortion
sexually transmitted diseases (STDs)
relationships and intimacy
sexual anatomy
menstruation
fertility cycles
physical changes at puberty
basic romantic or relationship attraction dynamics
reproductive functions
establishing relationships and dating
    etiquette
refusal techniques
problem sexual behaviors (rape, violence,
    drugs)
language of sex (including street
    language)

A basic understanding of these needs is useful in selecting suitable sex education materials for school library media collections.

Modern-day approaches to sex education vary in terms of content, values, and pedagogy. The three major approaches in the United States today can be termed *comprehensive*, *abstinence-only*, and *abstinence-plus* sex education.

Values are important in each approach. Comprehensive programs stress building a sense of responsibility, positive attitudes about sex and sexual behavior and language, and concern for others, including sexual partners. Comprehensive program advocates suggest the use of age-appropriate materials about pregnancy, contraception, and STDs. Avoiding pregnancy and preparing for adult life are also covered.

Abstinence-only programs typically emphasize family values. Character building and refusal skills are taught. Discussion of contraceptives or safer sex is generally avoided, although adverse side effects and inadequacies of contraception methods may be covered. Sexual activity outside of marriage is discouraged.

Abstinence-plus curricula include information on abstinence as well as on contraception. Although they teach that sexual abstinence until marriage is the best option, they recognize that an abstinence-only approach will not meet the needs of all adolescents.

Regardless of the emphasis of the school's instructional policies, comprehensive sex education materials should be available in the school library media center. Censorship questions may certainly arise, but well-constructed official materials selection policies should address such issues. School media center librarians, administrators, and parents should not forget that the U.S. Supreme Court in *Board of Education v. Pico* 457 U.S. 853 (1982) offered school library media collections some degree of protection from having materials removed without sound educational reasons for doing so.

Some authorities on sex education have claimed that, historically, materials on sex education have presented sex as a reproductive function only, separated from life as a whole, and have viewed sex from a rigid standard of morality. They see such an approach as ineffective, favoring instead an informational and nonjudgmental approach to sexual issues. These critics have also been concerned that traditional sex education materials have not addressed sex outside of marriage, including premarital relationships and homosexuality.

The issue of how homosexuality has historically been addressed has attracted particular attention in recent years. When homosexuality was mentioned at all in early books it was viewed as a sin. Later it was discussed in psychological terms as a mental illness. In recent years it has been presented as a freely chosen but erroneous lifestyle. Comprehensive sex educators today prefer that homosexuality be discussed as an innate human orientation. Such variations in interpretations and social values add to the controversy surrounding sex education discussions and information provided for youth.

The subject of premarital relationships has likewise proven problematic. Early sex education materials labeled premarital relations a sin. Today's more comprehensive sex education materials address it in terms of making correct decisions based on proper information and attitudes, a strong sense of self-understanding, and a commitment to responsible behavior.

Critics have also expressed concern about the selective nature of some types of information in traditional sex education materials for youth and the outright omission of other information. Topics such as abortion, birth control, and legal rights of minors were intentionally omitted to the detriment of young people. Illustrations have also been criticized for being unclear, uninformative, or distorted.

Within this context, the evaluation of sex information materials increases in importance. As society and culture change, sex education materials must reflect those changes. The moral dimensions of sex need to be addressed as well. Morality here is defined as responsible behavior and attitudes, and concern for others. Related problem behaviors also need to be covered. These include sex abuse, rape, incest, and other forms of sexual dysfunction that bring harm to self and others.

SOURCE: Adapted from W. Bernard Lukenbill, *Collection Development for a New Century in the School Library Media Center* (Westport, Conn.: Greenwood, 2002), 150–155. Used with permission.

How does your garden grow?
Pruning vs. weeding

by Hilda K. Weisburg and Ruth Toor

Do you ever wonder why administrators and faculty react so negatively whenever you weed your collection? It may be a matter of semantics. You know what you mean and why you are doing it, but others are likely to apply their version of the Merriam-Webster 10th Collegiate Dictionary (online) and think of a weed as "a plant that is not valued where it is growing and is usually of vigorous growth."

From that perspective, the question is, why would you have bought something that is "not valued"? Moreover, if it is "vigorous" why are you getting rid of it? As the staff sees what you are throwing out, they point to what is still good in the books and somehow miss the dated misinformation or the fact that students just don't want to use something looking that old.

To enlist allies rather than spend time defending your actions, start referring to the task as "pruning." This is defined by the above source as "to cut off or cut back parts for better shape or more fruitful growth." Collections need to be freed from the drab and tired volumes, printed before computers offered a relatively inexpensive way to vary typefaces, add color blocks, insert sidebars, and make information more easily and interestingly accessible.

Pruning reference makes more sense than weeding. Historical atlases don't go out of date but do become dated. Literary biography and criticism may continue to be valid (even though the author may be reappraised differently over time) but a densely written tome will almost never be used. Even annual almanacs should not be left on the shelves for too many years.

Professional collections are another area in dire need of pruning. The techniques of the 1970s may still work in today's classrooms but new approaches and terminology have superseded the materials purchased in that long ago time when ESEA Title II was a fully funded government subsidy. Any of your professional books written before the importance of collaborative planning with teachers was delineated in *Information Power* should not take up space on your shelves. Look carefully through your technology titles, because so much has changed in just a few years that most will be out of date.

Fiction is impossible to "weed." Almost nothing in this section is dated in the sense that newer information has replaced it. However, stories that innocently use the slang of 30 or more years ago are not going to capture your students' attention. Covers that portray clothing that was all the rage when Woodstock was a "current event" will be ignored. While some works really do stand the test of time, many more don't.

Titles that have remained popular over the decades often become shabby from heavy use. It is time to discard and replace these treasures. Your students deserve books that look good. Paperbacks usually require more replacing than hardcovers. When the pages are yellowed and cracking, you need to dump them—no matter how high the quality of the text is. Sometimes, spending some of your book money on refurbishing beat-up looking titles pays lots of dividends as students gravitate to anything that looks new.

Managing the process

While pruning (or weeding) is definitely a professional task, you can simplify it considerably by delegating it to one of your conscientious volunteers or a clerk. Be sure to explain the purpose and give criteria such as a copyright date, the dust level, or the condition of the volume. Pull some in advance to use as examples.

The person assigned to the job makes the initial selection only. Books should be put on a cart, in the back room, or any other location where you can peruse them at your leisure. Remove those that you feel should remain on the shelf and explain your reasons. Take out book cards from the ones you want to replace (if you have abandoned book cards, tear out the title page) and have someone prepare an order.

Physically getting rid of these books may still prove a problem. Among the possibilities are ripping off covers before putting them in large wastebaskets. If you are at a middle school or higher, give the job to your students after explaining why you are tossing the titles out. The activity is a great one for getting rid of excess anger and hostility.

After deleting the books from your collection, find out what limits, if any, your district places on disposing of them. If you are permitted to do so, invite faculty and students to choose what they like. Call the display "Take Home a Blast from the Past" or "Mine for Old Gold." The lighthearted tone serves to give you an opening to inform everyone about why both students and the collection will benefit from your pruning.

SOURCE: Adapted from Hilda K. Weisburg and Ruth Toor, "Problems in Librarianship: How Does Your Garden Grow? Pruning vs. Weeding," *The School Librarian's Workshop* 21, no. 5 (January 2001): 4–5. Used with permission.

The pros and cons of squelching library theft

by Paul Wartenberg

Book theft

Every librarian has suffered it, whether frantically hunting the shelves for a lost copy or decrying the missing pages torn from another copy. It has been the lot of all librarians since the day the Romans showed up at the Library of Alexandria and plundered copies of *Invading Gaul and Other Popular Moves: Winning Friends the Julius Caesar Way.*

My library is no different. After having to replace the missing chapter on book theft in our copy of *Libraries for Dummies*, I realized how horrendous the situation had become; so I decided to solve the problem, confronting at last the dreaded species known as Book Thieves.

Pondering this ponderment led to a number of possible solutions. Although some of these ideas seem fantastic, a technically proficient bibliographic expert armed with the right tools and government grants can make them a reality.

Possible solution: Placing an electronic security tag on each and every page, rather than one spot in the book that can be easily torn off.

Pro: Will protect each page from the Missing Pages Syndrome so common in popular reference books.

Con: Cost of magnetic strips and tags will skyrocket as supplies are used up, leading to pitched battles between neighboring libraries, eventually creating a library black market ruled by organized crime.

Possible solution: Creating dummy books out of a gummy substance, to place as a decoy in the subject areas hardest hit. The gum melts under human contact and sticks the Book Thief's hands together.

Pro: Makes it easier to cart the Book Thief off to the electric chair (valid in Florida only).

Con: Makes it hard to reshelve the dummy book; if air conditioning goes bye-bye, so does your collection.

Possible solution: Wiring up an extensive in-house surveillance system to watch over the shelves, especially those areas hardest hit by Book Thieves.

Pro: The noticeable overhead cameras should scare off your novice Book Thief; also helps in spotting staffers who keep sneaking a smoke in the far corners.

Con: Considering the current voyeuristic mood of young lovers, surveillance cameras will most likely encourage them (depending on how cute the couple is, this might be listed as a Pro); professional Book Thieves will steal the books on scrambling electronic signals and use that knowledge against us.

Possible solution: Highly trained guard dogs that sniff bags for the bindery glue used in bookmaking.

Pro: Nothing scares a Book Thief like a drooling, snarling Rottweiler.

Con: Dogs will get addicted to the glue.

Possible solution: Developing a nontoxic chemical sprayed onto each page, which when passing through the electronic gates causes paper to explode.

Pro: Should swiftly eliminate most of the Book Thief population; gives librarians a satisfying "That ought to teach 'em" feeling.

Con: Goes against librarians' basic pacifist beliefs; someone stealing a Norman Mailer book could conceivably blow up the entire building.

Possible solution: Hiring an elite team of ninjas to hunt down Book Thieves.

Pro: Ninjas will certainly get the job done.

Con: Elite ninja teams don't come cheap; law enforcement frowns on such vigilantism.

Possible solution: Advertising the problem of book theft to the public, asking your patrons politely to be considerate of other patrons who need these books.

Pro: It's the humane, *Star Trek* way of doing things.

Con: Book Thieves? Considerate? Since when?!?

SOURCE: Adapted from Paul Wartenberg, "The Pros and Cons of Squelching Library Theft," *American Libraries* (February 2000): 48–49.

A door half open:
Young people's access to fiction
related to homosexuality

by Laurel Anne Clyde and Marjorie Lobban

Sarah, the young lesbian character in Jenny Pausacker's *How to Tell Your Parents That You're Straight*, observes, "I've read heaps of books about this stuff—libraries don't get freaked by tough questions the way people do." It's a great endorsement for libraries, but how far do school and other libraries really go in providing collections, services, and programs for gay, lesbian, and bisexual young people? It is much less certain how systematically these books are acquired, promoted, and used in school and public library collections aimed at young people.

This article focuses on the work we have carried out over a number of years for the publication *Out of the Closet and Into the Classroom: Homosexuality in Books for Young People*. Fiction books related to homosexuality that are available for children and young people are discussed. We also discuss the evidence available for the inclusion of these books in library collections where they might be available to children and young people.

Throughout the 20th century, the number of adult books that portrayed homosexual characters and described homosexual relationships increased (Young, 1982; Grier, 1981). From the late 1960s and early 1970s, there has been a similar development in literature for young people. Apart from early books such as *Tom Brown's School-Days* by Thomas Hughes (1857) and *The Lass of the Silver Sword* by Mary Constance DuBois (1910), there are only two books for young people that predate 1970. They are *The Chinese Garden* by Rosemary Manning (1962) and *I'll Get There. It Better Be Worth the Trip* by John Donovan (1969). Since then, and particularly from the 1980s, the number of titles has continued to increase, with no sign of any falling off. The first edition of *Out of the Closet and Into the Classroom* listed 120 titles to the end of 1991; the second edition listed an additional 73 titles to the end of 1994 (with a further four titles from 1995), bringing the total to 193, an increase of around 60%. Since 1995, another 110 titles have already been identified for inclusion in a third edition.

Just as adult books dealing with homosexuality have been available for much longer than books for adolescents that deal with this topic, so books for young children appeared rather later than books for teenagers. The first picture book for young children, Susanne Bösche's *Jenny Lives with Eric and Martin* did not appear (in English translation) until 1983. The first edition of *Out of the Closet and Into the Classroom* listed 10 picture books. The second edition included 27 in all. Many of these titles appear to be aimed particularly, although not exclusively, at children growing up as part of gay or lesbian families. Since 1996, however, the number of new picture books appears to have declined.

Characteristics of the books

Most, but not all, of the books listed in *Out of the Closet and Into the Classroom* have at least one homosexual character. Books were categorized according to whether the gay or lesbian character was the main character, a supporting character, or a background character. In books in the first category, the main character (usually a teenager) is homosexual, has homosexual tendencies, or discovers that he or she is homosexual. Some of these, such as *Out of the Shadows* (Sue Hines), might be described as "coming out" novels. In books in the second category, the homosexual character is a secondary or supporting character or there is a homosexual incident that involves a supporting character. In each case, this has an influence on the main character and on the plot of the

book. The secondary characters might be parents or guardians; uncles or aunts, or brothers or sisters, or other close relatives; teachers, friends, or neighbors. The third category relates to those books in which a background character is homosexual or where a homosexual incident involves a background character. Again, this usually has some influence on the development of the plot.

Christine A. Jenkins (1993) has commented that "one of the most noticeable patterns in the young adult novelistic portrayal of gay/lesbian people is the predominance of males, both as teens and as adults." In the books listed in the second edition of *Out of the Closet and Into the Classroom*, significant male homosexual characters had been created by 21 female writers, but just one novel written by a male writer had a significant lesbian character.

What do the books tell young people about being homosexual? In novels or short stories for teenagers, being gay or lesbian and young is almost universally shown to be hard. Sometimes the difficulty lies in the young gay or lesbian not wanting to accept his or her own sexuality. More often, it is the real or imagined reactions of friends or family that fill the young gay or lesbian with apprehension.

Gay and lesbian adults, however, fare much better. They are often idealized individuals, loving, perceptive, sensitive, and supportive. Lesbians tend to be depicted in warm, stable relationships or as well-adjusted individuals, nurturing children. Gay men are mentors and role models.

If novels and picture books suggest ways of being to readers, then generally speaking, these books present a conservative picture of "being gay or lesbian." In children's and young adult books, the gay man or youth is usually a very "straight" gay, not effeminate, just a "regular guy" who happens to love guys. Even those teenage boys who are taunted for being a "fag" or a "poofter" are far from being outrageous in their behavior. Gay men are not presented as "screaming queens." Among the lesbians, there are no "diesel dykes" or super-butches.

Young people's access to the books

Identifying and listing books for children and young adults that deal with homosexuality or have gay or lesbian characters has sometimes been a difficult task. To what extent, then, do young people themselves have access to these books, for example, through their local libraries? Writing about collection development in libraries of all kinds, Cal Gough and Ellen Greenblatt note that:

> The abundance and variety of books written by, for, and about lesbians and gay men has increased enormously within the past 30 years. Neither this abundance nor this variety is reflected in most library collections, however. Recent studies show this to be the case regardless of the type of library collection examined or the availability of reviews for the materials.

They further suggest that a "persistent, widespread resistance to routinely collecting materials of interest or usefulness to lesbian and gay library users" disadvantages those users. It also means that heterosexual library users are less likely to come into contact with books that provide insights into the lives of homosexuals and/or their families.

James H. Sweetland and Peter G. Christensen compared the 1992 gay/lesbian oriented Lambda Book Award titles (plus a sample of titles reviewed in *Lambda Book Report*) with a control group of titles listed in *Publishers Weekly* and found that although the Lambda-listed titles were reviewed as often as the control group, they were held in significantly fewer OCLC libraries (as shown in the OCLC library catalog databases). In a study of 250 U.S. public and college libraries, Eric Bryant (1995) found that half had fewer than 30 books with lesbigay characters or themes, and whereas 10% of the libraries had at least 500 such books, a greater number (14%) had no books at all that had lesbigay characters or themes. James V. Carmichael Jr. confirmed that "lesbigay collections in small and medium sized public libraries are underrepresentative, if they exist at all."

The United States is not alone in this regard. Even in those places where collections were considered to be better than the norm, the services based on them often come in for some criticism. A survey by Steven Joyce and Alvin M. Schrader of gay male users of the Edmonton Public Library in Alberta, Canada, supported the results of an earlier central Canadian study by Janet A. E. Creelman and Roma M. Harris of lesbian library users. They found that although libraries were seen as an important source of coming out information and a significant ongoing information resource, there was nevertheless "a general lack of satisfaction with the library in terms of providing services concerning homosexuality." Ann Curry's British research has shown that throughout the 1990s, Section 28 of the local authorities legislation of 1988 (which prohibits the "promotion" of homosexuality) has in fact "promoted increasing self-censorship" among librarians and an unwillingness to stock "material that alludes positively to lesbians and gays and their lifestyle." One of the British public libraries that has continued to provide a special lesbian, gay, and bisexual collection, despite Section 28, is Brighton and Hove Libraries. Yet even here, although Mark Norman's (1999) study showed that the special collection was well used and appreciated by the city's diverse lesbian, gay, and bisexual community, and there was a core of satisfied users, nevertheless a significant minority of users (close to 40% in some instances) was dissatisfied with aspects of the collection and service—and this among people who do use the library.

Our work for *Out of the Closet and Into the Classroom* indicates that, just as there has been an increase in the total number of books with lesbian/gay characters and themes over the last three decades, so there has also been a corresponding increase in the number of such books for young people, although the trend in relation to books for young people started later. In addition, the professional and research literature indicates that, just as public library collections in general fail to provide sufficient books to meet the needs of gay/lesbian users of all ages or to provide representative coverage of gay/lesbian lifestyles and issues, so collections developed specifically for young users also generally fail in this regard.

In 1999, Alex Spence reported on a study of "Gay young adult fiction in the public library," in which he took Christine Jenkins' (1998) list of 99 young adult novels with "gay/lesbian/queer content" and checked the titles against the holdings of 10 U.S. and 9 Canadian urban public library system catalogs. The holdings varied a great deal among the libraries (whether expressed as total holdings or copies per capita), with some libraries having "substantial" collections and others holding few copies of few of the titles. Spence's work here is generally supported by the results of a study by Paulette M. Rothbauer and Lynne E. F. McKechnie (1999), which was also based on Jenkins' 1998 list of titles and which investigated holdings of 40 large- and medium-sized Canadian public libraries.

In 2000, Spence published the results of another study in this field, this time looking at the children's picture books with gay or lesbian characters or gay- or lesbian-related contents held by 101 public library systems in the United States, Canada, New Zealand, Australia, and the United Kingdom. For this study, the main source of titles for the checklist was the second edition of our *Out of the Closet and Into the Classroom*. Again, the libraries varied a great deal both in their holdings of the titles and the number of copies of the titles. Even the best of these collections represents a limited availability of lesbian- and gay-related picture books for the population served, a finding that partly reflects the relatively small number of relevant English-language picture book titles from among which the libraries could select in the first place (30 titles verified by Spence), but does not excuse the number of copies of the titles held.

Although Bott and Woog indicate that some school librarians have been supportive and even proactive in developing collections that include gay/lesbian-related material and materials that reflect different sexual orientations, Schrader suggests that other school librarians have reportedly given in to the widespread "pressure to censor materials" in school libraries. There is little anonymity for individuals, and students would be unlikely to identify with an openly gay group or service if it existed. Identification and support are much more likely to be informal and ad hoc, based on relationships between individual teachers and students, rather than formalized.

As Alvin Schrader (1996) has suggested, censorship and challenges to library materials can affect young people's access to books with homosexual content or themes. The American Library Association's Office of Intellectual Freedom, which monitors and records attempts to censor library materials,

produces an annual list of the books that are the "most challenged" in libraries around the country. In 1991, 40 of the challenges were related to books with homosexual characters or content; by 1993, the number had risen to 111, and it continued to remain high through the 1990s.

The catalog can be a powerful tool in bringing together readers and books. But equally, the failure to assign a subject heading such as Homosexuality—Fiction may mean that a book never connects with a potential reader. We are not aware of any research study that investigates the subject headings assigned to books with gay/lesbian/bisexual themes and characters and the influence of these subject headings on the accessibility of the books to potential readers. The Internet bookstore Amazon.com does

assign relevant subject headings to fiction titles with gay/lesbian content and/or characters, but whether young people use these to locate relevant reading material is not known.

Why should books with gay/lesbian/bisexual content and/or themes be available in school library collections, and available in such a way that students can readily identify the books? One argument is that the collection and services should support gay, lesbian, and bisexual students as they begin to explore their sexual identity. Another justification is to support children of gay or lesbian parents or with other gay/lesbian relatives. Still another argument in favor is that it is important to have these titles represented in school library collections to broaden straight students' view of the world and of sexuality and so to inform their interactions with lesbian/gay students or students with lesbian/gay parents. It would be interesting and useful to see a large-scale research study that investigated school library holdings of relevant titles.

Conclusion

For young people and their books, is it really the case that they have come "out of the closet and into the classroom"? At present, it seems that the closet door is no more than about half open. Certainly, since the late 1960s, we have seen the publication of a large number of books for young people in which homosexuality is the theme or in which gay or lesbian characters appear. However, these books often prove difficult to identify through reviewing sources, bookshops, and other standard sources of information, and this situation does not seem to be changing. There are comparatively few picture books or other books for young children and no books targeted at slow or reluctant readers. The images of gays and lesbians that are presented in the books are generally conservative. Although a positive aspect of the presentation of homosexual adults is that negative stereotypes are usually avoided, it is nevertheless unrealistic that all these adults should be responsible, sensitive, caring, and good at relating to children. More of the books deal with male homosexuality than with female, even when written by women. Regardless of their literary value or the images of gays and lesbians that they present, young people may not have

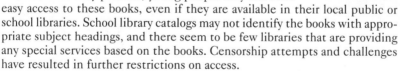

easy access to these books, even if they are available in their local public or school libraries. School library catalogs may not identify the books with appropriate subject headings, and there seem to be few libraries that are providing any special services based on the books. Censorship attempts and challenges have resulted in further restrictions on access.

Although this article cites a number of research projects that have investigated aspects of this topic, more research is needed. We know something of the inclusion of these books in public library collections, but little about this aspect of collection development in school libraries. The relationship between the coverage of the books in standard review sources and their inclusion in school libraries is unclear. Almost nothing is known about school librarians' knowledge of these books or about how they make purchase decisions related to the books. Do teacher-librarians and teachers have opportunities to explore and discuss these books as part of their professional education? Although there seems to be a relationship between censorship and access to these books in libraries, how strong is this relationship, how does it work, and does it affect some places and people more than others? How are these books cataloged in school libraries and how does the cataloging affect access to them? To what extent are very young children exposed to the picture books through the adults who care for them, and what factors influence this? What influence do publishers, reviewers, and booksellers really have on ensuring that children and young adults have access to books with homosexual themes or with gay or lesbian characters? And finally, what strategies can be used to improve the situation described in the paragraph above so that homosexuality in books for young people does move "out of the closet and into the classroom"?

SOURCE: Adapted from Laurel A. Clyde and Marjorie Lobban, "A Door Half Open: Young People's Access to Fiction Related to Homosexuality," *School Libraries Worldwide* 7, no. 2 (July 2001): 17–30. Used with permission.

Before you ask "Why a copy of the International Federation of Library Associations and Institutions' school library *Manifesto* when most of the readers of this book have *Information Power* in their offices?" think about our global community and how school librarians in the United States fit there. A better question might be "What are the similarities and differences between this document created by a global community and *Information Power* with its national perspective?" remembering that U.S. delegates to the IFLA School Libraries and Resource Centers Section participated in the preparation of the *Manifesto*. It is placed in full here because most school librarians are unaware of its existence.

IFLA School Libraries Section guidelines

by Tove Pemmer Sætre with Glenys Willars

The IFLA/UNESCO *School Library Manifesto: The School Library in Teaching and Learning for All* was published in 2000. It has been extremely well received all over the world and translated into many languages. New translations continue to be made and librarians all over the world are using the manifesto to raise the profile of school libraries in their own schools, own regions, and own countries.

The manifesto states:

> Governments, through their ministries responsible for education, are urged to develop strategies, policies and plans which implement the principles of this Manifesto.

These new guidelines have been produced to inform decision makers at national and local levels around the world, and to give support and guidance to the library community. They have been written to help schools to implement the principles expressed in the manifesto.

The drafting of the guidelines involved many people from many countries, with very different local situations, to try and satisfy the needs of all types of school. The guidelines will need to be read and used within a local context.

Workshops have been organized during IFLA conferences; meetings have taken place, and discussions held between library experts in person and using e-mail. The resulting guidelines are the product of much debate and consultation, for which the editors are very indebted and grateful. They also acknowledge the contributions of members of the standing committee of the section of school libraries and resource centers, and the guidelines from many countries that have informed the IFLA/UNESCO guidelines, especially *The Public Library Guidelines* published by IFLA in 2001.

The section has also published *The School Library: Today and Tomorrow*, during 2002. We hope that the manifesto, visions, and guidelines together will form a foundation for excellent school libraries everywhere.

Mission and policy

The school library in teaching and learning for all.

Mission. The school library provides information and ideas that are fundamental to functioning successfully in our increasingly information- and knowledge-based present-day society. The school library equips students with lifelong learning skills and develops their imagination, thereby enabling them to live as responsible citizens.

Policy. The school library should be managed within a clearly structured policy framework. The library policy should be devised bearing in mind the overarching policies and needs of the school and should reflect its ethos, aims, and objectives as well as its reality.

The policy will specify when, where, for whom, and by whom the full potential of the library will be realized. The library policy will become feasible if the whole school community supports and contributes to the aims and objectives set out in the policy. Therefore it should be written with as much involvement as viable, with as much consultation as practicable, and it should be as widely shared as possible in its printed form. In this way, the philosophy, the ideas, the concept, and the intentions for practice and development will become clear and will be commonly understood and endorsed, and will thus be ready to be put into practice effectually and enthusiastically.

The policy must be comprehensive and workable. It should not be drafted by the school librarian alone, but jointly with the teaching staff and senior managers. The draft should be consulted widely throughout the school and supported by exhaustive open discussion. The document and subsequent plans will specify the role of the library in relation to the following aspects:

- the school curriculum
- learning methods in the school
- satisfying national and local standards and criteria
- students' learning and personal development needs
- staff's teaching needs
- raising levels of achievement

The components which contribute to effective, successful, well-managed school libraries are the following:

- finance and budgeting
- accommodation
- resources
- organization
- staffing
- library use
- promotion

All these components are essential in a realistic policy framework and action plan. They will be considered throughout this document. The action plan should be made up of strategies, tasks, targets, monitoring and evaluation routines. The policy and plan should be an active document subject to regular review.

Monitoring and evaluation. In the process of attaining the goals of the school library, the management must continually monitor the performance in the services to ensure that the strategies are achieving the specified objectives. Statistical studies should be carried out periodically in order to identify trends. An annual evaluation should cover all the main areas of the plan document to ascertain the following points:

- whether they are achieving the objectives and declared goals of the library, the curriculum, and the school
- whether they are meeting the needs of the school community
- whether they are able to meet changing needs
- whether they are adequately resourced
- and whether they are cost effective

The following key performance indicators may prove useful tools for monitoring and evaluating the achievement of the library goals:

Usage indicators

- loans per member of school community (specified per student and per staff member)
- total library visits per member of the school community (specified per student and per staff member)
- loans per item (i.e., turnover resources)
- loans per opening hour (during school hours and after school)
- reference enquiries per member of school community (specified per student and per staff member)
- use of computers and online information sources

Resource indicators

- total book stock per member of school community
- provision of terminals/personal computers per member of school community
- provision of online access computers per member of school community

Human resource indicators

- ratio of full-time equivalent staff to members of school community
- ratio of full-time equivalent staff to library use

Qualitative indicators

- user satisfaction surveys
- focus groups
- consultation activities

Cost indicators

- unit costs for functions, services and activities
- staff costs per function (e.g., book loans)
- total library costs per member of the school society

- total library costs expressed in percentage of total school budget
- media costs expressed in percentage of total library costs

Comparative indicators

- Benchmark statistical data against other relevant and comparable library services at other schools of similar size and characteristics.

Resources

The school library must have adequate and sustained funding for trained staff, materials, technologies, and facilities, and its access shall be free of charge.

Funding and budgeting for the school library. In order to ensure that the library receives its fair share of the school's financial resources, the following points are important:

- understand the school budgeting process
- be aware of the timetable for the budget cycle
- know who the key staff are
- make sure that the needs of the library are identified

The components of the budget plan will need to include the following:

- an amount for new resources (e.g., books, periodicals, and nonprinted material)
- an amount for promotional materials (e.g., posters)
- an amount for stationery and administrative materials
- an amount for promotional events
- the costs of using Information Communication Technology (ICT equipment, software, and licensing costs, if these are not included in a general ICT budget for the school)

As a general rule, the school library material budget should be at least 5% of the per student expenditure for the school system, exclusive of all salaries, special education expenses, transportation, and capital improvement funds.

Staff costs may be included in the library budget but, at some schools, it may be more appropriate to have them included in the general staff budget. It is, however, important to emphasize that estimating staff costs for the library is a task which the school librarian should be involved in. The amount of money available for staffing is closely related to important issues such as how many opening hours the school library can manage and what standard and range of services it can offer. Special projects and other developments such as new shelving may require a separate bid for funds.

Spending of the budget should be carefully planned for the whole year and be related to the policy framework. Annual reports should throw light on how the library budget has been used and clarify whether the amount of money spent on the library has been enough to cover its tasks and attain the policy targets.

The school librarian must be clear about the importance of an adequate budget for the library, and may need to convey this to the senior management as the library serves the whole school community. It may be worth justifying an increase in financial support along the following lines:

- the size of school library's staff and collection is the best school predictor of academic achievement

- students who score higher on standardized tests tend to come from schools with more school library staff and more books, periodicals, and video material regardless of other factors such as economic ones

Location and space. The strong educational role of the school library must be reflected in the facilities, furniture, and equipment. It is of vital importance that the function and use of the school library is incorporated when planning new school buildings and reorganizing existing ones.

There is no one universal measurement for school library facilities but it is useful and helpful to have some kind of formula on which to base planning estimates so that any new or newly designed library meets the needs of the school in the most effective way. The following considerations need to be included in the planning process:

4

- central location, on the ground floor if possible
- accessibility and proximity, being close to all teaching areas
- noise factors, with at least some parts of the library free from external noise
- appropriate and sufficient light, both through windows and artificial light
- appropriate room temperature (e.g., air-conditioning, heating) to ensure good working conditions all year round as well as the preservation of the collections
- appropriate design to meet the special needs of disabled library users
- adequate size to give space for the collection of books, fiction, nonfiction, hardback and paperback, newspapers and magazines, nonprint resources and storage, study spaces, reading areas, computer workstations, display areas, staff work areas, and a library desk

Missouri Dept. of Elementary & Secondary Education

- flexibility to allow multiplicity of activities and future changes in curriculum and technology

The following list of different areas may also be worth considering when planning a new library:

- study and research area space for information desk, catalogs, online stations, study and research tables, reference materials, and basic collections
- informal reading area space for books and periodicals that encourage literacy, lifelong learning, and reading for pleasure
- instructional area space with seats catering to small groups, large groups, and whole classroom formal instruction, "teaching wall" with appropriate instructional technology and display space
- production and group project area space for functional work and meetings of individuals, teams, and classes, as well as facilities for media production

- administrative area space for circulation desk, office area, space for processing of library media materials, audiovisual equipment storage, and storage space for supplies and materials

Furniture and equipment. The design of the school library plays a central role in how well the library serves the school. The aesthetic appearance contributes to the feeling of welcome as well as the desire for the school community to spend time in the library.

An appropriately equipped school library should have the following characteristics:

- safety
- good lighting
- designed to accommodate furniture that is sturdy, durable, and functional as well as meeting the specific space, activity, and user requirements of the library
- designed to accommodate the special requirements of the school population in the least restrictive manner
- designed to accommodate changes in library programs and the school's instructional program as well as emerging audio, video, and data technology
- designed to enable proper use, care, and security of furnishings, equipment, supplies, and materials
- arranged and managed to provide equitable and timely access to an organized and diverse collection of resources
- arranged and managed so that it is aesthetically appealing to the user and conducive to leisure and learning, with clear, attractive guiding and signposting

Electronic and AV equipment. The school library serves an important function as a gateway to our information-based present-day society. For this reason, it must provide access to all necessary electronic, computer, and audiovisual equipment. This equipment will include the following:

- computer workstations with Internet access
- public access catalogs adjusted to the different ages and levels of students
- tape recorders
- CD-ROM players
- scanning equipment
- video players
- computer equipment, specially adjusted to the visually or otherwise physically handicapped

Computer furniture should be designed for children and easy to adjust in order to fit their different sizes.

Material resources. A high standard of library accommodation and a wide range of high-quality resources are essential. For this reason, a collection management policy is vital. This policy defines the purpose, scope, and contents of the collection as well as access to external resources.

Collection management policy. The school library should provide access to a wide range of resources that meet the needs of the users regarding education, information, and personal development. It is imperative that collections continue to be developed on an ongoing basis to ensure that the users have constant choice of new materials.

The school library staff must cooperate with administrators and teachers in order to develop a common collection management policy. Such a policy statement must be based upon curriculum, particular needs and interests of the school community, and reflect the diversity of society outside the school. The following elements should be included in the policy statement:

- IFLA/UNESCO School Library Manifesto—the mission
- statements of intellectual freedom
- freedom of information
- purpose of the collection management policy and its relation to school and curriculum
- long- and short-term objectives

Materials collection. A reasonable collection of book resources should comprise 10 books per student. The smallest school should have at least 2,500 relevant and updated items to ensure a wide, balanced book stock for all ages, abilities, and backgrounds. At least 60% of the stock should consist of curriculum-related nonfiction resources.

In addition, a school library should acquire materials for leisure purposes such as popular novels, music, computer games, videocassettes, video laser disks, magazines, and posters. This kind of material may be selected in cooperation with the students to ensure it reflects their interests and culture, without crossing reasonable limits of ethical standards.

Electronic resources. The range of services must include access to electronic information resources which reflect the curriculum as well as the users' interests and culture. The electronic resources should include access to Internet, special reference, and full-text databases, as well as instruction-related computer software packages. These may be available in CD-ROM and DVD.

It is vital to choose a library catalog system which is applicable for classifying and cataloging the resources according to accepted international or national bibliographic standards. This facilitates their inclusion in wider networks. In many places around the world, school libraries within a local community benefit from being linked together in a union catalog. Such collaboration may increase the efficiency and quality of book processing and make it easy to combine resources for maximum effect.

Staffing

The school librarian is the professionally qualified staff member responsible for planning and managing the school library, supported by as adequate staffing as possible, working together with all members of the school community, and liaising with the public library and others.

The library staff. The richness and quality of the library provision depend upon staffing resources available within and beyond the school library. For this reason, it is of paramount importance to have a well-trained and highly motivated staff, made up of a sufficient number of members according to the size of the school and its special needs for library services. The term *staff* means, in this context, qualified librarians and library assistants. In addition, there may be supporting staff, such as teachers, technicians, parents, and other kinds of volunteers. School librarians should be professionally trained and qualified, with additional training in educational theory and learning methodology.

One of the main objectives for staff management in school libraries should be that all staff members have a clear understanding of library service policy, well-defined duties and responsibilities, and properly regulated conditions of employment and competitive salaries which reflect the professionalism of the job.

Volunteers should not work as substitutes for paid staff, but may work as support based upon a contract that gives a formal framework for their involvement in the school library activities. Consultants at local or national level can be used as external advisers in matters concerning the development of the school library service.

The role of the school librarian. The librarian's main role is to contribute to the mission and goals of the school, including the evaluation procedures, and to develop and implement those of the school library. In cooperation with the senior school management, administrators, and teachers, the librarian is involved in the development of plans and the implementation of the curriculum. The librarian has the knowledge and skills regarding the provision of information and solution of information problems as well as the expertise in the use of all sources, both printed and electronic. Their knowledge, skills, and expertise meet the demands of a specific school society. In addition, the librarian should lead reading campaigns and the promotion of child literature, media, and culture.

The support of the school management is essential if the library is to carry out interdisciplinary activities. The librarian must report directly to the head teacher or deputy head. It is extremely important for the librar-

ian to be accepted as an equal member of the professional staff and be entitled to participate in the teamwork and all meetings as the head of the library department.

The librarian should create an environment for leisure and learning which is attractive, welcoming, and accessible for everyone without fear or prejudice. Everyone who works in the school library should have a good rapport with children, young people, and adults.

The role of the library assistant. The library assistant reports to the librarians and supports them in their functions. This position requires clerical and technological knowledge and skills. The assistant should have prior basic library training. Otherwise, the library should provide it. Some of the duties of the job include routine functions, shelving, lending, returning, and processing library material.

Cooperation between teachers and school librarian. Cooperation between teachers and the school librarian is essential in maximizing the potential of the library services.

Teachers and librarians work together in order to achieve the following:

- develop, instruct, and evaluate pupils' learning across the curriculum
- develop and evaluate pupils' information skills and information knowledge
- develop lesson plans

- prepare and carry out special project work to be done in an extended learning environment, including the library
- prepare and carry out reading programs and cultural events
- integrate information technology in the curriculum
- make clear to parents the importance of the school library

Skills of the school library staff. The school library is a service addressed to all members of the school community: learners, teachers, administrators, counselors as well as parents. All these groups require special communication and cooperation skills. The main users are the learners and the teachers, but also other categories of professionals such as administrators and counselors should be included.

The fundamental qualities and skills expected from the school library staff can be defined as follows:

- the ability to communicate positively and open-mindedly with children and adults
- the ability to understand the needs of users
- the ability to cooperate with individuals and groups inside and outside the school community
- knowledge and understanding of cultural diversity
- knowledge of learning methodology and educational theory
- knowledge of information skills and of how to use information
- knowledge of the materials which compose the library collection and how to access it
- knowledge of child literature, media, and culture
- knowledge and skills in the fields of management and marketing
- knowledge and skills in the field of information technology

Duties of the school librarian. The school librarian is expected to do the following:

- analyze the resource and information needs of the school community
- formulate and implement policies for service development
- develop acquisition policies and systems for library resources
- catalog and classify library materials
- instruct in library use
- instruct in information knowledge and information skills
- assist students and teachers in the use of library resources and information technology
- answer reference and information enquiries using appropriate materials
- promote reading programs and cultural events
- participate in planning activities connected to the implementation of the curriculum
- participate in the preparation, implementation, and evaluation of learning activities
- promote the evaluation of library services as an ordinary part of the general school evaluation system
- build partnership with external organizations
- prepare and implement budgets
- design strategic planning
- manage and train library staff

Ethical standards. The school library staff has the responsibility to observe high ethical standards in their dealing with all members of the school community. All users should be dealt with on an equal basis regardless of their abilities and background. Services should be adjusted to match the needs of the individual user. In order to strengthen the role of the school library as an open and safe learning environment, the staff should emphasize their function as advisors rather than as instructors in the traditional sense. This implies, first and foremost, that they must try to adopt the user's perspective rather than let themselves be biased by their own attitudes and prejudices in providing library service.

Programs and activities

The school library is integral to the educational process.

Programs. In national curriculum and education development programs at the national level, school libraries should be considered as vital means for fulfilling ambitious goals regarding the following:

- information literacy for all, gradually developed and adopted through the school system
- availability of information resources for students at all educational levels
- open dissemination of information and knowledge for all student groups to exercise democratic and human rights

At national as well as local levels, it is advisable to have programs designed specifically for the purposes of school library development. These kinds of programs may involve different aims and actions related to the context they are in. Here are some examples of actions:

- develop and publish national (and local) standards and guidelines for school libraries
- provide model libraries to demonstrate "best practice"
- establish school library committees at national and local level
- design a formal framework for cooperation between school libraries and public libraries at national and local level
- initiate and offer professional school librarian training programs
- provide funding for school library projects such as reading campaigns
- initiate and fund research projects related to school library activities and development

Cooperation and resource sharing with public libraries. In order to improve library services for children and young persons in a given community, it may be a good idea for school libraries and public libraries to cooperate. A written cooperation agreement should include the following points:

- common measures for the cooperation
- specification and definition of cooperation areas
- clarification of economic implications and how to share costs
- scheduled time for cooperation period

Examples of cooperation areas are the following:

- sharing staff training

- cooperative collection development
- cooperative programming
- coordination of electronic services and networks
- cooperation in the development of learning tools and user education
- class visits to the public library
- joint reading and literacy promotion
- joint marketing of library services to children and young persons

Activities at school level. The school library should cover a wide range of activities and should be a main role player in achieving the mission and vision of the school. It should aim to serve all potential users within the school community and meet the particular needs of different target groups.

The programs and the activities must thus be designed in close cooperation with the following:

- principal/head teacher
- heads of departments
- teachers
- support staff
- students

The users' satisfaction depends on the ability of the school library to identify the needs of individuals and groups, and on its capability to develop services which reflect changing needs in the school community.

The principal and the school library. As the instructional leader of the school and the key person in providing a framework and climate for implementing the curriculum, the principal should acknowledge the importance of an effective school library service and encourage the use of it.

The principal should work closely with the library in the design of school development plans, especially within the fields of information literacy and reading promotion programs. When the plans are to be put into effect, the principal should ensure flexible scheduling of time and resources to allow teachers' and students' access to the library and its services.

The principal should also ensure cooperation between teaching staff and library staff. He or she must ensure that the school librarians are involved in instruction, curriculum planning, continuing staff development, program evaluation, and assessment of student learning.

In the evaluation of the whole school, the principal should integrate library evaluation (see "Mission" and "Policy") and highlight the vital contribution a strong school library service makes in the achievement of the established educational standards.

Heads of departments and the school library. As the main person in charge of professional activities each departmental head should cooperate with the library in order to ensure that its range of information resources and services cover the special needs of the subject areas of the department. Like the principal, the head of department should involve the library in development planning and direct attention to the library as a vital part of the learning environment and as a learning resource center.

Teachers and the library. Cooperation between teacher and librarian has already been addressed in "Cooperation between Teachers and School Librarian." Some complementary aspects are worth highlighting at this point.

The teachers' educational philosophy constitutes the ideological basis for their choice of teaching methods. Some of the methods that are based on a traditional view of the teacher and the textbook as the most important learning resources do not favor the role of the school library in learning processes. If this view is combined with a strong wish to keep the door of the classroom closed and to have strict control over the students' learning activities, the library may be even more shut out of the mind of the teacher as an important support for information. Even if most teachers favor such a "banking education ideology" and therefore look upon the students as passive stores to be filled up by transferring selected knowledge to them, it is still important for the library to find its role as a supporting service linked to the curriculum. A useful strategy to establish a partnership in learning within the frames of the ideology just described could be to promote the services of the library especially for the teachers. This promotion should highlight the following:

- ability to provide resources for teachers which will widen their subject knowledge or improve their teaching methodologies
- ability to provide resources for different evaluation and assessment strategies
- ability to be a working partner in planning the tasks to be done in the classroom
- ability to help teachers to cope with heterogeneous classroom situations by organizing specialized services to those who need more support and those who need more stimulation
- the library as a gateway to the global village through its interlibrary loans and electronic network

Teachers who have a more progressive and open educational ideology are likely to be keener library users. In addition to all the functions and possibilities mentioned above, they may include the library as a teaching place, and in so doing, move away from traditional teaching methods. In order to activate students in the learning process and develop their independent learning skills, teachers may cooperate with the library in fields such as the following:

- information literacy by developing the students' "spirit of inquiry" and educating them to be critical and creative users of information
- project work and assignments
- do reading motivation with students at all levels, for individuals or for groups

Students and the library. The students are the main target group of the school library. Cooperation with other members of the school community is important only because it is in the interest of the students.

Students can use the library for many different purposes. It should be experienced as an open, free, nonthreatening learning environment where they can work on all sorts of assignments, as both individuals and groups.

The students' activities in the library are likely to include the following:

- traditional homework
- project work and problem-solving tasks
- information seeking and information use

- production of portfolios and material to be presented to teacher and classmates

Use of the Internet. The new electronic resources are a special challenge for all library users. Using them can be very confusing. The librarian can provide the support to show that these resources are just tools in the learning and teaching process; they are means to an end and not an end in itself.

Library users become very frustrated when they look for information and think that, if they can access the Internet, then their information problems are resolved. The opposite is usually the case. The librarian can help users with the Internet and can also help minimize the frustrations resulting from information searches. What is important here is to select relevant and quality information from the Internet in the shortest time possible. The students themselves should gradually develop the ability to locate, synthesize, and integrate information and new knowledge from all subject areas in the resource collection. Initiating and carrying into effect information literacy programs are therefore among the most important tasks of the library (see the section "Teachers and the Library" above for further consideration).

The cultural function of the school library. The library can be used informally as an aesthetic, cultural, and stimulating environment containing a variety of journals, novels, publications, and audiovisual resources.

Special events can be organized in the library such as exhibitions, author visits, and international literacy days. If there is enough space, students can do literature inspired performances for parents and other students, and the librarian can organize book talks and storytelling for the younger students. The librarian should also stimulate interest in reading and organize reading promotion programs in order to develop the appreciation of literature. Activities addressed to encourage reading involve cultural as well as learning aspects. There is a direct link between reading level and learning results. Librarians should always be pragmatic and flexible in their approach when providing reading material to users and supporting the individual preferences of the readers by acknowledging their individual rights. By reading fiction and nonfiction literature which fits their needs and levels, students may be stimulated in their socialization process and identity development.

Cooperation with parents. The tradition of involving parents and careers in school activities varies across countries. The library can provide an opportunity for the parents' involvement in the school. As volunteers, they can help with practical tasks and support the library staff. They may also participate in reading promotion programs by being motivators at home in the reading activities of their children. They can also take part in literature discussion groups together with their children and thus contribute, in a way of master learning, to the outcome of reading activities.

Another way to involve the parents is to form a "friends of the library" group. This kind of group may provide extra funding for library activities and can assist the library in organizing special cultural events which require more resources than the library has at its disposal.

Promotion of the library and learning

Promotion. The services and facilities provided by the school library must be actively promoted so that the target groups are always aware of its essential role as a partner in learning and as a gateway to all kinds of information resources. The target groups have already been mentioned on several occasions in previous chapters. They are the principal and the other members of the school management group, heads of departments, teachers, students, governors, and parents. It is important to adjust the type of promotion to the nature of the school and to the different target groups.

Marketing policy. The school library should have a written marketing and promotion policy specifying objectives and strategies. It should be worked out in cooperation with the school management and teaching staff.

The policy document should include the following elements:

- objectives and strategies
- action plan which ensures that the objectives are attained
- evaluation methods

The actions that are needed will differ depending on aims and local circumstances. Some essential issues are provided in the following list as a way of illustration:

- starting and running school library websites which promote services and have linkages to and from related websites and portals
- organizing displays and exhibitions
- writing publications containing information about opening hours, services, and collections
- preparing and distributing resource lists and pamphlets linked to the curriculum, also for cross-curriculum topics
- giving information about the library at meetings for new students and their parents
- organizing "friends of the library" groups for parents and others
- organizing book fairs and reading and literacy campaigns
- providing effective interior and exterior signposting
- initiating liaison with other organizations in the area (e.g., public libraries, museum services, and local history associations)

The action plan should be evaluated, reviewed, and revised annually and the whole policy document should be discussed throughout at least once every second year.

User education. Library-based courses and programs aimed at teaching students and teachers how to use the library are perhaps the most effective marketing tool. For this reason, it is extremely important that these courses are well designed and have width and balance.

Because these programs play a key role in the library, it would also be appropriate to consider them in "Programs and Activities." The marketing aspect of all kinds of user education is, however, so essential that it may be even more suitable to deal with this topic in this chapter.

Courses specially designed for teachers should give them clear guidance on the role of the library in learning and teaching and on the support available from the library staff. These courses should especially emphasize the practical training in information seeking connected to the subject areas taught by the teachers. Through their own experiences in finding relevant resources, the teachers are likely to develop a deeper understanding of how the library can complement classroom work and be integrated within curriculum topics.

Like other learning programs at school, the various components of the student courses should be delivered in logical sequences to promote progression and continuity in the student's learning. This means that skills and resources must be introduced progressively through stages and levels. The school librarian should have the main responsibility for user education programs, but should cooperate with the teachers in order to link their different components as closely to the curriculum as possible. The teacher should always be present while students are having their library training programs and act as an adviser in cooperation with the librarian.

In user education, there are three main teaching areas to be considered:

- *knowledge* about the library: what is its purpose, what kinds of services are available, how it is organized, and what kinds of resources it has
- *skills* in information seeking and information using
- *motivations* for using the library in formal and informal learning projects

Model for a study skills and information literacy program

Philosophy. Information literate students should be competent independent learners. They should be aware of their information needs and actively engage in the world of ideas. They should display confidence in their ability to solve problems and know what is relevant information. They should be able to manage technology tools to access information and to communicate. They should be able to operate comfortably in situations where there are multiple answers, as well as those with no answers. They should hold high standards in their work and create quality products. Information literate students should be flexible, able to adapt to change, and able to function both individually and in groups.

Information literacy guidelines provide all students with a learning process that is transferable across content areas as well as from the academic environment to real life. These guidelines specify the following:

- the student should construct meaning from information
- the student should create a quality product
- the student should learn independently
- the student should participate effectively as a member of a work group
- the student should use information and information technology responsibly and ethically

Learning skills which may contribute to make this "philosophy" alive are included in the following list:

- self-directed learning skills
- cooperating skills
- planning skills
- locating and gathering skills
- selecting and appraising skills
- organizing and recording skills
- communicating and realizing skills
- evaluating skills

Self-directed learning skills. Self-directed learning skills are critical in the development of lifelong learners. Independent learners should be able to establish clear information goals and manage progress towards achieving them.

They should be able to use media sources for information and personal needs, seek answers to questions, consider alternative perspectives, and evaluate differing points of view. They should be able to ask for help and recognize the organization and structure of the library. The librarian plays a role as a learning partner, advising, not instructing, the students on their learning activities.

Cooperating skills. The school library is a place where individual differences mesh with the diversity of resources and technology. When students are working in a group, they learn how to defend opinions as well as how to criticize opinions constructively. They acknowledge diverse ideas and show respect for the others' background and learning styles. Furthermore they help to create projects that reflect differences among individuals and contribute to synthesize individual tasks into a finished product. The librarian can act as a group counselor and support them as much as necessary when they use the library as a resource in problem-solving activities.

Planning skills. Planning skills are an essential prerequisite for any research task, assignment, project, essay, or topic. At the initial stages of a learning process, activities like brainstorming, appropriate question framing, and keyword identification require creativity as well as regular practice.

A student with planning skills should be able to develop goals, spell out the problems to be solved, and design working methods to be used for that purpose. The librarian should be involved in the planning process to the extent the students wish. The librarian is expected to advise them on available resources and on the viability of any given assignment from the very beginning of the working process.

Locating and gathering skills. Locating and gathering are fundamental skills to be acquired by the students in order to be able to tackle information seeking at the library as independent learners. These skills include an understanding of alphabetical and numerical order, use of different kinds of tools for information seeking in computer databases and on the Internet. Reinforcement is required for these locating skills. They need to be related to the whole curriculum and developed progressively within a subject context. Exercises in these skills should involve the use of indexes, a wide variety of reference sources, and the full range of information technology. A competent student who masters these skills is able to integrate them when working with different methods of generating information such as survey, interview, experiment, observation, and study of sources. The librarian should design courses in locating and gathering skills which can be adjusted to meet the special needs of individuals and groups. The design should be carried out in cooperation with the teachers. In many ways, training in these skills represents the most essential part of user education at the library.

Selecting and appraising skills. Students need to develop critical and evaluative thinking skills. Together with the skills mentioned above, these skills are vital in order to obtain optimal results out of library use.

Programs designed to promote these skills should include exercise in the following:

- framing appropriate questions
- identifying likely resources
- using a variety of strategies
- building a reasonable timeline
- making ethical decisions

The librarian should especially focus on student guidance in how to find relevant updated authoritative information and in how to detect any bias or inaccuracy. A wide range of resources need to be consulted, compared, and appraised to ensure that hypotheses and conclusions are formed upon the widest possible knowledge base. The competent student should be able to identify criteria regarding authoritativeness, completeness, format and relevance, point of view, reliability, and timeliness.

Organizing and recording skills. Traditional conceptions about the function of a library are often limited to gathering and selecting information. The subsequent organization and use of this information has not been acknowledged in the same way. However, in a school library, this part of the process is just as important as the starting point. The librarian should also support the students in the development of these skills when they are working with projects and assignments. For this reason, the librarian should be an expert in the structural conventions of a project report and should give the students advice on how to write headings, chapters, and references. In addition, skills such as summarizing, quoting, and writing complete accurate bibliographies should be developed in the library and supported by the librarian. Competent students should be able to take notes, store information, and make it ready for use.

Communicating and realizing skills. Interpreting information and making use of it when working on projects and assignments are two of the most difficult learning skills. Through these skills, the students show whether they have a true understanding of the information they are providing or not. Transforming the information gathered into one's personal knowledge is indeed a challenging activity.

The competent student should be able to process information along the following lines:

- integrate information from a variety of sources
- make inferences
- draw conclusions
- construct meaning
- build connections to prior knowledge

Furthermore, the competent student should be able to do the following:

- communicate clearly
- reflect established aims and criteria
- demonstrate effective presentation skills

The librarian's role here is to advise and train students on these activities and provide a learning environment in the library which matches the students' support needs.

Evaluating skills. The final stage of a learning project consists of evaluating process and result. It is of vital importance that the students are able to do critical thinking about their effort and what they have achieved. Therefore the competent student should be able to accomplish the following:

- relate the finished product to the original plan and determine if the product has achieved its purpose
- determine the strengths and weaknesses of the learning project
- reflect on improvement and implications for future assignments

The librarian should be involved in the evaluation process together with the teachers for two reasons. One is to be informed about how the library managed to meet user needs. The second reason is to be able to function as an active learning partner who may contribute to throw light on the relationship between the learning process and the finished product.

Many countries, local authorities, and school libraries have worked out very successful plans for user education. Some of them are available on the Internet.

Selected references

American Association of School Librarians. *Information Power: Guidelines for School Library Media Programs.* Chicago: ALA, 1988.

Australian School Library Association, http://www.asla.org.au/. Policy statements on:

Information literacy
Electronic information literacy
Library and information services in schools
Privacy
Resource-based learning and the curriculum
Resource provision
Teacher librarian qualifications
School library resource center funding
School library bill of rights

Barrett, Lynn, and Jonathan Douglas, eds. *The CILIP Guidelines for Secondary School Libraries.* London: Facet, 2004.

Canadian School Library Association. *A Position Statement on Effective School Library Programs in Canada*, November 2000, http://www.cla.ca/divisions/csla/pub_3.htm.

Convention of Scottish Local Authorities. *Standards for School Library Resource Services in Scotland.* Edinburgh: COSLA, 1999.

Hannesdóttir, Sigrún Klara, ed. *School Librarians: Guidelines for Competency Requirements.* The Hague: IFLA, 1995.

Haycock, Ken, and Blanche Woolls. *School Librarianship: International Perspectives and Issues.* San Jose, Calif.: Hi Willow/IASL, 1997.

IFLA/UNESCO. *The School Library Manifesto: The School Library in Teaching and Learning for All.* The Hague: IFLA, 2000, http://www.ifla.org/VII/s11/pubs/manifest.htm.

Library and Information Services Council (Northern Ireland). *LISC Guidelines,* 2nd edition (forthcoming), http://www.liscni.co.uk.

Library Association of Ireland. *Policy Statement on School Library Services,* March 1996, http://www.libraryassociation.ie/policy/schools.htm.

Library Services for Education. *Central to Excellence: Guidelines for Effective School Libraries*. Rothley, England: Leicestershire County Council, 2002.

The Primary School Library Guidelines. London: CILIP, 2002, http://www .cilip.org.uk/professionalguidance/youngpeople/primaryguidelines.htm.

School Libraries: Guidelines for Good Practice. Dublin: Library Association of Ireland, 1994.

School Library Standards and Evaluation, list of American websites at http://www.sldirectory.com/libsf/resf/evaluate.html.

Scottish Consultative Council on the Curriculum, et al. *Taking a Closer Look at the School Library Resource Centre: Self-evaluation Using Performance Indicators*, August 1999, http://www.svtc.org.uk/sccc/closer/library.pdf.

South Africa, Department of Education. *A National Policy Framework for School Library Standards*, July 1997, http://education.pwv.gov.za/teli2/policydocuments/ library1.htm.

Stripling, Barbara K. *Learning and Libraries in an Information Age: Principles and Practice*. Englewood, Colo.: Libraries Unlimited, 1999.

National library associations are good sources of further information.

SOURCE: Adapted from Tove Pemmer Sætre and Glenys Willars, "The IFLA/UNESCO School Library Guidelines," *International Federation of Library Associations IFLA Professional Reports*, no. 77 (2002). Reprinted with permission.

EVALUATION
CHAPTER FIVE

Information power

Principle 6 of *Information Power* states, "Ongoing assessment for improvement is essential to the vitality of an effective library media program."

Goals for the school library media specialist

1. Remain current on all issues related to the use of information and information technology for learning and on methods and tools for assessing library media programs.
2. Collaborate with teachers, students, administrators, and others to develop and implement a comprehensive plan for identifying the information needs of the school community and assessing the program's role in meeting them.
3. Schedule regular, systematic data collection from a wide range of users and potential users of the library media program.
4. Use both quantitative and qualitative methods (e.g., both statistical information and observations and interviews) and both input and output measures to collect and analyze assessment data.
5. Make decisions based on the results of data analysis to develop plans and policies for the continuous improvement of the library media program.
6. Report the results of program assessment on a regular basis to teachers, students, administrators, and other community members.

SOURCE: Adapted from "Program Administration," chapter 6 in *Information Power: Building Partnerships for Learning* (Chicago: American Library Association, 1998), 108–109.

School library media centers (LMC) and academic achievement
by Keith Curry Lance and David V. Loertscher

Eleven major studies done since 2000 in almost 4,000 schools in the states of Alaska, Pennsylvania, Colorado (two studies), Texas, Oregon, New Mexico, Iowa, Michigan, Minnesota, and Missouri found:

> Strong school library media programs make a difference in academic achievement. This happens when the library media center has a high quality information-rich and technology-rich environment, easily

133

accessible to students and teachers, and when there is both professional and support personnel who provide leadership and tireless
partnering. Significant contributions happen in spite of the presence
of at-risk factors.

The strongest effects on quality education continue to be various at-risk
factors such as poverty and lack of English language skills. However, in spreading
the banquet table for young learners, the research says loudly that quality
library media programs are part of the main course rather than a side dish.

SOURCE: Adapted from Keith Curry Lance and David V. Loertscher, *Powering Achievement: School
Library Media Programs Make a Difference: The Evidence,* 2nd ed. (Salt Lake City: Hi
Willow, 2003). Used with permission. Studies listed above are listed and linked plus
updated as they appear at http://www.lmcsource.com under "free" resources.

Sources

The studies from
Colorado, Alaska,
and Pennsylvania are
summarized in Keith
Curry Lance and
David V. Loertscher,
*Powering Achievement:
School Library Media
Programs Make a
Difference: The
Evidence* (San Jose,
Calif.: Hi Willow,
2001).

The Texas and
Oregon studies can
be linked from
http://www.lrs.org/.

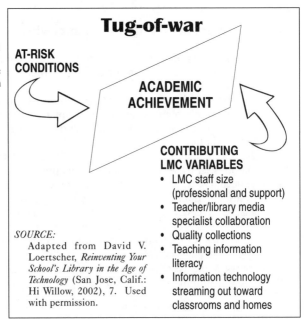

Tug-of-war

AT-RISK CONDITIONS

ACADEMIC ACHIEVEMENT

CONTRIBUTING LMC VARIABLES
- LMC staff size (professional and support)
- Teacher/library media specialist collaboration
- Quality collections
- Teaching information literacy
- Information technology streaming out toward classrooms and homes

SOURCE:
Adapted from David V.
Loertscher, *Reinventing Your
School's Library in the Age of
Technology* (San Jose, Calif.:
Hi Willow, 2002), 7. Used
with permission.

Accountability and the school teacher librarian

by David V. Loertscher and Blanche Woolls

Whether positions are reassigned or eliminated, funding to purchase materials and equipment that are essential if the school library is to play its major
role in the education of students may be lost. Too few teacher librarians
have conducted the appropriate studies to justify their programs or their
positions. One way this can happen is through the collection of action
research data.

Action research has been defined in many ways. One of the more recent definitions was given in workshop materials used by Richard Sagor, "Action research is a disciplined process of inquiry conducted *by* and *for* those taking the action. The primary reason for engaging in action research is to assist the 'actor' in improving and/or refining his or her actions."

If the results of action research are to be readily accepted by other educators and the school community, accountability measures we choose have more power if they are modeled after existing research studies. Many teacher librarians have little experience in conducting research and are more likely to make an error in design. A tested design used as a model is very helpful. One need only find the model.

Much, but not all, research related to school libraries is a product of governmental funded research projects and doctoral dissertations. Funded research is usually conducted in response to a formal request and may have a specific design testing specific needs for information. In reviewing this as a possible model, it is possible to expand as well as replicate the findings. When a government agency has funded research to look at the achievement of students in relationship to the presence of a teacher librarian and a good collection, this methodology can be and has been used as a model for others with funding. Doctoral dissertation research may provide another source for research design models.

Survivors of doctoral programs learn how to conduct research. Their task is to demonstrate to a committee that they are able to carry out a study from beginning questions through finished product. For those who are interested in research related to children and schools, being able to conduct a study becomes difficult because permission is needed to involve students. Many school officials consider required testing invasive and too time consuming even to consider an outside study. When the researcher is a member of the teaching staff of a school district, it is easier than it is for an "outsider" to propose the study. Being a "local" has its advantages.

This is one of the reasons the two authors of this paper originated the concept, Treasure Mountain Research Retreat, a short conference of practitioners and researchers meeting to discuss research and its application to the school library. Practitioners learn of the most recent research being conducted and researchers learn of research needed for the teacher librarian. Should collaborative projects evolve from Treasure Mountain, the researcher would not only be conducting needed research, but could also have a population available to "test," a win-win situation.

The last Treasure Mountain was held in spring 2002 with funding from the Institute of Museum and Library Services. Doctoral students were invited to attend and participate with other researchers at no personal expense. Remarks of three of the speakers, Keith Curry Lance, Ross Todd, and Ken Haycock, fit well as a platform for this discussion of accountability for they gave examples of research that had been conducted. If

Treasure Mountain, Utah

any school librarian prepares to tackle the challenge of accountability, their comments provide an introduction to action research possibilities.

Keith Curry Lance is well known for his national and state government funded studies of student achievement showing that professional teacher librarians and well stocked school libraries make a difference. His premise to the audience was that research in school libraries and their importance in the teaching and learning of students has a longer history than many teacher librarians realize. He cited Mary Virginia Gaver's study of children's reading reported in the early fifties. This study as do many others used an experimental research methodology making their replication in the school situation more difficult because of the requirement of a control group as well as an experimental group. This means that one group is given a "treatment" and another, the control group, is not. It is always difficult for a teacher librarian to deprive any student of a new experience, thus losing the control group aspect of the research. Lance's own research shows how studies may be conducted using available data rather than gathering new data with an experimental study.

Keith matches achievement test scores of students to the presence of a teacher librarian, an adequate collection, the amount of collaboration going on, the availability of information technology from the school library and moving into classrooms closer to learners, among other criteria. When you tie your research to published studies, you are paying attention to the competence of the respondent. Lance cautioned his Treasure Mountain audience to use research as a basis to build and pointed out that picking the right subjects for your research is critical. His suggestion was "Don't ask people who don't know the answer." Asking principals library management questions may generate more opinions than facts unless you are trying to point out the principal is uninformed about school library procedures. Choosing a methodology is another reason for the review of studies. Researchers learn one answer because they will have walked down one path to its conclusion. Using reports of their research can help you decide if you want to follow their path, walk parallel, take a different direction altogether, or ask a different question.

Another speaker, Ross Todd, discussed the challenge of changing the mindset of others. Their problem is one of ego versus student outcomes. The easy route remains "how we have always done this," and it takes strong evidence to overcome present practice. The emphasis is on image, support, rhetoric, funding, role/position, and being valued. He describes one solution as "evidence-based practice." Citing a process employed in medicine, Todd suggested that practice is justified in terms of evidence about the likely effects. Implicit in this are the concepts: "duty of care," "informed decision making," and "optimal outcomes."

To pre-plan optimal outcomes, teacher librarians must begin with the end in mind. Stephen Covey suggests, "To begin with the end in mind means to start with a clear understanding of your destination. It means to know where you are going so that you better understand where you are now so that the steps you take are always in the right direction." Beginning at the end is also advocated by Grant Wiggins and Jay McTighe who use it in relation to creating learning experiences. Determining what you want to accomplish and then planning how to collect the evidence you will need so you can report your degree of success becomes your model. If you want to chart your best course of action, you review the research detailing how others have accomplished what you wish to accomplish. At Treasure Mountain, Todd told the audience that putting research into practice involves conscientious, explicit, and judicious use of the current best research findings in making decisions about the performance of the day-to-day role of the school librarian. His remarks apply directly to the need to know research findings in order to build tests of accountability.

Day-to-day professional work is directed towards demonstrating the tangible impacts and outcomes of sound decision making. This involves local actions, local processes, and local immediate outcomes. It is, nevertheless, based on establishing a sound research-based framework for decision making. Teacher librarians should focus on the delivery of services based on stated goals and objectives with identified indicators of outcomes. Planning should be on systematically demonstrating outcomes and end points in tangible ways.

Dr. Todd's assumptions, confirmed by the Lance studies, are that information and information services make a difference. Specific learning outcomes matter. The practices of school librarians are linked to learning and learning outcomes, and school librarians should engage in evidence-based practice. In a new publication, Loertscher and Connie Champlin have provided some data sources of learning outcomes including assessment of information literacy:

> Rubric score that an individual used information literacy to enhance a project after being taught in use.
> Rubric score that content knowledge was enhanced through information literacy.
> Rubric score that the local standards for technology literacy and information literacy were met.

For the assessment of impact on reading:

> Evidence of individual progress in reading from measures other than state or standardized tests.
> Evidence from an attitudinal measure that the learner is both an avid and capable reader.
> Reading log analysis (including amount read).
> Points from electronic reading programs.
> Scores on writing assessments.

For assessment of the impact of technology:

> Rubric score for use of technology in a project.
> Rubric score that content knowledge was enhanced through technology.
> Rubric score that information literacy standards were met.

Loertscher suggests that teacher librarians regularly collect data from three sources: from the *organizational perspective* (size of facilities, equipment available, amount of funding provided, and size of collections or staff), from the *learning unit level* (various learning experiences that are designed by adults to interact with library materials and technology), and from the *learner level* (achievement test scores). Teacher librarians collect data using data instruments (daily, weekly, monthly measures), from the ongoing data collection to prepare reports or presentations, and from action research projects (studies within the school or district designed to answer local questions). Data may be collected in real time, periodically, and for special projects. The last of these, action research projects, require more planning and more time to execute.

The authors of this article have taught action research workshops and their training outline included writing a research question and designing a methodology to collect and analyze data, drawing conclusions, and reporting the results. However, Loertscher has added a new activity to this plan and includes the reflection piece before, during, and after action has occurred and results have been analyzed and reported.

Another new direction proposed by Loertscher is the triangulation of data-driven practice. Viewing the data from various vantage points is helpful when making action decisions. Creating data at the learner level involves all members of the collaborative team, teachers, teacher librarian, *and* students. Learners must have a significant part reporting from their perspective as well as the teacher and teacher librarian analysis so that students know what they know as well as their performance measures. Rubrics have been a great help to students in understanding where they are and where they need to go. This will help them understand if they are doing better over time and *why* this is happening. This can be supplemented by local and state tests. Teacher and teacher librarian will respond to their jointly developed checklists and questionnaires. They will also have student portfolios to judge, and they create their own learning unit level measures.

At the learning unit level, the teacher and teacher librarian keep collaboration logs, rubrics, and assessments of learning. These measures will help the teacher librarian assess whether collaboration between them has affected the teacher's methods. In assessing these, they will need measures of content, content learning, information literacy, and technology skills.

At the organizational level, not only do teacher librarians collect data, they need to share the findings with the community. When action research is based on other well-designed studies, the audience will recognize that quality and believe in the reported results. It will make the case for implementing the changes requested by the research.

The final speaker at Treasure Mountain, Ken Haycock, states the challenge to us that we have the evidence or can gather the evidence that we can make a difference. The conundrum is "Now we need only do it!"

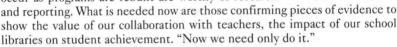

Teacher librarians and school libraries have survived tough times in the past. In fact, the improvements that occur as programs are rebuilt are worthy of research and reporting. What is needed now are those confirming pieces of evidence to show the value of our collaboration with teachers, the impact of our school libraries on student achievement. "Now we need only do it."

SOURCE: Adapted from David V. Loertscher and Blanche Woolls, "Accountability and the School Teacher Librarian," *School Libraries in Canada* 22, no. 2 (2002): 7–9. Used with permission.

Block scheduling: A survivor's guide

by Blanche Woolls and David V. Loertscher

Very little research has been reported testing the effectiveness of block scheduling and much that has been published is controversial. Furthermore, any reports that relate directly to school library media programs are most often just that—reports of activities or how we are implementing block scheduling or what we have heard someone else is doing. They have little research base. Yet this educational innovation provides an excellent opportunity for school library media specialists to exhibit leadership. Our article in *Knowledge Quest* in the March/April 1999 issue asked library media specialists who were going to be involved or were teaching in schools with block scheduling to document impact in ways other than impressions or observations.

This article provides some simple ways for conducting action research and comparing data to findings that have been previously published and that are beginning to show the effectiveness of the library media center program in support of block scheduling. Library media specialists who follow the directions, collect the data, and report their findings in their state association newsletters, at conferences, and in *Knowledge Quest* and other school library media journals will accomplish three goals:

1. to do action research
2. to add to the body of information
3. to help other library media specialists assume a leadership role while participating in planning and execution of block scheduling in their schools

To conduct your research study, you will need to know what action research can and cannot do, how to go about implementing a plan, what has been reported in the literature, and how you can use this to compare your results. According to S. Isaac and W. B. Michael, action research is designed "to develop new skills or new approaches and to solve problems with direct application to the classroom or other applied setting." R. Swisher and C. R. McClure compare action research to traditional research and common sense. The major differences among the goals of these methods are the following:

Action research is designed "to obtain knowledge that can be directly applied to the local library/information center to increase organizational effectiveness."

Traditional research is used "to obtain knowledge that is generalizable to a broad population and to develop and test theories."

Common sense is used "to make changes in the current situation that appear likely to improve the library/information center."

It does not require an advanced degree to be able to conduct action research studies. In fact, the research must be conducted by the library media specialist and be directly related to the effectiveness of the library media center. Some ground rules do exist. For instance, the best approach is to have goals and objectives for your media center program. You will be testing how well you meet these goals and objectives, looking at your situation to see how well your services and the resources available to your students and teachers meet their needs.

Steps to follow in conducting research include:

1. Determine what you wish to test.
2. Find out if anyone else has tested this problem and how the study was conducted.
3. Write your problem statement.

4. Decide how you will study this problem.
5. Consider what data you will collect.
6. Decide how you will analyze the data.
7. Choose how and to whom you will report your findings.
8. Determine what you will do to make the changes found in the research.

The remainder of this article discusses action research for one specific use: testing the effects of block scheduling on use of the library media center. If you are in the process of planning or implementing a block scheduling program, you will need to collect base data immediately. If block scheduling has been implemented in your school, you will report differences based upon new projects you introduce, recognizing that it will be more difficult to attribute success to block scheduling for the changes you find.

Background needed

Baseline data to be collected include the teaching styles of teachers, the pattern of block scheduling, the subject areas included, and the past pattern of usage of the library media center. It is impossible to credit differences unless you have a starting point.

What are the teaching styles of your teachers? Teachers who have spent the last 20 years lecturing to students for 45 minutes, who rely almost exclusively on the textbook, who state with pride that they are on the same page in their plan book that they were on last year at the same time, and who assess student progress through paper and pencil tests will move reluctantly into a different pattern. Their learning style is your first measurement. While teachers never fit totally into a single style, they will exhibit one style more than another.

Many tests exist for analyzing the interpersonal behaviors of individuals. It is often difficult to get teachers to participate in what they consider personality tests. Blanche Woolls uses the teaching/learning styles of Anthony Gregorc: concrete sequential, abstract random, abstract sequential, and concrete random. They are easy to identify. One can observe classrooms and limited teaching and still place teachers within the categories, remembering that everyone has some traits of each category.

Concrete sequential teachers work step by step, carefully following directions. They make lists and, one by one, move steadily to complete each of the carefully developed plans. They seat students in orderly rows in a quiet classroom. Concrete sequential teachers and students enjoy the order offered in computer programs.

Abstract sequential teachers are the inventive ones who thrive on abstract ideas, theories, and hypotheses. They are intellectual, logical, and rational, developing new ideas and inventions such as computers. They see the big picture and solve problems as a part of a system. Using an idea, they create blueprints demonstrating that they visualize the whole product.

Abstract random teachers think with their emotions. They are very interested in the ambiance of the classroom. Because they enjoy group work, student desks may be placed in groups of three or four. They may rebel against a structured environment. Compared to a concrete sequential teacher's classroom, the abstract random classroom appears chaotic.

Concrete random teachers want to know what makes things tick. They often cannot articulate the steps they follow to

go from beginning to end, yet they solve problems easily. They do not think conventionally. Willing to dismantle the computer to see how it works, they make good technicians in schools.

We surmise that many teachers fall into the concrete sequential category. They enjoy the structure of the classroom, the format of the school day, and the safety of the textbook. They look askance at the disarray they perceive to exist in an abstract random teacher's classroom. They mistrust the concrete random teacher (or student) because they weren't shown how the problem was solved.

Concrete random teachers will enjoy seeing how things tick and will be helpful in testing new products for their use in the classroom. Your abstract sequential teacher, being better able to see the whole picture, will work more easily toward across-the-curriculum units of instruction. By thinking through these teaching styles, you will be able to choose the best approach to help them change.

What is your pattern of block scheduling? Many patterns have been put into place. The 4×4 pattern includes four classes the first semester in 90-minute blocks with four different classes in 90-minute blocks for the second semester. Another pattern is the A/B schedule, with four classes in 90-minute segments meeting every other day for the entire year. "A" classes meet one day and "B" classes meet the second day. These classes continue for the entire year. Other schools have combined the 4×4 and A/B classes into a "combination block schedule." Another pattern is the combination of 4×4 and A/B classes with the class length varying each day. That is, on three of every five days, each class is 90 minutes in length. On the other two days, classes are 75 minutes in length and a "resource hour" is in place for 60 minutes. Other permutations exist with changes in the number of minutes or the rotation.

If this has not yet been implemented, teachers could be asked to analyze in a three-week period how much time they spend lecturing in their classes, working in group-related activities, and giving time to begin homework. When teachers have begun block scheduling they could discuss their plan books for one three-week period. If they happen to have kept their plan books from previous years, they could try to compare what they covered and how they spent the class periods. This cannot be a rigid review, so don't attempt precision. Rather, try to get a sense of the percentage of time in lecture and in other activities.

Are all subject areas involved in block scheduling, or just some subject areas? Some research shows that science teachers are very happy with this schedule as it gives them time to prepare and conduct full experiments. Teachers in other subject areas seem to find it difficult to fill the time. Are teachers fighting the block schedule because they fear they will lose their ability to plan thoroughly for each minute of the class period? Scheduling small group activities may make them feel they will lose control of the classroom.

When some subjects are placed in the block schedule and others have not been, a record of the reasons this division was made would be helpful in planning future tests of any library media activity to be planned.

What has been the pattern of usage of the library media center? This needs to be recorded before any changes are implemented. Fast change makes it easy to forget past patterns. Library media centers are heavily used only a small portion of the school year—during the annual research assignment for the junior or senior major paper and freshman research into careers. For the rest of the year, they are often a respite from the study hall. As you review your plan book, you can begin to analyze the number of classes using the library media center in proportion to the single students who come from a study hall or from classrooms.

The shift to collaboration with teachers and integration of information literacy skills into every subject is worthwhile to record. Library media specialists will need this information to use as confirmation of the need for a larger budget and for more staff. Your record of collaboration will provide ideas both for repeating a unit and for remembering those tasks or materials that were less successful.

Determining what to test

Once you have your baseline data, you begin the design of your action research. Choosing what to test should be a partnership arrangement. You will need to find co-teachers who want to work with you, although you need to remember that sometimes being a part of a study brings in a better performance simply because it is a study. For the beginning action researcher, starting small with a simple study will be better than a larger attempt with a longer time frame from beginning to completion.

Who else has tested this problem? To base your research on a model from the field is another way to reduce the amount of error you might encounter when starting from scratch. Our March/April 1999 article in *Knowledge Quest* provides you with some reports from the field that would be useful in finding out who else has studied this problem.

To translate findings into the question you wish to have answered, G. M. Mistretta and H. B. Polansky found the following advantages to properly implemented block scheduling:

1. Reduced number of class changes and transitions during any one school day;
2. Reduced duplication and increased efficiency;
3. Reduction in the number of students seen by each teacher daily;
4. Reduction in the number of teacher preparations per day;
5. Reduced fragmentation;
6. Flexible instructional environments; and
7. Variation of time based on the content area.

These advantages will be used to demonstrate how the action researcher can use someone else's findings to build a new study.

Writing your problem statements

Beginning with the first numbered item, your question might be, "How many reductions have occurred since the change to block scheduling?" It is a simple matter to record the number of class changes and transitions that occur with block scheduling. Students who have been assigned six or seven class periods in the six-hour school day will move six times, with a consequent loss of time spent going to lockers.

Other problem statements will be built around your objectives. One objective could be that your collaboration will increase by working with a certain number of teachers to build information literacy into their classroom assignments. Another might be that information literacy competencies of students will be increased. This one will be a more difficult one to assess, but it should be one for which you are constantly seeking evidence.

For Mistretta and Polansky's second item, your question is "How does the longer time in the library media center affect the way I teach information literacy?" Discovering the reduction in duplication and the increase in efficiency may take more time to record. When students are in the library media center to conduct research, the fact that you can give instructions and students can practice them immediately reduces time spent compared to the alternative method of 45-minute classes.

Shorter classes mean repeating much of the information at the beginning of the class. Students forget when they aren't able to put their learning into practice. Does the increased time allow them to generate their research question and test the resources for supporting evidence, or are they only able to do the first step? Have you planned reflection time? How could you "test" if their retention is higher? Could you compare the amount of time given to your lecture?

An increase in student learning time will be shown to result from the combination of teacher collaboration in planning and the longer time in the media center for putting instruction into practice. It will help you know if you have enough resources available.

How will you study these problems? What data will you collect? Selecting the design defines what data you will collect. Because we have been placing our study within the framework of Mistretta and Polansky, some of the data to collect falls easily into place. Collecting data can accomplish two objectives: It can actually collect data, and it can become an awareness tool to encourage collaboration among teachers.

What if the research project in a junior English class covered a topic being taught in the junior social studies classroom? Results could point out that an arbitrary assignment of an extended research paper needs continual re-teaching of information literacy skills while the application of a real topic increases interest in that topic, improves retention of research skills, and heads the student toward lifelong learning. Scheduling the research project as a joint project between two classrooms immerses students in the social studies topic and allows them to have their writing skills checked by a well-trained editor, the English teacher. Students also will have three critics for their papers—the English and social studies teachers and the library media specialist—each looking for both their major objectives, but also seeking to identify any writing or social studies content.

For this, one rubric would be built to assess student work and another to assess the value of teacher collaboration across the curriculum. The rubric to test the quality of student products would be developed by students, teachers, and library media specialist.

The reduction in the number of students seen by each teacher daily, the third item in the Mistretta and Polansky report, is an easily collected statistic. For the classroom teacher, collaboration with the library media specialist means that two adults are working with the students, resulting in an even smaller pupil/teacher ratio. While the number of students who come to the library media center may be the same for the library media specialist, the length of time spent with a single group lengthens even though others are in the center at the same time.

The fourth item in Mistretta and Polansky suggests that the number of daily teacher preparations may decrease. However, it may not cut down on the amount of time a teacher needs to prepare. Further, implementing block scheduling means that teacher and library media specialist need time for collaboration, and this time may not have been factored into the teaching days in past years.

At this point, the library media specialist begins to collect data on collaboration with teachers. Probably the easiest way to do this is through an electronic plan book that records your calendar for the day, the teachers who come into the media center to consult, and the name of the unit being discussed. As you begin to build units of instruction, your record of those actual units of instruction will be your evidence. While it is easier to save them on disk, keeping a hard copy in a notebook makes it readily available when someone comes into the media center.

Library media specialist as instructional designer

A RAND study was reported in "The Change Process and Alternative Scheduling." The study, which looked at successful urban schools, showed that external technical assistance was needed for coaching and strengthening staff skills through professional development. "New teaching strategies can require as much as fifty hours of instruction, practice, and coaching before teachers become comfortable with them."

One suggestion for library media specialists who wish to move into a leadership role is to be an integral part of the planning for practice and coaching experiences. If skills in instructional design are sufficient and if library media specialists have the proper rapport with their colleagues, providing the technical assistance may save the district money that would otherwise be needed to hire the appropriate consultant. In addition, the library media specialist now is well established as someone for a teacher to approach with education problems.

"Reduced fragmentation," the next item in Mistretta and Polansky, has always been a keystone for library media specialists. In our role, we see all of the students and all of the teachers all of the time. We have worked with all curricular areas and we can help teachers further reduce the fragmentation of courses taught in isolation. It is a difficult battle to win when school district administrators, parents, and the news media wait for the next report of testing done within a state. However, if we are to prepare students for life and work after their basic education is completed, helping teachers join together to relate learning in one classroom to learning in the next becomes our battle cry.

A calendar of teachers, units, and what they teach is a simple beginning to the process of helping teach across the curriculum. If you return to the example of the English teacher whose research report is based upon a topic covered in the social studies classroom, the model of collaboration across the curriculum begins. If one of your objectives for the year was to develop and implement at least one information literacy activity that would cross curriculum areas, you have met your objective.

Flexible instructional environments are challenges to the textbook/lecture teacher. Expanding lectures from 45 minutes to 90 minutes only increases the boredom of the audience. Library media specialists can help teachers build cooperative group activities and provide students time for reflection. Working together, library media specialist and teacher can see that every child in the class has assistance when questions arise. Modeling collaborative behavior in the media center with collaborative projects is one method of coaching teachers and demonstrating to students the value of working together. Collecting evidence of this adds to your growing stack of successful objective implementation.

How will you analyze your data? Most of your data will result in numbers that you can add and subtract. Just report those numbers. Whenever possible, you can turn them into percentages. Most readers readily understand what an average score means, and they will understand percentages of time spent on projects. If you feel that more expertise is needed to analyze your data, see if someone in your district is available to help you, or turn to a nearby college or university and locate someone who might be interested in helping you with your project. For many faculty members, being able to help you with your research will help them with their own research agenda. Research is a requirement for tenure, promotion, and salary increases in many institutions of higher education.

How and to whom will you report your findings? The wonderful thing about action research is that it belongs to you. You share it with the persons of your choice. Obviously, if findings are very positive, you will want to share it with the entire school. When the findings are less positive, you and your teacher cohorts will need to assess how to make the managerial and educational changes that will bring better results the next time.

If the problem is lack of materials, that statistic is reported to administration. For years, many school library media centers have had severely reduced funding to purchase resources and equipment. Your research reported in terms of student achievement and curriculum needs should strengthen your position, particularly if an educational innovation is under way.

Findings are reported to teachers to help them understand the role of the media center in student progress. When teachers who have not made use of the media center learn the results of classes that have, they will be eager to join the library media specialist and other teachers in collaborating on units of instruction.

Giving parents examples of the progress of students who are conducting research can be made through presentations at parent-teacher meetings, exhibits at open house for parents, newsletters sent home, and devices students themselves may create. With the attention being paid to parent participation in the education of their students, your information concerning increases in information literacy will be welcomed by all.

Providing your administrator(s) with evidence of research progress gives them ammunition to request additional funds from the site-based management pool. Administrators could be given the words and a PowerPoint presentation to encourage them to make presentations at their conferences and expand the attention given to the library media program as an integral part of the school curriculum.

The bottom line with this article is its context. It was to help you assess the impact of block scheduling on library media services. Your results need to be reported in your local area by sharing findings with your colleagues in your district. Next you should write short articles for your state association newsletter. Presenting a synopsis of what you have found on a list such as LM_NET can help you locate a colleague with similar interests with whom you might collaborate for an article in *Knowledge Quest*. Reporting to groups when opportunities arise allows you the opportunity to tell your audience about your research and to listen to their suggestions for improvements. Members of the audience often have success stories to relate that will expand the knowledge.

Adding to the skimpy research on the value of the library media center in block scheduling can be critical in the implementation of the innovation. It helps to establish the leadership role of the library media specialist and to create the need for additional resources. It allows the library media specialist to move teaching into a constructivist mode and it improves student attitudes about school, one of the findings of much of the research on block scheduling.

Comparing your data to other findings can confirm your present direction for resources and services. If, in the process of comparison, another way to implement appears to be more successful, it gives you an opportunity to try a new method. If what you are doing is confirmed in the literature, you have every support to continue to follow that path.

What will you do to make the changes found in the research? When the results of your research show problems and no similar study is reported for you to see what another library media specialist tried, meet with your cooperating teachers and discuss the situation. See if common sense can help you try a different approach. Engage other teachers in the discussion. This may encourage them to join you in a future project. Again, you may wish to consult with someone in a local university or with staff at your state department of education to select new methods. Those who are accustomed to using an e-mail list could surely post their questions to other library media specialists.

You are the key to successful change when block scheduling is implemented at your school. You need only engage the interest of your faculty and administration in leading the planning process. When you have collaborated with teachers, they become your best advocates for changes in scheduling, sharing of resources, reallocation of staff, and additional resources. As students recognize the use of information in their education, they build lifelong research skills. You must keep in mind that, as you change your role in the school and your program's services and resources to meet the changing needs of block scheduling, you will build on your base data. You will continue to add to your evidence of the effect of these changes on the teaching and learning in your building. When change shows improvement in student performance, or more collaboration between teachers and library media specialists or between teachers of different subjects or grade levels, you have demonstrated the positive effect of the library media center in a block scheduling environment.

SOURCE: Adapted from Blanche Woolls and David V. Loertscher, "Testing the Effect of the School Library Media Center in a Block Scheduling Environment," *Knowledge Quest* 28, no. 2 (November/December 1999): 16–25.

Internet skill rubrics for teachers

by Doug Johnson

Not long ago, formal instruction about the Internet focused primarily on how to use a wide variety of specialized tools for locating and retrieving files. Tools like gophers, newsreaders, e-mail programs, telnet, and ftp were all dedicated to single tasks and each required extensive training in its use. Now, most Internet resources can be easily accessed using a properly configured Internet browser like Netscape or Explorer. The specialized tools have become modules built into these powerful programs. For all but the most demanding Internet users, a web browser configured with some "helper applications" will be the only tool needed for Internet use.

The interface to the Internet has changed dramatically as well. "Streaming" is quickly allowing Internet users to play music and hear discussions. Using the Internet as a telephone is becoming more common. "Push" technologies deliver up-to-the-minute news, weather, and business information to one's desktop, relieving the user of the responsibility of finding and retrieving it.

These changes in access and content have allowed Internet instructional time to be spent less on:

How do I find files and data?
How do I use specific Internet tools?
How do I download the information to my computer?

and increasingly on:

How can I focus my searches?
How can I determine if the information is accurate?
How do I interpret and take meaning from the information?
How do I use and communicate the information within an educational setting?
How do I prepare my information so it can be displayed on the Internet?

The older skills, while at times frustrating to teach, were easier to master! While the needed skills for using the Internet seem to change almost daily, they can be used as a starting point for measuring staff competencies. Each of the rubrics has four levels:

Level 1: Pre-awareness
Level 2: Awareness
Level 3: Mastery
Level 4: Advanced

Prior to training, we assume most teachers are at level 1 or 2, and our district's training efforts are designed with that assumption. By the end of the training, we anticipate teachers will be at level 3 or 4 in most skill areas, and have gone up at least one level in all areas. At minimum, 30 hours of direct instruction are needed for the mastery of all ten competency areas. These rubrics, then, serve two purposes:

1. By asking teachers to complete an anonymous self-assessment using the rubrics before training and again after training, we can judge the effectiveness of our staff development efforts. Simple graphs showing the percentage of training participants at each level pre- and post-training are constructed. These results can be shared with staff development committees and the administration.

2. The rubrics also provide a "road map" for teachers wanting to improve their Internet skills. By examining the specific skills described, teachers know in what areas they need to practice or continue to take classes.

Please feel free to use and modify the rubrics for your district's specific needs and as technology changes.

Teacher instructions for Internet skill rubrics

Judge your level of achievement in each of the following competencies. Circle the number that best reflects your current level of skill attainment. (Be honest, but be kind.) At the end of the training program, you will complete the same set of rubrics that will reflect your level of skill attainment at that time. (Level 3 is considered mastery.) This tool is to help measure the effectiveness of our training program, and to help you do a self-analysis to determine the areas in which you should continue to learn and practice. Keep a copy of these rubrics to refer to during the training.

This is an anonymous assessment. You do not need to sign the pre- or post-evaluation tool. Individual results will be aggregated to determine how effective the program has been for the group as a whole. You should, however, keep track of your own individual progress.

1. Internet basics

Level 1—I do not understand how networks work, nor can I identify any

personal or professional uses for networks, including the Internet. I do not have an account on any network nor would I know how to get one.

Level 2—I can identify some personal or professional uses for networks, and understand they have a value to my students and me. I've read some articles about the Internet in the popular press. I can directly use network access to a library catalog or CD-ROM.

Level 3—I can describe what a computer network does and how it can be useful personally and professionally. I can distinguish between a local area network, a wide area network, and the Internet and can describe educational uses for each. I can describe the history of the Internet, recognize its international character, and know, to a degree, the extent of its resources. I have personal access to the Internet that allows me to receive and send e-mail, download files, and access the World Wide Web. I know that I must protect my password, and should restrict access by others to my account.

Level 4—I use networks on a daily basis to access and communicate information. I can serve as an active participant in a school or organizational planning group, giving advice and providing information about networks. I can recommend to others several ways of obtaining Internet access.

2. E-mail and electronic mailing lists
Level 1—I do not use e-mail.

Level 2—I understand the concept of e-mail and can explain some administrative and educational uses for it.

Level 3—I use e-mail regularly and can:

read and delete messages
send, forward, and reply to messages
create nicknames, mailing lists, and a signature file
send and receive attachments
use electronic mailing lists and understand the professional uses of them
read and contribute to a professional electronic mailing list

Level 4—I can send group mailings and feel confident that I could administer an electronic mailing list. I use activities that require e-mail in my teaching. I can locate lists of subject-oriented mailing lists.

3. The World Wide Web
Level 1—I do not use the World Wide Web.

Level 2—I am aware that the World Wide Web is a means of sharing information on the Internet. I can browse the Web for recreational purposes.

Level 3—I can use a web browser like Explorer or Netscape to find information on the World Wide Web and can list some of the Web's unique features. I can explain the terms hypertext, URL, http, and html. I can write URLs to share information locations with others. I can use web search engines to locate subject specific information and can create bookmarks to websites of educational value.

Level 4—I can configure my web browser with a variety of helper applications. I understand what "cookies" do and whether to keep them enabled. I can speak to the security issues of online commerce and data privacy.

4. Search tools
Level 1—I cannot locate any information on the Internet.

Level 2—I can occasionally locate useful information on the Internet by browsing or through remembered sources.

Level 3—I can conduct an efficient search of Internet resources using directories like Yahoo! or search engines like Google or Lycos. I can use advanced search commands to specify and limit the number of hits I get. I can state some guidelines for evaluating the information I find on the Internet and can write a bibliographic citation for information found.

Level 4—I can identify some specialized search tools for finding software and e-mail addresses. I can speculate on future developments in online information searching including know-bots and other kinds of search agents.

5. Newsgroups
Level 1—I have no knowledge of newsgroups.

Level 2—I know that there are resources in a variety of formats available on the Internet, but cannot confidently access them.

Level 3—I read the newsgroups that interest me on a regular basis, and I can contribute to newsgroups.

Level 4—I know how to find, configure, and use the specialized tools for newsgroups. I use the resources found in these areas with my students.

6. Obtaining, decompressing, and using files

Level 1—I cannot retrieve files from remote computers.

Level 2—I know that documents and computer programs that are useful to my students and me are stored on computers throughout the world. I cannot retrieve these files.

Level 3—I can transfer files and programs from remote locations to my computer, and can use programs or plug-ins that help me do this. I can extract compressed files, and know some utilities that help me view graphics and play sounds and movies. I understand the nature and danger of computer viruses, and know how to minimize my risk of contracting a computer virus.

Level 4—I use information I have retrieved as a resource for and with my students. I understand the concept of a network server and the functions it can serve in an organization. I can use an ftp client to upload files to a server.

7. Real-time and push technologies

Level 1—I use only static documents and files I retrieve from the Internet.

Level 2—I have some information sent to me on a regular basis through e-mail and I check some sites on a regular basis for information.

Level 3—I use chat rooms and customized news and information feeds. I can listen to music audio streamed from the Web. I know the hardware and software requirements for web-based videoconferencing.

Level 4—I can use real-time applications to design a "virtual" classroom or interactive learning experience. My students use videoconferencing for communication with experts and project collaboration with other students.

8. Web page construction

Level 1—I cannot create a page which can be viewed with a web browser.

Level 2—I can save text I've created as an html file with a command in my word processor. I know a few, simple html commands.

Level 3—Using hand-coded html or a web page authoring tool, I can view web pages as source documents; create a formatted web page that uses background color, font styles and alignment, graphics, and tables; include links to other parts of my document or other Internet sites in my page; and know basic guidelines for good web page construction and the district's web policies.

Level 4—I can use the Web as an interface to databases. When appropriate, I can register my pages with search engine sites. I can help write web creation policies for design, content, and use.

9. Learning opportunities using the Internet

Level 1—I am not aware of any ways the Internet can be used with students in my classroom.

Level 2—I occasionally allow my students to use the Internet to find information.

Level 3—I know a variety of projects and activities that effectively use the Internet to instruct and involve students. I know a source for collaborative projects, can direct students to online tutorials and learning resources, and encourage a variety of key-pal activities.

Level 4—I can design and implement an Internet project or maintain an educational Internet site.

10. Netiquette, online ethics, and current issues surrounding Internet use in K–12 schools

Level 1—I am not aware of any ethics or proprieties regarding the Internet, nor am I aware of any issues dealing with Internet use in a school setting.

Level 2—I understand a few rules that my students and I should follow when using the Internet. I understand that the Internet is sometimes a controversial resource which many educators and parents do not understand.

Level 3—I have read a guideline for Internet use such as Rinaldi's "The Net: User Guidelines and Netiquette" or other source, and follow the rules outlined. I know and read the FAQ files associated with sources on the Internet. I am aware that electronic communication is a new communications medium that may require new sensitivities. I can identify print and online resources that speak to current Internet issues like:

censorship/site blocking software
copyright
legal and illegal uses
data privacy
security

I can list some of the critical components of a good Acceptable Use Policy and know and use our district's.

Level 4—I can use my knowledge of the Internet to write good school policies and activities that help students develop good judgment and good information skills.

SOURCE: Adapted from Doug Johnson, "Internet Skill Rubrics for Teachers," *The Book Report* 17, no. 5 (March/April 1999): 37–40. *The Book Report* is now published as *Library Media Connection.* Used with permission.

Reading danger points

by David V. Loertscher

If any of the following describe or approximate what is going on in your school, red flags should be raised.

Students do not list reading on any list of fun things to do. Reading is not cool.

Book collections in the library media center are old, worn out, and unattractive.

Budgets are so small that the number of new books purchased each year is insignificant.

Books available don't match what children or teens would enjoy reading.

Students only check out one or two books a week from the library media center.

Classrooms contain few reading materials beyond textbooks.

Classroom collections are small, outdated, too limited, or stagnant.

Classroom collections and library media center collections are not connected and are funded separately.

Reading aloud, particularly as students get older, is sporadic or nonexistent.

There is wide concern that high school students are not good readers, but there is no schoolwide effort to do anything about it.

Teachers of science, social studies, physical education, art, and math don't feel they have any responsibility to teach reading.

Science, social studies, or other content areas require little or no reading beyond the few textbook paragraphs on a topic.

No program of sustained silent reading exists in the school; or, it has been tried but has been considered a failure.

Reading motivation "events" or programs are one-time or annual events of brief duration or are nonexistent.

There are very few books in students' homes.

Students do not have bed lamps or safe places to keep library media center books in the home.

Parents, care givers, or siblings do not read aloud to younger students on a regular basis.

SOURCE: Excerpted from David V. Loertscher, *Reinventing Your School's Library in the Age of Technology: A Guide for Principals and Superintendents* (San Jose, Calif.: Hi Willow, 2002), 34. Used with permission.

How administrators can evaluate school libraries

by David V. Loertscher

The research is very clear in outlining the key elements necessary to transform an outdated library program into one that competes strongly with at-risk conditions in any school. This article recommends four reasonably simple ways to monitor the investment versus its impact.

Technique #1: Measure the amount of collaborative planning done by library media specialists with teachers to plan, execute, and evaluate the impact of joint learning experiences. When a teacher is willing to move a learning experience from the classroom to the library media center, good things are likely to happen: there are now two teachers instead of one, an information-rich and technology-rich environment is at the elbow, and each learner can expect twice as much professional support for a given learning task.

Collaborative planning of exciting learning experiences in the library media center requires advance planning, creative transformation of a low-level learning experience to an improved one, innovative use of information and technology, and sound assessment of content knowledge, information literacy skills, and wise use of technology.

A key but simple measure is to request that library media specialists keep collaboration logs. (Examples of collaboration planning and evaluation forms are available at www.indiana.learns.org.) Into a notebook go the planning sheets used by library media specialists and teachers as they collaborate to build learning experiences. It belongs in the log *only if* the teacher and the library media specialist agree that the experience was superior to one that would have been conducted in the classroom alone. The number, spread across the disciplines and across the faculty, constitute the "gold star" learning experiences.

If the administrator notices unhealthy patterns of low frequency of collaboration or inadequate spread across disciplines or grade levels, the administrator can partner with the library media specialist to build this exciting intervention. As a collaborative pattern emerges in the library media center, certain observable activities will be happening. This will include brainstorming a curricular unit, developing plans, activities, and assessments for a learning experience, choosing the materials and technologies to support instruction, working side by side as the unit activities happen, jointly evaluating the success of the unit, and engaging in staff development to refine the collaborative process.

Technique #2: Ascertain the impact of information literacy as taught by the library media specialist during a collaboratively taught unit of instruction. Library media specialists are charged by their professional associations with teaching information literacy defined as the effective use of ideas and information. To do this, they are to equip learners with a research model where the novice learns to build a question, find high-quality information, internalize the information, synthesize/draw conclusions, communicate the findings, and reflect on the process and the learning.

How do the teacher and the library media specialist know that a learner has made progress? One most promising assessment is fairly simple. Include on the rubric for any library-based project both content-related items and process-related items (information literacy). Learners will understand that they must master knowledge about their topic, but they will have to show some competence in the effective use of the research process. For a specific project the teacher would rate the content knowledge part of the rubric and the library media specialist would rate the items on process. At the learner level, the percentage of learners who succeeded on both categories would be known and could be reported across various units that were moved to the library media center.

Technique #3: Ascertain the impact of technology on collaboratively taught units of instruction. When a teacher is overwhelmed by technology because the classroom contains too little for too many learners, moving a unit to the library media center learning laboratory where there is not only more technology but also more adults to assist is an attractive notion indeed. In this scenario, the computer space in the library media center becomes a learning laboratory. Creative ideas for the effective use of technology build over time because of the parade of units passing through the center. A range of the mundane to excellent presents itself and better ideas tend to emerge. The assessment of whether, in fact, technology has contributed both to the learning of content and to the process of learning can be assessed at the learner level if the rubric contains items related to the effective use of technology. In addition, the checklists from the International Society for Technology in Education (ISTE) standards for student use of technology can be quite useful to the administrator seeking the worth of technology investment.

Technique #4: Ascertain the amount of reading being stimulated through the library media program. The research is quite clear, that the more students read, the higher they will score on almost any measure in almost any discipline. (See NCRTEC *Scoring Guide for Student Products* at http://www.ncrtec.org/tl/sgsp/how.htm.) Here is an area of traditional expertise for the library media specialist. However, some assessment of effectiveness is in order. First, test access.

> What percentage of students would say they are reading a "library book or two" right now?
>
> Can students check out unlimited quantities of library books?
>
> Are the abuses of electronic reading programs under control?
>
> Are there mountains of fascinating, exciting, and interesting books to read stocked in the library media center, in rotating classroom collections, and at every other appropriate place in the school?

Money spent to purchase books kids want to read affects reading scores since students read more. For each collaboratively taught unit in the library media center, rubric items connected with the amount read can encourage students to read far beyond a few paragraphs in the textbook with obvious results.

A concluding story and a few conclusions. Recently, the author conducted a graduate class in two spectacular school library media center facilities. In both schools, no expense had been spared to build a 21st-century facility complete with high technology, lavish furnishings, and an elegant ambience. In the first, the principal and the library media specialist made a pact that no teacher would schedule a visit to the library media center without first doing advance planning with the library media specialist. Because all the teachers were new at the school's opening, they thought that collaboration was "just how it works around here." The library media center in this school is filled with exciting learning experiences from morning through afternoon. In the second school, the principal opted to staff the center with a clerical. This library media center is a lavish babysitting facility. The tourist in either stands in awe. The realist is outraged because of the inequity.

Across the United States, thousands of school library media specialists who were educated in the 1970s are currently retiring. These folks were educated at a time when audiovisual materials were just starting to be added to library book collections. Today, their replacements need to be high-tech wizards, learning consultants, collaborative partners, and focused on making a difference in learning. The challenge, of course, is to find such a person and to release persons who have not kept up with the vision of what a school library media program can do to increase achievement. Wise administrators seek out an exemplary teacher and commit him or her to get a library media/technology credential. You may lose a good teacher, but you gain the influence that teacher will have on the entire school. If your library media center is the hub of the school and if it is contributing to achievement, it will be your fault!

SOURCE: Adapted from David V. Loertscher, *Reinventing Your School's Library in the Age of Technology: A Guide for Principals and Superintendents* (San Jose, Calif.: Hi Willow, 2002). Used with permission.

Student assessment: A critical function of the school library media specialist

by Marilyn Miller with Dianne Hopkins

Competent school library media specialists fully accept the responsibility for the evaluation of the media program, collections, and learning activities cooperatively planned with teachers. Research and subsequent developments in teaching and learning theories have led, particularly in the decade of the nineties, to the explication of the intrinsic component of the assessment of learning in the model of performance-based education. School library scholars have responded with thoughtful writings on the role of the school library media specialist in student assessment. These writings are reflected in *Information Power: Building Partnerships for Learning*, which states unequivocally that program and student assessment are responsibilities of library media specialists.

Although student assessment is implied throughout the guidelines, the greatest specific attention is paid to the subject in Appendix E, Student Performance Assessment. Appendix E defines student assessment and describes the various processes and strategies that library media specialists have available to them. In Chapter 6 on Program Administration (pp. 108–109), Principle 6 states that "ongoing assessment for improvement is essential to the vitality of an effective library media program." The narrative provides specific directions and goals for the library media specialist to use in meeting this principle.

Dianne Hopkins, professor at the School of Library and Information Studies, University of Wisconsin–Madison, prepared an excellent background summary of current thought on assessment for the Vision Committee charged with developing IP2. I have always thought the paper needed wider dissemination. It is clearly developed and expressed and presents a cogent rationale for assessment. Library media specialists who may be overwhelmed by this role in evaluation will find it helpful. I am sharing Hopkins' working paper with her permission.

A summary of current work on assessment

1. Assessment should be formative and summative. The primary basis for evaluation of the program relates to its ability to meet the needs of the students collectively and individually. As part of a planning process, the library media program is evaluated on a regular basis to review overall mission, goals, and functions in relation to user and instructional needs and to assess the efficiency and effectiveness of specific activities:

Input and output measures are included in evaluation, including the collection, intellectual access, flexible scheduling, expectations of the principal for a curriculum-involved library media center, student-based inquiry, the facility design.

Within the collection and technology, there is recognition that each medium embodies a cluster of attributes that cause the medium to be either more or less able to support certain learning tasks for individual learners.

The extent to which the library media center encourages cooperative learning within a learning community is evaluated. Cooperative learning may be encouraged through student inquiries and teacher/student-generated content questions.

2. The process of evaluating the program involves not only the library media specialist but also and especially classroom teachers and students. A key to evaluation is the nature of the collaboration between the library media specialist and the teacher. Others involved in evaluation include the school principal, the school's site-based management team (where applicable), parents, and selected community members.

3. The library media specialist is a continual learner who provides leadership for a student-centered library media center program. The library media specialist models and promotes collaborative and effective planning, learning, and teaching.

4. The evaluation of a student-centered library media program is based on sound principles in which there is widespread agreement, such as:

the importance of collaboration between the library media specialist and teachers;

the importance of information literacy skills incorporated into content learning;

learning theories including diverse rates of learning for students, diverse student abilities, diverse styles of learning, variety of student needs;

a recognition that learning depends on a variety of intertwining learning strands—content knowledge, knowledge of information-seeking processes, problem solving, and critical thinking; and

the importance of links to the larger learning community through electronic access, and partnerships with other libraries and with other cultural institutions.

5. The evaluation of library media center programs involves a holistic approach to student learning that builds upon and recognizes the importance of the library media center program as a central part of the learning community of which the student is central.

6. The results of library media center program evaluation impact the student as learner. Thus library media center programs recognize, and take into account, that students' new learning is affected by their prior learning. There is also recognition that learning is a process of self-directed restructuring of new learning with the old.

7. The library media center program should be a part of a total school community in which student learning is central. As such, an inquiry-based approach is important.

8. The library media center and the library media specialist are essential in authentic assessment.

9. The library media specialist collaborates with the classroom teacher and other members of the learning community to assess student learning (students' achievement?).

10. The library media specialist, in collaboration with the learning community, establishes policies that ensure equitable access to ideas and information. These policies reflect legal and ethical standards in policies, procedures, and practices.

11. Program and personnel evaluations follow districtwide policies and procedures, focus on performance, and are based upon appropriately collected data.

12. Evaluation is part of an ongoing planning process during which mission, goals, and functions in relation to user and instructional needs as well as the efficiency and effectiveness of specific activities are reviewed. Library media center mission, goals, and objectives are complementary to the school's mission of student learning through its educational goals and objectives.

13. In order for evaluation to be successful, the mission, goals, and objectives of the library media program must be clearly understood and fully supported by the administration and educational staff, students, and the community.

Dianne Hopkins reviewed the following documents in preparing her background summary:

American Association of School Librarians and Association for Educational Communications and Technology, *Information Power: Guidelines for School Library Media Programs* (Chicago: American Library Association, 1988).

School Improvement Office, Division of Instruction and Staff Development, "BETTER: Information Literacy: Outcomes of the School Library Media Program" (Baltimore: Maryland State Department of Education, 1997).

B. K. Stripling, "Assessment of Student Performance: The Fourth Step in the Instructional Design Process," in *Assessment and the School Library Media Center*, ed. Carol C. Kuhlthau (Englewood, Colo.: Libraries Unlimited, 1994), 77–85.

SOURCE: Adapted from Marilyn Miller, "Student Assessment: A Critical Function of the School Library Media Specialist," *Knowledge Quest* 28, no. 4 (2000): 27–28.

Irrefutable evidence

by Ross J. Todd

Di Wilson is on a mission. She's spent the last 15 years hoarding evidence—the kind of information that proves her relevance to student learning. Wilson understands that colleagues at her K–12 girls' school want proof that she's valuable, and she's more than willing to comply. She already has a portfolio stuffed with papers, everything from students' test scores to surveys to checklists, anything that will chart her vital role as a school librarian.

Wilson knows that evidence-based practice—the process of carefully documenting how school librarians make a difference in learning—is key to being recognized. A big part of her work is devoted to creating assignments that tie the library to the classroom curriculum. Whenever there's good news to report, Wilson brings it to the attention of her teaching colleagues and parents. Her most recent success story includes a two-year project exploring plagiarism in her school in Melbourne, Australia. Wilson surveyed students and colleagues and discovered that the main culprit was a lack of clear instruction on note-taking skills, particularly in grades seven through nine. That prompted her to create lessons on correct citation and note-taking styles, and they were eventually adopted by the school's teachers.

"I keep very busy working with teachers from a wide range of subjects, both revising [lessons] we have done in the past and creating new ones," Wilson says. "If school librarians can lead by example, by using the skills and resources at their fingertips to explore curriculum [connections], then I think they gain the respect of the teaching staff." School-wide respect, coupled with her collaborative programs, has made it far easier for Wilson to secure a decent budget.

Most educators don't recognize a direct link between the daily activities of school librarians and improved student achievement, despite several important statewide studies by Colorado University's Keith Curry Lance linking ample school library services with increased student success on standardized test scores (see "Dick and Jane Go to the Head of the Class," *School Library Journal*, April 2000, pp. 44–47). Why? Because the evidence isn't directly linked to local student success and isn't readily documented or available. To gain the support of your administrators, principals, teachers, and parents, show them your impact on student learning. They want to know how their students benefit from their own school library services. Move away from advocating the value of school libraries and start documenting tangible outcomes. Taking concrete action will help you gain the respect you deserve and eventually play a huge role in budgetary decisions that affect your media center.

What is evidence-based practice and how can it work for you? First coined by the medical profession in the early 1990s, evidence-based practice can now be applied to what you do to show how and why your services are important to student learning. Start by familiarizing yourself with existing research on how school libraries can optimize learning. Then make sure you systematically focus on gathering meaningful evidence on the impact of your instructional role on student achievement.

Incorporating evidence-based practice doesn't require extraordinary investigative skills. All that's needed are simple strategies to help gather proof that your library lessons help students become better learners. When I was a school librarian, I'd administer quick exercises at the end of each information literacy lesson, asking students to jot down the three most important things they learned, how my lesson improved the way they previously conducted research, and how I could further help them. The answers I received provided clear insights into the impact of my lessons and ways I could continue helping students. In short, the questionnaires helped justify my work and gave me ideas for future information literacy lessons. Proving your worth can be that simple.

Some school librarians say that proving their worth detracts from completing their day-to-day work. But if school librarians are already engaged in collaborative teaching efforts, why not simply document their impact on student achievement? If student learning is our most important objective, then evidence-based practice is not about proving our worth, it's about demonstrating the vitality of our contributions to learning.

Start engaging in evidence-based practice by teaching students the fundamentals of inquiry-based research, which lays the foundation for your documentation. School libraries aren't just repositories of information—a certified media specialist needs to provide quality instruction. Like any good investigator, start by gathering the most essential evidence—how information literacy teaches kids to develop critical-thinking skills. Inquiry-based research trains kids to think beyond prescribed answers to come up with analytical answers to questions. "It takes students out of the predigested format of the textbook and rote memorization into the process of learning from a variety of sources to construct their own understandings," says Carol Kuhlthau, professor of library and information science at Rutgers University and the author of *Teaching the Library Research Process: A Step-by-Step Program for Secondary School Students* (Center for Applied Research in Education, 1985). Kuhlthau recommends giving assignments that avoid simple yes or no answers. Get kids to examine their existing knowledge and determine what additional information they need to learn. And get them to explore inconsistencies in their current knowledge and expectations and to formulate questions that will help them develop their own theses. These student appraisals will guide classroom teachers and librarians in the planning, implementation, and assessment of future assignments.

If you overlook this critical stage of information-literacy instruction, students will fail to gain ownership of their research and never learn the correct way to evaluate or locate quality information. An evidence-based approach provides a rich opportunity for school librarians to ensure that their lessons make a real contribution to student learning.

There's no standard approach to getting started with evidence-based practice, and strategies will vary from school to school depending on the learning goals of individual districts. But media specialists must develop paper trails to prove their worth. This documentation can include samples of students' work, lesson plans, surveys, and test scores, anything that will help justify your job. While planning your lessons, focus on the need to explicitly identify what you are teaching and how to prove you were successful. A good starting point is to focus on any collaborative lessons with your colleagues. When teachers and school librarians work together, principals and the school board see firsthand evidence of your value. And when teachers see that you make a difference in student learning, they become your biggest advocates.

School librarian Sue Healey at Tintern Grammar School in Australia, for example, recently devised a collaborative lesson with a history teacher to help kids develop more effective Internet search strategies. Healey created a checklist asking students to describe their search techniques for the assignment. Then she showed them all the flaws in their techniques and gave them a lesson in how to properly uncover primary documents and other quality resources. When the librarian surveyed students on how the lesson helped them prepare better research papers, she was able to demonstrate that her lesson improved the quality of students' projects. Charting what students have learned—the instructional outcomes— is a critical component of evidence-based practice. You must make clear statements based on concrete evidence that your students have benefited from your lessons. To help you do so, refer to the following information literacy strategies offered in *Information Power* (American Library Association, 1998):

Simple checklist strategies: Check students' levels of information literacy skills, technical skills, knowledge, and attitudes before and after the library instruction.

Rubric strategies: Evaluate students based on a set of criteria that clearly defines the impact of your lessons.

Conferencing strategies: Devise activities where students can reflect on their work, their skills, and the benefits of the library instruction.

Journaling strategies: Document your instruction and the outcome of your instruction.

Portfolio strategies: Gather samples of students' work over a period of time and match them to your school's curriculum goals and information-literacy requirements.

These strategies ensure that information literacy is embedded into your lessons and will help you identify how the library has made a difference in student learning.

About 50 ninth graders at the K–12 Gill St. Bernard's School in Gladstone, N.J., helped media specialist Randi Schmidt prove that point. The students were involved in a four-week research project to improve their print and online research skills. After Schmidt taught them how to ask the right questions, analyze and synthesize available resources, and develop well-thought-out theses, students were asked to write a one-page report on how the librarian's instruction helped them create a more comprehensive final project. The responses were full of rich detail about how information-literacy instruction helped them write better papers. One student said the lesson helped him weed out bad information, while another said she could better formulate her own views. Other students said the lessons helped them become independent researchers and taught them to stay focused on the questions being asked. These comments, taken directly from students' own voices, provide clear-cut evidence that information-literacy instruction was put to good use.

It's important to understand that evidence-based practice takes assessment to a higher level. By developing information-literacy lessons and detailing the explicit lessons learned, the contributions of the school library move beyond observation to powerful evidence about its central role in the school. It proves that students actually benefit from the librarian's daily activities. Over time, the multidimensional role you play will become clear to your teaching colleagues.

How do we know evidence-based practice actually works? We've already seen significant results. Kuhlthau and I are currently undertaking a survey of 10,000 K–12 students in Ohio to determine how school libraries there have explicitly helped students learn. This project, funded by the Ohio Educational Library Media Association, will move beyond test scores to examine the qualitative and quantitative ways school librarians help kids find quality resources and use that information to produce exemplary research projects. Our overall goal is to determine how media specialists help students with everything from technology to independent thinking and research to reading skills. The results of our findings, expected this fall, will present a clear picture about how effective school libraries improve students' skills.

Evidence-based practice certainly requires effort, but the skills needed to engage in this practice stem directly from the information-literacy processes that we preach. What's important is that the gathered evidence highlights how the librarian plays a crucial role in boosting student achievement, in shaping important attitudes and values, in contributing to the development of self-esteem, and in creating a more effective learning environment.

How to get started . . .

Teach students the fundamentals of inquiry-based research. This lays the foundation for your documentation.

While planning your lesson, explicitly focus on identifying what you are teaching and how to prove you were successful. Start by focusing on any collaborative lessons with teachers.

Develop a paper trail. This can include samples of students' work, lesson plans, surveys, test scores, and checklists.

Chart what students have learned. *Information Power* offers a helpful checklist of strategies (visit www.ala.org/aasl/ip_nine.html).

SOURCE: Adapted from Ross J. Todd, "Irrefutable Evidence," *School Library Journal* 49 (April 1, 2003): 52–54. Courtesy of *School Library Journal.*

5

CREDENTIALS

CHAPTER SIX

ALA/AASL standards
for school library media specialists

The following is from the ALA/AASL *Standards for Initial Programs for School Library Media Specialist Preparation: Initial Preparation for the Master's Degree.* The standards are directly applied to those programs wishing accreditation by the National Council for Accreditation of Teacher Education (NCATE).

Introduction to the program standard

The School Library Media Specialist (SLMS) Preparation Program is predicated on the philosophy and mission of the national guidelines for school library media programs of the American Association of School Librarians (AASL): "to ensure that students and staff are effective users of ideas and information." To carry out that mission, successful candidates:

- provide intellectual and physical access to materials in all formats;
- provide instruction to foster competence and stimulate interest in reading, viewing, and using information and ideas;
- work with other educators to design learning strategies to meet the needs of individual students.

School Library Media Specialist candidates have the potential to be effective teachers as well as effective information specialists. Within this construct, the elements of collaboration, leadership, and technology are integral to every aspect of the school library media program and the school library media specialist's role. The basic goal of the SLMS Preparation Program is clear: to prepare candidates for service and leadership as school library media specialists serving pre-K–12 students. The program addresses the philosophy, principles, and ethics of the field: to ensure that students and staff are effective users of ideas and information through teaching and learning, information access and delivery, reading advocacy, and program administration. It values research, reading, teaching, and services to the field; and it determines the role of library services in a diverse and changing society.

To ensure that programs prepare candidates to meet these challenging expectations, the American Association of School Librarians, on behalf of the American Library Association, has developed rigorous standards based on research findings, national and state professional documents, expert opinion, and accepted best practices in the field. The master's degree in librarianship from a program accredited by the American Library Association or a master's degree with a specialty in school library media from an educational unit accredited by NCATE is the appropriate first professional degree for school

163

library media specialists (adopted July 6, 1988, by ALA Council). With this new set of standards, only institutions offering master's degrees to prepare school library media specialists will be considered for recognition. However, given that some states have undergraduate and certification programs prior to the master's level, ALA/AASL will review undergraduate and post-baccalaureate certification programs for quality of programs, when requested, but will not grant recognition in publications or on the ALA/AASL website.

Conceptual framework

Program standards: Philosophy, beliefs, values. The primary goal of the School Library Media Specialist Preparation Program Standards is to prepare graduate students for service as certified school library media specialists, grades pre-K–12. The program standards are intended to meet state and national standards for School Library Media Specialists (SLMS) and to ensure that candidates are able to carry out the mission and goals of school library media programs as set forth by the American Association of School Librarians (AASL): "to ensure that students and staff are effective users of ideas and information." Successful candidates thus address three critical areas of service provided in effective library media programs:

teaching and learning
information access and delivery
program administration

Program knowledge base. The specific goals of school library media specialists fall within the larger concept of librarianship. Librarianship has as its goal, to develop and use skills and knowledge in the areas of information resources, information access, technology, management, and research as a basis for providing library and information services.

A fundamental aspect of school librarianship is *information literacy:* the ability to access, evaluate, and use information from a variety of sources and in a variety of formats. According to AASL's standards, an information literate student is also an independent and socially responsible learner. This learner will need practice in communication, critical thinking, and problem-solving skills in order to be prepared to work in today's world. Information literacy extends to lifelong engagement with information and ideas for personal fulfillment.

Information access and delivery is the first of three critical areas of services for today's school library media specialists. Historically, school libraries have housed resources for the school; however, as resource-based and constructivist learning approaches gained credence, the need for intellectual and physical access to information became more critical. The school library media specialist who has a solid foundation in evaluating information, has technological expertise in retrieving and organizing information, and maintains a commitment to intellectual freedom, is able to create an information-rich learning environment within the school. The library media program needs to support and stimulate goals and spontaneous interests and inquiry of children.

Teaching and learning is the second aspect of school librarianship. Earlier versions of the school library media specialist program focused on a consultancy role and stressed locational guidance, but current practice demands a true partnership role, in which the school library media specialist and classroom teacher are engaged together throughout the instructional process. The school library media specialist brings a unique perspective to instructional collaboration, because the library program reaches all students and all curricular areas. Research has shown that student achievement increases with collaborative planning and teaching; therefore the school library media specialist must be willing to assume a leading role in curriculum and instructional development.

Program administration constitutes the third rung of the knowledge base: "the ability to manage resource center programs, services and staff in order that these services may contribute to the stated educational goals of the school." The school library media specialist must understand management and change, must communicate clearly, and must be prepared to take tactical risks. In addition, librarians must advocate for support and must create an environment that contributes to student achievement. Effective library media programs will contribute to academic success, reading improvement, and an enhanced school culture. The school library media program will contribute to the development of a habit of lifelong learning by providing access to resources within and beyond the school. School library media specialists also need to participate in staff development opportunities. Therefore, the effective school library media specialist will exhibit leadership skills among colleagues, in essence by "leading from the middle," as they position themselves to be recognized as leaders among equals.

Standard 1: Use of information and ideas

School library media candidates encourage reading and lifelong learning by stimulating interests and fostering competencies in the effective use of ideas and information. They apply a variety of strategies to ensure access to resources and information in a variety of formats to all members of the learning community. Candidates promote efficient and ethical information-seeking behavior as part of the school library media program and its services.

Efficient and ethical information-seeking behavior
Target: Candidates advocate for and demonstrate effective use of current and relevant information processes and resources, including emerging technologies. Candidates model a variety of effective strategies to locate, evaluate, and use information in a variety of formats for diverse purposes. Candidates plan reference services, using traditional and electronic services that are comprehensive and address the needs of all users. Candidates model and teach legal and ethical practices.

Literacy and reading
Target: Candidates are knowledgeable about historical and contemporary trends and multicultural issues in reading material for children and young adults. Candidates analyze and apply research in literacy and reading in order to select and recommend diverse materials in formats and at levels that facilitate the reading process and the development of fluency in readers. They collaborate with teachers to integrate literature into curriculum. Candidates instill a sense of enjoyment in reading in others that leads to lifelong reading habits.

Access to information
Target: Candidates analyze and implement library media program scheduling options for different needs by developing flexible and open access for the library media center and its services. Candidates plan strategically to ensure

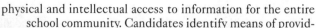

physical and intellectual access to information for the entire school community. Candidates identify means of providing remote access to information. Candidates model and promote the tenets of privacy, confidentiality, intellectual property, and intellectual freedom.

Stimulating learning environment
Target: Candidates demonstrate collaborative techniques as they create and maintain an attractive, positive educational climate in a technology-rich library media center. Candidates use research-based data, including action research, to analyze and improve services.

Standard 2: Teaching and learning

School library media candidates model and promote collaborative planning with classroom teachers in order to teach concepts and skills of information processes integrated with classroom content. They partner with other education professionals to develop and deliver an integrated information skills curriculum. Candidates design and implement instruction that engages the students' interests, passions, and needs which drive their learning.

Knowledge of learners and learning
Target: Candidates ensure that the library media curriculum is documented as significant to the overall academic success of all students.

Effective and knowledgeable teacher
Target: Candidates can document and communicate the impact of collaborative instruction on student achievement. Candidates develop a regular communication procedure between home and school.

Information literacy curriculum
Target: Candidates work to ensure that responsibility for an integrated information literacy curriculum is shared across curricular areas throughout the school. Candidates advocate for the information skills curriculum in order to ensure appropriate learning experiences for all students, and to address the academic needs of the school community.

Standard 3: Collaboration and leadership

School library media candidates provide leadership and establish connections with the greater library and education community to create school library media programs that focus on students' learning and achievement, encourage the personal and professional growth of teachers and other educators, and model the efficient and effective use of information and ideas.

Connection with the library community
Target: Candidates employ strategies to ensure connections between the school community and the larger library world of public, academic, special libraries, and information centers. Candidates participate in professional associations.

Instructional partner
Target: Candidates anticipate providing leadership to school and district committees. Candidates share expertise in the design of appropriate instruction and assessment activities with other professional colleagues.

Educational leader
Target: Candidates develop a library media program that reflects the best practices of education and librarianship. They have a thorough understanding of current trends and issues in education. Candidates write a plan for professional growth that justifies their own professional choices. Candidates engage in school improvement activities by partnering with administrators to help teachers learn and practice new ways of teaching. Candidates share information, apply research results, and engage in action research.

Standard 4: Program administration

School library media candidates administer the library media program in order to support the mission of the school, and according to the principles of best practice in library science and program administration.

Managing information resources: Selecting, organizing, using
Target: Candidates utilize collection analysis and evaluation research techniques to ensure a balanced collection which reflects diversity of format and content, reflecting our multicultural society. Candidates design plans for collection development and analysis and policies that ensure flexible and equitable access to facilities and resources. Candidates develop procedures to analyze the effectiveness of library media policies, procedures, and operations. Candidates ensure that policies and procedures are in place to support intellectual freedom and the privacy of users of all ages.

Managing program resources: Human, financial, physical
Target: Candidates organize, manage, and assess all human, financial, and physical resources of the library media program. Candidates advocate for ongoing administrative support for the library media program and policies. Candidates actively seek alternative sources for funding the library media program, both within and outside the school community.

Comprehensive and collaborative strategic planning and assessment
Target: Candidates collaborate with teachers, administrators, students, and others in the school community to develop, implement, and assess long-term strategic plans. Candidates are able to align the library media program with the information literacy standards and the school's goals, objectives, and content standards. Candidates use quantitative and qualitative methods of data collection and analysis to assess data and make decisions on which to base plans and policies.

School library media program standards glossary

Access—Access to the school library media program and resources is defined in three ways. Physical access refers to the ability of all users to easily make use of the library media center facilities and resources. Intellectual access ensures that all users will find materials on their reading, interest, and comprehension levels. Economic access refers to the removal of all barriers to library materials and services based on the user's ability to pay.

Advocacy—The coordinated and comprehensive process by which support for the library media program is created within the greater community.

Challenged materials—Books and other resources that are identified by concerned citizen(s) with an expressed desire to remove them from the library collection.

Collaboration—In a collaborative instructional information skills unit, the school library media specialist works closely with other teachers in the school to co-plan, co-teach, and co-assess information skills.

Collection development—The systematic process of gathering input on user needs, identifying materials to meet those needs, and acquiring those materials for the library collection.

Confidentiality—The legal expectation by patrons that their reading, viewing, and listening of library resources is not revealed to others without their permission.

Cooperative collection development—Two or more libraries, possibly of different types (such as public, academic, school, or special) working together to jointly acquire materials.

Digital divide—Term used to refer to the growing gap between those who have access and can use information technology and those who cannot.

Diversity—The NCATE definition of diversity is "differences among groups of people and individuals based on ethnicity, race, socioeconomic status, gender, exceptionalities, language, religion, sexual orientation, and geographic area." A diverse library media program extends that concept to apply to the library collection, to issues of access to the library media center, and to design and delivery of information skills instruction.

Fixed scheduling—A method of assigning each class in the school a set time to use the library each week. This is usually done to provide the  classroom teacher with a planning period. This method prevents the school library media specialist and the classroom teacher from collaboration, especially in larger schools.

Flexible access—The opposite of fixed scheduling, the school library media program is not used as a method of providing the teacher's planning period. Classes are scheduled as a result of instructional need.

Format—Refers to the variety of ways in which information is packaged. Common formats are books, videotapes, electronic, audio recordings, etc.

Information ethics—Use of information in accordance with both legal and moral precepts. The library patron's right to privacy, to full access of information, and the right to expect that other patrons will respect ownership of information are included.

Information literacy—The ability to locate and use information in all formats.

Information Power—The national guidelines for school library media programs first published by AASL in conjunction with the Association for Educational Communication and Technology in 1986 and revised in 1998.

Information retrieval—Usually electronic, information retrieval refers to the process of identifying, locating, and accessing the full text of information, in all formats, and wherever located.

Information specialist—Person with professional training in the organization, storage, and retrieval of information.

Information technology—Commonly used to refer to the computer and other technology used to store or retrieve information.

Instructional partner—The concept of the school library media specialist as an active participant in the instructional life of the school, and in the education of each student.

Integrated information skills curriculum—The alignment of the identified information skills curriculum with subject area curricula.

Intellectual freedom—The right of each patron to access information and ideas according to their needs or interests.

Life-long reading—The creation of a strong desire to read that continues throughout the student's life.

Location and access—Limiting information skills instruction to the identification of materials and their placement in the library. Does not typically include instruction in the comprehension, use, or synthesis of the information.

Mission—The mission of the school library media program in the school is to "ensure that students and staff are effective users of ideas and information." This mission was first developed for the 1986 edition of *Information Power*, the national guidelines for school library media programs, and has remained the mission.

Open access—Users are welcomed in the library media center before, during, and after the school day without barriers.

Organization of information—Term used to refer to the standard protocols by which information is arranged. Other terms that are sometimes used are cataloging and classification, technical services, etc.

Outcomes-based learning—Identifying what students will know and be able to do at the end of an educational process.

Privacy—The legal expectation by patrons that their reading, viewing, and listening of library resources is not revealed to others without their permission.

Program administration—The role of the school library media specialist centering on the management of the school library media facility and services.

Reading habit—The creation of a strong desire to read that continues throughout the student's life.

Resource-based learning—Using materials in a variety of formats to teach, illustrate, or support the curriculum concepts.

School library media center—Usually refers to the room in the school that houses the school library media facility.

School library media program—The integration of the services coordinated by the school library media specialist including but not limited to those within the school library media center.

School library media specialist—The professional licensed school library media teacher with specialized training and education in the school library media profession.

Selection policy—Formal statement guiding the identification of materials to be included in the school library media collection, and the school collection of instructional resources.

Selection tools—Established books, review journals, and other aids that are recognized by the library field as valid and reliable sources of information to assist the school library media specialist in the identification of resources.

Technical services—The assorted skills associated with preparing information resources for use by patrons, including cataloging and classification, database management, and other skills.

National Board standards for library media specialists

by Sharon Coatney

What do good teachers know? What do they do? How do they effect change in their schools and foster learning in their students? These questions that confront all of us in the field of education are central to the mission of the National Board for Professional Teaching Standards (NBPTS):

> The mission of the National Board for Professional Teaching Standards is to establish high and rigorous standards for what accomplished teachers should know and be able to do, to develop and operate a national voluntary system to assess and certify teachers who meet these standards, and to advance related education reforms for the purpose of improving student learning in American schools.

A group of teacher librarians, school library educators, and library supervisors met in Washington, D.C., to write the certifying standards that will enable school library media specialists in this country to become nationally certified. This process, sponsored by the NBPTS, has been both interesting and challenging. The group, like all subject area certifying groups convened by the National Board, was quite diverse. Most of the members were working school library media specialists, but they came from all types of schools and school libraries. Some represented wealthy suburban districts, others rural, and still others urban. The schools represented reflected many types of library programs and philosophies. The daunting task of coming up with standards that were exemplary, but could be met by library media specialists in many different circumstances, was difficult though not impossible. Through discussion and exercises planned to bring about consensus, while simultaneously encouraging divergent thought, the school library professionals defined the standards that will identify the characteristics of accomplished library media specialists. These standards, as all others endorsed by the Board, are not for the novice, but are to recognize those experienced librarians who exemplify accomplished excellence in the teaching field of school library media. The group finished a third draft with the final writing completed by a professional writer employed by the NBPTS. The 63-member Board then approved the standards. The standards were then circulated for national comment by the school library media field.

NEW Independent Study Confirms the Effectiveness of National Board Certification®

Background

The National Board for Professional Teaching Standards was created in 1987 as an answer to studies such as *A Nation at Risk* that contained statements like this: "If an unfriendly foreign power had attempted to impose on America the mediocre educational performance that exists today, we might well have viewed it as an act of war." The Carnegie Task Force on Teaching as a Profession suggested, as a possible solution to the problems indicated in the *Nation at Risk,* the creation of "a profession equal to the task—a profession of well-educated teachers prepared to assume new powers and responsibilities to re-design schools for the future." Coming out of this milieu, the NBPTS is an independent nonprofit group governed by a national board, most of whose members are working classroom teachers. Funding for the board comes from a combination of grants from major private foundations and federal funds.

Expert teachers in the certifying areas develop their own profession's stan-dards. Standards reflect the five core propositions endorsed by the NBPTS:

1. Teachers are committed to students and their learning.
2. Teachers know the subjects they teach and how to teach those subjects to students.
3. Teachers are responsible for managing and monitoring student learning.
4. Teachers think systematically about their practice and learn from expe-rience.
5. Teachers are members of learning communities.

These standards have become the basis for the performance-based certify-ing assessments that will enable library media specialists to become nationally certified. This is very important for our field. We must continually reinforce our role as teacher in order that we remain indispensable to schools in the continuing process of fostering student achievement.

SOURCE: Adapted from Sharon Coatney, "National Board Standards for Library Media Special-ists," *Knowledge Quest* 28, no. 1 (September/October 1999): 40–41.

National Board effects on library education

by Gail Dickinson

The National Board for Professional Teaching Standards (NBPTS) was formed in 1987 in response to the publication of *A Nation at Risk.* Two of the problems that a subsequent Carnegie report identified as reasons why teachers left the classroom were the lack of a career ladder for teachers and poor pay and ben-efits. NBPTS addressed these and other issues by creating rigorous standards for the teaching profession, devising a voluntary system of identifying accom-plished teachers, and encouraging policy changes to reward and sustain those skilled teachers in the classroom.

To date, there are nearly 24,000 National Board Certified Teachers (NBCTs). Library media as a certification area first became available in 2002. The first class of candidates produced approximately 435 library media-cer-tified teachers, although there may be others with library media licensure who are board-certified in areas such as early- or middle-childhood generalists.

If one were told that Jones Middle School was a good library program, the immediate response might be, "What do they *have?*" The assumption is that good school library media programs have financial resources and supports—good facilities, sound and stable budget streams, current materials and technologies, and administrative backing (evidenced by best practices such as flexible access). The National Board standards take the opposite approach by examining school library media specialist (SLMS) performance irrespective of resources. The influence on school library media research and practice will be profound.

SLMSs who achieve accomplished teacher status through National Board Certification (NBC) are judged against the same rigorous standards as classroom teachers. They demonstrate outstanding competence at collaborating with classroom teachers to teach information skills, integrate technology, and encourage reading and love of literature. They exhibit knowledge of management practices, technology basics, children's and YA literature, collection development, ethical and legal tenets, and information literacy. There is good reason to be proud of those in our profession who have met and exceeded such high standards. Still, amidst the cheers, there are those of us who wonder what this means for school library media preparation programs and practices.

As awareness of the NBC process increases and more states follow North Carolina's pattern of having at least one certified teacher in each school, questions will arise on how to align school library media preparation programs with NBPTS standards. What and when should students be encouraged to apply? How should the NBPTS process be supported?

Accreditation of teacher education programs

The National Council for the Accreditation of Teacher Education (NCATE) offers an accreditation process for teacher education programs. Required in some states, but voluntary in most, NCATE's core propositions of what teachers should know and be able to do and their subject-specific standards also affect teacher preparation. In addition to covering the syllabi, schools of education must demonstrate that prospective teacher candidates, in NCATE's words, "know and can do" the basic building blocks of teaching. Phrases such as "performance-based," "conceptual frameworks," "knowledge, skills, and dispositions," and "assessment systems" are constantly revisited in faculty meetings in university and college preparation programs.

NCATE accredits teacher education units at both beginning and advanced levels. For initial licensure programs (first-time teachers), NCATE suggests alignment with the Interstate New Teacher Assessment and Support Consortium (INTASC) standards for beginning teachers. INTASC represents a group of state education agencies and national educational organizations dedicated to the reform of the preparation, licensing, and ongoing professional development of teachers. For advanced programs (licensed teachers seeking master's or post-baccalaureate degrees), NCATE advocates alignment with NBPTS standards. This poses an interesting dilemma.

School library media preparation programs are designed for beginning SLMSs, whether they are at the undergraduate or graduate level. In some states, SLMSs are required to hold a teaching license in another subject or grade level. In other words, they must have been a classroom teacher (or at least done practice-teaching) before they can begin their school library media career. In several states, no such previous licensure is required; first-time SLMSs are also new teachers. In contrast, NCATE states that preparation of SLMSs should always be considered advanced. If we are preparing first-time educators, then surely INTASC standards are more relevant. On the other hand, NBPTS library media standards are more applicable to the library media skills needed. Since NBPTS library media standards are for accomplished teachers, its place in school library media licensure is unclear. It is unreasonable to expect novice students to become accomplished media specialists within the short library school or graduate degree experience. An extensive dialogue among school library media educators is needed to agree upon the extent to which our preparation programs should be aligned with various standards, including NBPTS.

The role of preparation programs in supporting candidates

Teachers need at least three years of experience before applying for NBC, but prior state licensure in their certification area is not required. For example, students new to library media but experienced as teachers can apply for certification in library media or in any other certificate area. How should school library media educators respond when their students ask for assistance or advice concerning their application for NBC?

There are compelling reasons to seek licensure immediately. Experienced teachers may not want to wait for three years after graduation to apply for library media certification. One important consideration is that concepts and content underlying the field are fresh to current students. Three years later, a high school librarian will have to review areas that relate to elementary education, such as literature for young children. Similarly, certain aspects of learning theory, information literacy, and technology may need refreshing.

Secondly, as more school library media preparation programs become performance based, the assignments and activities used in preparation programs will grow to align closely with NBPTS requirements. If required to develop a literature-based instructional activity as part of a children's literature course, students working on their certification portfolio may want to enhance that same activity to submit for the literature appreciation portfolio entry.

Further, as a library school student, one has access to academic resources, learning opportunities, and mentors. While a professor may not be the best critical friend to read a portfolio entry, that person remains a source of information and advice.

Finally, students in library school are in a milieu in which writing, reading, and being assessed are everyday occurrences. After leaving graduate school, the emotional aspect of writing for another's review may feel like a difficult hurdle.

There are equally good reasons to discourage application for certification while in library school. First, NBPTS is designed to identify accomplished practice. While prospective SLMSs may show evidence that they will become accomplished library media specialists, they are not, yet. It is an oxymoron to designate inexperienced SLMSs as accomplished. Of future concern, if states begin to accept NBC in lieu of state licensure, SLMSs could become certified with only minimal training in the library profession.

Secondly, the focus of NBPTS is on teaching standards. While tying the program administration role firmly to student learning makes partial sense, some parts of an SLMS's job relate more closely to library science than teaching.

Will alignment with NBPTS standards weigh the school library media field too heavily toward education, minimizing the important role that we play in the library and information sciences?

In addition, support for unsuccessful candidates is somewhat murky. While a certification candidate who does not achieve a passing overall score can bank passing scores and retake low-scoring sections, teacher education programs rarely take responsibility for NBPTS candidates who do not pass on the first try. NBPTS feedback is sketchy; a candidate may only learn that he or she did not provide "clear, consistent, and convincing evidence" of the required knowledge and skills. A "banker" may need guidance in designing a plan for improvement of an entry. School library media educators must ask themselves if they are prepared to accept responsibility for a graduate banker's NBPTS portfolio or assessment center exercises. Should continuing education be offered to retake candidates on children's and YA literature, collaboration, learning styles, or technology?

Compounding these issues is the fact that little information is available about the areas in which NBPTS candidates score poorly. Those who achieve certification are listed on the NBPTS website and publicly applauded. Retake candidates, already reeling from not achieving certification, must self-identify to receive assistance.

What if the knowledge needed is related more to education than library science? The school library media field asserts that teaching is an important role of the SLMS. How credible is it for educators in preparation programs to say, "Not our problem," if pedagogical expertise needs to be revisited by the candidate?

Further, we are long overdue for a discussion about the integration of education and library and information science precepts, principles, and practices in school library media education. Are students equally prepared as educators and library and information science professionals? Should they be? In discussion, we could clarify these issues. Unfortunately, these questions have not yet been articulated, much less discussed, in some programs.

Meeting multiple goals

In raising these questions, I am not suggesting that we ignore NBPTS requirements, nor completely redefine our preparation programs. Rather, many programs can incorporate the beginning skills without difficulty. For example, a typical assignment for a curriculum class asks a school library media candidate to develop a lesson plan that can be taught in a collaborative setting. To turn that into a performance-based assignment to satisfy NBPTS requirements, the candidate would be asked for evidence of developing and implementing a collaborative unit. By partnering with a classroom teacher and collaborating to develop and implement an information skills unit integrated into classroom content, the candidate would also satisfy NBPTS entry 1 on instructional collaboration. To further align some of the basic skills required for NBPTS entries, a preparation program could require a videotape of instruction and a reflective writing piece.

In teacher education programs, professors can lay the groundwork for writing, teaching, and action research in the early education courses, perhaps as early as the freshman year in college. Throughout the junior and senior years, these skills can be scaffolded. After teaching for a few years, the experienced but still fresh teacher could return for a master's degree, which could build upon both the academic base and the practical experience. Teacher as writer, teacher as researcher, teacher as leader—typical courses in an MEd program—align with NBPTS standards.

In an ALA-accredited program, only a few courses are designed specifically for the SLMS. Additional scaffolding is rare. If state regulations allow school library media licensure without previous teacher certification, those courses have to lay massive groundwork. The rare individual with an undergraduate degree in school library media may decide to return to school for an ALA-accredited MLIS or an advanced education degree. However, the former is considered to be an entry-level degree, while the latter may not even mention school library media.

Another significant difference concerns a shift in focus from working with teachers and content to focusing primarily on students. SLMS education programs ask the library school student to start the collaborative effort by identifying a teacher with whom they would work well, or by choosing a curricular area in which they are comfortable. In contrast, NBPTS applicants almost never write about the collaborating teacher or the subject area. Instead, they focus on the makeup of the class, student learning styles, demographics, special needs, and personality characteristics. In later entries they analyze the learning of one or two students. Turning from collaborating with teachers to teaching students alone requires a shift in thinking. Assessing the achievement of one student's learning of information skills is different from analyzing large-scale assessments of the impact of the library media center program.

Scholarly research opportunities

The school library media field has experienced two major shifts in preparation programs. The first was the Knapp School Libraries Project, which provided models of school library media programs as well as insight into the preparation of SLMSs. Along with the impetus provided by the 1960 standards, the Knapp Project was responsible for defining the modern school library media program. Similarly, in the late 1980s and early 1990s, Library Power, a major school library initiative funded by the DeWitt Wallace–Reader's Digest Foundation, provided documentation and affirmation of collaborative work with teachers and administrators both in instruction and in program administration. Library Power and *Information Power* set the stage for the modern library media program.

NBC may represent a third major shift in the field. With both the Knapp Project and Library Power, emphasis was placed on building the structure of the library program. Adequate resources, budgets, facilities, technologies, and staff development for classroom teachers and administrators were seen as essential for the successful school library media program. If excellence in school library media programming fell short, it was because it was a good instructional program but lacked an adequate facility, or it had a superb facility but little technology; or wonderful technology and staff but no flexible access.

Now academic researchers can begin to answer questions about how the SLMS affects that equation. Through the portfolio entries, they have a window into how the SLMS encourages reading, collaborates with a classroom teacher, and integrates technology, regardless of grade levels, physical plant, budgets, community demographics, or other factors. Can SLMSs achieve excellence with a poor budget, few resources, and an unsupportive administration?

A proactive response

As a first step, educators in school library media preparation programs need to become informed about NBPTS library media standards and portfolio entries. Then, we must find natural congruencies between the NCATE and NBPTS standards. The third step involves assessing which skills required by the NBPTS process can be incorporated into the school library media preparation programs.

Let us begin a national conversation about the role of school library media preparation in NBC. Preparation programs should lead the way in carefully planned, research-based approaches to school library media certification candidacy. Our school library media students are demonstrating their expertise as accomplished teachers. Our role, as yet undefined, could determine their next steps as leaders in the profession.

SOURCE: Adapted from Gail Dickinson, "National Board Effects on School Library Media Education," *Knowledge Quest* 32, no. 3 (January/February 2004): 18–21.

Information power

Technology is a primary tool used by the library media specialist to forge connections between the program and the learning community. Technology has always played a critical role in school library media programs. Using the concepts and skills embedded in instructional technology, school library media specialists collaborate with teachers to develop and manage effective instruction and to evaluate processes and resources for learning. They jointly create learning experiences that integrate the information literacy standards for student learning with subject-matter content. Using principles of sound instructional design, school library media specialists and teachers analyze learner need, design and implement instruction to meet that need, and evaluate and revise plans for future improvement. This process provides the school library media specialist with the framework for building critical in-school relationships, and it strengthens the program's connections to resources and information beyond the school.

SOURCE: Adapted from "Connections to the Learning Community," chapter 7 in *Information Power: Building Partnerships for Learning* (Chicago: American Library Association, 1998), 128.

Who should be running your district's technology department?

by Doug Johnson

At the building level, the addition of technologies to schools has already resulted in new and changed job responsibilities for many media specialists and often the addition of new personnel to take care of technical duties. Technology means changes at the district level as well. And the choice in leadership for the implementation and use of technology in a district will determine whether it is a real asset to students, staff, and parents, or just an expensive boondoggle.

In her must-read book, *Failure to Connect*, Jane M. Healy reports on her visits to a variety of schools where technology is being used. And you can guess what she finds: technology is being used as everything from a babysitter to a genuine educational tool that fosters higher-level thinking and communication. In some schools, Healy reports, technology is being used to reinforce the "factory model of education" with "a teacher (or software) firmly in charge, dispensing a well-defined body of knowledge, and preparing a workforce accustomed to lining-up, doing what they are told and not asking too many questions" to a "learner-centered" approach in which the teacher is a "coach" and students ask questions and "actively pursue learning because it is important or interesting to them." Why, she asks, are there such differences in schools?

One thing she observes: "one energetic and visionary educator who knows what teaching should look like and had the energy to make it happen." My guess is that every building in your district has one or more of these educators. But how many districts have them in administrative positions that have responsibility for technology throughout the district?

There is both a hard and soft side of technology administration, and school technology leaders often have different concerns. The hard side technologists ask questions like:

How can I keep it running?
How much will it cost to implement or replace?
Can I guarantee the system and data it contains will be secure?
Are the administrative functions of state reporting, payroll, grading, scheduling, and transportation being accurately carried out?

Those responsible for the soft side of the technology equation often worry about:

How do I train teachers to use the equipment effectively?
How can I encourage the use of technology to stimulate creative lessons and activities?
What kinds of things should students be doing with technology?
Is technology making a difference in the performance of our students?
How do I know if technology is providing more learning opportunities for more students?

Notice that the concerns of each side are not in opposition; they are only different. It is apparent that neither side can function effectively without the other. It is imperative for a technology department to have both hard and soft experts on staff. And the key to whether they work well together is that they are housed together and they report to the same boss. The best decisions we make in our district are joint decisions that take into account curriculum and staff development as well as hardware and networking realities. Both sides really need to listen to each other.

So what qualifications does this techno-boss need in order to be effective? J. M. Healy's attributes (one energetic and visionary educator who knows what teaching should look like and has the energy and dedication to make it happen) are a good place to begin:

Above all else, this techno-boss needs to be an experienced, successful educator. He or she understands that all technology efforts are directed to meet educational goals. This is a person who has been a teacher and possibly an administrator and can empathize with both. This person can articulate a clear educational philosophy and the place of technology within it.

The techno-boss should have a whole-district view of technology. He or she understands what problems the district has and the goals it is trying to meet. The techno-boss sees technology as part of the solution, not a separate entity undertaken for its own sake. This person can represent the district at community, state, and national organization functions.

The techno-boss needs to be an efficient manager. He or she may not need to know how to program a computer, extract data from the health services database, or replace the toner cartridge in a laser printer, but does know the person in the district who can and sees that it gets done when needed. And lets them do it with a maximum amount of trust and freedom.

The techno-boss understands the ethical dimensions of technology use. He or she understands how technology has impacted the rules regarding copyright, materials selection, intellectual freedom, and privacy.

The techno-boss above all needs to be a leader. It means creating and sharing a practical vision of a better system of schooling that serves more children in better ways. It means, as Tom Landry reminds us, getting folks to do things they do not want to do in order to accomplish the things they want to accomplish. It means getting people to see and address their problems in effective ways, and helping them grow in the process. It means getting people to talk and work together, to be empathetic and patient. It means risk, criticism, continuous self-evaluation, and the acceptance that life will always be one long, steep, learning curve.

7

No techno-boss embodies all these characteristics, but the best come very close. A technology director establishes good communications and finds ways to be interdependent.

SOURCE: Adapted from Doug Johnson, "Who Should Be Running Your District's Technology Department?" *Knowledge Quest* 28, no. 4 (March/April 2000): 43–45.

Imitation on the Web: Flattery, fair use, or felony?

by Debra Kay Logan

Have you ever searched for your own website on the Internet? Searching for your site can answer many questions. Will students be able to locate the website from home without the exact URL? Is the new address showing up on the search engines yet? Has someone else copied your site and represented it as his or her own work?

What would it be like to find page after page of your work copied and repackaged by another library professional? How could it ever happen? What should you do? Are there ways to protect your work?

Those were the questions that I dealt with when I found the bulk of my website copied. The background was different, a few words were changed, and a handful of links were added or taken away; but the work was fundamentally mine. At first I was puzzled by how I had happened to stumble on the pilfered pages. Our school's name had been removed, the copyright notice with my name had been cut from the bottom of each page, and I had not been credited in any way on the copied pages. With the identifying information gone, why had the search engine listed the duplicate site as a hit when I searched our school name? Upon opening one of the purloined pages to look at its underlying coding, I had the answer to the first of many questions. The metatags I had written as I created each page were still in place. These tags included my name as the site's author and our school's name as one of the keywords. Since the metatags were my primary proof of authorship, I immediately began preserving them by printing copies of both the pages and the underlying codes for each page. After I had made electronic copies of the site, it was time to let someone know that I wanted the copied site off the Internet.

Even though the Internet is new and confusing territory, it seemed unlikely that a library professional could intentionally remove copyright notices from the bottom of six pages without knowing that he or she was violating copyright. With that in mind, I chose to notify the district's superintendent instead of dealing directly with the webmaster. The metatags made it possible for the school system to immediately verify the identity of the actual author. The people I dealt with were professional, apologetic, and anxious to correct the situation. The plagiarized pages were withdrawn from the Internet as quickly as possible. Still, I was left with some of the questions I had originally asked upon finding the problem pages. Web experts like Diane Kovacs and Kathy Schrock were very helpful as I tried to answer my questions.

How could it ever happen? With photocopy machines, VCRs, tape recorders, and computers, making copies has become an increasingly simple process. Often the difficulties are in knowing when it is or is not acceptable to copy, or how copies can be fairly used in an educational setting. Copyright confusion is compounded when dealing with a new and relatively unfamiliar format like the Internet. Even websites specializing in Internet copyright do not always agree on what is and is not legal. What is certain is that the United States copyright laws do protect web resources.

As soon as *any* original piece of writing or artwork is put into a tangible form, it is protected under United States copyright law. Once a website is saved to disk, it is protected (Library of Congress, "Copyright Basics," United States Copyright Office, http://lcweb.loc.gov/copyright/circs/circ1.html, accessed February 23, 2000). Ideas, facts, and links are not protected by copyright, but wording is (T. G. Field Jr., *Copyright on the Internet*, http://www.fplc.edu/tfield/cOpyNet.htm, accessed February 23, 2000).

As the de facto guardians of copyright in a school setting, school librarians/media specialists should be first in line to support ethical and fair use of Internet resources and the last to contemplate their abuse.

What should you do when dealing with plagiarism? First, document what you have found. Save and print copies of the copied site. Unless there is reason to believe that the copying was done knowingly, contact the webmaster. When writing to the webmaster, try to remember that imitation is a form of flattery and that a person copying a library resource site is trying to meet the needs of students and teachers. Contact the webmaster with polite but firm expectations. Clearly inform the webmaster that you want the copied items removed as quickly as possible. Invite the webmaster to link to your site. Give permission to use the original website in instructional settings. Tell the webmaster that the principal and then the superintendent will be contacted if the situation is not resolved satisfactorily. (If using e-mail, allow a week before contacting administrators—some people do not read their e-mail daily.) Remind the webmasters of the potential legal ramifications of their actions. Copyright violation can be a felony under certain circumstances.

If contacting the webmaster does not result in the removal of the plagiarized material, do contact the principal, superintendent, district webmaster, and/or the owner of the server. Have documentation available to present to these parties. Documentation might consist of such items as dated printouts of web pages or copies of dated e-mail requesting (or, better yet, granting) permission to link to sites.

What is called a "Poor Man's Copyright" also could be used to document a site's precedence. A "Poor Man's Copyright" is created by printing the site's pages, mailing them to yourself via certified mail, saving the receipt, and not opening the envelope. While this practice is called "Poor Man's Copyright," actually registering a site is still needed to bring suit for infringement and damages.

Do not be surprised if the plagiarist makes excuses or untrue claims. No matter how outrageous, ridiculous, feeble, and/or obviously untrue such statements are, I have learned that it is best to ignore them and simply restate that the goal is for the copied material to be removed from the Internet as soon as possible.

Are there ways to protect your work? Yes! Tell the world that your site is protected. Put a copyright notice at the bottom of each page. The notice should include "©" or "Copyright," the work's original date or a span of years like 1997–2000, and the author's name. T. S. Eggleston, in *What Every Webmaster Needs to Know about Copyright,* recommends putting the words "All Rights Reserved" underneath the notice. The forms for actually registering a site can be

easily downloaded from the U.S. Copyright Office website. Form TX is the correct form for registering most websites. When a site is officially registered, the owner can sue for infringement and damages. Unlike the contents of a printed book, the contents of a website can be updated daily. Those changes are not covered by a previous registration. That does not necessarily mean that a website has to be re-registered after each change to protect the author's rights.

Make locating violations easy when writing your site by including an esoteric link or some distinctive wording in your site. Deliberately misspell a word or two. Field, in *Copyright for Computer Authors*, suggests hiding a purposeless loop in the coding. Include meta-words when creating your site. Use unique wording when tagging images. If creating your own images, look into image watermarks. Like watermarked paper, watermarked images have identifying information buried in them. Specialized software can embed/watermark images with such information as names, dates, and other identifiers. Software that will not allow images to be copied is being introduced to the market at this time. Periodically search for the ownership clues using search engines. All engines and some directories search metatags.

The Internet is predicated around the sharing of information and ideas. Unchecked, plagiarism may ultimately limit what is made available on the

Internet. Most webmasters are usually flattered when asked to share resources and are willing to have their sites quoted, cached, or browsed offline for fair and educational use. Some will make requests for links back or other forms of acknowledgments. With the ability to link to a site, copying and posting it is not only illegal, it is totally unnecessary. While imitation is a form of flattery, it also can be a felony.

SOURCE: Adapted from Debra Kay Logan, "Imitation on the Web: Flattery, Fair Use, or Felony?" *Knowledge Quest* 28, no. 5 (May/June 2000): 16–18.

Evaluating information on the Internet

by Merran Ware

This is an exciting time for teacher-librarians and classroom teachers. The Internet offers an important opportunity to teach evaluation skills where they will be instantly recognized by students as necessary and relevant. As teachers struggle to cope with the information explosion themselves, it is an opportune time to model the skills needed to evaluate what is found and to reduce the information overload. Technology has made the mechanics of searching easier than ever before, but has increased dramatically the need for critical thinking in the development of search strategies to enhance the validity of search outcomes and sift through the plethora of information available.

The need for evaluation skills is obvious. The increasing amount of literature available on the subject attests to this fact. This need has always existed, but the Internet has demonstrated such skills to be paramount. Children show signs of blossoming evaluation skills with questions some parents dread: *Why? How? When?* But as their schooling progresses, students seem to become more accepting and passive absorbers of data. We need to teach them to question what they are reading, hearing, and seeing—that what is presented is not always truthful, without bias or manipulation. Evaluation criteria provide a systematic approach for searchers to assess the quality of the information they encounter. A checklist of criteria can clearly indicate potential problem areas and raise awareness of such problems as bias, authority, and currency.

The advent of the Internet as an information source has essentially not changed the problems students previously encountered with print and electronic resources such as CD-ROMs and databases. However, these materials have generally undergone scrutiny by editors and publishing companies before being made available. Anyone can author anything on the Internet, and so now there must be even more awareness of the need to examine this material critically.

Many students perceive the Internet as the only useful resource, providing the most current, most prolific amount of information on every conceivable topic, and the fastest means of obtaining that information. However, in practice, Celeste McNicholas and Ross J. Todd report research has shown that students found their Internet searching frustrating and time-consuming for little productive result, due to lack of appropriate searching strategies and poor search technique. They have not comprehended that the Internet is riddled with misinformation, and that more than ever evaluation skills are necessary to decipher the good from the bad and indifferent. According to Barbara Ripp Safford, skepticism is a useful filter to be applied.

Students' searching problems

Delia Neuman found that students had problems generating search terms, designing effective search strategies, and overcoming mismatches between personal ideas of how information is organized and how information is actually organized in electronic databases. Although Neuman's research was based on CD-ROMs, her conclusions can be related to similar problems found in Internet searching, and indeed to print resources. McNicholas and Todd commented that student Internet searchers experienced frustration due to lack of selection skills. Library materials preselected for their relevance to the curriculum provided a shortcut to useful information. When faced with the information overload of the Internet, students did not have the discriminatory or evaluative skills to reduce their information retrieval to a manageable result.

Students lack strategies to deal with the information they find. Library instruction, according to Theresa Wesley, tends to concentrate on where to look, but not on what to do with the information found.

Characteristics of search engines

The tools to unlock information from the Internet are the search engines, subject directories, and meta-indexes, which provide access via keywords or search strings. Diane Walster proposes that students lack knowledge of search engine characteristics, and this will affect the results they obtain when using such tools. Strategies such as determining what sources are actually searched by the search engine, analyzing the quality of the information found, and understanding the rules and idiosyncrasies of each search engine are essential for successfully locating desired material.

Susan Feldman suggests the advice from the literature regarding search engine use is not to rely on searching from one database alone, as understanding the strengths and weaknesses of each determines the success of locating the information required. Debbie Abilock provides a matching of information need (such as requiring a broad overview of a topic) to a search engine suitable for that purpose (Yahoo! as a subject directory). This diagnostic form of selecting search engines is particularly useful in aiding students to become independent information users.

Website evaluation criteria

In evaluating websites, two aspects need to be considered—the site design and the information presented on the site. Gene Wilkinson, Lisa T. Bennett, and Kevin M. Oliver have drawn up a list of 11 criteria with matching indicators of quality that were ranked according to their importance by a review panel of experienced Internet users. These criteria are:

    site accessibility and usability
    resource identification and documentation
    author identification

authority of author
information structure and design
relevance and scope of content
validity of content
accuracy and balance of content
navigation within the document
quality of links
aesthetic and affective aspects

Sites and pages on the Internet should be evaluated in terms of their authority, balance and objectivity, currency, accuracy, coverage, purpose, and site organization and design.

Identifying misinformation

Students need to be aware that information on the Internet may be false or misleading. Misinformation includes incomplete information, pranks, contradictions, out-of-date information, data improperly translated across different machines or systems, software incompatibility that sometimes leads to fragmentation, unauthorized revisions, factual errors, biased information, and scholarly misconduct.

According to Mary Ann Fitzgerald, the following triggers may indicate misinformation:

payment demands
contradictions and inconsistencies within the article
author credentials not matching the subject matter
appeals to the emotions—flattery, fear messages, language stirring guilt or
    sympathy
opinion markers—words such as *could, might, would, believe, "I think," assume,*
    etc.
misleading or unsound arguments that sound plausible
oversimplification
unstated assumptions
"pass" messages—instructions to pass a communication on to other people,
    similar to chain letters
lack of evidence to support claims

Conclusion

Evaluation is a vital component of the search process, keeping the process on course, preventing sidetracks and distractions from diverting the attention away from the task at hand. Together with analysis and synthesis, evaluation is a higher-order skill necessary to construct personal meaning and understanding from gathered information.

If higher-order thinking styles are required, information problems must be worded to require those levels of thinking. Assessment must include the steps taken to accomplish the final product if the importance of the information search process is to be recognized. This will necessitate more effective planning and collaboration between the teacher-librarian and the classroom teacher to use many of the strategies outlined in this literature review. There are lessons available on the Web that can be tailored to the needs of school communities, which include teachers as well as students. In many cases, teachers have more fear of the unknown with electronic media, and they need the reassurance that support is available to them.

Teaching and learning are the responsibility of the entire school staff, but there is a leadership role for the teacher-librarian to lobby and promote the need for a whole-school commitment to information literacy and information skills across the curriculum. There is an opportunity now for teacher-librarians to be proactive, to take the initiative for teaching evaluation skills in context, in the development of the information-literate student.

SOURCE: Adapted from Merran Ware, "Evaluating Information on the Internet," *School Libraries Worldwide* 7, no. 2 (2001): 39–48. Used with permission.

Student rights and the freedom to read
by Terrence E. Young Jr.

> Intellectual freedom is freedom of the mind, and as such, it is both a personal liberty and a prerequisite for all freedoms leading to action. . . . Intellectual freedom is the right of every individual to both seek and receive information from all points of view without restriction. It provides for free access to all expressions of ideas through which any and all sides of a question, cause or movement may be explored. (*Intellectual Freedom Manual*, 5th ed.)

Lest we forget how precious a liberty we have in our "freedom to read," libraries, bookstores, schools at all levels, and civil liberties organizations host numerous literary events each year during Banned Books Week (http://www.ala.org/bbooks/) to celebrate the importance of the First Amendment. The 1999 Banned Books Week was celebrated September 25–October 2, 1999. Try Ray Bradbury's *Fahrenheit 451*, Ernest Hemingway's *A Farewell to Arms*, John Steinbeck's *Of Mice and Men*, Maya Angelou's *I Know Why the Caged Bird Sings*, J. D. Salinger's *Catcher in the Rye*, Kurt Vonnegut's *Slaughterhouse Five*, or Alice Walker's *The Color Purple*. They all have been banned somewhere in America at one time or other. Currently controversy rages about the Harry Potter books.

Whereas once books were the main source of censorship in the school library media center, the addition of the Internet as a library resource tool has introduced us to "electronic information freedom." The same big issues are at work here. Sex, profanity, violence, language, and racism remain the primary targets and are labeled with such terms as "sexually explicit," "offensive language," "unsuited to age group," "pornographic," and "occult theme or promoting the occult or Satanism" among others. Many banned book titles are removed from school libraries because they are considered inappropriate, they don't conform to curriculums, or they conflict with the values of the community. But how do you apply these criteria to the Internet?

In today's school library media centers, computers, CD-ROMs, and videos compete for space once limited to the printed word. Schools may serve *in loco parentis*, and attempt to inculcate societal values. The reason school censors are successful is they are ready, willing, and able to do battle to promote their ideology and theology. Until parents and school patrons who abhor censorship are willing to be equally committed to protecting school books and libraries, our students' educational horizons will continue to narrow. Wherever an alliance of administrators, teachers, parents, business leaders, and clergy is formed against censorship, objectors cannot prevail. Vigilance is the only safeguard.

Vigilance begins with a collection development policy that includes, where appropriate, the media center's policy on questions of intellectual freedom. Many school library media centers have found it helpful to quote the ALA statement on freedom to read, and have a formal procedure for handling complaints—both of these could appropriately appear in the collection development policy.

Many school library media specialists are familiar with intellectual freedom through the "Library Bill of Rights" (http://www.ala.org/work/freedom/lbr.html) or ALA's Code of Ethics (http://www.ala.org/alaorg/oif/ethics.html). ALA maintains several other useful and informative intellectual freedom sites:

ALA's Resolution on the Use of Filtering Software in Libraries: http://www.ala.org/alaorg/oif/filt_res.html.

Office for Intellectual Freedom (OIF), http://www.ala.org/oif.html, is charged with implementing ALA policies concerning the concept of intellectual freedom as embodied in the Library Bill of Rights, the association's basic policy on free access to libraries and library materials. The goal of the office is to educate librarians and the general public about the nature and importance of intellectual freedom in libraries.

Intellectual Freedom Action Network (http://www.ala.org/alaorg/oif/ifan_inf.html) maintained by ALA's Office for Intellectual Freedom (OIF).

School library media specialists have several choices when it comes to "electronic intellectual freedom." Most will adopt the ALA position, which "affirms that the use of filtering software by libraries to block access to constitutionally protected speech violates the Library Bill of Rights" (http://www.ala.org/alaorg/oif/filt_res.html). Some will take the pro-choice position of some public libraries: filters on terminals that can be turned on or off by the student, with "off" being the default setting. Still others will direct students to filtering search engines that allow students to search the entire Web rather than just through a handpicked selection of kid-safe sites. Results then are filtered to remove possibly objectionable materials to filter their searches.

School library media specialists usually are the only voice of intellectual freedom in the school setting. After we educate them, it is their responsibility to educate their school administrators.

@your library

As we consider this Internet technology and the role that school library media centers might assume in the cyberspace of tomorrow, we also must remember why libraries are maintained throughout all levels of society. Schools and school library media centers must continue to be places where students' minds can grow and not be stunted for lack of intellectual freedom. We must continually ensure that advances in information technology be used to provide freely accessible information to all who seek it. Only by boldly and firmly grasping the impacts of technology will school library media centers emerge stronger and more central to our culture than ever before.

SOURCE: Adapted from Terrence E. Young Jr., "The Big IF: Electronic Intellectual Freedom— What Are a Student's Rights to Information?" *Knowledge Quest* 28, no. 3 (January/February 2000): 42–43.

10 reasons why the Internet is no substitute for a library
by Mark Y. Herring

"Reading," said the great English essayist Matthew Arnold, "is culture." Given the condition of reading test scores among schoolchildren nationwide, it isn't surprising to find both our nation and our culture in trouble. Further, the rush to Internetize all schools, particularly K–12, adds to our downward spiral. If it were not for the Harry Potter books, one might lose all hope who languishes here. Then, suddenly, you realize libraries really are in trouble, grave danger, when important higher-education officials opine, "Don't you know the Internet has made libraries obsolete?" Gadzooks! as Harry himself might say.

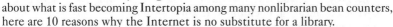

In an effort to save our culture, strike a blow for reading, and, above all, correct the well-intentioned but horribly misguided notions about what is fast becoming Intertopia among many nonlibrarian bean counters, here are 10 reasons why the Internet is no substitute for a library.

   1. Not everything is on the Internet. With over one billion web pages you couldn't tell it by looking. Nevertheless, very few *substantive* materials are on the Internet *for free*. For example, only about *8%* of all journals are on the Web, and an even smaller fraction of books are there. Both are costly! If you want *Physics Today*, you'll pay, and to the tune of many dollars.

   2. The needle (your search) in the haystack (the Web). The Internet is like a vast uncataloged library. Whether you're using Hotbot, Dogpile, Infoseek, or any one of a dozen other search or metasearch engines, you're not searching the entire Web. Sites often promise to search everything but they can't deliver. Moreover, what they do search is not updated daily, weekly, or even monthly, regardless of what's advertised. If a librarian told you, "Here are 10 articles on Native Americans. We have 40 others, but we're not going to let you see them, not now, not yet, not until you've tried another search in another library," you'd throw a fit. The Internet does this routinely and no one seems to mind.

   3. Quality control doesn't exist. Yes, we need the Internet, but in addition to all the scientific, medical, and historical information (when accurate), there is also a cesspool of waste. When young people aren't getting their sex education off XXX-rated sites, they're learning politics from the Freeman web page, or race relations from Klan sites. There is no quality control on the Web, and there isn't likely to be any. Unlike libraries where vanity press publications are rarely, if ever, collected, vanity is often what drives the Internet. Any fool can put up anything on the Web, and, to my accounting, all have.

4. What you don't know really does hurt you. The great boon to libraries has been the digitization of journals. But full-text sites, while grand, aren't always full. What you don't know can hurt you: (a) articles on these sites are often missing, among other things, footnotes; (b) tables, graphs, and formulae do not often show up in a readable fashion (especially when printed); and (c) journal titles in a digitized package change regularly, often without warning. A library may begin with X number of journals in September and end with Y number in May. Trouble is, those titles aren't the same from September to May. Although the library may have paid $100,000 for the access, it's rarely notified of any changes. I would not trade access to digitized journals for anything in the world, but their use must be a judicious, planned, and measured one, not full, total, and exclusive reliance.

5. States can now buy one book and distribute to every library on the Web—not! Yes, and we could have one national high school, a national university, and a small cadre of faculty teaching everybody over streaming video. Let's take this one step further and have only digitized sports teams for *real* savings! (Okay, I know, I've insulted the national religion.) Since 1970 about 50,000 academic titles have been published every year. Of these 1.5 million titles, fewer than a couple thousand are available. What is on the Net are about 20,000 titles published before 1925. Why? No copyright restrictions that cause prices to soar to two or three times their printed costs. Finally, vendors delivering e-books allow only one digitized copy per library. If you check out an e-book over the Web, I can't have it until you return it. Go figure, as they say. And if you're late getting the book back, there is no dog-ate-my-homework argument. It's charged to your credit card *automatically*.

6. Hey, bud, you forgot about e-book readers. Most of us have forgotten what we said about microfilm ("It would shrink libraries to shoebox size"), or when educational television was invented ("We'll need fewer teachers in the future"). Try reading an e-book reader for more than a half-hour. Headaches and eyestrain are the best results. Besides, if what you're reading is more than two pages long, what do you do? Print it. Where's a tree hugger when you really need one? Moreover, the cost of readers runs from $200 to $2,000, the cheaper ones being harder on the eyes. Will this change? Doubtless, but right now there's no market forces making it change. Will it change in less than 75 years? Unlikely!

7. Aren't there library-less universities now? No. The newest state  university in California at Monterey Bay opened without a library building a few years ago. For the last two years, they've been buying books by the tens of thousands because—surprise, surprise—they couldn't find what they needed on the Internet. California Polytechnic State University, home of the world's highest concentration of engineers and computer geeks, explored the possibility of a virtual (fully electronic) library for

CSU Monterey Bay library

two years. Their solution was a $42-million traditional library with, of course, a strong electronic component. In other words, a fully virtualized library just can't be done. Not yet, not now, not in our lifetimes.

8. But a virtual state library would do it, right? Do what, bankrupt the state? Yes, it would. The cost of having everything digitized is incredibly high, costing tens of millions of dollars just in copyright releases. And this buys only one virtual library at one university. Questia Media, the biggest such outfit, just spent $125 million digitizing 50,000 books released (but not to libraries!) in January. At this rate, to virtualize a medium-sized library of 400,000 volumes would cost a mere $1,000,000,000! Then you need to make sure students have equitable access everywhere they need it, when they need it. Finally, what do you do with rare and valuable primary sources once they are digitized? Take them to the dump? And you must hope the power never, ever goes out. Sure, students could still read by candlelight, but what would they be reading?

9. The Internet: A mile wide, an inch (or less) deep. Looking into the abyss of the Internet is like vertigo over a void. But the void has to do not only with what's there, but also with what isn't. Not much on the Internet is more than 15 years old. Vendors offering magazine access routinely add a new year while dropping an earlier one. Access to older material is very expensive. It'll be useful, in coming years, for students to know (and have access to) more than just the scholarly materials written in the last 10 to 15 years.

10. The Internet is ubiquitous but books are portable. In a recent survey of those who buy electronic books, more than 80% said they like buying paper books over the Internet, not reading them on the Web. We have nearly 1,000 years of reading print in our bloodstream and that's not likely to change in the next 75. Granted, there will be changes in the delivery of electronic materials now, and those changes, most of them anyway, will be hugely beneficial. But humankind, being what it is, will always want to curl up with a good book—not a laptop—at least for the foreseeable future.

The Web is great, but it's a woefully poor substitute for a full-service library. It is mad idolatry to make it more than a tool. Libraries are icons of our cultural intellect, totems to the totality of knowledge. If we make them obsolete, we've signed the death warrant to our collective national conscience, not to mention sentencing what's left of our culture to the waste bin of history. No one knows better than librarians just how much it costs to run a library. We're always looking for ways to trim expenses while not contracting service. The Internet is marvelous, but to claim, as some now do, that it's making libraries obsolete is as silly as saying shoes have made feet unnecessary.

SOURCE: Adapted from Mark Y. Herring, "10 Reasons Why the Internet Is No Substitute for a Library," *American Libraries* (April 2001): 76–78.

Networks for school librarians: IASL-LINK and LM_NET

What is IASL-LINK?

IASL-LINK is a closed listserv/group for members of the International Association of School Librarianship (that is, its membership is restricted to the membership of the Association), and as such, is one of the benefits of membership. IASL-LINK is for communication between members of the Association throughout the world, and for the distribution of announcements and links to discussion papers, articles, news, information about projects, and information from IASL conferences and meetings. It supports the aims and objectives of the Association by providing a communications link and a means of disseminating information. It is not intended to replace other activities of the Association, like the *IASL Newsletter*, but rather to add another dimension to the Association's communications channels.

IASL-LINK is a group on Yahoo! Groups. IASL-LINK messages can be read as e-mail, or read on the IASL-LINK page on the Yahoo! Groups website. All messages remain at the Yahoo! Groups website for reference (unless a message is deleted by the original sender or the Group moderator). Our Yahoo! Group is searchable on the Yahoo! Groups site.

Joining and participating. IASL has two levels of participation.

1. Participation by e-mail. IASL members can use IASL-LINK as a listserv and participate by sending and receiving the e-mail messages. New members of IASL will be automatically added to IASL-LINK when they join the association. Other members will be added as requested. To be added to IASL-LINK, send an e-mail message to the following e-mail address (with nothing in the body of the message):

> IASL-LINK-subscribe@yahoogroups.com

The moderators of IASL-LINK will receive a message to add you to IASL-LINK. Once your membership in IASL is verified, you will be added to IASL-LINK. This process is very quick, usually within a day. Using IASL-LINK in this manner will allow you access to the listserv capabilities of the Yahoo! Group, but not the variety of other features offered by Yahoo!

To communicate with everyone on IASL-LINK, send an e-mail message to:

> IASL-LINK@yahoogroups.com

Make sure that you use a subject line that is descriptive because this subject will appear not only on your message but also on links to the stored message on the Yahoo! Groups site. Your message will be sent automatically to all of the members of the listserv, usually within minutes.

If you want to respond to a message that was sent to IASL-LINK by someone else, use the function of your electronic mail software in the usual way, and the reply will go just to the person who sent the message to IASL-LINK. Sometimes it might be more appropriate to reply to the whole group, in which case, address your reply to IASL-LINK@yahoogroups.com.

Please note that messages with attachments should not be posted to IASL-LINK. One of our goals is to reduce or eliminate spam and viruses. *Never* open any IASL-LINK message that contains an attachment. Documents and other files can be stored at the group web page at Yahoo! Groups, but may not be transmitted. Directions follow explaining how to join Yahoo! and link yourself to the group called IASL-LINK so that you can use these features.

2. Become a member of Yahoo! and have full access to the Yahoo! Groups section. This allows for the listserv (e-mail) capabilities, and also offers other features such as file sharing, opinion polls, photo galleries, bookmarks, archived and indexed messages, and a few things we are still learning about!

If you wish to fully utilize all the capabilities the Yahoo! Group IASL-LINK has to offer, you must become a Yahoo! member by registering, verifying, and activating your e-mail address with Yahoo! You must use the e-mail address on file with IASL-LINK or the one you plan to use when joining IASL-LINK.

IASL-LINK is located at: http://groups.yahoo.com/group/IASL-LINK/.

Follow this link to IASL-LINK at Yahoo! Groups. Assuming you are *not* already a member of Yahoo!, you will need to click the link "Join this Group"—it will lead you to a new window where you will need to click on "Sign up now." The initial process is a bit cumbersome . . . so please be patient! We recommend that you have these instructions available and use them as a guide when joining.

You will need to select a Yahoo! ID and a password. This can be whatever you desire. You will also set up a security question and answer.

One very "tricky" point on this page is in the box labeled "Alternative Email"—you *must* enter the e-mail you use or wish to use for IASL-LINK. The concept of "Alternative Email" means alternative to Yahoo! e-mail . . . in other words, your regular e-mail address. Yahoo! refers to this as "alternative" to your options of having a free web-based e-mail at Yahoo!

Another point of information: *If* you check the Interests boxes near the bottom, you *will* get unsolicited e-mails. We highly recommend that you *do not* check those boxes!

Last step on this page is a Word Verification . . . follow the directions.

You will need to submit the form and you will then receive a Welcome message; it will welcome you by whatever Yahoo! ID you selected.

The next step is to Verify your e-mail. Yahoo! will send an e-mail to the e-mail address you listed in the "Alternative Email" box. The e-mail you receive will have a code in it. You need that code to complete the Verify page.

The final step is to click on "Activate your membership." This will link your selected Yahoo! ID and your Verified e-mail address to IASL-LINK and give you all the capabilities the Group has to offer.

Leaving IASL-LINK. If you want to leave IASL-LINK, then send an email message to the listserv computer at

IASL-LINK-unsubscribe@yahoogroups.com

Nothing should appear in the subject line or the body of the message.

Subscribing to LM_NET

To subscribe to LM_NET, Peter Milbury suggests you just do this:

1. Send an e-mail message to:

LISTSERV@LISTSERV.SYR.EDU

2. In the first line of the message, type:

SUBSCRIBE LM_NET Firstname Lastname

(Of course, you would substitute your actual name in the line, such as "SUBSCRIBE LM_NET Jo Librarian." No quotes necessary.)

The LM_NET listserv computer will respond with an informative message, which will ask for a confirmation. You will then be added if you properly follow the directions.

If you ever set yourself to "no mail" or mail has stopped arriving from LM_NET, and you are wondering if you are still subscribed, you can check your status by doing this:

1. Send a message to:

LISTSERV@LISTSERV.SYR.EDU

2. On the first line of your message type:

q lm_net

(Do not include your ID or signature file in the message.)

A few minutes later you should receive a message from LM_NET listserver. It will either tell you that you are not subscribed, or it will give you a status report such as this one:

From: "L-Soft list server at Syracuse University (1.8d)"
LISTSERV@LISTSERV.SYR.EDU
To: yourname@yoursite.state.us

Subject: Output of your job "pmilbury"
q lm_net
Subscription options for yourname@your site.state.us, list LM_NET:
DIGEST—You receive list digests, rather than individual postings
MIME—You prefer to receive messages in MIME format
SHORTHDR—Short mail headers with only "human friendly" fields
REPRO—You receive a copy of your own postings
NOACK—No acknowledgment of successfully processed postings
Subscription date: 17 Sep 2000
Summary of resource utilization

CPU time: 0.211 sec
Overhead CPU: 0.471 sec
CPU model: 150MHz Pentium (96M)
Job origin: pmilbury@cusd.chico.k12.ca.us

If you have been unable to find what you are seeking about LM_NET, please contact Peter Milbury by e-mail: pmilbury@ericir.syr.edu.

SOURCE: Adapted from School Libraries Online, "IASL-LINK," International Association of School Librarianship (IASL), http://www.iasl-slo.org/iasl-link.html; and "Welcome to LM_NET on the World Wide Web!" http://www.eduref.org/lm_net/ (accessed August 4, 2004).

Remaking your website
in seven easy steps
by Walter Minkel

Here's how to create a terrific site that is easy to navigate, presents clear information, and provides links to great websites, while giving users quick access to your catalog and subscription databases. You'll end up with a site that conveys the implicit message that libraries are essential and that skillful librarians are ready to guide students, teachers, and parents through the overwhelming world of information.

Follow these seven "commandments" to get started on a successful web makeover:

1. **Create a standard template to ensure that every page has a consistent layout and style, and is readily identifiable as part of your site.** Every

page should include your library's name and logo (keep them small) and a navigation bar (on the top or left-hand side of each page) that enables visitors to move easily throughout the site. To make sure your site meets these basic requirements, try the "search-engine test": If a page that's buried deep within your site—say, a booklist or a toddler-time calendar—was to turn up on Google or on another search engine, would visitors know immediately that it was your site?

2. Put yourself in your users' shoes. Find out what they most want from your website. Kids always want public libraries to provide a page of links to online games, and students want school libraries to offer a list of online resources that's tied to homework assignments. Both public and school library websites should always provide annotated lists of homework sites and recommended books by grade level.

3. Organize all text into brief chunks. The most important bits of information should appear as soon as an online visitor arrives at your home page. And almost every paragraph on your home page should include at least one hyperlink. Why? Research shows that online visitors spend 90 seconds or less viewing a page. They want to find the information they need, and move on quickly. Also, make sure that your home page includes those things that are most essential to what your library offers, including links to available databases with brief descriptions.

4. Get rid of all generic clip art and animated images, or GIFs. They distract viewers, and generic images say nothing about your particular library. Instead, use small digital photographs (no larger than 35k) and other images, such as your logo and mascot, which are representative of your library and its personality. To assist visually handicapped users, be sure to accompany each image with an "ALT" tag—those are the tags that display small boxes of text over each image when you place your mouse pointer on the picture.

5. The more your site's pages resemble the pages of a book, the easier they will be to read, especially by those who are visually impaired. Make sure that every page has a white background with black text, or at the very least, that there is sufficient contrast between the background and text. Avoid using a textured or multicolored background, as well as light-colored text against a black background.

6. Follow the "cat box" rule. If you want frequent visitors to your site, you must keep changing it. Most resources on your site should be permanent, but there should also be a place where there's new information—seasonal, topic-related, or fun stuff that remains on your site no longer than a month.

7. Design your pages so visitors can tell your library is the coolest ever, and they could miss something important if they're not regular visitors. To do that, explain in simple, user-friendly language what your library has to offer. If possible, try to include something on your home page that no other site has.

SOURCE: Adapted from Walter Minkel, "Remaking Your Web Site in Seven Easy Steps," *School Library Journal* 48, no. 5 (May 2002): 46–49. Courtesy of *School Library Journal.*

OPERATIONS
CHAPTER EIGHT

Information power

Principle 10 of *Information Power* details effective management of human, financial, and physical resources as the basis of a strong library media program.

Goals for the school library media specialist

1. Maintain expertise in strategies and techniques of budgeting, supervision, scheduling, and all other areas of management responsibility.
2. Serve on the school's management team, and collaborate regularly with teachers and administrators through other formal and informal mechanisms to maintain the visibility and quality of the program's management.
3. Report regularly to administrators and others regarding the program's holdings, services, uses, and finances.
4. Participate in hiring, training, and evaluating all program staff, and maintain responsibility for assigning and scheduling staff and volunteers.
5. Administer the program budget and oversee acquisition and use of space, furnishings, equipment, and resources.
6. Oversee all aspects of the daily operation of the library media program.

SOURCE: Excerpted from "Program Administration," chapter 6 in *Information Power: Building Partnerships for Learning* (Chicago: American Library Association, 1998), 113–114.

School libraries: Inviting spaces for learning

by Dianne Oberg

My interest in the design of school libraries started in the early 1980s with the challenges I experienced in planning a library renovation. I learned more from coping with a new library facility and from working on school library program evaluations with Eunice Easton, then the school library consultant for the Province of Alberta. During our years in the field, Eunice and I were enraged, amused, and mystified by some of the library designs we found in Alberta schools.

Many of these "special" design features survived, by the way, only until the official opening of the new or renovated library was over and until the school could find enough money to remove or change the feature that took too much space, that caused concerns for the safety of students and teachers, or that limited library accessibility for students and teachers with disabilities.

Inviting to the mind, body, and soul

The library staff in those and other such poorly designed facilities have found ways to provide exemplary school library programs in spite of the obstacles created by such facilities. Furthermore, the physical plan and layout of the library represents only one of the three elements that contribute to an inviting and welcoming library facility.

A library needs to be inviting to the minds and souls as well as to the bodies of its users. In addition to being comfortable, spacious, and barrier free, a library should be an intellectually stimulating and psychologically welcoming place. That is, the library should provide the materials and programs that support teachers and students in the difficult, complex, and exciting work of teaching and learning. The library should provide an atmosphere within which all teachers and students feel they belong and are respected. The library should be a place where the emphasis is on what you can do, rather than what you cannot do, and where there is respect for young people, their teachers, and their families and communities.

The primary practical reason for providing inviting and welcoming libraries is that students who feel cared for and encouraged are more likely to be motivated to do their best as learners and that teachers who feel respected are more likely to do their best as teachers. Teaching and learning for the Information Age, in the classroom and the library, need to be centered around developing information skills, around students learning to use information for creative and innovative thinking, for problem solving, and decision making.

Vicki Hancock reports that the school that is effectively preparing students for the Information Age is characterized by interactivity, self-initiated learning, a changing role for teachers, a central role for librarians and technology specialists, continuous evaluation, and a changed environment. As Mark Dressman points out, it is a place where the desires of the young people as readers have priority over the desires of the teachers, or the librarian for that matter. Dressman argues that the classroom is a private space for "literacy as work" while the library is a public place for "literacy as pursuit of pleasure." Dressman acknowledges that his argument does not address the library as a place where students complete inquiry-based activities planned by teachers and librarians, but he does raise some interesting questions about the school as a place for young people to make choices about what they read and view and about what they learn.

Literacy as pursuit of pleasure

Practical considerations for creating inviting libraries include the following:

Providing an accessible and flexible physical facility. In the little research available on school library facilities, Blanche Woolls reports that librarians who liked their libraries gave reasons such as "attractiveness" and "plenty of space"; those who didn't cited reasons such as "lack of space" and "inconvenient structural features." Open-area libraries (libraries without walls or doors) were not liked by librarians because of problems such as traffic control, book loss, and visual distractions. Libraries on one level with few inner walls and supporting columns offer the flexibility needed to adapt the library space to program needs and to allow ease of access to all teachers and students.

Planning and rearranging the space within the library continues to be an important task for teacher librarians as programs change, as new technologies are acquired, and as the number of teachers and students using canes, crutches, and manual or electric wheelchairs increases. There should be no stairs limiting access into or within the library. Library furniture should be movable and multipurpose. Stacks should be at least 900 mm (36 in.) apart and there should be maneuvering space at the ends of aisles of at least 1,200 mm × 1,200 mm (4 ft. × 4 ft.) for wheelchair users.

The integration of computer technologies continues to be a pressing problem in school libraries. Technology goes with the library throughout the entire writing process, from gathering to publishing. Wendy Scott suggests that literature can be appreciated and shared through the technology as well. According to Robert A. French, a library should not become a computer lab, but technology should be a strong component of a school library program.

Supporting engaging learning programs. Studies done with teachers and students indicate architectural design is not nearly as important to them as the nature of the program and services being offered. Technology offers many new program opportunities as well as making it easier to expand access to information beyond those materials we own and have on hand in the library. However, as pointed out above, print and audiovisual items will continue to play an important role in our school libraries.

When students are carrying out meaningful learning projects that involve them in authentic, difficult, and current real-world problems, teacher librarians will need to be there ready to support them with resources both from within and beyond the library's own collection. This will be a demanding task when students are initiating their own learning, asking their own questions rather than waiting for teachers to ask the questions, when students are the "active shapers" rather than the "passive receivers" of their learning. In this case, it may be that library-based learning becomes closer to "literacy as pursuit of pleasure" rather than "literacy as work."

In *School Matters: The Junior Years*, Peter Mortimore, Pamela Sammons, Louise Stoll, David Lewis, and Russell Ecob suggest that schools that are good places where students want to be provide: challenging interesting work, higher order inquiry, a learning-centered environment, focused curriculum, and maximum learning-related communication between teachers and students and among students. These factors also express what constitutes best practice in school library programs and what makes libraries good places where students want to be.

Supporting a diverse community of learners. Teacher librarians in most schools are working with an ever more diverse community of students that goes far beyond diverse learning styles to diversity related to such aspects as class, race, culture, and religion. Teacher librarians work to understand and make connections with the world in which students live outside of school, the world of their homes and families.

In such ways, the school library environment can complement, enhance, and show respect for the perspectives on life and learning found in students' families and communities. However, the school library and its programs are also capable of violating and devaluing these perspectives. For example, when developing home reading programs, teacher librarians of middle-class backgrounds may not take into account that many working-class parents and their children value reading for information more highly than reading for pleasure. Teacher librarians not sensitized to the need for inclusive definitions of family may not search out materials that offer positive representations of single-parent families or families with "two mommies." Teacher librarians with no interest in religion may never think to include novels where personal faith in God is an important part of the characters' lives in the recreational reading section of the library. Jean Donham Van Deusen found that teacher librarians, using their experience gained in their "insider-outsider" position within schools, also can work as advocates for more welcoming schools overall.

SOURCE: Adapted from Dianne Oberg, "School Libraries: Inviting Spaces for Learning," *School Libraries in Canada* 19, no. 1 (1999): 4–6. *School Libraries in Canada*, the journal of the Canadian School Library Association, Copyright 1999. Used with permission.

Breaking out of the box: Reinventing a juvenile-center library

by Veronica A. Davis

Libraries are portals to new worlds. They serve up possibility, learning, and, in a word, freedom. In this sense libraries run counter to the spirit and intent of the average prison, where jailers scrutinize every portal, every possibility, and every freedom, including the figurative ones offered in the quiet refuge of the library. The effects are often deleterious, if not disastrous, and they make the job of any prison librarian challenging. Still, with the proper administrative support, prudent planning, and a firm commitment to education, a prison library can serve its clients effectively.

I became the first media specialist of the Beaumont Expansion School of the Beaumont (Virginia) Juvenile Correctional Center in July 1997, just in time to realize the dream of a lifetime—creating a library from scratch.

Library within walls

My first challenge was determining how to liven up a 20-by-25-foot room of plain white concrete walls. When a coworker asked me what I expected a correctional library to look like, my response was, "Home." The library is the one place where young inmates should not be reminded of their confinement. After all, the library is the heart of any academic environment; and isn't home where the heart is?

It wouldn't be easy, however. It was difficult to envision how Beaumont's population of young men could study and research effectively in a space that made me feel as if I were standing in one of their cells.

I saw my mission as combining technology with modern appeal. A library should be as inviting to the eye as it is to the mind, an especially important consideration when working with a captive audience of reluctant readers. But accomplishing this was easier said than done, since safety and security issues in a juvenile correctional center dictate that the smallest detail cannot go overlooked.

I placed Beaumont's furniture order with Virginia's correctional department vendor, Jill Nelson, who remarked after seeing my plan, "It's about time that correctional libraries shed their image of being cold, dark, and unfriendly. Just because this population is incarcerated, they should not receive less." With that in mind, Jill adjusted my design to meet security guidelines, paying close attention to the height and weight of the furniture, metal pieces that might be exposed, space between tables and shelving units, and the arrangement of computer equipment.

Beaumont Expansion
School library

The shelving we were slated to purchase was identified as industrial quality. But after some research, I realized that industrial shelving posed a security risk: A disaffected patron could easily remove nuts and bolts of no specified use or metal shelf guides hanging from the sides of units and use them as weapons.

New ideas, new technology

Then there was the matter of stocking the library. Our goal, of course was to provide wards with the tools that would enable them to improve their reading ability, afford them the technology that would help mainstream them back into public schools when they are released, and provide them with resources to enrich their lives. But there was one catch: I had to meet the needs of students between the ages of 13 and 20½, with reading levels ranging from kindergarten to postgraduate, on a start-up budget of $186,000.

It soon became apparent, however, that an educational program that isn't inclusive of different learning styles will neither challenge gifted students nor interest those with learning disabilities. Institutional librarians found that their patrons' lack of motivation to learn stemmed from a lack of motivation to read, and they began drifting back to a leisure-reading mode in an effort to engage their clientele. Still, students in correctional centers as well as other public schools continued to score on the low end of literacy tests—scores that could not go overlooked.

In response, the State Department of Education implemented the Standards of Learning in 1996, which mandated that every public school set measurable academic standards that students must meet for a school to retain its accreditation. The standards gave juvenile correctional schools a new lifeline in their efforts to redirect a population running out of options.

My aim was to give Beaumont residents a sense of what they could expect to see, hear, and retrieve, in real time, online through curriculum-based electronic resources that the library would create and/or select. I bought multimedia equipment comparable to that available in public settings and established an electronic network linked to three public workstations that offered access to the OPAC, educational software, and an electronic reference and serials collection.

Just the beginning

Quality education depends on, among other things, libraries that can comfortably meet their clients' ever-increasing and changing demands. Libraries within correctional facilities, then, should be even more poised to fulfill their mission, since their clients face greater challenges than those frequenting public facilities do.

The benefits ripple across many boundaries and are being recognized by all members of the prison staff and others. "The Beaumont Expansion Correctional Center's library is definitely one that not only accommodates those who use it, but also serves as a model for others who wish to more adequately address their students' educational needs," said Denwood Barksdale, language-arts department chairman of the Blandford School, which shares the Beaumont campus.

SOURCE: Adapted from Veronica A. Davis, "Breaking Out of the Box: Reinventing a Juvenile-Center Library," *American Libraries* 31, no. 10 (November 2000): 58–61.

Designing a school library
edited by Lillian Carefoot

The planning process: Educational specifications and design

Planning for a new or renovated school library should be a systematic process that includes identification of the planning team, information gathering and needs assessment, and development of educational specifications. Development of the educational specifications is the most important part of the planning process. Educational specifications define the educational function of the school library, interpret the program functions, and determine the spaces required for those functions. In particular they identify instructional functions, user functions, technical services functions, and administrative functions. For each identified space the following information should be included: name of space, size, number of people using the space, and a detailed description of its function. Typically, this description will include the relationship of the space to other areas of the school library and to the larger context of the school. It may also include other pertinent information like special furnishings, lighting needs, electrical requirements, cabling, shelving, and environmental concerns, among others.

The design process

The phases of the design process usually include the following: conceptual, schematic, design development, and construction documents. In the conceptual phase, the school building committee agrees on the educational specifications, ascertains needs, and plans the building/ renovation (building program). The architect begins to translate the building program into design. During the schematic phase, priorities are set for the major design considerations. These designs are usually in the form of diagrams, or bubble diagrams or models. Watch for:

- spatial relationships of the interior spaces
- circulation patterns

- inclusion of all functional areas
- visual control
- zoning of quiet and noisy areas
- size of spaces

In the design development phase, interior spaces are worked out in detail and exteriors are developed. Floor plans are created and artist's conceptions of the exterior are produced. This stage includes the development of structural, mechanical, and electrical systems. Watch for:

- windows
- doors
- elevations
- placement of electrical outlets
- furniture
- shelving
- height of windows
- wall coverings
- floor coverings
- conduit for future needs
- handicapped access
- sight lines
- lighting schemes

During the construction documents phase, minutely detailed and all-inclusive working drawings and specifications are created (blueprints). These drawings contain all the basic graphic, notational, and dimensional data required to describe to a contractor the nature and scope of the work to be performed. Blueprint reading involves understanding scale, lines, and drawing views.

Every drawing should include a plainly marked scale to which the drawing is made. The scale is usually inserted as part of or adjacent to the title block or else shown directly beneath a drawing title elsewhere on the sheet. Be aware that the scale may vary from drawing to drawing. A decimal inch scale is often divided into 10 equal parts—each part equals one inch. A metric scale is read like the decimal inch scale except in millimeters.

Each line in the blueprint has a particular meaning and represents something.

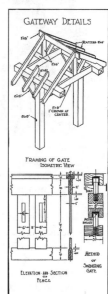

- Thick lines
    Used for an object; represent all edges and surfaces that can be seen when looking directly at the object
- Thin lines
    Hidden lines (a dashed line --------): All edges and surfaces that cannot be seen when looking directly at the object
    Center lines (long and short dashes): Locate the center of a circle or arc
    Extension lines (that extend from the object): Dimension lines that have the dimensions located on or near the line

Plans include four drawing views: The One View is always the front view and is the most important. The Two View can be the right-side view or the top view. The Three View offers a pictorial view of an object. It includes the front view, the top view, and the right-side view, drawn in a three-dimensional fashion. The final view, the Section View, shows the object as if it were cut in two. This is done to more clearly show the interior features of an object. Sectional views can be full, half, revolved through 90 degrees, or removed or detail (removed from its original position to a convenient space near the principal view). Section lining or cross-hatching is used in sectional views to indicate various materials of construction.

A working drawing will more than likely use symbols to convey detailed information. Symbols may indicate

types of material (e.g., concrete, brick, wood)
electrical features (e.g., types of electric receptacles, light fixtures, wiring, telephone outlets, computer receptacles, etc.)
mechanical features (e.g., heating, ventilating, and cooling systems)
architectural (these are mostly pictures of the object depicted as you would see it when looking at it from the angle or view shown on the drawing)
plumbing (e.g., pipe, fittings, and fixtures)

The title block is usually placed in the lower right-hand corner of the drawing. It can contain drawing information: drawing title, drawing number, scale used, dimension notation, page number.

Written specifications that accompany some drawings are the descriptions of work involved, types and grades of materials, and other pertinent information to help the completion of the project. An ideal set of specifications for building construction will clearly and precisely describe the essential and practical limits of the quantities of work and material needed.

Other criteria in the planning process include some general design considerations such as form follows function, designing for maximum flexibility now and in the future, and a warm and welcoming atmosphere inviting use. Access considerations include providing handicapped access to all areas of the library. For acoustic control, use carpeting in high noise areas. Conference, seminar, production, and work rooms should have special acoustical treatment. Provide for water in the work room.

For the best climate control, the entire school library should have a separate climate control for heat and air if possible with ideal humidity at 60%. Return air vents should be positioned high on walls or installed in the ceiling to allow maximum wall space for shelving.

Doors should be light enough in weight to be opened by students and should have no thresholds to facilitate movement of heavy AV carts. Provide a door to the outside corridor in the AV equipment room.

Electrical outlets should be spaced throughout the library: the recommendation is 110v duplex outlets every 10 feet of available wall. Locate wall-mounted electrical outlets in the kick space, not in the shelving. Install floor outlets in instructional, listening, and viewing areas. Locate 110v dedicated surge suppressed circuit isolation transformer/voltage regulators at the circulation desk and the automated library catalog. Locate double duplex electrical outlets, each with a dedicated circuit, at all computer workstations. Install closed circuit television outlets as appropriate and a cable television distribution system with connecting outlets as appropriate. Areas with built-in counters should have 110v strip outlets at 5-foot intervals. Install ceiling-mounted electric projection screens in instructional areas, and install video surveillance cameras as appropriate.

Flooring treatment should have continuous carpeting where equipment is moved on rolling carts. Use carpeting in the following areas: circulation, display, reading, listening, viewing, group viewing, conference rooms, professional collection, offices, workroom, large group instruction, primary/storytelling. Use vinyl or tile flooring in the following areas: main entrance, audiovisual storage, audiovisual production, television studio, head end, darkroom, media production area.

In today's library, consider installing a television distribution system, cable distribution system, intercom system, telephone system, and computer network server(s). It appears that consideration should be given to a wireless network. To be able to teach in the library, provide

- whiteboard
- electrical outlets
- computer network connection
- light control
- adequate seating for a full class (no more than four students per table)
- visual control of the whole library from the teaching station
- electric or manual projection screen
- LCD projector
- video projector
- ability for teleconferencing

Lighting considerations include providing some connection to the outside via windows (over shelving, not at floor level), skylights, an atrium, or other means. Provide separate lighting controls for various areas of the school library.

Location and spatial considerations

Locate away from noisy activity areas, such as the gym, multipurpose room, lunchroom, and band room. Locate in an area that is easily accessible to the entire school. For reading and browsing, allow 25 square feet per student. For safety, allow a minimum of 3 ft. between stacks; 4 ft. between tables in nontraffic areas; and 6 ft. between tables in high-traffic areas. Consider ergonomic principles when designing computer areas. If you are going to have a security system, locate it away from computers or shield computers. Safeguard the collection by locating high-demand materials in controlled access areas, locating the circulation desk near the entrance/exit and away from stack areas, providing an outside drop for return of materials, and limiting the number of exits/entrances.

Be careful of sight lines. Make sure you can see the whole library from the circulation desk. If shelving is freestanding, keep it low enough to see over it.

Design for future expansion of the facility. Plan for the incorporation of future technologies, and plan for flexible use. For storage areas, provide work area for preventive maintenance. Provide an adequate power supply in the AV storage area with no windows, provide space for movable carts, and use wall-to-wall, floor to ceiling, adjustable shelving of varying depths. Install telephone lines with jacks around the library for telephone use and/or for computer modems.

Finish walls with a tackable surface in a neutral color, providing ample area for display of student work. Provide ample signage and graphics, and install pegboard in the AV storage room. The walls between conference rooms can be movable or folding.

Observation windows in offices and workrooms should begin 45 in. from the floor. Since peripheral, wall-mounted shelving is more desirable than free-standing shelving, most of the exterior windows should begin at least 72 in. from the floor and take a minimum of wall space. Consider alternative means of providing natural light. Light control blinds must be provided in areas where natural light enters the library.

General considerations

For books, estimate 30 standard size, 60 picture books, 15–18 reference books, or 3 magazines per 36-in. shelf. One square foot of floor space equals 15 standard book volumes. For carrels, allow 16 square feet each. Computer work areas require surfaces at least 42 in. wide by 30 in. deep. A computer mouse requires a space at least 10 in. by 12 in. Counter height for secondary students should be 38–40 in.; for intermediate students, 36 in.; and for primary students, 28–30 in. Provide seating for 15% of the student body but no more than 100 students in one area. Allow 25 square feet per student (browsing, reading, listening/viewing, individual study, computing).

The recommended specifications for shelving are:

average shelving section: 36 in. wide
charts, prints, and posters: approximately 38 in. high × 40 in.
    wide × 36 in. deep
elementary schools: 42 in. and 60 in. high
middle schools (junior high): 60 in., 72 in., and 82 in. high
multimedia: 14–16 in. deep
periodicals: 14-in. sloping shelf with 12-in. space from top to
    bottom of shelf
primary shelving: 42 in. high; shelves 15 in. apart; shelf partitions
    8 in. apart
reference (elementary): 39 in. high, 14 in. deep
reference (secondary): 42 in. high, 14 in. deep
senior high (secondary): 60 in., 72 in., and 82 in. high

Adjustable shelving 42 in. high with three shelves per 36-in. unit will hold 90 volumes per section. Shelving 60 in. high with five shelves per 36-in. unit holds 150 volumes per section. Shelving 82 in. high with six shelves per 36-in. unit will hold 210 volumes per section. Shelving 96 in. high with seven shelves per 36-in. unit holds 240 volumes per section. Shelving should have a depth of 10 in. for standard-sized books, 12–16 in. for oversize and picture books, 12 in. for magazines, 16 in. for audiovisual materials, and 14 in. for reference books.

Freestanding, island-type shelves should be 36–46 in. high. Allow 36–40 in. between stacks. In high-traffic areas, allow 5 ft. between rows of furniture and shelving. Shelving should not exceed 15 ft. in length.

Tips from teacher librarians

Always go with the industry standard. Look ahead but don't design for technology that does not yet exist; remember that older technologies are seldom replaced by new technologies. Check and recheck at every stage of the process. Do not take anything for granted. Get all agreed-upon changes in writing.

All shelving should be flexible, not fixed. All furniture and shelving must be on a scale that is functional to the age group of the students. Design for easy supervision and convenient traffic flow. Many teacher librarians do not like a mezzanine because it requires more supervision, moving resources up the stairs is difficult, video surveillance cameras need to be monitored on an ongoing basis, and another security system may have to be installed at the mezzanine level.

Try for a floor plan that does not have large pillars holding up the ceiling. Oddly shaped rooms may be visually appealing but can be difficult to use efficiently. Define how your computers will be used. If they will be used for research purposes, they can be facing a wall. If they are a teaching station, you may want to arrange them so that you can walk around them. Make sure that you can see the computer monitors easily and that the monitors do not face a light source. Have one or more computers dedicated for your automated library catalog. Install a dedicated data plug for your printers.

Design your circulation desk with the circulation computer toward the middle of the desk. That way you can place materials on either side of the computer. Remember to install a dedicated outlet for the photocopier and any other large pieces of electrical equipment. Check the number of electrical circuits in addition to the number of electrical outlets.

When selecting your shelving, make sure that the material will be strong enough to bear the load of the materials. Have a 4- to 6-in. kick board below the bottom shelf. Avoid slick shelf surfaces. Select the right bookends for the type of shelving. Choose shelves with backs or ledges to prevent books from falling behind the shelving. The span of a shelf should not exceed 36 inches. If you have a combination of adjustable and fixed shelving, plan to shelve fiction in the nonadjustable shelving (fiction books tend to be a uniform height).

When moving your collection, measure and log off the amount of shelf space needed for each section of books before you pack them in boxes. Add at least one quarter of the length of space allowed on each shelf for future expansion. Log the call numbers and the height of the tallest book in the box. If possible, do not use the bottom shelves of tall shelving units.

The ceiling lighting should not be parallel to freestanding shelving. There will be fewer shadows if lights run at right angles to the shelving. Consider stackable chairs for greater flexibility. If given a choice, students prefer round

tables and paperback books. Plan for no more than four students at each table because a greater number tends to promote too much sociability.

Furniture checklist

Consider the following furniture items: book return bin, book truck, and cabinet units. Side chairs for adults should be 32 in. high, 18 in. wide, and 18 in. deep. Youth chairs should be 27 in. high, 16 in. wide, and 16 in. deep. Juvenile chairs should be 25 in. high, 16 in. wide, and 14 in. deep. Chairs for children 5–7 years old are 13½ in. high and for children 3–5 years old, 11½ in. high. Stacking chairs may be heights of 10 in., 12 in., 14 in., 16 in., or 18 in. Office chairs should be ergonomic. The circulation desk should be 42 in. high to 32 in. high. Computer workstation heights are 27½ in., 29 in., and 32 in.

Include display and directory boards, display dividers, display panels, a lectern, and lounge furniture (chairs, couches, and occasional tables should be considered).

Shelving and storage considerations include an atlas reference shelving unit or atlas stand; audiovisual equipment shelving/storage; big book storage/display for elementary schools; book return bins; book trucks and AV carts; CD-ROM storage and display; chart/poster/art print shelving; computer disk storage; dictionary/reference shelving unit or stand; display units and display cabinets; easy or picture book shelving with dividers; map files; miscellaneous storage for toys, realia, and models; newspaper shelving; oversize storage and display; paperback storage and display; periodical and reference shelving; and videocassette and CD storage and display. Include a step stool. For study carrel(s) and tables, adult height is 29 in.; wheelchair height, 32 in.; youth height, 27½ in.; juvenile height, 25 in. Reference tables are 42 in. high, 72 in. wide, and 24 in. deep.

Functional areas

- administration
- archives
- audiovisual equipment storage and distribution
- browsing/reading area
- cable television drop
- circulation
- computer lab (adjacent or integral)
- conference rooms
- display
- drama/presentation
- group viewing
- instruction area
- Internet and online access
- large group instruction
- librarian's office
- library catalog

- library workroom
- multipurpose area
- parents/community collection
- primary/storytelling
- production of multimedia, including a television studio
- professional collection
- public address system
- reference/information services
- security system
- seminar/conference/meeting rooms
- signage
- small group instruction
- stacks/shelving
- storage
- storage for computer servers
- teacher's resource room/work area
- teaching area
- technical services
- textbook storage
- video conferencing
- video distribution system
- viewing/listening

SOURCE: Adapted from Lillian Carefoot, ed., "Designing a School Library," *School Libraries in Canada* 19, no. 1 (1999): 14 (4-page insert). *School Libraries in Canada* is the journal of the Canadian School Library Association. Used with permission.

8

Building digital libraries for analog people: 10 common design pitfalls and how to avoid them

by Doug Johnson

1. Not planning for a physical library media center at all. For some reason, remodeling tends to bring out the "visionary" in school planners and architects—especially when that vision involves cutting construction costs by shrinking or eliminating the library media center from the building project. What these folks forget is that while some information resources might become digital, the folks who use them will remain "analog" for a very long time. And these analog people will continue to need a physical facility in which to place their analog bodies and gather to meet very human needs.

Even if all books suddenly disappeared tomorrow, we will still need physical library media centers. We sometimes forget that society has given our K–12 schools three major charges:

Teach young people academic and technical skills.
Help socialize its future citizens.
Contain and protect its children while Mom and Pop are busy (and keep children out of shops and off the streets).

Each of these societal charges is becoming more important, not less. Consequently, we have all-day kindergarten, longer school days and school years, latchkey programs, etc.

The physical space of the library media center helps schools meet each of these charges and other curriculum initiatives. For instance, in most schools, there is an increasing amount of project-based, collaborative work done by students at all grade levels, often required by state standards. There are increasing needs for students to have access to digital technologies that help them access data and communicate information. Flexible learning opportunities like online course work, interdisciplinary units, extended school days, service learning, and secondary/postsecondary class schedules create needs for school spaces unlike the traditional classroom.

We are social creatures and social learners. Although we have the Internet, we still gather at shopping malls and libraries. We may have e-mail, but we still telephone and visit. We can watch movies on our VCRs at home, but we still go to motion picture theaters in record numbers. Our analog selves like physical places to gather, to work, and to learn.

2. Not having a planning team. A steering committee with a variety of stakeholder interests can help design a library media space that does more than just fit in an existing program—it also allows for an envisioned program to happen. Your committee should visit new, exemplary school media centers and programs and ask, "What's right" and "What's wrong" of the people actually working in those centers.

Involve the architect as early as possible, because a good one will ask you the right questions. Rather than supplying him or her with a layout or floor plan, you and the planning team should be able to describe the activities that will take place in the media center, the kinds and quantities of resources, and how many people you serve. Share your media program's philosophy, mission, and goal statements. Be open to innovation, but make certain that "form" follows "function."

Progressive planners will invite other departments, programs, or public agencies to share their new area. Think about spaces for the gifted and talented program, a study center, or a community access television station in your media center. Having lots of adults working in the media center tends to help make a more productive center. For instance, does your library media center plan have a work area for teachers, complete with laminator, telephone, sink, comfy chairs, and coffee pot?

3. Planning for only one kind of learning. The amount of physical floor space necessary can only be answered by determining how the new facility will be used and by whom. How many students and classes should be able to work in the media center at one time? Will future class assignments make more or less demand on library media center resources and space? (Be careful. Library media centers with too much seating tend to become study halls, test-taking centers, and/or dumping grounds.) The number of students and classes working productively at one time will depend on the level of staffing in your media center. One professional will have a difficult time helping more than two classes conduct research at the same time.

Today, the library media center still needs to allow for different kinds of student use—individual, small group, and large group. Consequently, the space needs to accommodate conference rooms, enough tables and chairs in one area to seat a class, and upholstered chairs in which individuals can read and study.

Storage for and access to all information formats and communication methods need to be provided, including print, audio, video, and digitized resources. Plan sufficient space to house an adequate print collection by purchasing shelving for your current print collection, plus 20%. Buy all the shelving at the time of construction, because it will not match if you buy some now and some later. Trust me. As long as video remains analog, a wet carrel with a small video recorder, monitor, and headsets needs to be available.

At least one of the building's general-use computer labs should be part of the media center area, preferably separated by well-windowed walls for visual supervision and for sound containment. While the current (and correct) recommendation is to place as many computers in individual classrooms as possible, most teachers still like to use a lab occasionally for whole class instruction. Every building should have at least *one*.

In addition to a large lab, the media center should provide a generous number of research and productivity terminals for individual users. There also should be an area for individuals and smaller groups of students to use technology to complete multimedia projects. The following technologies, too costly for purchase for every classroom, should be readily available to students and teachers:

scanners
laser printers
digital and analog video cameras
microphones
digital and analog video editors
digital still cameras
graphics pads or tablets
drawing, painting, and photo editing software
desktop publishing, presentation, and hypermedia authoring software
writable CD-ROM drives

Remember that *all* areas and resources need to be accessible to the physically challenged. Pay particular attention to shelving height, aisle widths, and floors on multiple levels that need ramps.

If your media center needs to expand, is there a logical wall that can be removed to accommodate that growth? Don't laugh. Our local bookstore just removed all its computer software in order to make room for computer *book* offerings.

4. Designing the library media center for only school use. If possible, locate the new library media center near the classes that use it and its technology labs often. Locate the center away from the noises from the band room, technology education shops, gymnasiums, cafeterias, or air-handling units that create unnecessary distractions.

Another "location" factor is becoming increasingly important. If we want to pass bond or operating referendums, we need to market our schools as resources that can be used in the evenings, on weekends, and throughout the summer by community organizations.

This means that, rather than having the entire school building accessible, we may want a library media center that can function as a stand-alone facility (with its own bathrooms, drinking fountains, and climate control) for after-school use. Does the library media center need an outside entrance located near parking? Air conditioning the area will permit year-round use by staff, students, and the community.

5. Designing for technologies that do not yet exist. Look ahead, but do not design the facility for technologies that do not yet exist or have not proven to work in a school setting. Remember that older technologies are rarely replaced by new technologies. The book, radio, telephone, motion picture, television, and CD-ROM technologies as well as the Internet all currently provide people with information and will continue to do so into the foreseeable future. Place video, voice, and data drops throughout the area, particularly on walls and columns. Install a ten-foot-by-ten-foot electrical and data floor grid for maximum flexibility. Also, ease your mind by installing only conditioned electrical outlets. Avoid visible goofs like placing the electrical plates and video jacks near the floor instead of close to the ceiling-mounted television monitors. Those wires and extension cords running down the wall look tacky.

Whole building network technologies need to be accommodated. The library media center is a practical place for the network wiring closet, including a work area for file server placement and maintenance as well as the video head end. In a controlled space in the library media center, this equipment can be easily monitored and accessed by the library media specialists and the technicians.

Learn to read the architectural plans. Double- and triple-check the location of data, electricity, and telephone lines as well as light switches. While you are at it, make sure the doors and windows are in the right places, also.

6. Creating media centers that are difficult to supervise. Include:

> areas of the media center that can be restricted from student and/or public use;
> conference rooms, computer labs, and production areas that can be locked;
> windows for viewing into conference rooms, computer labs, and production areas;
> student entrances that can be easily monitored; and
> security system installation if needed.

Seek to eliminate:

> areas that cannot be seen from a single location such as the circulation desk;
> two-story library media center plans;
> freestanding floor shelving more than 30 inches high;
> computers with Internet access placed where they cannot be easily monitored;
> (and especially) *high-walled study carrels!*

Check the floor plan to look for unsupervisable blind spots.

7. Designing library media centers that have poor traffic patterns. Lay out any proposed floor plan on a large table. Get your favorite Monopoly piece and walk through a typical day using the plan. For instance, get a piece of audiovisual equipment, answer the telephone, answer a reference question, plan with a teacher, and help with an Internet question. Now go through the same procedure as a library media center user who is getting or returning a book, reading a magazine, coming in with a class to use the computer lab, and using the catalog or other digital resources.

Do the traffic patterns make sense? Are the circulation areas and the computer labs near the entrance? Is equipment storage near a hallway or are you wheeling it the length of the center? Is the reading/study area away from high-traffic areas where users will repeatedly be distracted? Will you have to walk a long distance to answer a reference question? Is the media center easily accessible from the rest of the building, but not a convenient passage between areas of the building?

8. Forgetting the importance of good lighting and sound dampening. As anyone who has used a computer for extended lengths of time can tell you, the importance of good lighting is more important to our physical comfort in the digital age than ever before.

Lighting needs to be both adequate and nonglare. Architects have the lumen numbers and nifty gadgets to determine the amount of light in places like stacks and reference areas. Make certain light levels are checked in the final walk-through. Light diffusers need to be located to reduce reflection and glare, especially from computer monitors. Are there natural light sources that will not fade the carpet, destroy materials, or create glare? The media center should have a specific area that can be separately darkened for projected presentations, with light switches in a single bank located in a controlled area.

Make certain the furniture you choose has a matte finish to reduce glare and eyestrain. Light-colored woods are easiest on the eyes be- cause they provide the least contrast with white paper.

Good carpeting and ceiling tiles help mute the necessary noises associated with learning. The days of the deadly quiet library are past, but it is still difficult for both students and the library media specialist to work in a very noisy room. Ask your architect about placing floor tile in the high-traffic areas and laying carpet in the rest of the library media center for more uniform wear throughout the room.

9. Ignoring aesthetics. The first rule of decorating is to never let someone who is not a professional select the color of anything. Even if someone on your committee thinks he or she has taste, double-check with a real interior designer. It is money well spent.

Consideration needs to be given to the aesthetic qualities of the area. Are colors coordinated? Is there visual interest in the architectural design and texture variety? Have you added warmth through fabrics and woods in your seating and shelving? Are there display areas for student work and new materials near the entrance to help personalize a library media center? Discuss with a design professional the type of atmosphere you are trying to create as well as how you want the user to feel when entering. Do not forget to include an office where you would be happy working—one that is pleasant, comfortable, and practical.

Taking the time and making the effort to ensure that your library media center will be functional and attractive sends a very clear message to your patron—I respect and care about you.

10. Forgetting about all those things that will drive you nuts day in and day out. Here's my short checklist:

No nightlight by the door. You have to stumble through the dark, knocking your shins to get to the bank of light switches.

No backs on shelving. Books slip back and down.

Too-tall, nonadjustable shelving.

No area for the display and reading of current magazines and newspapers.

No dedicated story area in an elementary library media center.

Low-quality furniture that does not resist scratching and marring. Buy good laminate and strong legs.

No upholstered chairs for comfortable reading and studying.

No office or semiprivate work area for the library media specialist.

No after-hours book drop.

No coat closet or place for the library media staff to store dripping umbrellas.

No sink.

No water fountain.

Conclusion

I like visionaries. Without them I would never have gotten to dream about beeburgers, personal helicopters, self-cleaning houses, or all-digital libraries. When it comes to facility design, however, let practicality take the front seat. Bricks and mortar last a very long time. And remember, even if the future is digital, it is where you will be spending the rest of your analog life.

SOURCE: Adapted from Doug Johnson, "Building Digital Libraries for Analog People: Ten Common Design Pitfalls and How to Avoid Them," *Knowledge Quest* 28, no. 5 (May/June 2000): 10–15.

Making the library accessible: An inclusive approach

by Rolf Erickson and Carolyn Markuson

Americans with Disabilities Act (ADA)

Signed into law in 1990, the Americans with Disabilities Act (ADA) is a comprehensive civil rights law that prohibits discrimination on the basis of disability. Titles II and III of the ADA mandate handicapped access to public facilities. The intent of the law is to ensure that facilities are accessible to and usable by people with disabilities by making those facilities barrier free. The Architectural and Transportation Barriers Compliance Board (Access Board) is responsible for developing accessibility guidelines (ADAAG) for newly constructed and renovated buildings. The initial guidelines were issued in 1991. The ADAAG provide guidance to the Department of Justice, which is responsible for enforcement of Titles II and III of the ADA. Noncompliance is treated as a form of discrimination. The Access Board may from time to time amend the ADAAG, and the Department

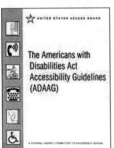

The Americans with Disabilities Act Accessibility Guidelines (ADAAG)

of Justice may amend its own regulations implementing the ADA by adopting these new accessibility guidelines.

The original accessibility guidelines were based on adult dimensions and did not include children's dimensions even for facilities designed for use primarily by children. In 1986, the Access Board recommended accessibility guidelines for physically handicapped children in elementary schools. New accessibility guidelines approved in July 1999 provide further options based on children's dimensions as exceptions to specifications based on accepted adult dimensions. These optional specifications are discretionary, not mandatory, and they focus on certain elements designed and constructed primarily for use by children ages 2 through 12.

Much confusion exists about many aspects of the ADA, and it can be difficult to interpret. Architects do not always know all the rules. School librarians involved in building projects must have a basic knowledge of ADA requirements in order to ask intelligent questions and to monitor progress with respect to the ADA. If barrier-free design is not incorporated into the plan at the beginning of the process, you will be faced with extra costs down the road.

To understand ADA requirements, you must be familiar with certain principles and definitions upon which they are based:

1. According to the ADA, an adult wheelchair needs clear floor space 48 inches deep by 30 inches wide. Because actual dimensions of wheelchairs vary, be aware that this space may not always be adequate, especially for some motorized wheelchairs.
2. Any reach above 5 feet or below 20 inches is not accessible to a person in a wheelchair.
3. To make a right or left turn in a wheelchair, a space 36 inches by 36 inches is needed; to make a smooth U-turn, the space needed is 78 inches by 60 inches.

You should be aware of several ADAAG requirements that have specific application in libraries:

1. Entry and all interior doors must be at least 32 inches wide. Thresholds must be beveled with a thickness of no more than one-half inch.
2. Door hardware must be operable with one hand, with no twisting of the wrist required and must be mounted no more than 48 inches above the finished floor.
3. A wheelchair user must be able to enter and exit through any theft-prevention system or an alternative entry and exit must be provided.
4. Any library on more than one building level must have elevator access available for all levels.
5. Floor surfaces must be smooth and covered with firmly fastened, nonslip materials. Carpeting must have a hard pile (one-half-inch maximum thickness) with a firm, stable, and slip-resistant finish, and it must have a firm or no-cushion backing or pad.
6. Accessible routes must connect all spaces within the library. These routes, including aisles between book stacks, must be at least three feet wide. The ADAAG express a strong preference

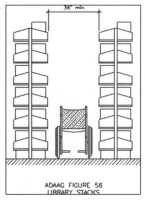

ADAAG FIGURE 56
LIBRARY STACKS

for a 42-inch aisle. If your library is designed with the minimum space between stacks, pay particular attention to exact shelf dimensions. A shelf with a depth of 10 inches may take up more floor space than 10 inches, and end panels may extend beyond the dimension of the shelf.

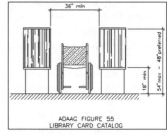

ADAAG FIGURE 55
LIBRARY CARD CATALOG

7. At least 5%, or a minimum of each element of fixed seating, tables, and carrels, must comply with ADAAG requirements. This applies to all public areas of the library. Accessible routes must lead to and through these areas of seating. Clearance between tables and carrels must be at least 36 inches. When planning areas of lounge seating, clear space should be made available to accommodate users of wheelchairs.

8. Floor space at a table or workstation must be a minimum of 30 inches wide by 48 inches deep. Only 19 inches of the depth is allowed to be underneath the work surface.

9. Knee space beneath a work surface must be at least 27 inches high, 30 inches wide, and 19 inches deep. For children age 12 and younger, the minimum height is 24 inches.

10. Where wheelchair seating space is provided, work surfaces must be 28 to 34 inches above the finished floor. For children age 12 and younger, the minimum height is 26 inches. Consider the use of some height-adjustable tables or carrels to meet this requirement.

11. Clear aisle space at displays of periodicals, new books, and so on must be at least 36 inches; maximum reach height must be no more than 54 inches from a side reach and no more than 48 inches from a front reach, with 48 inches preferred irrespective of approach. Book-stack heights are unrestricted.

12. The circulation desk must be on an accessible route. The desk must have a countertop that is at least 36 inches long and a maximum of 36 inches above the finished floor. If students are checking out materials and are required to sign their name or write something, you must have a surface no higher than 34 inches, with knee space so a wheelchair can fit under it.

13. The maximum height for placement of light switches is 48 inches.

14. If the bottom edge of an object that protrudes into a passageway is more than 27 inches but less than 80 inches above the floor, the object must not protrude more than 4 inches into the passageway.

In addition to becoming familiar with the ADA, perhaps the best way to make the library free of barriers is to consult students with disabilities. Ask them what features would be most useful in a new library facility. When planning a new school library facility, you should attempt not just to follow the mandated requirements, but to make the library as accessible as possible to everyone. Keep in mind that making a library facility more usable for disabled patrons will make it more usable for everyone.

Signage

Signage is an integral part of the interior design of a school library. Too often it is either ignored altogether or overdone, creating visual clutter that defeats the purpose.

Planning. Signage should be planned along with the design of the library facility and the selection of furnishings. Some designers recommend that signage not be planned until after the new facility is occupied, the argument being that traffic patterns and usage can then be better observed. Dangers accompany this approach, however. First, good quality sign systems are not inexpensive. The best way to guarantee a good system is to plan it in advance and include it in the furnishings budget; otherwise, finding the necessary funds later may prove difficult or impossible. Second, the wait-and-see approach often results in a haphazard system of signs that are handmade, look makeshift, and spoil the library's appearance.

The signage for a school library is not complicated to plan. Not many signs are needed, and, if you've planned for a natural traffic flow, it will be clear where signs will be the most helpful. The sign system you purchase should be one that can be updated or modified easily and economically. If you choose to wait and plan signage after the facility is finished, do so only if you have a guaranteed budget at your discretion.

The planning for a sign system should begin when you are visiting other libraries to get ideas for your new facility. During these visits, take note of what you like or dislike about the signage. Catalogs from companies that specialize in signage will give you some idea of the range of available products.

The signage in the school library should make it easier for users to find what they need. The format, color, and type style should be consistent, and the signs must complement the setting. Avoid clutter: If there are too many signs, they tend to become invisible.

Common signs. The signs most commonly needed in school libraries identify the circulation desk, the areas of the collection (fiction, nonfiction, reference, periodicals, and so on), and the range of books found in each shelf unit. Range finders will most likely need frequent updating, so it is very important to purchase signs that can be easily changed in-house. Range finders commonly have protective covers over the labels, and the covers can be secured with screw-type locks to prevent tampering. These covers should have a matte finish to avoid glare.

Terminology. The terminology for signs should be based on common sense and should be easily understood and meaningful to everyone. Avoid professional jargon. For example, if your library has a reference desk, consider identifying it with a sign that says simply *Information*; for the circulation desk, consider using the terms *Checkout* and *Return*. Give the terminology some thought, and solicit ideas and opinions from students and teachers. Be creative and maybe just a bit daring. Don't think it always has to be done the same old way.

Design elements. In addition to signs, helping users find their way in the library can be enhanced by the use of design elements. Changes of color on the floor, for example, can be especially effective to designate traffic lanes and functional areas. Again, be creative.

ADA requirements. Signage must also meet ADA guidelines.

Permanent rooms and spaces must be identified with signs. These signs must have tactile lettering (a minimum of 1/32 of an inch thick). Lettering must be between 5/8 inch and 2 inches tall, and must include grade 2 braille. Permanent room signs must be mounted on the same side of the door as the door handle, 48 to 60 inches from the center of the sign to the floor, and far enough to the side of the door frame that a person reading the sign, at a distance of 3 inches from the door, will not be hit by the opening door.

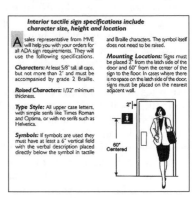

Interior tactile sign specifications include character size, height and location

A sales representative from MVE will help you with your orders for all ADA sign requirements. They will use the following specifications.

Characters: At least 5/8" tall, all caps, but not more than 2" and must be accompanied by grade 2 Braille.

Raised Characters: 1/32" minimum thickness.

Type Style: All upper case letters, with simple serifs like Times Roman and Optima, or with no serifs such as Helvetica.

Symbols: If symbols are used they must have at least a 6" vertical field with the verbal description placed directly below the symbol in tactile

and Braille characters. The symbol itself does not need to be raised.

Mounting Locations: Signs must be placed 2" from the latch side of the door and 60" from the center of the sign to the floor. In cases where there is no space on the latch side of the door, signs must be placed on the nearest adjacent wall.

2"

60" Centered

All permanent, directional, and identification signs must have a nonglare finish and sharp contrast between the colors of the letters and the background.

All overhead signs must have letters at least 3 inches high, and must be hung a minimum of 80 inches above the finished floor.

Learning styles

Teaching methods have changed considerably in recent years as we have discovered much more about the brain and learning. Designers of educational facilities have been slower to address this new knowledge. When a new or renovated school library facility is planned, it is important to apply what we know about the brain and learning to the design process. The new facility should provide an effective learning environment, one that supports different learning styles.

Once again, the role of the school librarian, as well as other school personnel, is critical. Do not assume architects and interior designers are familiar with how people learn, or with the changes in how schools function today compared with 10 or more years ago. This is why we see new school library facilities that are still designed on an outmoded educational model. This is why you must be involved.

Flexibility. Any new school library facility should have elements incorporated into its design that allow students to work in cooperative groups. Spaces should be provided for this, and furniture should be selected to facilitate this kind of learning activity. Square tables are more effective than rectangular tables, because they allow students to sit closer together, which also helps to lower noise levels. Flexibility is paramount. Small tables that seat two or at most four students work well; when larger table configurations are needed, the tables can be easily combined.

Storage. A final consideration is storage. New trends in assessment emphasize portfolio development to demonstrate academic growth. Providing spaces for the construction and storage of student portfolios and student-created multimedia projects should not be overlooked in the planning process. School libraries, as central depositories of information, can provide storage for these student activities. Because librarians are the information storage and retrieval experts within the school system, it is incumbent on us to raise this issue in the planning process—we may be the only ones to think about it.

Safety issues

Providing for the safety of students using the library as well as of library staff members should be included in the planning process. Location of the library within the school plays a role in safety. The library should not be tucked away in some remote corner from which a quick and easy evacuation is difficult. How the library is designed in terms of supervision is also critical. The shape of the library should be such that no spaces are hidden from view. Stacks should be configured to facilitate supervision of aisles, and staff work areas must include windows so a staff member can supervise outside adjacent spaces.

Local building codes will usually determine how some safety issues must be addressed. Meeting these codes is the responsibility of the architectural firm. The ADA also has guidelines for safety features that must be met. Some of these safety issues, including floor covering, protruding objects, adequate aisle space, and furniture design, affect accessibility. The school library should be equipped with an alarm system that is both audible and visual. Alarms must be at least 80 inches above the floor, and at least 6 inches below the ceiling. Because the requirements specified by the ADA for alarm systems are very technical, it is important that the company that supplies the system guarantees compliance with existing laws. Emergency exits must be provided as well as exit signs and lights.

Once the facility is complete and ready for use, you must have an emergency management plan, and any such plan must address the needs of the disabled. Being prepared for an emergency is probably the most important step to take in terms of safety. Evacuation procedures must be clear to users of the library, so they can act quickly in any emergency, and staff members must be fully prepared to implement emergency procedures.

SOURCE: Adapted from Rolf Erickson and Carolyn Markuson, *Designing a School Library Media Center for the Future* (Chicago: American Library Association, 2001), 70–75.

Remodeling the media center

by Steven M. Baule

Your dream of remodeling your library media center has become a reality. You quickly must focus on the many items that need your attention. The locations for various parts of the media center, electrical and data wiring needs, light, security, and reuse of existing furniture and equipment are just a few. If you are to gut the media center, but stay inside the existing space, consider where you presently run into problems retrieving equipment and materials. List all of the functional areas that you want to have. Next, contemplate a "normal day" in the library media center. At what points are you pulled in two or more directions? What equipment seems to be in awkward locations? What areas need to be next to each other and what areas should not be adjacent? Determine the amount of space needed for each area. Remember that the print collection probably won't get any smaller in the near future, but the reference collection will most likely become almost entirely electronic in the next 10 years. Now that you have determined the types of spaces needed, which should be in adjacent locations, and what size each should be, you are ready to turn that information over to the architect to develop a couple of alternate designs for your review.

Electrical and data wiring will be significantly advanced. Provide for students and teachers bringing in their own computers. Plan for future needs based upon present laptop configurations and power requirements. Because many of the emerging laptops have much longer battery lives, you may not need electrical outlets at each student table. Wireless data networking requires pulling the wire during remodeling, much less expensive than pulling the cable later. You should consider not only the number of computers you will have in the library media center but also the number of fax machines, printers, and phones.

Lighting is another issue that needs more attention. Indirect lighting will work better than direct lighting near computer monitors where direct light can cause glare. Ensure that windows are not situated in such a way to cause glare at different times of the day. Slightly tinting outside windows can eliminate the negative effects of the sun's rays. To set up an area for computer projection devices, make sure that the area's lighting controls are separate from the rest of the library media center's controls. Where possible, divide the light banks into three areas and put one or two sections on dimmer controls. This will give you almost unlimited control over the amount of light in the projection area.

Security and supervision also need to be part of any remodeling plan. Ensuring a single entrance and exit for students allows for the easiest setup and maintenance of a security system for library materials. When determining how to arrange shelving and computer terminals, you also should keep supervision in the forefront. If possible, try to have all computer screens visible from one direction. This not only will help you instruct students on computer use but also will help you monitor what they are doing. In the same way, in a perfect design, one staff member could view the entire library from a central location, such as the circulation desk.

When remodeling, always spend your budget on facilities issues first. Equipment can come in later budget cycles, but additional facility modifications are rarely going to be viewed favorably after a major remodeling project. Following that advice may land you in a beautiful new library media center with the same old mismatched furniture. One solution for metal furniture is electrostatic painting. Given a color sample from your new color scheme, a painter can match it exactly. This will allow you to keep your old gray and black filing cabinets and brown metal desk without destroying the look of your new library media center. You could even paint old metal shelving.

The key to remodeling a library media center is in the detail. Don't leave anything to chance. Work closely with the architect or designer, and make sure your voice is heard. Plan for functionality, then adjust for daily use. And don't forget to allow for the possibilities that the future holds. Finally, develop a good plan to move all of your resources out of the library media center for the renovation and have a plan to get them back in place before the school year starts. Good luck.

SOURCE: Adapted from Steven M. Baule, "Remodeling the Media Center," *The Book Report* 17, no. 1 (May/June 1998): 24–25. *The Book Report* is now published as *Library Media Connection.* Used with permission.

Developing bid specifications for facilities projects
by Steven M. Baule

An important aspect of the facilities design process is the development of good competitive bid specifications or a well-defined request for proposal. In all cases, the facilities design team should not expect to develop the bid requirements without assistance from the business manager and an outside consultant. From a legal standpoint it is critical that bid specifications be developed to allow all bidders to be judged on equal terms.

In general, bid specifications have two important aspects: to ensure that they address the specific equipment, materials, or services required, including warranties, training to be provided, and other considerations, and to determine that the bidder is capable and qualified to provide the equipment, material, or services requested. Large bid specifications are built around four basic sections: general conditions, special conditions, a table of values, and information about the bidder's company and employees who might work on the project.

General conditions refer to the situation: the hours the vendors will have access to the school, who checks them in when they arrive, who is responsible for cleaning up after work is done, the acceptable size of trucks coming to a loading dock, and so forth. Many school districts have standard sets of general conditions, compiled with the help of an architect or general contractor, that they use for all construction and renovation projects. Special conditions cover items where there is a change from the general conditions. For instance, you may need to identify who is responsible for moving out old shelving or how boxes of books will be labeled.

The table of values is the heart of the bid. It includes each item or service requested and the cost to the district for the item or service. Many smaller requests for proposals or bids only include this section. Bid documents should itemize each thing to be provided. This may be done by describing a standard that the equipment must meet or by specifying a proprietary item: specifying a brand name and model number. Many schools and government agencies prefer to provide descriptive standards because this seems fairer. However, development along proprietary lines is a simple way to develop a bid specification, and as long as multiple suppliers can furnish the brand requested, the bid process is not compromised.

In many states you can reject a bid because the company does not have adequate experience in the type of work you need done. This section of the bid document should identify any certifications or other information about the vendor that you need to determine the bidders' expertise.

Once standards have been set, the specifications can be closed. That means that only the exact product requested in the specifications should be provided—no substitutions are allowed. In other cases, you may want to allow multiple options from which the bidder can choose; any product from a designated list would be acceptable; you may specify "or equivalent," which gives the bidder the option to provide an alternative item meeting standards specified. This is risky when bidding technology-related items, as it is nearly impossible to judge multiple facets among many alternatives in comparison to a specified item. Generally you should allow for a newer generation of the same product to be bid without penalty.

In furniture bidding, the use of equivalent items is often a benefit, as a bidder may find an identical item with the exact same performance from another vendor at a lower price. In some cases, you can require that any alternative submission must be approved prior to the bid. This allows you to determine whether a substitution will be satisfactory on an item-by-item basis. Further, the bid specifications should include the level and length of warranty to be provided by the bidder. In general, you should require that vendors bring in samples of furniture you are interested in using. It is important that your design team has the opportunity to test drive chairs and tables, not just look at them in a catalog. In the best-case scenario, vendors leave their samples for a week or two so that your design team can review and inspect them without pressure.

No matter what method you decide to use for determining specifications, you should request that bidders provide both a unit price for each item and the total extension for each line of the bid. This will assist your team and the business office in determining the successful bid proposal in a timely manner. As a contingency, you should request a unit price for any additional number of the item that you might consider purchasing (e.g., you order the 35 chairs you can afford, but a lower bid allows you to buy additional chairs at the same price as the original bid). Installation and delivery costs should be included within the bid for each group of items. Further, the bidder should indicate how long the quoted prices stand so that if you obtain additional funds three months later, you can purchase additional furniture without having to renegotiate the cost. As tax-exempt institutions, schools should instruct bidders not to include taxes within their quotes.

The second aspect of the bid specification should gather enough information about the vendor to determine whether or not the bidder will be able to complete the work or deliver the equipment specified. You will want to specify that any bidder must be an authorized reseller for any equipment quoted. Bidders who are not authorized resellers should be automatically disqualified. In the same manner, when you are bidding large projects, bidders should provide general financial information, the length of time they have been in business, their ability to service the products requested, and the number of qualified installers and service people on their staff.

In doing wiring or electrical work, the bidder enumerates certifications or union affiliations. Require a number of references based upon work done in a similar school or library setting by the same project manager. If the vendor provides references for a project team that will not be assigned to do the work at your location, request references for the specific project manager who will be assigned. You should retain the right to reject a bidder based upon poor references. In many states, the vendors will also need to identify that they are supportive of a drug-free workplace, pay prevailing wages based upon union wage scales, and comply with other state and federal regulations.

On large projects, you should develop a prequalification procedure to eliminate any bidders without sufficient experience, staff, or positive references to properly complete the project being bid. Further, a prebid walkthrough or survey is vital. In this situation, all of the vendors hoping to bid on the project are required to come to the work site, walk through the facility with the bid specifications, and ask questions about the project. Such a walkthrough will help ensure that bidders have a good understanding of the project. This will avoid a vendor's claim that he or she didn't understand the scope of the construction and therefore needs money to complete the project. During the walkthrough, a school representative should keep a running list of all questions and provide bidders with an official response to each question later.

In some cases, where the project's scope is large or some variables may exist in its final stages, the school may set a fixed amount, called an owner's contingency, within the bid itself. When the school's governing body requires that all projects stay within or under budget, such a contingency will allow room for changes that are likely to emerge during the course of a large project. When a few drop locations are added in a sizable wiring project, the owner's contingency will permit those drops without going over budget. In some cases, this contingency may be expressed as a percentage of the total project, but an exact dollar amount is more common and easier to compare among bidders.

If equipment needs to be installed or specific work is to be done, the bid specifications should include a preliminary timeline. As soon as the bid has been awarded, the successful bidder should submit a comprehensive project timeline that can be referred to in the weekly construction meetings to determine whether or not the project is continuing on schedule. In some cases, you may want to add a liquidated damages clause. Liquidated damages require the bidder to forfeit a certain amount of money for each day beyond the original completion date that it takes to finish the project.

When the project is moderate to large in scope, it is advisable to break the project bids into several groups. For example, basic furniture can be considered as one group and computer furniture, another. This allows the school more flexibility in selecting vendors than if a single bidder must be chosen. Be aware that awarding the bids to several vendors will require more coordination. To help with this coordination, specify that successful bidders must attend weekly or bimonthly coordination meetings. In practice, most construction or renovation projects have a preconstruction meeting immediately after the bid is awarded, ensuring that everyone begins on the same page.

The time and place of the bid opening are defined in the initial bid notice. Bids are opened and the table of values read. Then the school team thanks everyone attending. Until you and the business office have a chance to review each bid, you should not assume that the lowest bid is the winning bid. That vendor may have forgotten an item or made a calculation error in the final total. After you have had a chance to review all bids, you or the business manager should write a letter of recommendation to the governing board as to which vendor should be awarded the contract.

Remember, you do not have to go it alone. Before you begin to draft your own documents, check with your neighboring districts, regional libraries, or state association to see models of their sample bids or requests for proposals. In some cases, a trusted vendor can be asked to assist you in developing bid specifications. Many vendors are willing to do this because they feel it will give them an edge in the bid process. Furniture vendors are particularly willing to do this. Nonetheless, you should always insist that such work be done as a contract, and pay the vendor for the work. This eliminates any charge of collusion. Your architect and your business manager should also be able to help you develop detailed bid specifications. However, it is important that you take ownership of the process and advocate for your needs since you are the one who will be working in the library for the next decade. Good luck.

SOURCE: Adapted from Steve Baule, "Developing Bid Specifications for Facilities Projects," *Knowledge Quest* 31, no. 1 (September/October 2002): 14–17.

Give yourself a behavior management makeover

by Geoff Dubber

Library behavior is affected by many things. It isn't all your fault! School morale, the buildings, students' perceptions of themselves, teaching and learning styles, and, of course, outside social factors all play a crucial part. Patterns of behavior and student attitudes are a mixture of all these things, over many

of which you have little direct control. On the other hand, library behavior is also linked to library perception. The way the students think of you and the library is much more under your control.

How about first giving a thought to yourself? To an extent you embody the library! How do you feel? If you smile, the school will smile with you. Scowl and everyone avoids you. After all, you spend a good deal of time in the library and maybe you feel that school life often passes you by.

So start by giving yourself a makeover. A massage or an evening out will help but not yet. I have other things in mind to be done first. Create a vision of what you want and devise three key strategies to achieve it. Remember the library is the hub of school information and the key learning area in the school. Go to see the principal and demand that long overdue meeting to discuss your progress and plans. Don't take "no" for an answer. Book up for a useful course. Decide to close the library for one break-time a week and have coffee in the staffroom. Talk with teaching colleagues. Try to achieve three positive moves to improve your status, expertise, and self-esteem by the end of the day. Above all, talk positive and smile! That will make *you* feel better; teaching colleagues will respond more positively, and so will the students. Behavior will improve, too.

Library atmosphere

Now think about your library environment and atmosphere. Is it as good as you can make it? What do you *want* it to be like? How about changing the posters and displays of books? Could you design some brighter and clearer signs? Play some quiet background music? Get that old printer mended?

Insist from now on that nobody, just nobody, moves chairs about at any time, including Mr. Smith's class and the sixth graders. Close a little earlier at lunchtime to give yourself time to clear up. Put the fiction books on the opposite side of the room. Place the reference material nearer the checkout counter. Beg, borrow, or buy some new plants. Can you have better control of the entrance or exit points?

Make a resolution not to admit more students than you can reasonably seat and supervise. Provide an inquiry book for complicated inquiries and deal with those later. Start that development plan you've promised yourself—and remember to tell the principal what you're doing.

The next step

What next? Cultivate an effective curriculum image. What do the students think the library is for? What do staff think it's for? Be honest. How many colleagues and students think the library is one or all of these: a substitute exam room, sick bay, lunch bar, common room, detention room, or hiding place when it's wet and cold outside?

Start talking to your principal about ways to cultivate this effective curriculum image. Do you and the library feature in the school's brochure? Is the library open during Parents' Evenings? Think carefully about curriculum time use and ways you can work more effectively with your teaching colleagues. Do you know enough about the school curriculum? Does your permission system work? Do you need one? Who does what when you have teacher-led classes or groups in the library (what's your role)? If the library has a positive curriculum image and effectively supports learning, then student behavior is likely to improve.

Psychology

Now get psychological! Think about the psychology that affects behavior management and the ways in which you can apply it to your situation. What do the experts tell us?

- The least effective way of managing behavior is to tell students they are doing wrong.
- Behavior is an attempt to communicate a need. It's important to look at why something is happening rather than just looking at what is happening.
- Behavior is learned and new behavior can be learned, too.
- It is usually impossible to control other people's behavior, but we can modify our own in the light of their actions and needs and thereby help to modify theirs.
- Respect is ultimately more important and more effective than control.

- The way you manage behavior situations reflects your belief in yourself, your trust in your situation, and your relationship with the people with whom you are dealing.

It makes good sense, doesn't it? So what can you do to turn theory into practice? Try to be assertive rather than aggressive. Stand back and review a difficult

situation before wading in. Don't shout but listen to reason and then talk firmly and calmly. Try to find something positive to say even if you're also finding fault. Stand your ground but be fair and attempt to come to a compromise if this is possible. Avoid issuing threats you can't carry out, or imposing sanctions that will be ignored. Practice using positive body language. Smile. Keep your eyes focused on the culprits and move them sideways rather than downward. Crouching down to their level can be useful and nonthreatening, but stand up very straight so that you can see the whites of the eyes of the bigger ones! Look determined but not threatening, and address everyone by name.

Think about the way you give instructions, too. Gerard Gordon suggests a useful sequence to use when talking to a large group:

- Give a clear instruction and expect compliance.
- Allow "waiting time."
- Look for positive behavior and paraphrase the instruction if necessary.
- Acknowledge appropriate behavior.

When dealing with a difficult student, try this strategy:

- Acknowledge good behavior elsewhere in the library.
- Increase your physical proximity to the culprit.
- Direct a private question, giving the student time to explain the problem or situation.
- Give a clear instruction and expect it to be carried out.

If there is still no cooperation:

- Remind the student of the instruction/rule.
- Offer a choice.
- If possible, give a cooling-off time.
- Remove the student, if all else fails!

Try to remember these strategies, and practice. Give yourself a pat on the back every time you use one of the strategies or implement the sequence.

Conclusion

Behavior management, then, is about much more than trying to keep noisy students quiet during wet and windy lunchtimes. It's about you, your self-esteem and status, the library environment, and knowing and practicing a bit of psychology. Once you've thought about all this, achieved some of it, and planned the rest, that's the time for your massage or evening out.

SOURCE: Adapted from Geoff Dubber, "Give Yourself a Behaviour Management Make-Over," *The School Librarian* 47, no. 3 (Autumn 1999): 121–122. First published in *The School Librarian,* journal of The School Library Association (UK and Ireland). Copyright 1999. To learn more about The School Library Association, go to http://www.sla.org.uk.

Good behavior: How school librarians can reap if they sow

by Siân Spink   ✱ 4 Rules

Who should discipline?

Should teachers or librarians be responsible for discipline in the school library? Perhaps it is preferable that the librarian remains outside the formal discipline process because a barrier may be created between the librarian and the pupils if the librarian deals with discipline directly. However, the librarian should never be denied the right to eject disruptive pupils from the library. Without the right to discipline pupils, the librarian will have reduced authority in the eyes of the children. Because it is an important part of teachers' skills, behavior management forms a significant element of teacher training.

Self-discipline

Because classroom experiences do not always prepare pupils for the less structured environment of the library, in today's "come-and-go" school library librarians have to plan policies and procedures that will encourage the development of self-control and self-discipline in pupils. The librarian should try to foster a positive atmosphere and establish controlled behavior by adopting certain attitudes. These should include believing in and valuing young people, respecting their dignity, and remembering to discipline, not to punish but to change behavior.

The more pupils assume responsibility for themselves, the more the librarian is free to help them. If pupils are encouraged to believe that the library is theirs, they may then increase their sense of self-worth and have an increased awareness and respect for the library, leading to a greater ability to control their behavior.

There are principles of good practice that are effective in creating and maintaining high standards of behavior in a school and these can be applied to the school library. These principles will contribute to the whole-school discipline policy, the school ethos, and classroom management skills, including reinforcement skills.

Approaches to discipline

The librarian should consider which approach to discipline is best. There are several to bear in mind:

A pupil-centered approach which assumes that disruptive behavior is a response to an inappropriate school environment.

An authoritarian teacher-dominant approach generally viewed as unworkable in a library where pupils come and go relatively freely. It is a method that would be used only if pupils or equipment were endangered.

An analytical approach usually found to be impractical in the school library because the librarian serves many people and is unable to devote much time to a single person. The long-term and ongoing individual attention required is impossible.

A teacher-student approach focusing on the dynamics working between teacher and pupil and calling for one-to-one discussion. This approach is again impractical in the library, for the same reasons as for an analytical approach. However, sometimes, a special rapport can develop between the librarian and a pupil.

The best approach for the librarian to adopt is the behaviorist approach, which recognizes that good behavior is a skill that can be taught. The librarian should try to look at things from the pupils' viewpoint, understanding their reasons for acting as they do. Children, like adults, have bad days and it is worth bearing in mind that, before coming to the library, pupils may have come from a lesson in which they have had to sit extremely quietly and now feel the need to be more active.

Reinforcement skills

Rules and consequences. Life is filled with demands and rules of all kinds and every person has to be responsible for his or her behavior in relation to those rules. Pupils need rules and regulations to help them behave until they are mature enough to establish behavior patterns of their own. The school library is no exception. A planned and predictable system of rules and consequences, together with generous use of praise and rewards, encourages pupils to use the library appropriately. Rules should be simple, consistent, few in number, contribute to the goals of the library, and always be worth enforcing. As far as possible they should be expressed in positive terms and be statements of pupils' responsibilities, explaining what pupils are expected to do rather than what they ought not to do.

Rewards and sanctions. The positive, lasting impact of rewards and privileges for good behavior outweigh sanctions applied for bad behavior. Pupils become more motivated and achieve more when their successes are rewarded rather than when the focus is on their failures and shortcomings. Flexibility is necessary in the way in which praise is given. Praise can be delivered in both formal and informal ways, in public or in private, awarded to individuals or to groups, and earned for steady maintenance of good standards as well as for particular achievements.

Having a choice of consequences ensures that librarians can be flexible when dealing with a particular situation, so retaining their credibility and consistency. Ideally, pupils should experience the consequences of their misbehavior and be made aware of alternative, acceptable behavior.

It is always tempting to respond to misbehavior by using detention or banning pupils from the library. However, neither method is effective in changing problem behavior. Detention is invariably ineffective because the inevitable time lapse breaks the link between the bad behavior and the punishment. If the library is seen as a pleasant and important place, pupils may see withdrawal of this privilege as a punishment but will not easily learn why their behavior was unacceptable. Using the library should always be sought after and penalties for loss should be well publicized so that students aren't surprised when rules, particularly behavior rules, are broken.

SOURCE: Adapted from Siân Spink, "Good Behaviour: How School Librarians Can Reap If They Sow," *The School Librarian* 48, no. 4 (Winter 2000): 175–176, 182. First published in *The School Librarian,* journal of The School Library Association (UK and Ireland). Copyright 2000. To learn more about The School Library Association, go to http://www.sla.org.uk.

The school shooter:
A threat assessment

by Mary Ellen O'Toole

The intervention process

A school cannot ignore any threat of violence. Plausible or not, every threat must be taken seriously, investigated, and responded to. A clear, vigorous response is essential for three reasons: first and most important, to make sure that students, teachers, and staff *are* safe (that is, that a threat will not be carried out); second, to assure that they will *feel safe*; and third, to assure that the person making the threat will be supervised and given the treatment that is appropriate and necessary to avoid future danger to others or himself.

The following discussion focuses on two specific issues: (1) the need for schools to adopt a well-thought-out system for responding to threats, and (2) guidelines for the role of law enforcement agencies in the threat-response process.

Threat management in schools

A clear, consistent, rational, and well-structured system for dealing with threats is vitally important in a school. If students or staff feel that threats are not addressed quickly and sensibly, or if school administrators appear overwhelmed and uncertain at every threat, confidence in the school's ability to maintain a safe environment will be seriously undermined. This in turn can seriously disrupt the school's educational program.

An effective threat management system will include a standardized method for evaluating threats, and consistent policies for responding to them. A standardized approach will help schools construct a database, with information on the types and frequency of threats, which may help evaluate the effectiveness of school policies. Consistency in threat response can deter future threats if students perceive that any threat will be reported, investigated, and dealt with firmly.

Here are some guidelines for establishing and implementing a threat management system:

Inform students and parents of school policies. A school should publicize its threat response and intervention program at the beginning of every school year (or to new students when they transfer into the school). The school should clearly explain what is expected of students—for example, students who know about a threat are expected to inform school authorities. The school should also make clear to parents that if their child makes a threat of any kind, they will be contacted and will be expected to provide information to help evaluate the threat.

Designate a threat assessment coordinator. One person in a school—or perhaps several in a large school—should be assigned to oversee and coordinate the school's response to all threats. The designated coordinator may be the principal, another administrator, a school psychologist, a resource officer, or any other staff member. The school should find appropriate threat assessment training programs for whoever is designated.

When any threat is made, whoever receives it or first becomes aware of it should refer it immediately to the designated coordinator, and school policy should explicitly give the coordinator the necessary authority to make or assist in making quick decisions on how to respond—including implementing the school's emergency response plan, if the threat warrants.

The coordinator's specific responsibilities will be determined in each school, in accord with the professional judgment of the principal and administrative staff. They could include: arranging for an initial assessment when a threat is received to determine the level of threat; conducting or overseeing an evaluation after the threatener is identified, using the Four-Pronged Assessment Model [see below]; developing and refining the threat management system; monitoring intervention in previous cases; establishing liaison with other school staff and outside experts; and maintaining consistency and continuity in the school's threat response procedures.

Consider forming a multidisciplinary team. As well as appointing a threat assessment coordinator, schools may decide to establish a multidisciplinary team as another component of the threat assessment system. Schools could draw team members from school staff and other professionals, including trained mental health professionals. The team would constitute an experienced, knowledgeable group that could review threats, consult with outside experts, and provide recommendations and advice to the coordinator and to the school administration. *It is strongly recommended that a law enforcement representative should either be included as a member of the team or regularly consulted as a resource person.* Making threats can be a criminal offense, depending on the threat and the laws of each state. Although most school threats may not lead to prosecution, school officials need informed, professional advice on when a criminal violation has occurred and what actions may be required by state or local laws.

The Four-Pronged Assessment Model

This innovative model is designed to assess someone who has made a threat and evaluate the likelihood that the threat will actually be carried out. Anyone can deliver a spoken or written message that sounds foreboding or sinister, but evaluating the threat alone will not establish if the person making it has the intention, the ability, or the means to act on the threat. To make that determination, assessing the threatener is critical.

Educators, law enforcement, mental health professionals, and others must realize they cannot handle threats in the same "old" way. Those tasked with assessing threats must be trained in the basic concepts of threat assessment, personality assessment, and risk assessment as presented in this monograph, and realize the importance of assessing all threats in a timely manner.

What information about students can help us tell which threateners are likely to carry out their threats? Their age? Their grades in chemistry class? Their socioeconomic level? The experience of the FBI's National Center for the Analysis of Violent Crime is that frequently, only limited information is known about someone being evaluated for threat assessment, or information may be available only in certain areas—a student's academic record, or family life, or health. All aspects of a threatener's life must be considered when evaluating whether a threat is likely to be carried out. This model provides a framework for evaluating a student in order to determine if he or she has the motivation, means, and intent to carry out a proclaimed threat. The assessment is based on the "totality of the circumstances" known about the student in four major areas:

Prong One: Personality of the student
Prong Two: Family dynamics
Prong Three: School dynamics and the student's role in those dynamics
Prong Four: Social dynamics

Here is how the Four-Pronged Assessment Model can be used when a threat is received at a school: A preliminary assessment is done on the threat itself. If the threatener's identity is known, a threat assessor quickly collects as much information as is available in the four categories. The assessor may be a school psychologist, counselor, or other staff member or specialist who has been designated and trained for this task. Information can come from the assessor's personal knowledge of the student or can be sought from teachers, staff, other students (when appropriate), parents, and other appropriate sources such as law enforcement agencies or mental health specialists.

If the student appears to have serious problems in the majority of the four prongs or areas and if the threat is assessed as high or medium level, the threat should be taken more seriously and appropriate intervention by school authorities and/or law enforcement should be initiated as quickly as possible.

In order to effect a rapid assessment, it may not be possible to evaluate a student thoroughly in each of the four prongs. Nonetheless, having as much information as possible about a student and his or her life is important in order to determine if that student is capable and under enough stressors to carry out a threat.

The following section outlines factors to be considered in each of the four prongs.

Personality of the student: Behavior characteristics and traits. According to Webster's, personality is "the pattern of collective character, behavioral, temperamental, emotional, and mental traits of an individual." This pattern is a product of both inherited temperament and environmental influences. Personality shapes how people consistently view the world and themselves and how they interact with others. Forming an accurate impression of someone's personality requires observing his or her behavior over a period of time and in a wide variety of situations.

Understanding adolescent personality development is extremely important in assessing any threat made by someone in that age group. An adolescent's personality is not yet crystallized. It is still developing. During adolescence, young people are likely to explore or engage in what others perceive as strange behavior. Adolescents struggle with vulnerability and acceptance ("Am I lovable and able to love?"), with questions of independence and dependence, and with how to deal with authority, among other difficult issues.

Clues to a student's personality can come from observing behavior when the student is:

coping with conflicts, disappointments, failures, insults, or other stresses encountered in everyday life

expressing anger or rage, frustration, disappointment, humiliation, sadness, or similar feelings

demonstrating or failing to demonstrate resiliency after a setback, a failure, real or perceived criticism, disappointment, or other negative experiences

demonstrating how the student feels about himself or herself, what kind of person the student imagines himself or herself to be, and how the student believes he or she appears to others

responding to rules, instruction, or authority figures

demonstrating and expressing a desire or need for control, attention, respect, admiration, confrontation, or other needs

demonstrating or failing to demonstrate empathy with the feelings and experiences of others

demonstrating his or her attitude toward others (for example, does the student view others as inferior or with disrespect?)

Assessors who have not been able to observe a student firsthand should seek information from those who knew the student before he or she made a threat.

Family dynamics. Family dynamics are patterns of behavior, thinking, beliefs, traditions, roles, customs, and values that exist in a family. When a student has made a threat, knowledge of the dynamics within the student's family—and how those dynamics are perceived by both the student and the parents—is a key factor in understanding circumstances and stresses in the student's life that could play a role in any decision to carry out the threat.

School dynamics. The relationship between school dynamics and threat assessment has not been empirically established and therefore its level of significance can either increase or decrease depending on additional research into these cases. *While it may be difficult for educators/assessors to "critique" their own school, it is necessary to have some level of understanding of the particular dynamics in their school because their school can ultimately become the scene of the crime.*

School dynamics are patterns of behavior, thinking, beliefs, customs, traditions, roles, and values that exist in a school's culture. Some of these patterns can be obvious, and others subtle. Identifying those behaviors which are formally or informally valued and rewarded in a school helps explain why some students get more approval and attention from school authorities and have more prestige among their fellow students. It can also explain the "role" a particular student is given by the school's culture, and how the student may see himself or herself fitting in, or failing to fit in, with the school's value system.

Students and staff may have very different perceptions of the culture, customs, and values in their school. Assessors need to be aware of how a school's dynamics are seen by students. A big discrepancy between students' perceptions and the administration's can itself be a significant piece of information for the assessor.

Social dynamics. Social dynamics are patterns of behavior, thinking, beliefs, customs, traditions, and roles that exist in the larger community where students live. These patterns also have an impact on students' behavior, their feelings about themselves, their outlook on life, attitudes, perceived options, and lifestyle practices. An adolescent's beliefs and opinions, his choices of friends, activities, entertainment, and reading material, and his attitudes toward such things as drugs, alcohol, and weapons will all reflect in some fashion the social dynamics of the community where he lives and goes to school.

Within the larger community, an adolescent's peer group plays an especially crucial role in influencing attitudes and behavior. Information about a student's choice of friends and relations with his peers can provide valuable clues to his attitudes, sense of identity, and possible decisions about acting or not acting on a threat.

SOURCE: Adapted from Mary Ellen O'Toole, *The School Shooter: A Threat Assessment Perspective* (Quantico, Va.: Critical Incident Response Group, National Center for the Analysis of Violent Crime, FBI Academy [2000]).

State school safety centers

[*Ed. note:* Starred states have school safety centers.]

California Safe Schools and Violence Prevention Office
California Department of Education
1430 N Street
Sacramento, CA 95814
Phone: (916) 319-0800
http://www.cde.ca.gov/ls/ss/

Colorado Center for the Study and Prevention of Violence
Institute of Behavior Science
University of Colorado at Boulder
439 UCB
Boulder, CO 80309-0439
Phone: (303) 492-8465
Fax: (303) 443-3297
http://www.colorado.edu/cspv/safeschools/

Connecticut Safe Schools and Communities Coalition (SSCC)
30 Arbor Street
Hartford, CT 06106
Phone: (860) 523-8042
Fax: (860) 236-9412
http://www.preventionworksct.org/sscc_home.html

Office of Safe and Healthy Schools
Florida Department of Education
325 W. Gaines Street, Room 301
Tallahassee, FL 32399-0400
Phone: (850) 245-0416
Fax: (850) 245-9978
http://www.firn.edu/doe/besss/safehome.htm

8

School Safety Project
Georgia Emergency Management Agency
P.O. Box 18055
Augusta, GA 30316-0055
Phone: (404) 635-7000
Fax: (404) 635-7205
http://www2.state.ga.us/GEMA/

Indiana School Safety Specialist Academy
Indiana Department of Education
Room 229 State House
Indianapolis, IN 46204-2798
Phone: (317) 234-0326
Fax: (317) 232-9140
http://doe.state.in.us/isssa/

Kentucky Center for School Safety (CSS)
Eastern Kentucky University
105 Stratton Building, 521 Lancaster Drive
Richmond, KY 40475-3102
Phone: (877) 805-4277
http://www.kysafeschools.org

Mississippi Department of Education
Office of Safe and Orderly Schools
P.O. Box 771
Jackson, MS 39205-0771
Phone: (601) 359-1028
Fax: (601) 359-3184
http://www.mde.k12.ms.us/lead/osos/

Missouri Center for Safe Schools
University of Missouri, Kansas City
5100 Rockhill Road
Kansas City, MO 64110-2499
Phone: (816) 235-5656
Fax: (816) 235-5270
http://www.umkc.edu/education/safe-school/

Missouri Safe Schools—Newsletter of the Missouri Center for Safe Schools
http://www.umkc.edu/safe-school/newsletter/index.asp

Nebraska School Safety Center
Nebraska Department of Education
301 Centennial Mall South
Lincoln, NE 68509-4987
Phone: (402) 471-1925
Fax: (402) 471-8127
http://www.nde.state.ne.us/safety/

New York State Center for School Safety
175 Route 32 North
New Paltz, NY 12561
Phone: (845) 255-8989
Fax: (845) 255-3836
http://int11.mhrcc.org/scss/

North Carolina Center for the Prevention of School Violence
North Carolina Department of Juvenile Justice and Delinquency
    Prevention
1801 Mail Service Center
Raleigh, NC 27699-1801
Phone: (800) 299-6054; (919) 733-3388, ext. 332
http://www.ncdjjdp.org/cpsv/

Ohio Resource Network for Safe and Drug Free Schools and Communities
P.O. Box 210109
Cincinnati, OH 45221-0109
Phone: (800) 788-7254 (opt #2); (513) 556-0782
Fax: (513) 556-3764
http://www.ebasedprevention.org

Oregon State School Safety Center
Institute on Violence and Destructive Behavior
University of Oregon
1265 University of Oregon
Eugene, OR 97403-1265
Phone: (541) 346-3592
Fax: (541) 346-2594
http://www.uoregon.edu/~ivdb/

8

Pennsylvania Center for Safe Schools
275 Grandview Avenue, Suite 200
Camp Hill, PA 17011
Phone: (717) 763-1661
Fax: (717) 763-2083
http://www.center-school.org/viol_prev/css/index.html

South Carolina Office of Safe Schools and Youth Services
South Carolina Department of Education
1429 Senate Street, Room 606
Columbia, SC 29201
Phone: (803) 734-8402
Fax: (803) 734-4458
http://www.myscschools.com/offices/ssys/

Tennessee School Safety Center

Tennessee Department of Education
7th Floor, Andrew Johnson Tower
710 James Robertson Parkway
Nashville, TN 37243-0375
Phone: (615) 741-3248
Fax: (615) 741-6638
http://www.state.tn.us/education/sp/sptscc.htm

Texas School Safety Center

Texas State University–San Marcos
601 University Drive, Suite 309
San Marcos, TX 78666
Phone: (512) 245-3696
Fax: (512) 245-9033
http://cscs.txstate.edu/TxSSC/default.html

Texas School Safety Center Newsletter
http://cscs.txstate.edu/TxSSC/newsletter.htm

Virginia Center for School Safety

c/o Department of Criminal Justice Services
805 East Broad Street, 10th Floor
Richmond, VA 23219
Phone: (804) 786-7684
http://www.dcjs.virginia.gov/vcss/index.cfm

Washington State School Safety Center

Office of Superintendent of Public Instruction
Old Capitol Building
P.O. Box 47200
Olympia, WA 98504-7200
Phone: (360) 725-6000
http://www.k12.wa.us/Safetycenter/

SOURCE: Much of this information is from "The SafetyZone," Northwest Regional Educational Laboratory's listing of state school safety centers at http://www.safetyzone.org/state_centers.html, current as of August 28, 2004. The authors acknowledge the speed with which URLs may change.

PROGRAM
CHAPTER NINE

For some students, and in certain schools this may be many students, the only library skill that they should have to acquire is an awareness, imprinted indelibly and happily upon them, that the library is a friendly place where the librarians are eager to help.

SOURCE: Adapted from Frances Henne, "Learning to Learn in School Libraries," *School Libraries* 15, no. 4 (May 1966): 17. Copyright 1966.

Information power

Principle 5 of *Information Power* states, "Comprehensive and collaborative long-range, strategic planning is essential to the effectiveness of the library media program."

Goals for the school library media specialist

1. Establish program planning as a priority and devote adequate time and resources to this process on an ongoing basis.
2. Participate on committees charged with developing and implementing long-range, strategic plans for the school (such as teams for site-based management, school improvement, technology planning, and curriculum development).
3. Work regularly with teachers, students, administrators, and other members of the learning community to develop and implement long-term, strategic plans that align the library media program and the information literacy standards for student learning with the school's goals, priorities, and national curriculum standards.
4. Create plans for the library media program that

   define the program's mission and goals and give direction to the allocation, organization, and management of human, physical, and financial resources

   shape the roles and responsibilities of all program staff and focus attention on program effectiveness and accountability

   accommodate changes in such critical areas as the nature of the school's population and the development and availability of new resources and technologies

SOURCE: From "Program Administration," chapter 6 in *Information Power: Building Partnerships for Learning* (Chicago: American Library Association, 1998), 106–108.

Biggest challenges for 2002, 2003, and 2004

by Kathy Ishizuka, Walter Minkel, Evan St. Lifer, and Debra Lau Whelan

2002: If you were to weigh all the aspects of your job, which would you choose as most critical to your short- and long-term success? To which pressing issues do you need to commit the most time and attention? The *School Library Journal* staff decided to help elucidate, and confirm, the front-burner issues for those professionals who provide library service to children and young adults. We observed, we listened, and we interviewed the profession, and then we took our findings and argued amongst ourselves. From that process, we distilled five themes that represent the profession's overriding challenges for 2002:

> educating individuals higher up in the food chain;
> making information literacy a higher priority among teachers and an essential, required research skill for students;
> stanching the flow of retiring librarians by using innovative methods to recruit new blood;
> managing effectively the challenge of accessing information despite a filtered information environment;
> dealing with sometimes unpredictable fiscal hardships due to a sagging economy.

2003: The biggest challenges for 2003 are how to partner with your principal, staying on top of technology, managing time effectively, recruiting qualified librarians, getting behind literacy efforts, and taking an advocacy stance.

2004: Making it through 2004 will mean school librarians must learn how to be effective, frontline players in the president's plan to improve literacy skills among our nation's children. The public libraries' influence on students will continue to rise, essential research on the librarian's impact on student achievement will continue, and the number of nonfiction series titles will continue to proliferate.

For the future, it would be wise to determine if the challenges for 2002, 2003, and 2004 have been met, or should even greater effort be made to solve the problems. Further, it would also be interesting to see if today's predictions are tomorrow's challenges for 2005.

SOURCE: Adapted from Kathy Ishizuka, Walter Minkel, and Evan St. Lifer, "Biggest Challenges for 2002," *School Library Journal* 48 (January 2002): 50–53; Debra Lau Whelan, "Greatest Challenges for 2003," *School Library Journal* 49 (January 2003): 48–50; and Evan St. Lifer, "What's in Store for 2004," *School Library Journal* 50 (January 2004): 13. Courtesy of *School Library Journal.*

Taking the lead in developing learning communities

by Violet H. Harada

The current landscape of educational reform, according to Deborah King, places enormous demands on instructional leaders "to function in a constantly changing environment and to serve students with greater and more diverse needs than ever before." Regardless of the specific type of reform, the bottom line is that we must reexamine what is worth learning and how we assess that learning. The paradigm shifts reflect a minimization of superficial and isolated learning experiences and a demonstration of each student's understanding of interdisciplinary concepts, principles, and processes. Reform scholars also challenge schools to connect such activities as forming grade-level teams and common preparation periods with the actual learning of both adults and students. Richard E. Elmore believes that without an understanding of how these practices link with student performance, these measures become largely symbolic activities that do not succeed because the people in the organization are clueless about why they are doing them.

Especially daunting, as well as exciting, is the fact that this reform effort is occurring in a millennium that David Thornburg describes as a "digital tornado of epic proportions." The advancements in communications technology have made globalization possible in every aspect of our lives. According to Jean Donham, an explosion of information and advances in instructional and information technologies indeed characterize the increasing complexity of learning reform.

Within this context, one fact becomes increasingly clear: the traditional model of classroom teachers working alone is no longer effective. Lifelong learning that includes the ability to make intelligent and responsible decisions about the quality of our lives and about society's well-being is inextricably linked to establishing communities where learning occurs for everyone. Problem solving and decision making, whether it involves a young child's learning experience or a teacher's pedagogical practice, are more effectively handled as dynamic, social exchanges. In short, learning at all levels is a social experience.

This article posits the importance of fostering learning communities in today's school reform movement and the potential role of the school library media specialist (SLMS) as a leader in building these collaborative networks.

Learning communities

Central to this concept of social learning is the notion of learning communities. Richard DuFour and Robert Eaker assert that such communities must foster mutual cooperation, emotional support, and personal growth as people work together to achieve what they cannot accomplish alone. Current research findings, as reported by Fred M. Newmann and Gary G. Wehlage, indicate that schools functioning as learning communities produce higher levels of student learning.

The establishment of collaborative relationships forms the bedrock for flourishing learning communities. Members must operate in networks of shared and complementary expertise. They must be encouraged to develop their own skills and contribute to the development of others' knowledge and skills.

In such communities, educators realize the power of teams. Teachers create informal study groups. Administrators provide planning and resource support. SLMSs and counselors are part of curricular development teams. Schools converse with other schools on related projects and issues. Teams connect with community agencies and organizations, including public libraries, universities, and businesses. They also reach out to district, state, national, and even international agencies for information and assistance.

Significance of collaboration

The ability to interact smoothly with others and to work together with one or more persons to achieve a goal is flagged as an essential skill in the North Central Regional Educational Laboratory's (NCREL) Twenty-First-Century Skills. NCREL elaborates:

> Successful collaboration is dependent on the individual's and group's ability to devise a strategy to divide a task into pieces based on the strengths of the individuals, yet ensure that each has a clear sense of the entire project in order to understand the expectations for the component pieces.

Ray Doiron believes that building consensus is at the core of successful collaborative initiatives. Rather than focusing only on short-term effects, teams must work on long-term results. In this process, curriculum must be viewed as holistic and dynamic rather than as static and linear. Figure 1 captures the salient features of collaborative learning communities and compares them with notions of traditional schooling.

Figure 1. Comparing Traditional and Collaborative Models

Traditional	Collaborative
Curriculum is fragmented.	Curriculum is integrated.
Learning focuses on isolated fact-gathering.	Learning embraces problem solving and decisions.
Textbooks are primary tools in the classroom.	Learning tools are varied and globally accessed.
Teachers work independently.	Teachers collaborate.
Environment is competitive and controlled.	Environment nurtures social interaction and consensus.

Collaboration and school library media centers

How does the notion of collaboration relate to the school library media center? *Information Power* states that in this digital information age, all of us are "interconnected in a lifelong quest to understand and meet our constantly changing information needs." The document further elaborates that merging current learning and information theories requires new communities that are "not limited by time, place, age, occupation, or disciplinary borders but [are] linked by interest, need, and a growing array of telecommunications technology." It identifies collaboration as one of the major building blocks for quality learning networks.

Other publications, such as David Loertscher's widely used taxonomy (see figure 2), flesh out the degrees and levels of collaborative involvement specific to school library media centers. At levels 1 through 3 of his taxonomy, there is little or no contact between the classroom teacher and the SLMS. The media center is a place divorced from the classroom and the teacher is an

---

Figure 2. The School Library Media Specialist's Taxonomy

---

10. Curriculum development. Along with the other educators, the library media specialist contributes to the planning and organization of what will actually be taught in the school or district.

9. The mature school library media center program. The school library media center program reaches the needs of every student and teacher who will accept its offerings in each of the four programmatic elements.

8. Implementation of the four major programmatic elements of the school library media center program. The four school library media center program elements—collaboration, reading literacy, enhancing learning through technology, and information literacy—are operational in the school. The school library media center is on its way to achieving its goal of contributing to academic achievement.

7. Evangelistic outreach and advocacy. A concerted effort is made to promote the philosophy of the school library media center program.

6. Planned gathering. Gathering of materials/access to important digital resources is done in advance of a class project upon teacher or student request.

5. Cursory planning. There is informal and brief planning with teachers and students for school library media center facilities or network use—usually done through casual contact in the school library media center, in the hall, in the teacher's lounge, in the lunchroom, or by e-mail.

4. Spontaneous interaction and gathering. Networks respond 24 hours a day and seven days a week to patron requests, and the school library media center facilities can be used by individuals and small groups with no advance notice.

3. Individual reference assistance. The school library media specialist serves as the human interface between information systems and the user.

2. Smoothly operating information infrastructure. Facilities, materials, networks, and information resources are available for the self-starter delivered to the point of need.

1. No involvement. The school library media center is bypassed entirely.

SOURCE: Figure 2 reprinted with permission from David V. Loertscher, *Taxonomies of the School Library Media Program,* 2nd ed. (San Jose, Calif.: Hi Willow, 2000).

9

---

independent user of the facility. At levels 4 through 6, there are spontaneous and sporadic links with teachers, but these are usually limited to fulfilling their requests for resources. In other words, the touch points are largely reactive, dependent on teachers' decisions to involve the SLMS, and supplemental to the actual classroom plans. At levels 7 through 10, however, SLMSs are actively engaged in instructional planning and teaching. While they continue to work at all levels of the taxonomy, clearly the goal for SLMSs is to function more frequently at these upper levels as valued members of curriculum planning teams.

According to Jean Donham, successful collaboration is characterized by teams working together on key aspects of instructional planning and delivery. These key aspects include: identifying student needs in accessing, evaluating, interpreting, and applying information; planning how and where these skills will be taught; relating these skills to disciplinary learning; teaching in partnership so that learning takes place in a timely and integrated manner; assessing the process of learning; assessing the products or demonstrations of learning; and reflecting on the collaborative process itself.

Studies conducted by Keith Curry Lance, Marcia J. Rodney, and Christine Hamilton-Pennell in Colorado, Alaska, Texas, and Pennsylvania school districts provide important research-based support for collaborative efforts. Their findings in these states indicated that the amount of planning time between SLMSs and teachers was a "highly positive indicator for higher student test scores." In their second Colorado study, for example, the research team reported that test scores rose in both elementary and middle schools as the SLMSs and teachers worked together on curricular projects and issues.

Linking collaboration and leadership

In *Information Power*, collaboration is integrally linked with the theme of leadership. Toni Buzzeo states that this marks a profound shift from the roles SLMSs have traditionally assumed as providers of resources and services to roles that challenge them to step forward and serve as equal partners and leaders in the teaching and learning interchange. SLMSs are uniquely qualified for this pivotal position. They bring singular experiences and perspectives that make them potentially powerful contributors and leaders in establishing collaborative learning communities.

First, SLMSs are teachers who have not only the means to access and share timely research on best practices, but also the skills to teach in partnership with their colleagues. Their particular knowledge skills cut across all curriculum areas because they deal with access and evaluation of information sources, development of effective search strategies, and applications of technology to information needs.

Second, they have always championed relevant and responsible uses of various information technologies. Books and more traditional forms of information remain critical sources; however, SLMSs have introduced their school communities to a rich array of new resources, including software programs and tools. Importantly, they have frequently served as trainers of other teachers in Internet use.

Third, they have the advantage of serving the entire school community. Donham suggests that by working with other teachers, SLMSs can share their understanding of the total system and help expand a collective view of how students function best in the context of their total school experience.

Finally, SLMSs are able to function both as participants and as observers on these teams. Donham describes them as being both "insiders" serving as members of the planning groups and as "outsiders" asking "naïve questions that encourage deliberation among teachers." They function as catalysts for thoughtful and introspective inquiry into effective teaching practices. This latter role encourages all team members to clarify their own thinking as they strive for more precise communication of ideas.

Assuming leadership also means honing skills that are aligned with three major phases of group development, including the initiation, facilitation, and sustenance of collaborative initiatives. The remainder of the article briefly describes leadership actions needed during each of these phases. Figure 3 renders a visual summary of these actions.

Initiating actions

Collaborative groups normally involve small numbers of people with complementary skills. According to Donham, this means that various members are

---

Figure 3. Developing Collaborative Teams

Initiating actions
  Agree on goals
  Connect goals with school's vision
  Invite full participation
  Build trust
  Collect baseline data for assessment
Facilitating actions
  Establish operating rules
  Maintain focus
  Document progress
  Capitalize on strengths
  Encourage open communication

Sustaining actions
  Ask probing questions
  Make reflection integral to the
    improvement process
  Expand the network
  Develop the abilities of all members

Note: The author also created a reference list of research and writings published over the last decade titled "Collaboration: Nuggets from Research and Writings" for an AASL preconference at the 2002 American Library Association Conference in Atlanta.

---

proficient at different aspects of the team's work. For example, one member in a project development team might have strong content area knowledge, another might have access to a range of relevant information resources, a third may have technological know-how, and a fourth may be adept at managing people and time. It is important to note that the tasks are not always evenly divided among all members. Karen Muronaga and Violet H. Harada suggest that division depends on the talents and expertise needed at any given time. Orchestration of these various talents capitalizes on the synergy of the group.

Collective motivation will not happen unless there is buy-in from all group members. They must share the same broader vision and reach consensus regarding the group's major goals. An initiator helps a team see how its work fits into the total school picture. For this to occur, people must participate equally in decisions. For example, a high school in Hawaii developed a junior research project that involved the English, social studies, and fine arts departments. The SLMSs who coordinated the effort helped the faculty members to articulate a common goal consonant with the school vision—to increase student proficiencies in reading and writing. This was achieved in several meetings where all members shared their expectations for students and examined each area's content standards. Priorities were established by mutual agreement before project planning commenced.

At this initial stage of group development, Ken Haycock indicates that fostering a feeling of mutual respect is essential. A handbook of the American Planning Association states that trust is the "fundamental glue" that holds these relationships together. Because teachers have traditionally been independent operators within their classrooms, it is no surprise that they often approach invitations to collaborate with hesitation and even trepidation. Trust-building begins with individuals knowing something of each other's personal histories before they are willing to take risks in a team and tackle inevitable disagreements. This involves getting to know one another as people with different experiences and working styles. To encourage camaraderie and to build a comfortable environment, leaders must exercise active listening and careful observation of individual and group behaviors. Rather than allowing team members to dwell on individual weaknesses, leaders focus on strengths of people and capitalize on what members *can* do.

Assessment is an integral aspect of curriculum work; therefore, the group must start a baseline profile to measure the desired outcomes. Pre- and post-test examinations are not the only means of gathering this data. Alternative assessment techniques, including journal entries, observation checklists, questionnaires, and rubrics, might be considered. For example, to assess what students already know about the information search process before embarking on a series of research assignments, an SLMS and a teacher might ask students to write a journal entry predicting the steps they would take to complete a research project. At the end of the semester, students would then compose another entry describing the steps they actually took in completing their research assignments.

Facilitating growth

Every team needs a facilitator. An effective facilitator helps a group set its expectations, plans meeting agendas with input from the team, and arranges for some kind of reporting or documentation of sessions. He or she continues to remind the team of its overall target goals, which can get easily lost in the forest of immediate details.

Much as building a house requires a sturdy foundation, forming collaborative communities necessitates structural guidelines that ensure continuing group effectiveness. Establishing ground rules for group operations includes identifying mutually agreed upon individual and team responsibilities and timelines. Edie L. Holcomb indicates that interaction within groups must also be sensitive and tactful. Her tips for group interaction include: pose questions using nonthreatening language; ensure that all members are heard; constantly clarify terms by paraphrasing and asking probing questions; keep the discussion focused; and remain open and flexible.

Sustaining change

For long-term sustainability, leaders must establish analysis and reflection as indispensable parts of the collaborative process. They ask hard questions about why and how things work or don't work. These include: What did we want students to gain? Did they attain the outcomes desired? Were the assessment measures valid and reliable? Did we erroneously assume that students possessed certain prerequisite skills? Were our intervention strategies effective? How might we modify or alter future experiences? Questions such as these generate professional inquiry that results in substantive improvement and ultimate empowerment. According to Linda Wolcott, by engaging in this form of self-examination, team members learn more about themselves and others as teachers and as learners. Leaders play an essential role in the team by helping the team get a clearer and deeper picture of the major target; checking assumptions; bringing resources and networks to the group; getting others involved; and developing the abilities of all team members.

Maintaining communication becomes a vital component of sustainable communities. For busy school practitioners who are concerned about lack of planning time, Marjorie L. Pappas and Ann E. Tepe suggest that technology might provide partial solutions. E-mail, electronic discussion groups, and threaded discussions can save time spent in face-to-face meetings. Bookmarked web resources can minimize time spent searching on the Internet. Additional instructional planning tools, such as templates that permit teachers and SLMSs to collaboratively plan lessons online, allow for asynchronous dialogue.

Conclusion

Collaborating on student learning experiences produces a richness and depth that teachers and SLMSs cannot achieve alone. Working together also promotes reflective insights into the team's individual and collective professional skills. Collaboration becomes a generative process. As Gail Bush explains, "The collaborative experience then serves to further strengthen those aspects of our professional identities that we value and we find ourselves seeking future partnership and collaborative efforts that reflect these strengths."

Harada indicates this was certainly the case for teachers and SLMSs who participated in a recent Hawaii partnerships project. By planning together, they identified new strategies to improve their teaching, increase student involvement, strengthen their own disciplinary knowledge, develop more precise assessments, and cultivate broader community support. They also discovered a fresh appreciation and respect for the diverse talents and skills of individual members.

To assume a visible and vital role in developing learning communities, SLMSs must move beyond the service role of the profession to one of instructional leadership. Collaborative communities require thoughtful nurturing and caring support. Are SLMSs ready for this challenge?

SOURCE: Adapted from Violet H. Harada, "Taking the Lead in Developing Learning Communities," *Knowledge Quest* 31, no. 2 (November/December 2002): 12–16.

9

Implementing change: What school library media specialists should know

by Sandra Hughes-Hassell

Implementing change is difficult and school library media specialists often find themselves overwhelmed by the magnitude and complexity of the process. Fortunately, there is a growing body of research in the education field about the multidimensional nature of the change process, the factors that facilitate or impede change, and the importance of change agents to successful change efforts. School library media specialists can gain insight from this research—insight they can use to develop and implement learning-centered library programs.

A school library media specialist's efforts implement a learning-centered library program with an understanding of educational change that can facilitate the change process. A list of practical ideas for implementing *Information Power: Building Partnerships for Learning* is suggested.

Planned educational change

Planned educational change has been the topic of many research studies during the last 20 years. Six theories or perspectives of educational change have emerged from these studies: the technological, the political, the cultural, the psychological, the environmental, and the structural. Researchers have used all six theories to understand educational change; however, empirical data suggest that no one theory fully explains the change process. Instead, as Sheila Rosenblum and K. S. Louis point out, change in complex organizations, such as school systems, is a multidimensional process, and each of the six theories highlights an important aspect of the change process:

- Change alters and is altered by the attitudes and skills of individuals (psychological dimension).
- Change alters and is altered by the culture of the school (cultural dimension).
- Change attracts and stimulates conflict and exchange of power (political dimension).
- Change involves changes in skills, materials, and methods (technological dimension).
- Change requires modification of structural elements (structural dimension).
- Change efforts are affected by the larger social context (environmental dimension).

Michael G. Fullan and Suzanne M. Stiegelbauer have drawn on these six theories to develop a multidimensional theory or model of educational change. The key elements of the model include:

Advocacy groups. Educational change never occurs without advocates. All major research on innovation and school effectiveness shows that support from principals strongly influences the likelihood of change. Principals' actions serve to legitimate the change. When principals understand an innovation, they are more able to understand teacher concerns and provide teachers with the psychological and professional support they need to implement it.

Power sharing. Change efforts are most successful when teachers are empowered. This means including them in the selection of innovations, giving them opportunities to define change, allowing them to alter innovations to fit the needs of the school, and permitting them to help plan how an innovation will be implemented.

Support. Ongoing, purposeful staff development is critical to the successful implementation of an innovation. The most appropriate staff development activities build a collaborative work culture that allows teachers to feel comfortable taking risks and provides them with psychological and professional support throughout the change process.

Vision building. In order for change efforts to be successful, a shared and sharable vision of how the school will look with the innovation in place must be developed. Creating a shared vision provides the drive, direction, motivation, and excitement for change.

Evolutionary planning. Successful change efforts are sensitive to the culture of the school. School improvement is not just based on what teachers think or do, but also on what goes on around them. Educational leaders must be responsive to the setting or culture in which an innovation is implemented.

Monitoring and problem solving. Monitoring the implementation process and actively solving problems as they arise are essential to successful change. Monitoring serves three important functions: (1) it provides access to ideas; (2) it exposes ideas to scrutiny, helping weed out mistakes and further develop promising practices; and (3) it makes it possible to overcome problems with implementation. Based on the feedback, the system or school can provide additional in-service and materials or modify plans, organizational arrangements, or the innovation itself.

Restructuring. Educational leaders must alter the structure of the school to include activities that have been shown to lead to successful innovation (e.g., team planning, shared decision making, collaborative work environments, and mentors or coaches).

Evaluating the innovation. Before educational leaders adopt an innovation, they must make sure the innovation is worthy of being adopted and implemented, meets the needs of the local school, and has proven benefits. The goals of the innovation must be clear so teachers will know how it will affect them personally and what change it will cause in their current teaching practice.

Change agent theory

Theorists, researchers, and practitioners generally recognize that change agents play a critical role in the successful initiation, implementation, and continuation of planned educational change. In a school system, the school board, superintendent, assistant superintendent, district-level coordinator, principal, assistant principal, or individual teacher can act as a local or internal agent of change. School systems also may recruit external change agents, or consultants, to help facilitate the change process. According to Lyle E. Schaller, "in one manner or another everyone is an agent of change. Some people are passive agents of change, and others are negative agents of change, and in increasing numbers some are becoming affirmative agents of change." Whether acting positively or negatively, change agents, both internal and external, attempt to influence the change process.

9

Roles of change agents

Depending on the school and classroom context, Charles F. Grossner, John T. Shirk, Ronald G. Havelock and Steven Zlotolow, and Everett M. Rogers and F. Floyd Shoemaker report change agents may act as one or more of the following:

Enablers who facilitate efforts, stimulate insight, and provide encouragement.
Catalysts who seek to prod and pressure the organization to make changes.
Solution givers who help the organization adopt a suggested solution.
Process helpers who help diagnose and set objectives, link the user to the appropriate resource systems, select or create solutions, adopt solutions, and evaluate results.
Stimulators/innovators who "exhibit a free-wheeling style involving many interorganizational linkages," and prod the organization to accept more effective approaches.
Resource linkers who bring together many resources that enable the system to become more functional.
Brokers who negotiate a network of social institutions for the organization interested in making change. Brokers "consummate the deal."

Gatekeepers who, seeking not to disrupt the status quo, control the flow of information into the system.

Social interactionists who are concerned with the process of innovation diffusion. In this role change agents are concerned with identifying and understanding which innovations will diffuse freely, and identifying and encouraging natural networks within the organization.

Advocates who take sides to effect change.

According to Fullan and Stiegelbauer, regardless of the role that change agents assume, their goal is to "fill the gaps in expertise and to assist in charting and implementing the courses of action." Assistance by change agents contributes to the development of support, technical help, and clarity about an innovation. Matthew B. Miles and A. Michael Huberman report that it also can lead to greater mastery, confidence, and ownership.

Characteristics of change agents

While the roles change agents assume differ depending on the context of the situation, there are certain characteristics that successful change agents share. Among these are knowledge, leadership skills and abilities, attitudes, and specific personality characteristics.

Knowledge. In order to be successful, change agents must possess knowledge of the innovation. They must be familiar with the content of the new practice, its purpose, and the benefits that will result from its use. This type of knowledge can be gained through experience or study.

A second type of knowledge involves knowledge of people. According to Gene E. Hall and Susan Loucks, change agents must be sensitive to human needs and must be aware of the psychological and professional support that individuals need as they attempt to implement change.

Change agents also must have a working knowledge of the environment. They must be familiar with the organization, its practices, policies, philosophy, and objectives. Seymour B. Sarason believes they must be cognizant of both the culture, or core beliefs and values, of the specific school, and the power structure, or different factions or coalitions, that exist within that school.

Lastly, change agents must possess knowledge of the change process. Although research on the role of change agents is becoming more prevalent, studies show that the main source of learning to be a change agent is on-the-job experience. As Fullan and Stiegelbauer note, most change agents, especially internal ones, still learn their skills incidentally through trial and error.

Leadership skills and abilities. Schaller argues that effective change agents are effective leaders. They are willing and able to submerge their own role in order to concentrate on supporting and leading others who are attempting to make change. As leaders, change agents provide opportunities for power sharing. They are effective at building a collaborative work environment where teachers feel comfortable and are motivated to take risks.

As Pat E. Feehan points out, successful change agents also possess the planning skills, personnel management skills, staff development skills, and technical competence needed to be effective leaders. They work with teachers to work out "bugs" and overcome obstacles.

Attitudes. Lee Grossman asserts that successful change agents "have a positive attitude, exude confidence, and encourage participation." By using imaginative ways to demonstrate the value of change, they help motivate others to visualize how much better the organization will be when the change is adopted and put to work. They help create a positive climate that increases the likelihood that the innovation will be successfully implemented and continued.

Personality characteristics. According to Gordon Lippitt and Ronald Lippitt, while change agents must possess intellectual abilities, aptitudes, and specific skills, they also must have personality characteristics that make it possible for them to work effectively with people. Successful change agents are usually described as sincere, honest, patient, perceptive, realistic, enthusiastic, empathetic, and trustworthy. Feehan notes that they have a "magnetic" personality that draws support for ideas and motivates people to become involved in change efforts.

Translating theory into practice: A case study

In 1993, I conducted a comparative case study to describe how the implementation of whole language was affecting four elementary school library programs in central Virginia. The experiences of one of the school library media specialists I studied illustrate how understanding the nature of the change process and the role of change agents can enable school library media specialists to successfully implement a learning-centered library program.

Ellen had been the school library media specialist at her school for 14 years. Although she had instituted flexible scheduling and open access, teachers still used the media center in traditional ways and viewed Ellen as a "special." When the school district adopted whole language, Ellen, understanding how a learning-centered library program overlaps and complements whole language, began to work ardently to change how teachers and students used the library.

Ellen was successful in her efforts for several reasons. First, Ellen realized that a thorough understanding of whole language was central to her efforts. According to Ellen, "I needed training to meet the needs of my kids and my teachers." She attended whole language conferences, enrolled in a class on balanced literacy, participated in reading workshops offered by the school district, and read widely in the professional literature. She also learned from the teachers in her building. Ellen commented, "The teachers were patient and understanding about helping me, guiding me along the way. I felt comfortable asking them for help." Over time, as Ellen's principal pointed out, Ellen came to be viewed as one of the whole language "experts" in the building. She facilitated the efforts of teachers who were struggling to understand whole language and to change their practice, and she motivated teachers who already had an understanding of the philosophy to begin to use the library in different ways.

Second, Ellen recognized the need to evaluate the current library program—to identify the strengths of the program and further develop them, and to identify problems and develop strategies for overcoming them. Rather than undertake this task alone, Ellen identified and involved the influential teachers in her school in the process. She did this through formal channels (the leadership team) and informal channels (lunch discussions). Ellen worked with teachers and the principal to create a shared vision for the school library program—a vision based on student needs, changes in teaching practice (the focus on

constructivist teaching and learning and authentic assessment), and the culture of the school.

Third, Ellen focused on changing teachers' perceptions and beliefs. She understood that changing policies and procedures was not enough—she needed to help teachers see how the goals of a learning-centered library program overlapped and complemented the principles and goals of whole language. She did this by working with individual teachers or teams of teachers, providing professional development for teachers, and contributing to the leadership team. Ellen reached out to resistant teachers carefully, being sensitive to their needs and concerns. According to Ellen, "I met teachers where they were and praised them for what they were doing, yet at the same time I broadened their understanding of how the library could best meet the needs of their students."

Fourth, Ellen's success was due in part to her personality and her positive attitude toward change. Teachers described Ellen as enthusiastic, patient, realistic, and trustworthy. Ellen found change exciting: "It gives you a chance to grow." She modeled for teachers a positive response to change—she stepped outside her area of expertise and became knowledgeable about whole language, worked collaboratively with others to create a vision for the school library program, and changed her teaching practice to include more constructivist approaches to teaching. Her excitement about whole language motivated other teachers to learn more about the philosophy and change their teaching practices.

Most importantly, Ellen recognized that her work as a change agent was never done. School library media programs are organic—changing as the school library media field advances and as school systems adopt new programs, curricula, instructional strategies, and assessment techniques. Ellen noted, "There will always be new things that keep coming up and you'll never know exactly what to be prepared for. Just be ready."

The nature of change and IP2

Information Power: Building Partnerships for Learning (IP2) articulates a bold vision for school library media programs that places student learning at the center of the rationale for school library media programs. Marilyn Miller suggests that IP2 emphasizes the need for school library media specialists to "embrace collaboration as a strategy for success, demonstrate visible leadership, and step boldly into the role of technologist." Implementing the vision is challenging. Below is a list of strategies school library media specialists can use to facilitate the implementation of IP2.

1. Understand the vision described in IP2. Know its purpose and be able to explain how it will benefit students, teachers, and community members. Know the research about the link between school library media programs and student achievement.
2. Understand the school library media program's primary responsibilities. Know your own program well. Identify the principles that are the strengths of your program.
3. Gain the support of your principal through advocacy. Show how a library media program based on IP2 will help the principal achieve his or her schoolwide goals.

4. Identify the opinion leaders in your school and engage them in the decision-making process. Work with this group to create a shared vision of the school library media program, develop an implementation plan, and establish a timetable for activities. This group should become the continuing core support for all library activities.

5. Assess your ability to act as a change agent. Ask yourself:

> Do teachers and administrators view me as knowledgeable and competent?
>
> Do teachers and administrators believe I am sincere, honest, patient, empathetic, and trustworthy?
>
> Do I project a positive and confident attitude?
>
> Am I willing to engage in power sharing and allow my colleagues to help make decisions about the school library media program?
>
> Am I capable of submerging my needs and supporting others as they attempt to make change?
>
> Do I have a network in place to provide me with the psychological and professional support I'll need during the change process?

6. Work with your principal to alter the structure of the school to include team planning and collaborative teaching. Involve the opinion leaders in the decision-making process.

7. Introduce IP2 to teachers. Include the principal and key teachers in the presentation.

8. Develop strategies for supporting teachers. Provide professional development on aspects of IP2 that may be new to them—information literacy standards, collaborative planning, authentic use of technology, and flexible scheduling.

9. Model the inquiry process, authentic use of technology, and collaborative planning for teachers.

10. Be aware of other instructional and administrative changes taking place in your school. Much of the current change pressure on teachers has to do with standards, student achievement, and accountability. Identify how IP2 overlaps and complements these efforts. Show the principal and teachers how IP2 helps them address these overwhelming concerns.

11. Be patient and expect resistance. Change takes time. Teachers will need time to learn about IP2 and how it will benefit their students, to adjust to new organizational structures such as flexible scheduling, and to negotiate new roles and relationships. Don't expect everyone to change at once. Instead, implement IP2 one teacher or grade level at a time.

12. Monitor the change process. Change needs to be focused on clear goals. Through ongoing evaluation: (a) identify promising practices and further develop them; and (b) identify problems and develop strategies for overcoming them.

Conclusion

Understanding the nature of planned educational change is essential to every school library media specialist. Changes in society and technology will continue to result in substantial changes in education and school library media ns. School library media specialists who understand the nature of the process and the role of change agents will be prepared to lead in edu-...nal reform.

SOURCE: Adapted from Sandra Hughes-Hassell, "Implementing Change: What School Library Media Specialists Should Know," *Knowledge Quest* 29, no. 2 (January/February 2001): 11–15.

Making flexible access and flexible scheduling work today

by Karen Browne Ohlrich

Explaining flexible access

A definition of flexible access involves three elements: access to the library media center's space, its resources, and its services. Access to the library media program is all-inclusive. Students, staff, and even community members use these three elements of the library media center as individuals, small groups, or classes at almost any time a need arises. This means students can easily go to the library media center when necessary. The time frame of their use varies, but students and others are encouraged to sit and read, work at tables, or be taught a lesson. More than one grade level can be in the center at a time. The characteristics of flexible access include:

First, flexible access allows individuals, small groups, and classes to come into the library media center.

Second, flexible access encourages patrons to come into the school library media center at any time the building is open.

Third, flexible access encourages the library media center to be set up as a self-serve library, allowing the checking out and returning of materials at any time.

Fourth, flexible access allows library media patrons to come into the library media center and check out materials by whatever process can be devised.

Fifth, flexible access highlights the fact that a teacher, assistant, parent volunteer, community volunteer, and even the principal can bring students to the library media center.

Sixth, flexible access suggests that library media patrons can use any part of the library media center that's not in use.

Seventh, flexible access suggests that library media patrons can use any part of the library media center's resources as long as the primary purpose of serving the students is not compromised.

Eighth, flexible access highlights the services offered by the library media center and by the library media specialist.

Explaining flexible scheduling

Flexible scheduling allows the appropriate teacher or teachers to instruct students in what they need to know when they need to know it. Any combination of the scheduling variables is good if it fits the needs of the students and their learning.

First, flexible scheduling allows a class to be taught in the point of need.

Second, flexible scheduling allows a lesson of curriculum content to be taught to any combination of students in any place for any number of minutes and as many times in a week as needed.

Third, flexible scheduling supports the integration of information literacy skills into the classroom curriculum.

Fourth, flexible scheduling supports collaboration between teachers and the library media specialist.

Fifth, flexible scheduling allows a lesson to be taught by any combination of people.

Sixth, flexible scheduling encourages the more efficient use of the library media specialist's time.

SOURCE: Adapted from Karen Browne Ohlrich, *Making Flexible Access and Flexible Scheduling Work Today* (Englewood, Colo.: Libraries Unlimited, 2001), 15–16, 20.

The marriage of literacy and libraries through collaboration

by Jody K. Howard and Linda Fiorella

Collaboration . . . is possibly the best guiding principle that schools can follow to improve student achievement. But what does collaboration mean for media specialists and classroom teachers? It certainly involves more than checking out books from the media center and assigning book reports by the teacher. Meaningful collaboration comprises a multitude of topics including writing, reading achievement, and research. Children's literature is the catalyst that enhances collaboration in all of these areas.

Writing

The implementation of the Writing Assessment component of the Colorado Student Assessment Program (CSAP) for grades three through nine has schools scrambling to improve their students' writing scores. Many schools have adopted Six Trait Writing, one means of improving and assessing both writing and instruction. Six Trait Writing focuses on traits that exemplify good writing: ideas, organization, word choice, sentence fluency, voice, and conventions. A tenet of Six Traits is presenting models of the traits to students by using picture books, trade books, articles, and resource books. This provides a perfect arena for collaboration between media specialists and classroom teachers. By consciously looking for books that illustrate each trait, the media specialist can be an active partner in writing improvement. Some media specialists have arranged resource shelves containing various models exemplifying the traits. The Six Trait program emphasizes the idea of showing, not telling, and books provide the most natural means of demonstrating this idea.

For example, the classroom teacher plans a lesson to teach the students the trait of voice. The teacher and the media specialist collaborate in book

selection. The media specialist might choose to share *The Three Little Pigs* and juxtapose the story with *The True Story of the Three Little Pigs by A. Wolf as told to Jon Scieszka*. The second title is told from the wolf's point of view. While the events remain the same, the wolf's perspective gives the reader an entirely different idea of what occurred. Some students even feel sorry for the poor old wolf. This book then provides students with a model for telling their own stories using various voices.

Organization is another trait of good writing. *The Big Storm* by Bruce Hiscock is a book that provides a powerful model for organization. This scientific picture book tracks a particularly powerful storm, and in doing so, explains the weather cycle. Teachers then ask their students to write their own storm stories that illustrate their understanding of the weather cycle.

Holes by Louis Sachar models the unique organization trait. This book is wonderful to read aloud to elementary and middle school children since discussion is focused on the organization of the book. *The View from Saturday* by E. L. Konigsburg also models unique organization, with the author's use of flashbacks for character introductions. The experience of the authors, however, has been that when media specialists and teachers talk about the traits among themselves, they create the most useful lists of models from their own collections.

Research

Research . . . what a dreaded word for all involved! Students are either frustrated by their ineffective research methods, or plagiarized writing frustrates teachers. Students should be introduced to research beginning in kindergarten. Research should not be a dreaded word, but should describe a fun process. Teachers and media specialists can amplify the excitement by collaborating. Teacher and media specialist discuss how they will work together on a project about animals. They decide that beyond simply obtaining facts, the students will analyze an essential question: how is their subject animal suited to live in its natural habitat?

Now the fun begins! Teacher and media specialist make certain the students understand the question. The teacher discusses with the students the knowledge they already have, what sources they might use, and how they will proceed. Then the media specialist shows the students the various sources in the media center: books, magazines, websites, online databases, and newspapers. The media specialist has already collaborated with the teacher and consulted professional resources. Keith Curry Lance's study, *How School Librarians Help Kids Achieve Standards: The Second Colorado Study* (Colorado State Library, 2000), found that having a well-developed library media center increases student achievement on standardized tests between 15% and 18%.

Now the students begin their search for information. Both teacher and media specialist work with the students to help find, analyze, access, and record information. This works well because both have collaborated on what the students should accomplish, how they should proceed, what requirements must be fulfilled, and what the final project will include. They have developed a rubric either by themselves or with the students.

As the students discuss their findings, teacher and media specialist help the students refine their answers. The teacher and the media specialist have both assumed the role of facilitator in helping the students find, analyze, synthesize, and report on their findings. This is true research accomplished through collaboration.

Summary

Children's literature is the catalyst that provides materials for writing, reading, and research. It has become a tool for collaboration between the classroom teacher and the school media specialist. Armed with this tool and the willingness to work together, the media specialist, the classroom teacher, and the student create a formidable learning team that improves student achievement.

SOURCE: Adapted from Jody K. Howard and Linda Fiorella, "The Marriage of Literacy and Libraries through Collaboration," *Colorado Libraries* 28, no. 1 (Spring 2002): 37–38. Used with permission.

Teaching information skills to students with disabilities: What works

by Janet Murray

Molly DeLemos reports that in countries worldwide, many disabled children attend their local school as a result of inclusion policies in education. The school library program can contribute immensely to the education of disabled students, and one area where there can be an impact is in the acquisition of information skills. For students with disabilities, acquiring skills that will enable them to access information that affects their lives is of the utmost importance. If students are to become information literate, access to an information skills program administered by a professional librarian is essential.

An Australian study, which evaluated school library services for students with disabilities attending mainstream schools, investigated the acquisition of information skills by these students. This article summarizes the literature relating to the context and findings of the study regarding the acquisition of information skills by students with disabilities.

The transition to inclusive education

Developments in special education over the last two decades have had an impact on the role of special education teachers. Linda Ware commented that "the need for collaboration between general and special educators has been recognized as the key barrier to improved delivery of services for students with special needs in mainstream settings." Alan Dyson sees a need for special educators to reflect on their own practices and redefine their roles in their school. Catherine Clark, Alan Dyson, and Alan Millward observed that some schools in the United Kingdom are seeking to reconceptualize the role of the special educator as a "teaching and learning coordinator" who assists teachers in increasing learning outcomes for all students.

Dorothy Lipsky and Alan Gartner, in discussing school reform, identify a change in the role of the teacher generally to becoming a coach and facilitator rather than an instructor, and working collaboratively with other professionals rather than in isolation. In an inclusive setting this will involve working with teacher aides, professionals, and paraprofessionals concerned with the educational provision for a student with a disability. Chriss Walther-Thomas, Mimi Bryant, and Sue Land describe teaching and planning models that facilitate the support of disabled students in mainstream classes. They find one of the most successful approaches to be co-teaching, which is based on "ongoing classroom participation by supporting colleagues." It involves teachers working together as partners in planning and delivering an educational program for a particular group of students. But for co-teaching to be successful, staff development and time for planning must be provided.

P. J. McGrath discusses the transition special education teachers have made in Australia from using withdrawal as the primary method to team-teaching with classroom teachers in supporting disabled students. She recommends that schools should have a policy that reinforces the role of specialist teachers such as special education teachers, teacher-librarians, and teachers of English as a second language. McGrath identifies a need for classroom teachers to understand the benefits of team-teaching, especially the benefits it brings to the targeted students without attaching any stigma to them. In a more recent British study, Barbara Lee found that special education staff had an important role in supporting individual students and groups of students or in working in the classroom alongside subject teachers.

Another trend involves the conversion of what were originally resource bases for the support of disabled students to learning support centers that are available to all students. In schools where this kind of amalgamation has been achieved, computers, software, books, curriculum materials, and teaching resources are available in one location alongside personnel who can provide learning support, information technology support, and expertise on resources.

Teaching information skills and Cooperative Curriculum Planning and Teaching (CCPT)

Paula Montgomery found that cognitive style is related to the level of cooperation that takes place between school librarians and classroom teachers in integrating information skills into the curriculum. Librarians who exhibit field dependent characteristics in cognitive style, such as a social orientation, an interest in people, and a preference for working with others rather than in isolation, made greater efforts to introduce CCPT with classroom teachers. School librarians who exhibited field independent characteristics such as being socially detached, relying on their own values and self-defined goals, and a preference to work alone, were not so successful.

McGrath has pointed out that special education teachers share the same problems as school librarians in gaining the support of classroom teachers in team-teaching particular sets of skills. The problems she describes as Support Teacher Learning Difficulties mirror the problems faced by school librarians: time to convince classroom teachers of the need to teach together; to plan, implement, and evaluate the units taught together; and to promote a team-teaching policy across the school.

Teaching information skills to students with special needs

Both special education and school librarianship literatures were searched for reference to the teaching of information skills to students with disabilities. Little of substance was found in either. References in the school library literature are sparse. Some of these references are now dated, but their content continues to be relevant. This literature, discussed in the remainder of this section, focused on several key areas: teaching methods, team-teaching, the use of electronic information resources and audiovisual media, and storytelling.

Philip Baker and David Bender identify the attitude of the teacher toward disability as a fundamental factor in successfully teaching information skills to students with disabilities. They emphasize the importance of ongoing assessment and the need to have alternative methods ready if initial activities fail to achieve the expected learning outcomes. Joyce Petrie emphasizes the need to break down tasks into small steps for some students. She maintains that individualized instruction is the optimal method of teaching students with learning disabilities, but advises that wherever possible it should be complemented by the inclusion of the student in group activities. She offers strategies for using cooperative learning in the information skills context. For working in pairs, three possible combinations are suggested: pairing students with a common need in skill development, pairing a strong student with a weak student, and pairing students with a common strength. Petrie suggests that the ideal combination for a larger group is one low-achieving student, one high-achieving student, and two average achievers, but recommends that such groups be monitored to ensure equitable role assumptions. Petrie places importance on ongoing assessment as an essential component of teaching information skills to students with learning disabilities. She draws attention to body language and appropriate use of the voice and language as important factors in teaching disabled students.

Caren Wesson and Margaret Keefe recommend strategies for teaching information skills to students with learning disabilities. They offer a hierarchy of information skills appropriate for disabled students and recommend that two to five skills be taught each year. They suggest ways of modifying teaching methods, teaching materials, and motivational techniques. Visual cues, such as pictures, in addition to words on signs and labels can be helpful. Assignments and tasks can be shortened or modified, or the student might work cooperatively with another student. Several reinforcers to motivate students to learn information skills are suggested, such as allowing students to issue materials, allowing them to earn a discarded book or magazine, or using charts to monitor progress with skills to be learned.

In a later publication, Wesson and Keefe emphasize the advantages of cooperative teaching of information skills by the school librarian and the special education teacher. Team-teaching can overcome the difficulty some students experience in performing a skill learned with one person for a second person. This "generalization" can be a problem in schools where the special education model is one of support classes, where the student has to make a transition from the support classroom to a mainstream classroom—in this case the library. Teaching information skills cooperatively has another advantage: the librarian becomes one more person with whom students with disabilities can interact, thereby increasing their social skills. This advantage may persuade the special education teacher to try cooperative approaches to teaching information skills.

Eileen Hansen suggests that school librarians can learn a great deal about teaching and communicating with disabled students by observing special education teachers. She found this curbed her habit of giving too much information to students at once, which can overwhelm students with certain disabilities. She also recommends consultation with support professionals such as speech therapists.

Special education research has demonstrated that students with learning disabilities respond better to auditory and visual stimuli than to print media. School librarians could use more multimedia in teaching information skills to such students. Research conducted by Roxanne Mendrinos showed that disabled students were "not only more motivated but more productive using CD-ROM technology for reference." This study showed that CD-ROM technology was a great leveler in enabling students to access information successfully, regardless of their academic ability. School librarians interviewed by Mendrinos found that students were able to more easily narrow their searches by using CD-ROM reference tools, to gain a better understanding of which subject headings or keywords to use, and then to transfer this knowledge to search other catalogs and indexes. Much of this leveling effect is attributed to how CD-ROM indexes divide topics into subtopics, which helps all students, not just disabled students, to define their topic and search for relevant information.

In a later work, Mendrinos commented that electronic tools could enable students to "map concepts, ideas, to outline terms visually as well as abstractly." Such mapping can be helpful to students with learning disabilities. It is particularly useful when students lack critical reading ability and initially have trouble identifying sources that are relevant to their topic because they find it hard to read for comprehension. Although scanning a printed text would be too complex for students with low reading ability, menu-driven CD-ROMs can help students understand how one search term is associated with another.

SOURCE: Adapted from Janet Murray, "Teaching Information Skills to Students with Disabilities: What Works," *School Libraries Worldwide* 7, no. 2 (July 2001): 1–16. Used with permission.

Indirect advocacy

by Gary Hartzell

An advocate, says the dictionary, is "one who pleads the cause of another, as before a tribunal or judicial court; one who defends or espouses any cause by argument; a pleader." It is a difficult role, and many people are uncomfortable in it—especially when they feel that the value and virtue of the things they must plead for are so self-evident that they shouldn't require advocacy.

Many school librarians feel this way. What can you do if you're one of these people? There's no question, given what we see around us every day, that library advocacy is essential to library effectiveness—essential even to library survival in some places. How can you protect your role in the school and make a contribution to library media advocacy if you just don't have the personality for up-front and out-front direct activism? The answer is that you can develop indirect advocacy, recruiting other educators to plead the library media center cause with the principal, superintendent, union, board members, parents, and community groups. A call for library support from a nonlibrarian can hardly be perceived as self-serving.

You're probably thinking, "That sounds good, but how do I make it happen? I have teachers now who won't collaborate with me. How will I ever get them to advocate for me?" The answer is: You won't. Those are the wrong teachers. Beginning an advocacy campaign by attempting to recruit teachers secure in the traditional teaching role is unlikely to enlist many vocal supporters.

The initial targets for advocacy recruitment are teachers whose professional confidence and security either have not yet been established or whose confidence and security have been shaken and need to be reestablished. Those are the people you look for. I'm not talking here about poor or even mediocre teachers. You want to have good teachers speaking on your behalf. But even the best of teachers—or those who will become the best of teachers—go through periods of vulnerability. A period of vulnerability is your window of opportunity.

A teacher in the process of transition is more likely to accept help from you than one who is not. In usual circumstances, teachers rarely admit that someone else might know more than they do about how to present a particular lesson or deal with a specific group of youngsters. Unlike medicine where practitioners seek second opinions, teachers individually decide the nature and flow of events in their classrooms. Problems and results are hidden by classroom isolation and teacher autonomy, and to admit a need for help in teaching is to admit a personal weakness or incompetence.

It takes a special circumstance to overcome an aversion to admitting a need for help. But, given the nature of schools in the last part of the 1990s, there are situations in which teachers are likely to experience a decline in confidence and a rise in anxiety severe enough that they will accept assistance. These situations center around periods of personal or institutional transition. Even then, teachers may not be willing to ask for help in making sense of and mastering their situations, but they are likely to be willing to accept help if it's offered.

Opening a relationship with a teacher you want to recruit as a library advocate rests on a dual ability foundation. One part of it is your ability to recognize the teacher's period of vulnerability; the other is your ability to initiate an offer of help in a way that eliminates the need for the teacher to admit any instructional deficiency.

Recognizing vulnerability isn't difficult if you consistently strive to do two things. The first is to know the members of your faculty, and to keep up to date on changes in their assignments and situations. This can be done through social as well as professional interactions. The second is to scan the schedule and environment each semester for any of five specific situations in which a teacher is most likely to accept help. These are when the teacher is (a) a brand-new teacher, (b) a veteran teacher just new to your school, (c) a teacher assigned outside the area of his or her university preparation, (d) a teacher whose assignment has been radically changed, or (e) part of a faculty involved in significant schoolwide change.

Offering nonthreatening assistance to a vulnerable teacher is a skill that takes planning and practice, because it runs counter to our natural inclination. Most of us turn to someone and say, "Call me if you need help." We can raise the odds of successfully opening a relationship by changing just a few words. Instead of saying, "Call me if you need help," we can open the dialogue by acknowledging the teacher's position and saying something along the lines of, "You're new here, and I know there's a whole lot to learn very quickly. I can help you with part of it"—or even the more gentle, "I see you have a new assignment this year. I have something you might be interested in."

This approach saves face for teachers because it doesn't box them in. In both cases, you offer only to provide something small. There's no arrogance or threat, no takeover, no questioning of teachers' professionalism. The impression is of two professionals interacting. The approach doesn't force them to take the first step and ask for help. It allows them to decline your offer if they wish. It allows them to accept it without having to say that they are accepting help. "Oh, how?" or "Like what?" opens the door for you.

Once the door is opened, you have your shot. If you can then deliver on something that helps them master the new situation in which they find themselves, two things happen: (1) they will be in your debt, and (2) they will tell others of what you've done.

The five great opportunities for indirect advocacy recruiting

1. A brand-new teacher. There is invariably a gap between what someone right out of the university expects teaching to be and what it really is like. One dimension is motivation of students. Not all students are as eager to learn as your professors said they were. New teachers are often unprepared to deal with the wide span of learning styles. It is a major challenge to develop a repertoire of teaching techniques that will motivate reluctant learners and address varieties of learning styles. You can be of immense assistance to a new teacher and capture lasting support if you can develop an opportunity to show that you can find ideas of every kind.

2. A veteran teacher new to your school. A veteran newcomer experiences some of the same uncertainties a beginning teacher experiences. Because every school has a distinct culture, when a teacher transfers from one school to another, even within the same district, a resocialization experience is part of the entry into the new situation. The newcomer will have developed attitudes and responses in the last school, especially to uncertainty or perceived threat, that may prejudice how the new school is viewed. It is sometimes very hard for a newcomer to suppress the inclination to respond to familiar stimuli with familiar patterns of behavior. What was acceptable at the old school may not work in the new environment where norms and values are different.

Continuing faculty members and administrators are likely to see experienced teachers coming in as needing far less orientation than beginners. They are expected to already be aware of those things beginners' training would provide or be able to find them out on their own and assimilate them. Newcomers are expected to be instantly competent and talented. The bottom line is that experienced teachers new to your school are also in a very vulnerable state. They are trying to make sense of the new situation. They may not be as much in need of new teaching ideas as beginning teachers, but they sorely need help in understanding the resources available, what gets rewarded, what gets punished, and how to make a positive impression. You can help them with all those things—and in doing so, develop an ally.

3. A teacher assigned outside the area of university preparation. This situation is more likely to occur at the secondary level, but it certainly is not exclusive to the higher grades, especially in K–8 settings. The problem is not in any lack of education on the part of teachers so assigned; it's in the lack of fit between what they were trained for and what they are called upon to do. Teachers in these situations are at even more of a loss and a disadvantage than beginning teachers and veteran newcomers assigned to grades and students for which they were trained.

These teachers may be the most desperate for help among all who find themselves in a vulnerable state, and you have the resources and skills to help them. In this situation, they might not know where to begin, what questions to ask, or what challenges they are to face. This is a fertile field for your labors.

4. A teacher whose assignment has been radically changed. Radical alteration of a schedule isn't quite as challenging as our other three persons, but it still shakes confidence and raises anxiety. The experience of moving from teaching second grade to teaching sixth, for example, takes a teacher out of one unique environment and into another. Not only are there subject matter differences, but the nature of the client has substantially changed. Such schedule changes also change adult relationships, as the bonds of common experience in teaching shift from interactions with one group to another.

You can be of real assistance to a teacher making such a change. A given teacher with, say, a decade's experience at one grade level may see no gain in working with you on a broad scale. The same teacher, however, moved to a level at which he or she has no experience on which to draw, may develop a whole new perspective on the breadth, depth, and value of library media services. Once more, helping someone make rapid sense of a new situation and become effective in a new environment creates a debt that may be translated into a commitment as it grows.

5. A teacher taking part in a schoolwide change. Lastly, there is one situation in which everyone on the faculty becomes vulnerable—and their "recruitability" increases. That is when the school is undergoing a major operational change. In such conditions, everyone is taken back to the beginner's level. In such instances, the usual sources of information and support are absent. This is a void into which you can step—especially if you have any warning that such a change is coming. For example, with a change to site-based management, the odds are that few if any of your faculty colleagues have had any experience in working in such a setting. In a sense, it makes all of them into veteran teachers coming into a new school setting. They all will be concerned with how well they will be able to meet its challenges. In short, they all will be vulnerable.

You will have a great opportunity here to capture lasting support from several if not many faculty members if you are ready to seize the moment. If you have warning a year or more in advance that your school is going to move into a particular activity or mode of operation, you can have the lead time you need to research model programs, discover best practices and pitfalls, and prepare materials and resources that will make a pivotal difference in your colleagues' ability to adjust to the new order. Armed with material and information that will help them succeed, you will gather debts and commitments to cash in on later.

What does it take to be ready for such opportunities?

Building an indirect advocacy system spares you the unpleasantness of engaging in organizational politics, lobbying, pleading, and making impassioned public statements before large and sometimes hostile groups. But the trade-off is a required vigilance. You must engage in activities that will allow you to gather the information you must have in order to be able to assess the vulnerability and needs of others. That means you must serve on committees where you will get access to long-range plans and scheduling decisions. You would do well to carve yourself a role in new employee orientation and mentoring programs, if not in the hiring process itself. You need to attend board meetings and interact with members of the teachers' organizations. These activities will help you build the knowledge base and relationships through which you will be able to analyze new developments and recognize the opportunities they will bring.

You may think that there's something wrong in a system where you must engage in any advocacy, direct or indirect. And perhaps there is. But it's not a choice at this point in the history of American education. The unfortunate reality is that knowledge, skill, resources, and dedication are not enough. Being ready, willing, and able represents only three-quarters of your potential for success. The fourth is having the chance to put talents and skills to work. To have that chance, library media programs must survive. To survive they need advocates. We all must contribute in the best way we can. If your talents lie in library media skills and not in traditional direct advocacy competencies, then your library media skills must be made to do double duty.

SOURCE: Adapted from Gary Hartzell, "Indirect Advocacy," *The Book Report* 18, no. 1 (May/June 1999): 8–11. *The Book Report* is now published as *Library Media Connection.* Used with permission.

Articulation from school to society

by Debbie Abilock

My school's middle and lower school teachers were discussing what they would like students to know and be able to do as they enter middle school and what our lower school can deliver. Without doubt, every educational institution is familiar with this conversation. Whether it is framed within a discussion of standards, accompanies a curriculum mapping process, or results from informal conversations among faculty, this articulation between levels, grades, and institutions is important work.

Such articulation starts with a clear understanding of current practice. Our school has been involved in a multiyear process of curriculum mapping. It was a laborious paper-and-pencil activity, but we now are recording information about what we teach each month into an online database. This will make it feasible to locate gaps and repetitions and to identify areas for potential integration. Our database includes fields into which faculty can input the major components of their levels, specialists, and classroom curriculum. There is room for units, projects, concepts, topics, big ideas, and essential questions. Teachers are retrospectively mapping disciplines (science or physical education), themes (the Silk Road, the Shape of Time, Turn-of-the-Century Child, Legacies), skills and habits of mind (multiplication, testing data, questioning, and monitoring one's thinking), and even school programs (service learning or wind ensemble). In the prekindergarten's emergent curriculum, the map can be used as a real-time diary record.

Sitting in this articulation meeting I was conscious of how the receiving institution drives the curriculum of the sending institution. One teacher commented, "It would be better if they have had scale and proportion when we teach them to use GIS [graphical information systems] software to map our property in fifth grade." "Teach them to hold their pencil correctly . . ." suggests a first-grade teacher. Or, as our community high schools know, "two years of laboratory science providing fundamental knowledge in at least two of these three disciplines: biology [which includes anatomy, physiology, marine biology, and aquatic biology], chemistry, and physics" are required to matriculate into the University of California system. Don't misinterpret me; there's nothing wrong with requirements. They are goals to work toward as we design backwards. However, this design process must be tempered by sensitivity to a child's developmental readiness and taught with an understanding of an individual's profile of intelligences and learning style.

I would like to propose that we school librarians who look across all the grades have a role in speaking from an even larger perspective. We can articulate the goals of our society within our schools. We should be asking our schools, "Are there essential elements that young citizens should develop as they move toward full participation in a democratic society?"

First I would suggest our society needs citizens who are literate. The 21st century demands that readers analyze, compare, evaluate, and interpret multiple representations, including texts, photographs, artwork, and data, from a variety of disciplines in order to make fundamental sense of ideas and communicate articulately. In *Intelligence Reframed*, Howard Gardner contends that "literacies, skills, and disciplines ought to be pursued as tools that allow us to enhance our understanding of important questions, topics, and themes." Thus, as reported in the North Central Regional Educational Laboratory's *21st Century Skills*, such reading processes as information literacy, visual literacy, scientific literacy, media literacy, and cultural literacy ought to be our basics.

Educators must learn to understand—then learn to teach—these literacies in multiple formats. For the school library media specialist (SLMS), Dennis Adams and Mary Hamm report that this involves learning the complexity of reading new media formats as well as how different cultures define literacy, and how reading multiple texts plays out in classroom practice or in social practice under new technological conditions. If you have any doubts about the challenges this presents, try reading David Reinking's "Me and My Hypertext:) A Multiple Digression Analysis of Technology and Literacy [sic]." SLMSs should be teaching these literacies.

Second, our society needs, according to Robert J. Sternberg and Elena Grigorenko, citizens who are thinkers. Each of us may define thinking differently: as a balance of analytical, creative, and practical abilities; as intellectual habits like open-mindedness; or as mental processes specific to a discipline. Whatever the definition, W. Lance Bennett suggests that all our citizens should be able to identify what Ron Powers terms "eyewitless news" and understand the distortions of television's manufactured news recreations in order to vote intelligently.

As a corollary, our citizens will be required to make smart choices. In studies of choice making, two social psychologists, Sheena S. Iyengar and Mark R. Lepper, have shown that when the number of alternatives becomes too large and the differences between them are small, people become overwhelmed and frustrated. (Sound like Internet search results?) In related studies, Barry Schwartz, a Swarthmore College psychology professor, has identified two types of choice makers: "maximizers," who want to find the very best option, even when there is an extensive array of choices; and "satisficers," who look for any choice that meets a set of criteria. (Sound like an Internet evaluation strategy?) Students must learn to use the appropriate choice-making behavior in different situations. Thus, school librarians need to teach thinking skills and strategic behavior.

Last, citizens must know how to apply democratic principles. The First Amendment cannot be just book learning; students must make concrete use of it in their daily lives. To begin negotiating the curriculum, Carole Edelsky suggests reviewing your book selection and Internet acceptable use policies with students and introducing the online resources of the Office of Intellectual Freedom. Discuss interpretations of the First Amendment that affect their lives. According to *Youth Guide to the First Amendment,* you should familiarize yourself with government information on the Internet and the primary functions and current political issues that federal agencies face so that you can help design curricula that move beyond learning how a bill becomes a law. Greg R. Notess points out that school librarians should learn how other educators have used critical literacy to construct a climate of social justice. With a functional understanding of their inalienable rights and the rights of every other citizen, and of government's role to protect those rights, students can champion the marketplace of ideas—the core of our library services.

SOURCE: Adapted from Debbie Abilock, "Articulation from School to Society," *Knowledge Quest* 30, no. 4 (March/April 2002): 9–10.

Book club on a budget

by Linda Jaeger and Shelia N. Demetriadis

A few years ago in our inner-city middle school, we asked two seventh-grade honor students, "What good books have you read this year?" The girls looked at each other quizzically. "None," they replied. When we asked other students the same question, most responded that reading was "wak" (translation: very uncool). It was clear these attitudes needed to change, not only to improve our students' grades, but perhaps more important, to help them envision a life beyond the confines of their struggling neighborhoods.

We immediately thought of forming a book club, a place with no grade pressure where peers could encourage each other to read for pleasure, and where students and teachers could come together on equal terms. There was just one problem. We couldn't start a club without money to buy multiple copies of books. Our school didn't have the money, and the donors we approached said they didn't want to support an individual school, as opposed to the district, for fear of showing favoritism.

A few months later, we read an article in the *ALAN Review* called "Literature Reading and Research in a Middle School Classroom" (Fall 1997, 51–58). The authors outlined a project in which students read different books, but researched the same topics or themes. It looked like our problem was solved. We convened a meeting of interested teachers and together planned monthly themes for the remainder of the school year. Then, using our school's collection, we identified books of various reading levels related to each month's theme.

For our first meeting, in January, the teachers donated snacks to give the event a festive air. We simply wanted to introduce students to the club and let them choose books. About 25 students showed up. At the second meeting, we began our actual discussions. Since it was February, the theme was Black History, and the books we read included Gary Paulsen's *Nightjohn* (Delacorte, 1993). We went around the room asking students and teachers to talk about their books. One girl had that "I-hope-they-don't-call-on-me" look. When her turn came, she confessed to not having finished her book. Our response was, "That's all right. Would you like to share what you've read so far?" Obviously relieved, she began to speak. When she was done, other students joined in, and we had a great discussion, sparked by *Nightjohn*.

To generate more interest in the club, we ran two contests. The first, "Bring a Friend," encouraged members to bring other students to read with us (the prize was a candy bar). By June, we had 30 regular members, eight of whom were boys. The other contest challenged students to see who could post the most reviews on our website each month. The prize was $5 toward a book-fair purchase. This, too, generated activity—by June, one student had written 16 reviews.

The students particularly liked having guest speakers. Our school's book-fair representative came to book-talk and to distribute paperbacks for members to review. At another meeting, two teachers who are publishing authors discussed their writing experiences. We've also been visited by the weather reporter from a local TV station, who had started her own on-air book club. The students were thrilled to hear their own book club mentioned on her program the following day.

To our surprise, some financial support arrived at Christmas, when a local Barnes & Noble store adopted our club in cooperation with the local PBS station. They threw club members a holiday party, complete with gift-wrapped books donated by customers.

We don't have hard numbers to attest to the book club's success. But we do know that once it began, students we never expected to see were coming to the library to talk about books. The club also gave members a healthy dose of self-esteem and prestige. Not only were they visited by special guests, but club members also got to do things like promote our school book fairs by

9

reading reviews and performing skits over the school intercom. The moral is that it doesn't take lots of money to start a book club—and that it's well worth it.

SOURCE: Adapted from Linda Jaeger and Shelia N. Demetriadis, "What Works—Book Club on a Budget," *School Library Journal* 48, no. 3 (March 1, 2002): 47. Courtesy of *School Library Journal.*

A visit to a university library
by Margaret Tabar

Many traditions have been established during the centennial history of St. Paul Academy and Summit School, an independent, nondenominational day school in St. Paul, Minnesota. Third graders look forward to the day their teacher sends them to the front door for the Mystery Bus Trip. Seventh graders anticipate a week of winter outdoor camping in northern Minnesota. Seniors contemplate the topic of the short speech each of them will present during an assembly. Juniors anticipate the challenge presented by the United States history research paper.

Our social studies curriculum has a research component that begins in sixth grade and culminates in the junior-year paper. To encourage the use of both the school library and local public libraries, we begin sixth graders with an investigation of the national monuments that they will visit during their class trip to Washington, D.C. Primary sources are introduced as part of History Day projects in the eighth and ninth grades. Tenth graders travel to a large public library in the process of completing their short research paper. These assignments pave the way for juniors to visit a university library as they tackle a more extensive research paper.

Planned and refined by the history teachers and myself, the United States history research paper has two major objectives for student research:

- to select a topic, design a thesis statement, locate pertinent primary and secondary resources, and write a well-documented, analytical research paper; and
- to gain the information skills necessary for college and university library research, including the use of historical journal indexes, academic electronic databases, and the Library of Congress classification system.

After I introduce possible sources of topics for their United States history research papers, students spend class time in the school library exploring these sources and familiarizing themselves with the topics. When they begin to narrow their choices, they use the state electronic system, MnLink, www.mnlink.org, to search the collections of the state public, academic, government, and specialized libraries, such as the Minnesota Historical Society and Hill Reference Library.

The next step is a field trip to visit the Wilson Library at the University of Minnesota. I confer with a member of the library staff prior to the trip. We discuss indexes and databases, special collections, arrangements for our visit, and any changes to the layout of the library since the last visit. I return to school with many handouts created by the library staff. Since few of the students have borrowing privileges at the Wilson Library, it is expedient for us to purchase photocopy cards in advance. At school, the teachers have filed the field trip paperwork, reserved buses, and recruited additional chaperones.

Before students arrive at Wilson Library, they learn how to navigate the facility so that they can make effective use of their time. Using maps from the library, I explain the layout of the floors and note where the major resources, such as print indexes, bound periodicals, microforms, and government documents, are located. Directions for finding the photocopy machines, computer stations, and restrooms are given. Using a data projector, I demonstrate search strategies for the university online catalog, www.lib.umn.edu/books/. We review the differences between the Dewey Decimal and Library of Congress classification systems, both of which are used in the Wilson Library. The students are given a homework assignment to prepare a call number listing for a minimum number of materials they wish to locate during their visit.

Since many of the students will return to the Wilson Library independently to continue their research, I put together a packet containing information about the location and hours of the many satellite libraries operated by the university. I remind them to bring along the essentials, such as pens and note cards, along with money for copy machines, parking, and snacks. They are encouraged to use school or home computers to presearch the university library catalog, as terminals at the library are likely to be filled when we are on campus.

A day before our visit, I e-mail a list of the topics the students have chosen to the reference librarians. We instruct the students to seek help first from one of their teachers, consulting the reference staff if they need further help. This thorough preplanning is essential—a visit to a four-story facility can seem overwhelming to students accustomed to a one-room library.

Most students are excited to find extensive material about their topics. The teachers and I see the results in terms of thorough, well-documented research papers. We believe that this successful instructional experience in a research library will encourage students to use the large library facilities they will encounter during college.

SOURCE: Adapted from Margaret Tabar, "Rite of Passage: A Visit to a University Library," *Knowledge Quest* 30, no. 4 (March/April 2002): 29–30.

Methods of teaching information literacy

by David V. Loertscher

Library media specialists teaching information literacy have sometimes succumbed to the temptation of teaching those skills as a course of instruction so that students would visit regularly for their "library lesson."

Such an approach has been rejected as time-consuming and inefficient. Rather, the professional literature recommends the integration of information literacy skills at the point when students will use them.

As the illustration at the top of figure 1 shows, sometimes this teaching will take place as a mini-lesson when students are assigned a project and come to the library media center to do research.

However, if the teacher is doing an inquiry unit or a major project, the information literacy teaching will form the scaffolding of the entire research process. There will be a number of information mini-lessons as the research progresses.

Figure 1

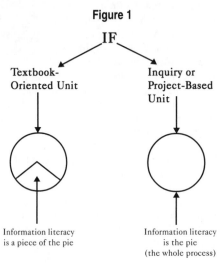

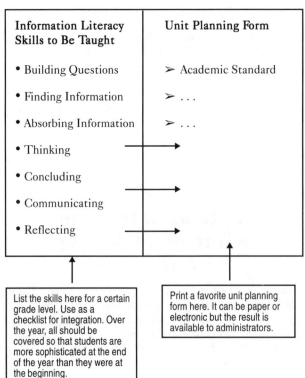

In either method, the illustration at the bottom of figure 1 shows how the two agendas are commingled to insure accountability for both educators.

SOURCE: Adapted from David V. Loertscher, *Reinventing Your School's Library in the Age of Technology* (San Jose, Calif.: Hi Willow, 2002), 58. Used with permission.

How would I recognize information literacy if I saw it in action?

by David V. Loertscher

If I walked by the library media center or briefly walked in for an observation, I might see at a cursory glance whether the library media center was full of students or empty, whether it was quiet or noisy, and whether the students were engaged. However, without a deeper probe, the significance of what was going on might well be elusive. The following observational checklist might help.

The library media specialist/teacher planning session may be in progress.
A class is doing research with both the teacher and the library media specialist assisting individuals or groups, or they might be jointly teaching.
Individual students or groups are obviously engaged in a research project and may not be "quiet."
Individuals, small groups, and whole classes might be doing research simultaneously with the library media specialists rotating around to several groups. The teacher would always be present when larger groups would be researching.

If a teacher were interviewed, signs that information literacy skills are being taught might include:

A lesson plan would have information literacy skills included.
The teacher would have had a planning session with the library media specialist in advance of the time in the library media center.
The teacher would be aware of an information literacy model being taught to all students in the school.
The teacher would understand what information literacy is, and that the library media program is taking the leadership in this activity.

If students were interviewed, knowledge about information literacy might include:

Recognition of the term "information literacy."
Knowledge about a helpful process or a procedure for doing research.
Knowledge about how the library media center and the technology of the school help them in their learning projects.
Recognition that both the teacher and the library media specialist guide them in the research process.
Knowledge that they are getting more and more particular about the quality of information they are finding.
Compliments for the information technology systems and their contribution to their education.

SOURCE: Adapted from David V. Loertscher, *Reinventing Your School's. Library in the Age of Technology* (San Jose, Calif.: Hi Willow, 2002), 59. Used with permission.

Rx for cut and clip

by David V. Loertscher and Douglas Achterman

Problem: Are learners cutting and clipping facts, paragraphs, articles, whole term papers from library books, periodicals, Internet sites and turning them in as their own work? Perhaps they have become creative and "dress up" the appearance of what they find and then turn it in. The bottom line is that they do very little thinking or learning. A zero educational experience.

Rx: With the library media specialist, build better questions for learners; have learners build better questions for themselves. The definition of a better question is one that cannot be answered through cut and clip mentality.

Examples

Invitations to cut and clip:

a list of fact questions to answer
an assignment where the "answer" is easily located in a periodical article, a book, or a website

Challenges to think:

Compare/contrast two opinion pieces.
Insert extracted data into a larger matrix, chart, diagram, mind map for analysis.
Look for trends across extracted sources.
Build in-class timelines, then look at the meaning, cause/effect.
Take on the persona of an important character; re-enact an event.

Ideas for other opportunities and challenges

Suggestions when teachers and library media specialists collaborate

Create good and clear assignments so students can begin immediately and stay engaged.
Include creative uses of technology that will contribute both to learning and to interest.
Require a wide variety of information sources to help students explore the rich world of information across the media.
Build the research process into the whole project so that students keep making progress toward becoming independent and more sophisticated learners over time.
Build in reflection along the way to help students assess what they know and how efficient their strategies are.

Activities likely to fail

spur-of-the-moment activities with little notice given to the library media staff
unclear assignments or directions to learners, causing them to waste time, become behavior problems, or wander in a state of stupor
competition for scarce information resources (when every other teacher is having students research the same topic your students are and at the same time)

assignments that do not require evaluation of information sources (you will get back information copied from the first hit of an Internet search, facts copied from an out-of-date reference source, and other nonsense mindlessly regurgitated)

SOURCE: Adapted from David V. Loertscher and Douglas Achterman, *Increasing Academic Achievement through the Library Media Center: A Guide for Teachers,* 2nd ed. (San Jose, Calif.: Hi Willow, 2003), 28. Used with permission.

Tools for learning
by David V. Loertscher and Douglas Achterman

Many times, a simple set of flash cards is just as good as a $3,000 machine—and more reliable. Technological sophistication is not automatically the answer. Theoretically, technology should help students learn more and learn more efficiently.

Numerous publications tout effective ways to enhance learning through technology. In reality, they are idea starters. Each teaching team, library media specialist, and student group should, through trial and error, test a variety of techniques and showcase the best. Emphasize technology-based projects where substance is more important than glitz; deep learning over surface learning. Consider the following strategies as a starter list:

Collaborative data collection and analysis. Various student groups in the same school, in the community, state, nation, or internationally, collect data to solve an engaging problem.

Real problems. Numerous technologies allow students to handle "real" data to solve real problems. The data can be historical or contemporary, or obtained instantly through sensing devices.

A transparent learning tool. When technology is properly used, it often becomes transparent to the learning task at hand. It becomes a true learning tool, not an end in itself. Matching the appropriate technology to the learning task helps ensure that transparent match.

The novelty of technology. Enduring a steady diet of the same teaching strategies is boring. The use of a new technology or a fresh approach to an older technology can stimulate interest both in the technology itself and in the subject matter to be mastered. Implementing new teaching strategies matched to appropriate technologies keeps the learning fresh.

Capitalizing on media characteristics. Each different kind of technology has its own unique characteristics that can contribute to learning. Films have motion and color; books allow easy skimming and scanning; the Internet allows worldwide, almost instantaneous communication; online databases often allow full-text searches; distance education allows participation from afar. When teachers and students use a particular medium for its strengths, concept delivery and understanding are likely to be enhanced.

Multiple data sources. The Internet, online databases, books, periodicals, video sources, and connections to other libraries help students experience a wide variety of information on the topic or question they are seeking. There is something for every student at every level.

Simulations. Simulations, including simulation gaming, provide a way to come close to reality without encountering the dangers, the impossibilities of traveling in time or space, the "what ifs," or the risks.

9

Communication beyond the school. The Internet, the amplified telephone, and e-mail allow students to communicate around the world, to other schools, experts, governments, agencies, libraries, museums, businesses, and a host of other sources. This communication supports the learners as they explore ideas, concepts, and important issues.

Background building. Before students can deal intelligently with an engaging problem, they can build the needed background knowledge from a wide variety of media and technology sources in a relatively short period of time.

Efficient learners. Because of technology assists, students write more, produce better products, edit their work more carefully, use more information resources, and integrate them into their work. Using the technology to gather as well as organize information and data helps the learner bring order and relevance to the subject matter.

SOURCE: Adapted from David V. Loertscher and Douglas Achterman, *Increasing Academic Achievement through the Library Media Center: A Guide for Teachers* (San Jose, Calif.: Hi Willow, 2002), 54. Used with permission.

Book bags and curiosity kits: An idea for the early grades

by David V. Loertscher and Douglas Achterman

Goal:		Result:
Each child from kindergarten through second grade reads **500+** books per year.		Every reader will read at or above grade level and have a habit of reading.

Try book bags. Each classroom acquires enough canvas book bags (either from commercial sources or by making them) for each child in the classroom, plus a few extras. Each book bag is numbered and can be decorated. Once a month, the class goes to the LMC, where the children help select the books for the book bags. Into each book bag goes a book that children can "read for themselves" (a wordless picture book, an alphabet book, books with a few words, highly illustrated books, etc.) and one book that can be read to the child by an older sibling, parent, friend, or caregiver (a good read-aloud picture book, a folktale, a nonfiction animal book, etc.). Back in the classroom, the book bags are hung on hooks or put in cubbyholes. Each day as the children go home they take a different book bag, rotating throughout the month. The teacher keeps a list on a clipboard to record the book bag number next to the child's name. The homework for a kindergartner through second grader is to read two books a day. If the child forgets to bring the book bag back, the spares can be used. In no case is a child denied access to a book bag, because reading practice is considered essential. The management of this program is considered a success when both the teacher and the library media specialist agree that the system requires very little monitoring. At the end of the month, the revisits the LMC, where the books are exchanged for new ones. Books book bag program are checked out to the room. No individual circulation r are kept for these books.

Schools using this system report extremely low loss rates and damage, counting the cost of either as the cost of doing business. In addition to using the book bags, the class comes to the library once a month to choose books for the classroom collection (a minimum of 100 books at a time). And the students make other visits during the month to select their own personal books to take home in addition to the book bags. The typical kindergartener, first or second grader should have read a minimum of 500 books during the school year and then linked into the public library system for regular reading during vacation periods.

Curiosity kits. A variant on the book bag program is the creation of curiosity kits where each child creates a book bag filled with 2+ books on a theme that they think other members of the class might be interested in: whales, riddles, drawing books, hobbies, paper airplanes, kite flying, etc.

Theme bags. During a month when the children will be studying a topic, they fill a third or half of the bags with books on the topic.

SOURCE: Adapted from David V. Loertscher and Douglas Achterman, *Increasing Academic Achievement through the Library Media Center: A Guide for Teachers* (San Jose, Calif.: Hi Willow, 2002), 38. Used with permission.

Critical thinking 101 : The basics of evaluating information

by Mary Ann Fitzgerald

9

Information Power: Building Partnerships for Learning contains nine information literacy standards for teaching one of the most important skills that students should gain from modern education. This article focuses strictly upon the second standard, one that is at the heart of information literacy: "The student who is information literate evaluates information critically and competently." Students may know how to access and locate, interpret, and apply information. However, if they do not invest any time in evaluating the information they use, their efforts often result in a low-quality product. Worse, failure to evaluate may result in unfavorable outcomes due to bad decision making based on flawed information.

Unfortunately, evaluating information is not a simple task. Many studies from the psychology, social psychology, and decision-making research areas demonstrate that it is extremely complex. Evaluation consists of a number of component processes and is influenced by a host of contextual factors. For example, the simple act of reading a newspaper article may involve some or all of the following:

Which newspaper does the article appear in, and how credible is this newspaper?
What is the reader's original opinion about the topic discussed in the article?
Is this the first time the reader has encountered the topic, or is the reader
    quite familiar with it?

What kind of mood is the reader in?
What kind of writing style did the author use?
How long is the article?
What other articles and advertisements appear on the same page as the article?

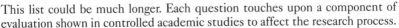

Who is the author, what are the author's credentials, and what opinion does the reader have about the author?
What evidence does the author present to support the major points of the article? Is this evidence valid in the reader's eyes?

This list could be much longer. Each question touches upon a component of evaluation shown in controlled academic studies to affect the research process.

So how do we teach students to perform this complicated operation? Experience with children and adolescents should convince any educator that simply directing a fifth-grader to evaluate a newspaper article is not an effective teaching strategy. Most young students are unable to verbalize what evaluation means or describe how it should be carried out. They know few concrete strategies with which they can start evaluating information.

Evaluation: A type of critical thinking

According to Carol C. Kuhlthau, evaluation is one of several types of critical thinking, along with problem solving, decision making, and analysis. It consists of a cluster of skills, but theorists do not agree exactly what these skills are. Robert H. Ennis indicates that most writers include such processes as finding inconsistencies, comparing and contrasting, and judging by criteria. The target of evaluation can be an object (as in a piece of art), an idea, or a person. Our focus here is information as the object of evaluation. When evaluating information, a person studies it for reliability, quality, credibility, and personal usefulness. These qualities overlap in meaning, but together they describe factors a person considers when judging information.

THOUSANDS OF BUSHELS OF POP-CORN STORED IN AN OLD WARE-HOUSE "POPPED" SO HARD AS TO WRECK THE ROOF OF THE BUILDING! THE OWNER BLAMED "SPONTANEOUS COMBUSTION INSIDE THE CORN" FOR THE TROUBLE!

Although adults also would probably benefit from learning how to better evaluate information, there is evidence that children are particularly gullible. Anyone who works with young children knows that they believe much of what they hear and read, unless explicitly told that a story is fiction. There are a number of psychological reasons for this gullibility. Adults train children to trust authority. Young people not only must obey but are expected to believe the information that adults give them, and those who do not do so are punished. Patricia M. King and Karen S. Kitchener say that children up to the age of adolescence tend to believe in the absolute reality of what they observe. Ellen M. Markman suggests that children may fail to detect inconsistencies because they are searching for perceptually false statements. John H. Flavell believes another problem is that children have poor metacognitive ability.

The gullibility of children has become a threatening issue now that information is more widely available at faster speeds than ever before. Parents have always warned children not to speak with strangers, but parental supervision has become problematic. Parents still bear the major responsibility for the safety of their children, but a recent poll conducted by Mike Snider found that 72% of parents monitor their children's use of the Internet only moderately or not at all. The same poll revealed that 18% of children surveyed planned to meet someone they met over the Internet. The danger of such intentions, according to Kevin Murphy, is demonstrated by criminal cases in which adults, posing as youngsters, entice children or teenagers to meet them away from their homes. Predators now have another avenue for deception, and children continue to be vulnerable. While even the best critical thinking skills will not prevent all cases of deception and predation, improving the ability to evaluate information may be one of a child's best methods of defense.

In the school setting, educators might be tempted to solve Internet and other misinformation difficulties by eliminating, labeling, or filtering. Access to web resources and the networking of K–12 environments resulted in a resurgence of censorship owing to concern for children's exposure to inappropriate materials over the Internet. While censorship is not the focus of this article, it must be noted that it is no substitute for teaching students to evaluate information. Dubious, inflammatory, or inappropriate information can theoretically be limited, but to what extent? Who decides when information is problematic? Eventually, everyone must independently apply critical thinking for personal purposes. It is essential that schools prepare students for this role.

General recommendations

Students should be involved in information inquiry projects from an early age as often as possible. Topics for information projects should come from across the curriculum, with some kind of relationship to the interest and curiosity of the individual student. While these principles are basic to most information process models, agreed upon by many scholars, personal conversations with teachers and library media specialists reveal that students do not yet conduct research as a common activity in all schools.

Library media specialists, teachers, and students need to be aware of how important and how complex the skill of evaluation is. We cannot assume that kids know how to do it, or that they can do it naturally. Students should understand that evaluation is difficult and that it is often not possible to be certain of the correctness of a judgment. While this perpetual uncertainty may feel uncomfortable to young students, it is a necessary part of intellectual development.

Evaluation should be incorporated seamlessly into whatever information search process is used. Most popular research models include an evaluation component. Some suggest several concrete evaluation strategies.

Questions of censorship often arise when discussing information quality. Instead of going to a great deal of trouble to teach children these skills, why not simply enable Internet filtering software? Library media specialists can refer to *Information Power* for a license to teach critical thinking. Now that there is national level support to include critical thinking as an information skill, library media specialists can use these standards to support their professional practice.

Finally, evaluation is a skill that should be instilled in students over a period of years. Teachers usually have students only for a single year, but library media specialists can influence children over time. The long-term teaching of such thinking skills has the potential of influencing both teaching and learning and the nature of K–12 education.

Specific recommendations

Students need a repertoire of evaluative strategies. A checklist approach is an excellent and easily implemented starting point for information evaluation. Students can find a suitable, ready-made checklist such as Kathy Schrock's for websites at http://school.discovery.com/schrockguide/eval.html, or they can compose their own. Checklists do not fit all evaluative situations, but they are an excellent way to begin using strategies.

Hilda Weisburg and Ruth Toor recommend that because of the importance of prior knowledge, students should be encouraged to read as widely as possible within subject areas. They should grow to understand that, while it is impossible to have domain knowledge about all topics, it is important to have some domain knowledge to help with important decisions and projects.

Further, even young children can be taught to pay attention to their thinking if they feel surprised or confused. By raising metacognitive awareness of their own mental operations, students can learn to monitor their process and become more reflective. As Deanna Kuhn notes, although metacognitive thinking in the youngest children is crude at best, the groundwork for later competence can be laid.

Students should learn to notice emotional aspects of information as well. Although we would like to think of information as objective and free of emotional influence, it is in truth difficult for authors, researchers, and journalists to remove their biases completely from their writings. Sensitivity to the subtle emotions expressed in a document alerts students to the writer's point of view, and may reveal problems like stereotyping, bias, and emotional manipulation. Regular analysis of the tone of the writing and the author's possible motivating factors can develop sophistication in students' reading and own writing.

Encourage students to use information in all formats. Their initial searches should be broad, providing them with appropriate resources regardless of format. They can learn to recognize that it is negligent to ignore disliked formats merely because of their inconvenience or unwieldiness. They should also be taught that some formats have a level of inherent reliability as a function of editing, peer review, or journalistic validation.

As part of their self-monitoring, students should learn that different strategies are appropriate depending upon which phase of information use they are currently in. In performing initial searches during the first phase of information use, they should look for relevant features that they have identified in advance, such as specific keywords or names of authors. By considering the context and length of any piece found before deciding to access, copy, or check out the item, they are using strategies that will guarantee greater success. For example, while the magazines *People, Biography Magazine, US,* and *Current Biography* all may have entries for the same person, they each connote a different level of credibility and usefulness.

In phase two, when students are absorbing a piece of information for the first time, they should continue to consider whether the piece is relevant. This involves being alert to inconsistencies, especially inconsistencies between the piece and the students' existing prior knowledge. Close monitoring of their own confusion, surprise, and disagreement are important metacognitive cues to be investigated.

In phase three, the students will have greater topic background, which should stimulate their reassessment of the points made by previously read articles. Ideas that seemed valid on first reading may now be inconsistent with something the student learned subsequently. Students will grapple with inconsistencies. Through middle and high school, greater emphasis should be placed on evaluating differing perspectives than on arriving at unswerving conclusions or truths. Teachers and library media specialists should accept products in which the "jury is still out" on an issue, as long as there is a thorough treatment of divergent perspectives.

Finally, teach relevance judging as a separate process from evaluation. Older students can learn to perform relevance and quality judgments concurrently if three conditions are met:

- they are proficient at performing both relevance judging and evaluation in isolation;
- they are able to verbalize the difference between these processes; and
- they are aware of the natural tendency to grab highly relevant information regardless of quality.

Instructional strategies for school library media specialists and classroom teachers

The following suggestions provide concrete teaching strategies that may begin to help students think evaluatively. Obviously, these will be most effective if collaboratively implemented by both library media specialists and teachers. Since evaluation is a complex process learned best over time, the library media specialist is in a unique position to ensure that this ability is developed in all students during their schooling. Small, steady doses of coaching in the evaluation process over the years will develop this overall critical thinking ability.

9

- Teach evaluation strategies one or several at a time, beginning with the most concrete.
- Encourage students to respond to signals and doubts that occur while reading because formal evaluation of all information is both overwhelming and impractical.
- Provide examples of types of misinformation, such as fake websites.
- Reduce the cognitive load by breaking the skill down into smaller parts and by beginning new skills in familiar contexts when a skill is introduced or when students seem to be having difficulty applying a skill.

- As suggested by Markman, locate short, curriculum-relevant texts for the classroom teacher that allow children to exercise such evaluation strategies as recognizing inconsistency or exaggeration. Later these can be reinforced and extended during extended research projects.
- Instruct students in how to seek the explanations behind points or actions described in information sources. As reported by Craig A. Anderson, research shows that people evaluate more effectively if causes are revealed where available.

✓ As Kuhn suggests, design curriculum-related activities or projects that involve formal argumentation, including the evaluation of evidence. To develop flexibility in thinking, students can switch sides and argue opposite positions. King and Kitchener note that debates, mock trials, and editorials present excellent vehicles for practicing evaluation skills.

✓ Allow students to create different types of media (video, multimedia, traditional arts, web pages, etc.) as public displays of learning that benefit both producers and consumers. Production experiences are particularly valuable in relation to evaluative skill for two reasons. First, the expression of learning in a concrete product stimulates students to articulate their thoughts in an ordered, logical manner; expressing logical thought is one avenue toward appreciating and critiquing the logic of others. Second, working with a particular medium demonstrates the characteristics of that medium. For example, when students edit video, they may discover how easy it is to manipulate context and create false messages.

✓ Encourage informal discussion among students so that they can gain additional perspectives and better formulate their thinking.

It makes sense for educators to understand the evaluation process. In an information-rich democratic society, the ability to evaluate information is an essential one. Marketplace decisions, jury trials, debates over social issues, and voting are all common activities that involve the evaluation of information. Fortunately, *Information Power* emphasizes the importance of this critical thinking skill by including it among the nine information literacy standards.

Scholarly literature has long discussed the attributes of critical thinkers and the components of higher-order thinking. Several writers have proposed programs for building critical thinking and for assessing it. However, few have written about it in concrete terms. Young students need the sort of specific and explicit directions about how and when to evaluate information discussed here.

Most important, library media specialists must recognize their role in building the skill of information evaluation. In the current national climate, basic skills and content area standards often crowd higher-order thinking from the curriculum. Through collaboration with teachers, integration of challenging inquiry projects into content areas, and regular use of powerful information technologies, library media specialists can profoundly influence the thinking patterns of students. In fact, they are arguably the professionals best positioned to ensure that evaluation becomes a cognitive tool for every student.

SOURCE: Adapted from Mary Ann Fitzgerald, "Critical Thinking 101: The Basics of Evaluating Information," *Knowledge Quest* 29, no. 2 (November/December 2000): 13–20.

Tell me a story

by Connie Rockman

In 1899, a pioneering librarian named Charlotte Keith took over the West End Branch of the Carnegie Library of Pittsburgh. Shortly thereafter, she advertised in local schools that a storytime would be held on Friday afternoons and that sixth, seventh, and eighth graders were invited to attend. On the first Friday, 300 children showed up to hear Miss Keith tell the story of *The Merchant of Venice*. When they left, not a single Shakespeare storybook was left on the shelves. More than a hundred years later, one chilly night in February, 120 children made their way to the Mark Twain Public Library, nestled in the wooded countryside of Redding, Connecticut. They were elementary-school children, from grades K–5, dressed in pajamas and carting their favorite blankets and stuffed animals. As the local paper reported a few days later, the children had

Young readers from the West End Branch of Carnegie Library of Pittsburgh.

come to hear a storyteller, who "shared tales from Africa and Appalachia and [of] characters ranging from a clumsy bullfrog to the mighty Casey at the Bat."

What drew those parents and children away from their TV sets and computers in 2001 was the same lure that fascinated Charlotte Keith's audience in 1899: the sharing of imaginative stories between teller and listener.

Storytelling, particularly for children beyond preschool age, is a craft too often ignored by today's librarians, immersed in their daily tasks and overwhelmed by the demands of a constantly changing profession. But in fact, telling stories to elementary and middle school students, and teaching them to express themselves through story, can yield wonderful results: increased attention spans, imaginative writing, good group dynamics, and enhanced self-esteem, to name a few.

Becoming a storyteller

How does a busy librarian, media specialist, or teacher fit storytelling into the school day or library schedule? First of all, we have to view storytelling as something everyone can do. In her book, *Storyteller, Storyteacher*, Marni Gillard talks about a "story continuum," on which one can trace a direct line from "artful self-expression" to the fine art of storytelling. The first step on the continuum might simply be a conversational anecdote emerging from the need to make sense of an occasion or experience. As you share these everyday events with friends and family, be aware of how you are shaping your stories to engage your listeners. Many professional tellers now include performance-quality personal tales in their repertoires, and you can be sure they all began as anecdotal material.

Finding stories

The most important ingredient in successful storytelling—a tip that you will read in all the how-to books—is that you must choose a story that you love. You may need to read many collections of stories to find the one that speaks to you, that makes you want to spend time learning it. It may help to listen to storytelling tapes while driving or walking—it's often easier to connect with a story that you have heard rather than read.

For many people, folk tales are the easiest stories to learn. Coming from an oral tradition, they have been honed through the years to a fast-moving, straightforward plot. They have stock characters and a minimum of description. They are free of pretense, contain a childlike sense of wonder about the natural

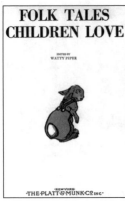

FOLK TALES CHILDREN LOVE

EDITED BY
WATTY PIPER

NEW YORK
·THE·PLATT·&·MUNK·C9·INC·

world, and can be interpreted on so many levels that each listener takes from the story what is most important for him or her. Often, folk tales have a robust humor even as they convey subtle messages about human behavior.

Folk tales are not the only source for story material. Many children enjoy stories from real life, and the biography section of your library is rich in this material. Five years ago, while reviewing a book on the history of the modern Olympic Games, I found myself fascinated by the stories of some of the legendary athletes who have emerged since the modern Olympics began in 1896. I developed a program to present in schools and libraries about James B. Connolly, the first gold medalist in track events. That was followed by the story of Jim Thorpe, the great Native American track star who was stripped of his gold medals through a technicality (they were restored to his heirs many years later), and Jesse Owens, whose record-breaking scores rankled Hitler in the 1936 Games. For me, the heart of Jesse Owens's story, the real human drama, was the spontaneous friendship he developed with one of the German athletes, the mutual respect and joy in each other's company that grew between a black sharecropper's son from America and a young white man from Nazi Germany. Finding the vivid details in a biographical sketch and the anecdotes that define personality can be a rewarding challenge.

Possibilities for storytelling abound in collections and single editions of literary tales, as well. One such story has been with me for 30 years, ever since I first heard a classmate tell it in a storytelling course at the University of Pittsburgh. My classmate told "The Mousewife," a story published by Rumer Godden. (Godden had found the story in a journal of Dorothy Wordsworth, sister of the poet William Wordsworth.) This strange tale of the friendship between a house mouse and a captured dove touched us all in the class, especially when the teller became choked with emotion as she related it. On a child's level, the story is about friendship and the mouse freeing the dove from a cage, but as I learned the story myself, it took on greater meaning about the importance of true friends in my own life.

Years later, I told the story in the living room of a group home for girls in Westport, Connecticut. Eight teenage girls, whose lives had been disrupted by various problems at home, listened intently as the dove told the mousewife about life in the wild and the mousewife came to understand the dove's world beyond the window and his need to be free. When the story ended, there was a hushed silence until one of the girls said, "That's a story about therapy."

The best stories meet us where we are and create meaning for our lives.

Tell often

When you have made the effort to learn a story, you will want many opportunities to tell it, to make it an integral part of you. If you are a librarian, you can tell it to many different groups as part of classroom visits. If you are a teacher, you can offer to tell your story in other classrooms. The more you tell the story, the more you make it your own. Each audience will teach you something about the story. They may start chanting a refrain, and you will find you have a participatory story. They may laugh where you think the story is poignant.

They may become hushed and thoughtful where you didn't expect that reaction. Whatever happens, you will learn from them and incorporate what you learn into subsequent tellings.

Storytelling at its best is a cooperative venture between teller and audience. Invite professional storytellers to your schools and libraries, by all means. Use their appearances to inspire your staff with the power of story. But do build on the excitement engendered by these events by featuring storytelling in your own classroom or library. The power of story can make a world of difference in your library, your classroom, and your students' lives.

SOURCE: Adapted from Connie Rockman, "Tell Me a Story," *School Library Journal* (August 2001): 46–49. Courtesy of *School Library Journal.*

9

PROMOTION
CHAPTER TEN

Information Power: Advocacy

The school library media specialist is the chief advocate for the library media program and documents its effectiveness so that the full learning community recognizes its value and supports its role. Seeking both formal and informal opportunities to raise public awareness, the library media specialist uses a variety of techniques to demonstrate the program's significance. Through regular administrative reporting, as well as ongoing advocacy, the library media specialist conveys the program's leadership in fostering information literacy, in encouraging collaborative teaching and learning, and in developing sophisticated uses of information technology.

SOURCE: Adapted from "Program Administration," chapter 6 in *Information Power: Building Partnerships for Learning* (Chicago: American Library Association, 1998), 113.

It's time to dispel some myths
by Marilyn Miller

Myths abound concerning nearly every aspect of library services, and school libraries are no exception. The first of several misconceptions I want to address is the notion that school library media specialists should no longer be considered librarians—a misperception often held by school library media specialists themselves as well as by other librarians. Some say that their identity as librarians who deliver certain services and programs is blurred by emphasis on their roles as teachers of finding and using information, and by the significant work some of them perform in curriculum development. I, for one, support the dual role of teacher and provider of instructional support to both students and teachers. The school librarian has been a pioneer in redefining the role of all librarians who work with people in a society heavily dominated by huge amounts of information and technology; and today, in fact, public service librarians in every type of library have a teaching role.

There are specific reasons why the title of teacher is seen to overshadow that of librarian in a school setting.

New visibility, new name

The first is the evolution of the once barely visible school library into the library media center of today. At the end of World War II, the school library was viewed in *School Libraries for Today and Tomorrow* as "an integral part of the educational program which it serves." Since then, school librarians have faced

unremitting challenges and changes. They have learned to select, organize, and circulate all types of learning materials and equipment deemed valuable in the education of elementary-school students. Their title was changed from school librarian to school media specialist, and when it was found that many people did not know what that meant, the word "library" was put back and they became school library media specialists.

I will always believe that the change in title was a major error practically, politically, and philosophically. The school library no longer resembles a mini-public library but looks more like a learning laboratory that invites the use of a wide range of resources and technologies. Its design must accommodate individuals, small groups, and entire classes, and it is no longer just a location but a school-wide part of the instructional program. What is delivered by the school library, and what happens because its applications are so pervasive, is more important than where it happens. As research and practice have brought new directions in teaching the use of resources and have identified their value for learners, the roles of school library media specialists have expanded and, according to *Information Power*, now include teacher, instructional partner, information specialist, and program administrator. To fulfill each role, the school librarian uses the principles, knowledge, and abilities taught by library education.

School librarians also emphasize their teaching role out of political necessity. Title and certification affect pay scales as well as credibility, and being seen as a teacher provides a safeguard when staff cuts are being made. School library media specialists must be certified or licensed in the state in which they work. That certification depends on teacher certification, and membership in teacher associations or unions is usually required.

A third reason why the teacher role model tends to overshadow the school librarian role can be found in the rise of single-purpose professional associations for school librarians. In the late '60s and early '70s, school librarians began to move away from state library associations to form their own organizations or joint organizations with colleagues specializing in nonprint educational media; one result was that other librarians sometimes considered them disloyal to the profession or uninterested in the fortunes of other types of libraries. In some states, school library associations have joined with other types of libraries in cooperative projects and conferences, while in others there is barely any professional interaction. This separatism has been politically and economically detrimental, and in an age of technology and complex systems that demand collaboration and partnership, it may become even more counterproductive.

Although some school librarians think of themselves as a group apart, without the expertise acquired by their study of librarianship their value to the students and teachers they serve will be lost or greatly diminished. School librarians provide millions of children with their first opportunity to savor the satisfaction and self-confidence that awaits them when they become competent readers and start down the path to self-directed learning. They must respect and project their role in creating awareness of the library—every library—as the source of lifelong learning and one of history's great social institutions.

Reading is still the key to success

The second misconception I would like to address is the notion that as technology plays a larger and larger role in the school library, we can put student reading on a back burner. Heavy workloads give weight to the false impression that technology makes media specialists' work with reading irrelevant. School administrators and other educators may contribute to this with ill-considered observations such as, "Kids don't need to read now that they have computers." The growth of electronic reading programs may offer another excuse for not making more time for creative, non-rote reading activities or working with teachers to supplement reading instruction.

The four major conveyors of information to students in today's schools are teachers, books (reading), videos, and computers. Reading is the only one of the four identified by researchers as the key to academic success (and most would add economic success as well). Voluntary, free, self-motivated reading has also been identified as key to the development of lifelong readers.

The school library media specialist must play a major role in the school's reading-development program. Reading guidance, with its opportunities for creative group activities and individual attention, is the area in which the school librarian reaches the most children and can collaborate most easily and most effectively with the teacher. Classroom teachers are struggling to teach reading skills to children who may have little foundation of enjoyment, expressive language, grasp of meaning, or motivation for decoding. Growing emphasis on skills and testing requires that reading teachers have a partner who can provide the sense of discovery and motivation needed to develop high-level literates equipped for leadership.

The school librarian serves as a bridge to all the students. Children leave a teacher at the end of the year, but the librarian can follow them from grade to grade, get to know some of them well, and become a positive adult influence. Given the national concern that the public, parents, and policymakers have about literacy, school librarians should step up their enhancement of reading.

10

Is education keeping up with reality?

My third concern relates to the perceived problems surrounding curriculum in library education programs and its relationship to the expressed needs of the field. Are library schools preparing students with the knowledge of key elements in the history and development of the American library and an understanding of its enormous potential role? The past is prologue: Can we survive as a profession if future practitioners aren't introduced to the roots of today's expanding mission? Specifically, where are new children's and youth librarians to come from? Is the move toward more technology courses a move away from those who serve society's future citizens? The last of the school librarians recruited in the mid-'60s are retiring; are state-supported library/media education programs preparing to deal with these shortages in the face of increasing demand for librarians trained to serve early childhood, families, youth, and students?

These serious questions must be addressed by the entire library profession. As child-serving agencies seek more partnerships with public libraries,

libraries have more difficulty securing youth librarians to work with them. In some areas, charter schools are placing incredible pressures on stretched and limited children's departments. When will public library directors and faculties in state-supported library education programs face this crisis situation and demand solutions?

It is a dangerous myth that the ALA, state associations, state libraries, and the profession in the field have no power in determining what library education must provide to serve our growing, diverse constituency. Pressure can be brought to bear on the state institutions of higher education with library schools to effect real change—pressure exerted with skill and political clout. This will include data about projected needs, numbers, demographics, and changes in clientele and service patterns. In addition, we must present, truthfully and graphically, what the disastrous outcomes for the society (not to mention for libraries themselves) will be if we fail to meet the challenge, and we must couple that with an equally truthful vision of what libraries of all types can accomplish if we will only equip them with the staff and other resources they need.

SOURCE: Adapted from Marilyn Miller, "As School Libraries Race Forward, It's Time to Dispel Some Myths," *American Libraries* 31, no. 11 (December 2000): 42–43.

Celebrate @ your library

by Hilda K. Weisburg and Ruth Toor

Let everyone know what is happening at your media center by latching on to the American Library Association's catchy advocacy campaign. The theme "@ your library" was launched at the Midwinter meeting in Washington, D.C., along with a website, www.ala.org/@yourlibrary. Tie the logo to whatever message you want to send. The impact will be reinforced by the countless ways it will be repeated as libraries around the country remind their patrons that public and school libraries are a national treasure.

If you can't think of a slogan, go to the campaign's page and find suggestions. For example, promote studying with "Make the grade @ your library." Another idea is "Get more out of class @ your library." Use it to encourage genre reading with "Find mystery @ your library" or promote Internet access with "Get wired @ your library."

Hold a contest and have students create messages with the logo. You can reward all suggestions with "@ your library" pencils available for $10 per dozen at the ALA store. Members get a 10% discount. One of the most eye-catching offerings is the "Ultimate Search Engine @ your library" bookmark and poster which allows you to use a digital camera to insert your own picture—for YOU are the ultimate search engine.

For free . . . but . . .

Even if you don't have extra funds to purchase items, you can get on board the campaign. The logo can be downloaded in so many different formats and sizes you are bound to find one that will work with your machines.

Print-ready artwork in Post-Script or Acrobat formats can also be downloaded. Those of you who have the software and printer capability have access to posters and bookmarks with an assortment of clever slogans ranging from "Nothing but Net @ your library" to "From Shaq to Shakespeare @ your library."

Although the logo is free, trademark rules apply. Before you download, you are reminded that

> libraries may use the trademark "@ your library" in American Typewriter Medium weight typeface, in either black, or red and blue as shown on this Web site, followed by a ™, for the purpose of promoting library use. The trademark may be used on signage, brochures, or other promotional documents or on merchandise intended for sale at the library or at a physical location within the community served by the library, but not through mail order, e-commerce, or other distribution methods. Any other uses, and any use by parties other than libraries, are subject to the prior written approval of ALA.

Become an advocate

Explore the website further and find "Quotable Quotes" about libraries. Choose your favorites and make them into large signs, posting them where they can be seen by everyone. Learn the key messages and talking points that will help you become an advocate for library media programs.

Over the past years, state library media associations have become more aware of the impact of legislation and advocacy as a means of keeping media centers a vital force in the schools. You need to become equally skilled at the building level. With the tools available at the campaign's website, you too can become a leader "@ your library."

SOURCE: Adapted from Hilda K. Weisburg and Ruth Toor, "Celebrate @ Your Library," *The School Librarian's Workshop* 21, no. 8 (April 2001): 14–15. Copyright 2001. Used with permission.

Marketing the changing role of the SLMS

10

by Judith Freels, Claire Kruse, David Richards, and Laura Sophiea

Recognizing that the 21st-century school library media programs should look different than programs of the past, the school library media specialists (SLMSs) in our suburban school district began to address what we felt the program could become. As a first step we looked at our roles as facilitators, teachers, and technologists. We identified our key roles as SLMSs, then compared our programs. This process led to the realization that the district's programs and roles differed from building to building. Eighteen different programs and perceptions of the school library media program were evident.

We decided that it was crucial for our group to come to a consensus about the key roles of SLMSs in successful school library media programs. Using the AASL's *Information Power,* we identified the following roles: information specialist, instructional partner, and program administrator. Next we decided that educating administrators, staff members, and community members was essential, so we created a brochure promoting the school library media program in the schools. The brochure's publication has prompted an extensive public relations campaign to promote the value of the school library media program in our district.

The first group we targeted was our district's administrators. Informal discussions revealed that their administrative graduate work gave them little understanding of the role of the school library media program. Many of their perceptions and understanding of the program were based on their personal experiences as students. Along with the brochure, we gave a presentation to the district administrators, allowing them time to reflect on their perceptions of a successful school library media program. This opened a dialogue between building administrators and their respective media specialists.

Teachers and building staff were the next groups targeted. SLMSs learned the skill of self-promotion as they distributed brochures to teachers. The brochures and subsequent discussions led to a new appreciation by building-level educators of the value of SLMSs and their programs. Most recently, SLMSs have taken the brochure to parent groups. Eventually, our marketing campaign will target the entire learning community.

In addition to the brochure, every school library media center in the district has created a web page during the past year. By connecting all of the media centers in our district, building-level isolation has been mitigated. These Web pages celebrate both a common vision and the unique attributes of each site.

SOURCE: Adapted from Judith Freels, Claire Kruse, David Richards, and Laura Sophiea, "Marketing the Changing Role of the SLMS," *Knowledge Quest* 30, no. 1 (September/October 2001): 19.

The hole truth: Librarians need to emphasize what they have to offer

by Gary Hartzell

"People don't buy a quarter-inch drill bit because they want a quarter-inch drill bit," points out Doug Johnson of the Mankato (MN) Area Public Schools. "They buy a quarter-inch drill bit because they want to create a quarter-inch hole." Similarly, board members and administrators aren't interested in good library media programs because they want good libraries. They're interested in libraries because they want students to read better, learn more, and improve achievement. What implications does this have for those of us who are library advocates?

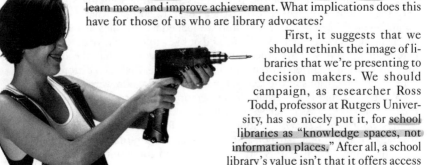

First, it suggests that we should rethink the image of libraries that we're presenting to decision makers. We should campaign, as researcher Ross Todd, professor at Rutgers University, has so nicely put it, for school libraries as "knowledge spaces, not information places." After all, a school library's value isn't that it offers access to information. Students and teachers don't seek information for information's sake; they seek it to generate useful knowledge.

The notion that it's the hole we're after rather than the drill bit also suggests another idea that Todd neatly voices: When we advocate on behalf of school libraries, we should emphasize "connections, not collections." In other words, the value of a library's collection is that it's able to *connect* students and teachers to the information they are seeking.

Part of the difficulty with the educational process is that it often disaggregates, or artificially separates, reality in order to study its constituent parts in a more manageable form. That means that mathematics, chemistry, physics, biology, and other fundamental disciplines are disconnected and studied in isolation from one another—despite the fact that they are inextricably integrated in our daily lives. The best educators constantly struggle to emphasize connectivity. The library is the only place in the school where there is a confluence of all of the various disciplines. A librarian's stock in trade is making significant interdisciplinary connections, connections between learners and the knowledge they are searching for.

Finally, focusing on the hole instead of the drill bit implies that librarians ought to strike a new stance when campaigning for additional school funds and personnel. We should never state that the resources will be used to hire staff or purchase books, magazines, CD-ROMs, computers, and licenses without stating what those resources are needed for. Buying the drill bit buys the hole; buying resources buys improved student achievement. Unless library supporters take that tack, board members and administrators will continue to view libraries and librarians as an expense rather than as a necessary investment.

Make no mistake. Our efforts at championing school libraries and persuading others that librarians continue to play an essential role in the educational process will be challenged. This will be a difficult fight because we know from social psychology research that it's harder to change an existing concept and relationship than it is to create a new one. We'll need to bring persuasive research evidence into play and be prepared to communicate it often and in as many ways as we possibly can. The evidence is available.

It's important to keep in mind that legislators, board members, and administrators—like the rest of us—make decisions on the basis of perceptions. If our advocacy efforts misguidedly reinforce stereotypical perceptions of libraries and librarians, we may lose ground instead of gaining it and find ourselves falling through a professional hole much bigger than a quarter-inch in diameter.

SOURCE: Adapted from Gary Hartzell, "The Hole Truth," *School Library Journal* 48 (July 2002): 31. Courtesy of *School Library Journal.*

Promoting library advocacy and information literacy from an "invisible library"

by Kathy Lehman

How does a new teacher-librarian keep visible when the collection is boxed up in an auxiliary gym? The author's information campaign to keep library news and services alive could help other librarians plan their advocacy programs.

FYI's

Weekly notices were put in faculty mailboxes announcing procedures for checking out equipment and videos, available public library and online services,

copyright information, Internet searching tips, and my vision of a "virtual" library. The Thomas Dale High School in Chester, Virginia, is "home of the Knights" and we found the perfect logo on a clip art disk to put on all library notices—a cartoon knight with a shield large enough to change the message inside. Soon students and staff began to associate the library knight with messages from the library resource center. To keep our principal informed of our efforts, we submit a report each month detailing instructional, administrative, and professional activities as well as circulation and usage statistics.

Faculty meetings

Whenever possible I made announcements and demonstrated, with laptop and LCD projector, the emerging virtual library and its potential for providing students with information resources while the library remained closed. I asked to be on the agenda at the Advisory Council meetings (a monthly meeting of department heads and administrators) and invited myself to department meetings. It took months to get on the agenda for some departments, but I never gave up. Not only did I present the online resources available, but I used modules built into the website to illustrate Boolean searching, research models, copyright guidelines, collaborative planning, and student research guides. Teaming with the assistant librarian, I ventured into classrooms and labs to demonstrate research strategies with students.

More significantly, I drew on my experience as a technology trainer in my previous school and offered teachers assistance to complete their final projects for a county-mandated technology portfolio. These projects, referred to as technology integration units, demonstrate a teacher's competence in nine strands of computer/technology applications. By collaborating with me to create a website for their class, teachers could fulfill this obligation. With every project, teachers completed a requirement for renewal of their state teaching license, I added another page to the virtual library, and students gained a

guided research project online. These web pages are available to students 24/7. It's a win, win, win situation.

The virtual library takes off

As with all websites, ours began one page at a time. I looked at model sites, talked to colleagues for suggestions and began collecting sites on electronic notepad pages as I surfed the Internet. I started the website with links to fee-based subscription sites, our school system's site, our state database, and trials of other databases.

We also linked to online services available through our public library. With their public library card number, students have remote access from our school library web page to the collection database and most licensed resources subscribed to by the public library.

Our virtual library branches to pages listing additional reference sources, other virtual libraries, recommended staff sites, and, most important, the Class Lists. These are web pages designed collaboratively with teachers to guide students through specific classroom research objectives. The early pages were designed simply to help students locate preselected, curriculum-specific websites. These allowed students to locate information without losing valuable class lab time mistyping URLs or surfing through inappropriate and misleading information. Following each session in school, students could enjoy the sites again as reinforcement from home.

The superior quality of information found in licensed databases quickly became apparent when students compared findings from our databases to Internet search engines. Every student using the licensed databases found solid material on his or her topic and completed the assignment in one session. English students were asked to compare results from licensed databases to their previous results from the Internet. One comment was "I like using the licensed databases better than the regular Internet because the information is deeper and more concise."

Clearly students recognize the value of edited, authoritative material. Teachers remarked that students were more focused using the class web pages. Everyone is equally engaged at the same time.

Articles published

10

To be sure students and staff know about the resources available and take advantage of our program, we have submitted articles to every publication available to us. *The Knightly News* is our student newspaper and student reporters have run articles regularly about the library's progress and the Virtual Library. *Knightline* is the newsletter for parents and we publish an article in every issue. Our local newspaper has been extremely supportive and published an article detailing our cooperation with the public library.

I wrote an article for our state librarians' journal describing my determination to be the "visible librarian with an invisible library." We have done our best to reach every student and staff member and offer our services and expertise to help them succeed. Keeping the school community informed is critical to securing philosophical and monetary support for library resource programs.

Community support

The overall success of our 10 months without a library is due to the amazing support of our school community. Teachers welcomed us into their classrooms and were willing to collaborate with us to try a new online approach to research. We continually added modules and pages to the Virtual Library to meet new instructional needs, demonstrate research models, and streamline the research process. Even today with our library open, new links are being added to the Virtual Library as we discover new appropriate sites. Teachers constantly stop us in the halls with suggestions or send students to the library with lists of websites to add to their class pages.

We truly have the best of both worlds: a well-rounded print collection with more than 20,000 items and a growing website with unlimited resources. We are knocking down the "walls" of the library and working to prepare our students to be information literate in the 21st century.

SOURCE: Adapted from Kathy Lehman, "Promoting Library Advocacy and Information Literacy from an 'Invisible Library,'" *Teacher Librarian* 29, no. 4 (April 2002): 27–28, 30. Copyright 2002. Used with permission.

At least 101 ways to put the ACTIVE in proactive!

by Debra Kay Logan

[*Ed. Note:* In this article, Debra gives us 126 ways to assume our leadership roles in the school, to put "active" into being proactive, and to place us in the center of teaching and learning, step by simple step.]

Smile at everyone who enters the library!
Collaborate.
Be visible.
Integrate instruction.
Help teachers find information when they are taking classes.
Share articles on how school libraries/media centers impact student achievement with administrators and teachers.
Key lesson plan to state learner outcomes.
Let the collaborating teacher take the kudos for a successful project.
Build an e-library for the school.
Be active in your profession.
Do programs for community groups.
Remember birthdays.

Assure teachers it is not their fault when a bulb blows.
Keep a candy basket for teachers in the library.
Attend extracurricular events.
Respond to advocacy calls to action and call, phone, or e-mail when needed.
Eat in the teacher's lounge.
Refrain from discussing colleagues with other coworkers.
Be professional.
Entice teachers to see new books and resources on display in the library.
Present at library and non-library conferences.
Call or write parents to compliment their children when appropriate.
Invite the press to special events.
Turn the circulation computer back on to check out one more book at the end of the day.

Replace bulbs ASAP with a smile.

After a successful project, ask the collaborating teacher to tell others about working with you.

Offer to help grade projects.

Help chaperone dances.

Drop what you are doing to help people.

Listen.

Anticipate research projects.

Offer discarded materials to teachers.

Volunteer to serve on building and district committees.

Pick up posters at conferences and give them to teachers.

Be gracious when meetings are held in the library media center.

Advertise special events.

Be enthusiastic.

Always have spare pencils for students.

Invite teachers and/or administrators to co-present at conferences.

Do a year-end report.

Write articles for non-library professional journals.

Be accurate.

Keep copies of district policies and curriculums in the library.

Decorate the library/media center.

Write news stories for local papers highlighting special library-related activities.

Help with young author programs.

Compliment students.

Promote services.

Maintain your sense of humor . . . no matter what.

Display new resources during parent–teacher conferences.

Watch for articles of interest to share with students and colleagues.

Write articles on what is happening in the library for parent newsletters.

Subscribe to *ALAWON*, the ALA Washington Office Electronic Newsletter.

Have a book discussion group for coworkers.

Invite elected officials to visit your library.

Collect hard data to support requests.

Troubleshoot AV equipment.

Be loyal.

Have special reading events.

Let teachers know when the kind of book they love is available in the library.

Make coworkers aware of great new software.

Attend conference sessions that will help colleagues.

Say "thank you" for support.

Give orientation tours to new teachers.

Align library goals and objectives with the district's continuous improvement plan.

Help teachers create their own classroom web pages.

Do in-services for staff on electronic resources.

Offer to put links for teachers' lessons on an Internet Project Page.

Offer to help with projects.

Frequently check in on new teachers and offer to help them.

10

Be the "go to" person in your building.

Bring conference handouts and goodies back to staff members and students.

Have shoulders that can be cried on.

Be discreet.

Involve staff in collection development decisions.

Accept responsibility.

Be willing to help other teachers find information for personal projects.

Start a paperback book exchange for teachers.

Sponsor a book discussion group for students.

Stay a bit late or come in early to help with a project.

Be ready to help readers find the perfect book.

Have an overdue amnesty day.

Help with service projects.

Offer to grade bibliographies.

Base library planning on building goals and needs.

Use surveys to evaluate your efforts and program.

Help with field trips.

Use an instant messaging program to help troubleshoot classroom computers when you cannot leave the library.

Involve staff members in library policy decisions.

Serve on as many curriculum committees as possible.

Read.

Troubleshoot classroom computers when the Tech Squad is not available.

Display student projects in the library.

Subscribe to your state organization.

Display diplomacy.

Keep up-to-date on current educational research.

Invite groups to use the library for after-school meetings.

Be firm, consistent, and fair.

Have a spare calculator for student use.

Do lesson plans like the other teachers in the school.

Be in charge of celebrations.

Be the first to learn how to use new technologies.

Attend faculty events.

Don't whine!

Help with multimedia projects.

Keep a coffee pot in the library.

Encourage teachers to work in the library.

Involve staff in library planning.

Display collaborative projects in the board room/administration building.

Handle your own discipline whenever possible.

Include classified personnel in special events.

Be a part of the solution.

Invite the board to meet in the library/media center.

Become one of the school's technology gurus.

Feed the teachers.

Ask students their opinions.

Be flexible.

Never stop learning about the newest educational technologies.

Invite staff and community members to help with library planning.

Promote National Library Week.
Write professional articles.
Display a library schedule in a prominent place
    like over the copier.
Publish a newsletter.
Keep a copier in the library.
Anticipate needs.
Put people ahead of things.
And do all this for $27,500 a year!

SOURCE: Adapted from Debra Kay Logan, "At Least 101 Ways to Put the ACTIVE in Proactive!" *Ohio Media Spectrum* 54, no. 2 (Spring 2002): 12–13. Used with permission.

Priming the pump

by Alice H. Yucht

There's an old story about a parched traveler who stumbled over an old water-pump in the middle of the desert. The traveler desperately pumped on the handle, but no water came out. Finally the traveler noticed some scratches on the spigot. Peering closer, he saw the words "dig under rock" and an arrow pointing to the left where he found a battered canteen filled with water and a note that read:

> This pump will work good after you pour the whole canteen of water down the pipe to get it going. But you have to prime the pump first— give *it* some water before you can have any for yourself. Just remember to put the refilled canteen and this note back where you found them for the next thirsty traveler.

"Priming the pump" means encouraging action by first providing a similar substance or lubricant to facilitate the desired results. You've got to do something to make it work, to give of yourself before you can hope to get anything in return. All good public relations programs work on the same principle: make valuable deposits *into* the "favor bank" before you can begin to withdraw any benefits.

Practice positive professionalism. "Share" should be the mantra of all librarians; we lose nothing by giving information away. Be the consummate info-pro: always peering ahead for possibilities and publications that might be useful to your colleagues and students. Forward current articles and hotlinks to teachers and administrators, send resource reviews to subject specialists, and promote new acquisitions and projects to the Powers-that-Be. Always provide service with a smile, no matter what. You want the library to be known as the primary resource center of your building, the "place to go for those in the know."

Recognize reality. "If only" accomplishes nothing. Make the best of what you've got. Cramped for space and can't push out a wall? Eliminate as much clutter and deadwood as possible to make your facility more attractive. No clerical help? Streamline your procedures so your students can check materials out without adult assistance. Remember you were hired to work, not whine. Requests for improvements or additions should be

10

predicated on the ensuing benefits for the whole school, not just the librarian!

Invest intelligently. Think before you spend time *or* money. What will give you the best, and most long-term, return on your investment? With book prices soaring and budgets shrinking, do you need multiple hard-cover copies or can you wait for paperbacks? Working on a collaborative project with an enthusiastic and influential colleague will pay more dividends than pulling books off the shelves for a teacher who never actually brings her classes into the library.

Market your materials and methods. Effective sales strategies do more than tell just what the product is; they also demonstrate *why* the consumer should want that product in particular. Think of ways to make your constituents want/need your products.

Do mini-booktalks at faculty meetings. Put together a page of practical websites for the parent newsletter. Provide booklists for recreational reading. Do a workshop on Internet search skills for your Parent–Teacher organization. Make sure everyone remembers the library as an integral part of the educational process when it's time to vote on the school budget!

Explore and extend. Remember that you need to get "wet," too. The information landscape is constantly shifting these days. Bring in new ideas and possibilities from exploring and reading widely. Attend conferences and courses, try new products, and make new contacts. Education works both ways; extend a hand to a new teacher or librarian, and you'll find yourself learning, too.

Priming the pump isn't really very hard. You just have to be willing to give, before you get . . . and then the rewards are great!

SOURCE: Adapted from Alice H. Yucht, "Priming the Pump," *Teacher Librarian* 29, no. 1 (October 2001): 47–48. Used with permission.

How to gain support from your board and administration

by Steven M. Baule and Laura Blair Bertani

When library media specialists gather, they often talk about their feeling that local school boards and administrators don't fully support the library media program. Underlying this perception is often a kernel of truth. If there is a lack of support for our programs, the reason is often that, as library media specialists, we haven't done enough to inform and persuade. Marketing our programs is a necessity in today's educational environment.

If your board of education and your school district administration are not fully aware of what you do, they cannot be fully supportive. Fortunately, in most districts, the days of "us and them"—teachers vs. administrators—are past. Teamwork and interdepartmental efforts are increasing, and collaborative management styles are more the norm than the exception. So what does this "changed environment" mean to the school library media specialist? More than likely, it means there has never been a better time for librarians to look to their administrators and boards for support.

Capitalize on this new environment by drawing attention to your programs. Market yourselves! Cultivate the support of your school's leadership.

Align your library goals with district goals; then market your program. First, learn what is important to the board and administration. Find out what short- and long-term goals they have established for the school district. Then make sure you address those goals when you design your own library media program goals. For example, if the board and administrative focus is on improved student achievement, emphasize the library's potential to help students toward higher achievement.

Once articulated and in writing, your library media program goals will be your road map for the year. Aligning your goals with the school district's goals will show how the library program is integral to the strategic direction of the district. Let those goals serve as the springboard for all your communications and marketing efforts. Some common ideas for increasing exposure of your program are outlined below. These ideas—along with your own—can become part of your marketing efforts.

Host your district's board meeting. To focus attention on your program, create situations for the board, administration, and other school leaders to visit your school media center. Nothing speaks louder than firsthand experience! In many school districts, the board of education holds its regular meetings in school libraries throughout the district. If your school district does not take this opportunity, then suggest it. If regular meetings in the library are not feasible for your board, then suggest hosting one meeting per year. Perhaps schedule that meeting to coincide with National Library Week or another such event. Have your librarians and media specialists attend the board meeting. Offer to present a short tour to board members prior to the meeting. Consider having student hosts explain how they use your library services. Credible comments spoken by a "customer"—especially a student—will speak volumes about your program's value to the school district.

Design a "fast facts" flyer. Design a one-page flyer— a set of bullet points—that can be your "brag sheet." Distribute your flyer to the board members and others. Ask the principal to include it in a start-of-school mailing to students and parents. Have copies always available at your checkout counter.

When writing and designing your flyer, be as professional as possible. Use the opportunity to showcase desktop publishing capabilities through your technology. Use one of the professionally designed templates available in much of the software. Use clip art or graphics, but use them sparingly. Make the type font consistent throughout your flyer. Write headlines that attract the reader. In deciding what to write, always consider what your customers need to know about your services rather than what you want them to know (in many cases, the same things). Keep sentences short; bullet points are easy for the hurried reader to scan.

Showcase everyday life. Invite board members and administrators in to see your day-to-day operations while students are using your facilities. Schedule a day in which they can see a range of your normal activities. Don't try to impress them with out-of-the-normal activities. Do impress them with how well you do your regular job and how that has a direct impact on student learning and the instructional process. Remember, the main topic of the conversation is student learning. That is our business and that will nearly always get the attention of a board member or administrator.

Send a library newsletter. If you don't presently send out a library newsletter to your staff, consider doing so. Consider publishing it monthly or quarterly. Be consistent. In time, staff will come to expect this regular news item from your office. A library newsletter will remind readers of your programs and the fact that you are a vital, integral member of the educational community.

Again, brevity is best. Keep your newsletter short: one page front and back will do. Focus on the services your library has to offer. Use your newsletter as a teaching tool. Provide information that teachers can use now. Plug a new technology service, feature a teacher who has used library services to create an interesting lesson, or provide tips on "where to find what" in the library. Consider quoting a student or staff member in each issue to help publicize your services. Your customers' words carry great credibility. Share news about interesting websites, including information that appeals to staff members personally; for example, in the last issue of the school year, include an article on where to find inexpensive summer airfares. In addition to distributing your newsletter in staff mailboxes, send copies to your district administration and ask the superintendent to include copies in routine mailings to board members.

Share highlights in an annual report. Develop an annual report for the board and administration. Sharing year-in-review highlights—where you were at the beginning of the year vs. where you are now—is good publicity for your constituents as well as a practical assessment tool for you. In a simple format, view your program over the course of the year. Include statistics to show the student and staff usage of your services. Include charts and graphs. Describe changes and upgrades in your services and facilities over the year.

Your annual report could be designed as a four-page document replacing your end-of-the-year newsletter, saving you from having to write and design two publications at that busy time of year. Again, use desktop publishing to design your annual report. Include graphics, photos, and headlines that attract the reader. When writing, keep your reader in mind. Will he care about this topic? Why should she be interested? How does this news impact your readers? What's in it for them?

Create a website. Promote your program on the Web by creating a web page for your school library program. E-commerce is the way of the future! A good library web page should serve as a gateway to electronic and community reference resources and should highlight parent information sources as well. If possible, provide a method for feedback to improve your services and link to the community. Remember, community members often have more influence with board members and administration than you do.

Capitalize on existing special events. Use National Library Week and other calendar events to highlight the role of the library media program. Hold a reception for the board, administration, and staff in the library media center. Such an event provides an informal opportunity for them to mingle with the library staff (even if only one staff member) and see the library. Make sure you have plenty of student materials on display, along with new titles. Enlist the help of teachers. Perhaps one of them would be willing to present a classroom assignment for your audience. Where possible, have students make poster presentations explaining some of the research they have completed using library resources and assistance.

Use "networking"—good, old-fashioned face-to-face salesmanship. Networking is a new-millennium buzzword for an age-old concept: Work face-to-face with people to develop wide support for the library program among the rest of your staff. Too often, library staff members work their entire days in the library, isolated from the rest of the school staff. Involve yourselves in the wider school community. Volunteer on committees. Speak up in faculty and staff meetings. Be a visible presence, spokesperson, and advocate for your programs.

Enlist others. When the English department chair or the third-grade teacher speaks on behalf of the library media program, his or her words carry great credibility. Board members and administrators expect the library media specialist to advocate for the library program, but when classroom teachers speak in your favor, it carries an extra endorsement.

Make a formal presentation to the board of education. Another way to market your program is to seek an opportunity to meet with the board in a formal presentation. Ask your superintendent if there is a board meeting at which you could present the library program—in 20 minutes or less. Streamline your presentation, focusing on how your programs and services contribute to student learning. Showcase your technological abilities by using PowerPoint, slides, or video in your presentation.

Again, for credibility—and variety—devote most of your short time to having teachers and students tell how they have effectively used the library to support their teaching and learning. Introduce, set the stage for their remarks, and conclude. Avoid library and media jargon and technology acronyms. (For example, talk about removing old materials from the collection, not "weeding.") Have fun; encourage staff and students to smile and talk about ways they enjoy the library.

Dress for success when you make that board presentation. Wear a business suit or otherwise present a highly professional appearance. It is important to present yourself as a manager of a modern library and information literacy program, not simply the "library lady" or the "media man" that some board members may recall from their own school days.

Create an ongoing marketing plan. Your progress toward achieving your yearly goals can be included in the content of your monthly or quarterly newsletters and can be the focus of your library tours. The accomplishment of those goals can be what you write about in your annual report and what you present at a board of education meeting.

After your first year of operating with communications goals that support your library's goals, your marketing plan becomes cyclical. Create goals for the next year based on the prior year's goals, the actions that supported those goals, any evaluative measures you used to assess your efforts, and, of course, what your board of education and administration have identified as new goals for the next school year. The cycle can be fun! Good luck.

SOURCE: Adapted from Steven M. Baule and Laura Blair Bertani, "How to Gain Support from Your Board and Administration: Marketing 101 for Your Library Media Program," *The Book Report* 19, no. 3 (November/December 2000): 47–49. *The Book Report* is now published as *Library Media Connection.* Used with permission.

Advocacy in less than five pages

by Blanche Woolls

School librarians have often been perceived as "special" teachers, lumped with art, music, and physical education, to provide special services rather than necessities. This provides a unique challenge, and one that is ongoing, to tell the message of protecting access to information, meeting information needs, teaching information literacy skills, and providing, in many instances, a safe haven for students. What is your score on this advocacy scale?

PR checklist

Do you
- ___ know the names of all the students in your school (or most for the very large schools)?
- ___ attend special events at your school (i.e., sports events, choir concerts, class plays, puppet shows)?
- ___ have students help you write a regular column for the school and local newspaper?
- ___ have an up-to-date web page for the school library?
- ___ have students who find their assignments by going to your library home page?
- ___ have a logo for all your publications?
- ___ offer a "bookstore" look to your book collection, enticing readers?
- ___ regularly report successes in classroom interactions to your principal?
- ___ have an advisory committee with teachers, students, and a parent?

Are you
- ___ *not* the flagon with the dragon but the brew that is true? (With apologies to Danny Kaye in *The Court Jester*, 1956.)
- ___ invited to special events in classrooms (i.e., the third-grade puppet show or the science fair entries)?

Your library
- ___ is welcoming, with an entrance free of clutter.
- ___ has a floor plan with a logical flow to the traffic.
- ___ has good signage so that users can find areas and materials quickly.

The following persons have visited your library this year:
- ___ school board member
- ___ state legislator
- ___ superintendent

The following persons have visited your library in the past month:
- ___ parents
- ___ principal

The following persons have visited your library in the past two weeks:

___ 50% of the teachers

___ 75% of the students

For each check mark, give yourself 5 points.

0–10:   You need to be worried. No one will miss you if you are replaced with a clerk.

10–30:   Start planning to implement enough to move up a level. If you involve teachers in the planning, you will gain allies and support.

30–60:   You have room for much improvement. Ask your advisory committee to help you set priorities.

60–80:   You seem well on the way to a higher score. Think through how to raise a few more points.

80–90:   What are you missing? Should it be a priority?

90–105: If you have been honest in your answers, you are truly a platinum school librarian.

When is the last time a school board member came into your library?

When is the last time you told the Rotary that you are there to help students navigate through the reefs of misinformation? When is the last time you met the Google challenge?

Advocacy requires efforts for both the big picture of the universe and the small picture of your school, with the intermediate picture from your school district to the region, to the state, to the nation, and to the world. While efforts may be transferable among the three pictures, some are unique.

Small Scale: Which parent can speak to a school board member after church?

Intermediate Scale: Do you assist your legislators in their home offices and do you attend State Legislator's Day activities?

Large Scale: Do you belong to and attend meetings of a national school library media association? An international association?

General suggestions:

Keep up with the research on the impact of school librarians on student achievement, but make sure you repackage it to fit your situation.

Have a contest for students to design a logo for your library and then use it on everything from bookmarks to your business cards to . . .

Using your logo throughout, create a media book.

What is a media book?

As chair of the University of Pittsburgh's Senate Athletic Committee over a period of years, this author learned the tricks of the trade about promoting college sports. Members of the committee received copies of the media books created to give to radio and television broadcasters. These glitzy, full-color publications featured pictures and information about coaches and players, including hometowns, college degree sought, year in college, height and weight, position played, team wins and losses, any records held, and other vital statistics. Posed photos of individual players and team portraits were accompanied by exciting shots from events, all in living color on well-designed pages.

It isn't all that difficult to prepare such a fact book for our school libraries. We now have access to digital cameras and color printers. You can then transfer the information you have printed to your website. Technology gives us the ability to update and print upon demand. What do you feature? How much does your library "weigh"?

Your mission, goals, and objectives in relation to the district and school goals and objectives

Special events that will happen in the library during the year—author visits, state young readers award program

Your collection size (and $$ replacement including the cost of online databases if purchased in print), formats, and usage statistics (number of class visits per week, research papers generated using the collection and the technology, testimonials from students), and areas of strength (e.g., information about the 50 states for the fifth-grade U.S. assignment)

Types of collaborative research projects you've created working with teachers

Pictures, pictures, pictures (making sure you have written parental permission to use images of students)

Your background and the backgrounds of your staff members

Anything else that helps someone who can't visit your library understand what goes on there

In addition, your website should be engaging and updated frequently. You should have professional business cards with your library logo. These should not be created from a program, but should be professionally designed calling cards with your name, title, website, and e-mail address as well as school address.

SOURCE: Created by Blanche Woolls for this publication.

AASL advocacy toolkit

The school library media specialist

For many children, the school library media specialist is their first experience with a librarian. These information professionals play a critical role, teaching students how to select, use, and understand information in all formats. National guidelines recommend that every school building have at least one full-time certified library media professional with appropriate support staff. According to the National Center for Education Statistics (NCES),

there are 72,160 state-certified school library media specialists in U.S. schools;

nationally, 69% of schools have credentialed school library media specialists; and

the ratio of students to school library media specialists varies widely. Montana has one school library media specialist for every 287.4 public school students. California, with the worst ratio, has one media specialist per 942.1 pupils. The national average is one media specialist for every 591.3 students.

The school library media center: Quotable facts

Keith Curry Lance, Marcia J. Rodney, and Christine Hamilton-Pennell report that the highest achieving students come from schools with good library media centers. NCES reports that almost 36 million students visit school library media centers each week during the school year.

According to the Entertainment Software Association, sales of video games and other entertainment software in the U.S. reached $7 billion in 2003. This total, according to two sources (the Book Industry Study Group and an article by Marilyn I. Miller and Marilyn L. Shontz), is more than nine times the amount spent on books, periodicals, audiovisual, and other materials for school library media centers ($647 million in 2000).

Funding for schools comes primarily from local property taxes, with some funding from state and federal governments. The Improving Literacy through School Libraries grants made by the U.S. Department of Education in 2002 represent the first direct funding for school library materials in almost 40 years. Most schools spend about $16 per student, less than the average cost of a book, on print and nonprint library resources.

More than 90% of elementary schools and almost 100% of high school libraries are connected to the Internet. Unfortunately, this fact is often used to decrease budgets for books and other materials.

SOURCE: Adapted from the AASL Toolkit, http://www.ala.org/ala/aasl/aaslproftools/aasladvocacytools/aasladvocacy.htm and http://www.ala.org/ala/aasl/aaslproftools/aasladvocacytools/schoollibrary.htm.

10

Information power

Principle 7. Sufficient funding is fundamental to the success of the library media program.

Creating an information literate society is an expensive task. The school library media program requires a level of funding that will give all students adequate opportunities. In an era when access to information defines the difference between wealth and poverty, the library media program must provide access to all the information and instruction that students and others need for active, authentic, information-based learning. The school library media program requires a budget that supports the continuous collection of information in all formats and that provides the instructional infrastructure that will help students learn to use that information in creative, meaningful ways.

In close collaboration with teachers, administrators, and others, the school library media specialist takes a leading role in planning and managing a program budget that provides for the ongoing acquisition, updating, and expansion of hardware, software, and other materials to support curricular and other learning needs. The library media specialist also presents budget requests that are adequate to underwrite necessary facilities expansion and maintenance and support appropriate staffing and services so that the program can meet the growing and changing information needs of students, teachers, administrators, and others.

SOURCE: Adapted from "Program Administration," chapter 6 in *Information Power: Building Partnerships for Learning* (Chicago: American Library Association, 1998), 109–110.

Managing the budget

by Blanche Woolls

School library media centers expand or disintegrate depending on the amount of money allocated in the school district budget for purchases of needed resources, new materials, and equipment. District administrators plan the district budget and present it to the school board for approval. The type of budget prepared is usually dictated by the state education department and may be directly related to some trend outside education but adopted by educators.

Whatever the model the school district uses, school library media specialists must conform to that model whenever they have input in the budget process. Whenever school library media specialists respond to requests for budget input, they should show they have made a needs assessment and that the budget covers proposed activities for a year, with the supporting rationale for each activity.

Conflicts arise out of the realities of the school district's financial situation, usually defined by level of local taxation, and the practical need to provide a wide variety of materials for students and teachers. These conflicts can occur at the district level, when the library budget is distributed from a central library budget, or in each school, if district funds are distributed to individual buildings. Because budget items for the library media program are part of the total school district budget, funding requests compete with other units such as academic requirements, art, athletics, and music programs. Budgets distributed in the local school will find the media specialist's requests competing with the classroom teachers' requests as well as with requests from other special programs.

Annual budgets for school districts are prepared early in one fiscal year for the next year's expenditures. The superintendent, usually with assistance from others who are asked for input, makes the final decision on items and amounts. Principals and the superintendent's central office staff are usually included in budget decisions; however, other participants may be included by demand rather than by request. An example would be the negotiators for the teachers' bargaining unit who may oversee the preparation of the budget to make sure no budget decrease will necessitate personnel reductions and to confirm the inclusion of salary increases and other benefits.

Once the budget is prepared, the superintendent presents it to the local school board for approval. In some states, the state board of education grants final approval. In other states, voters are asked to pass a referendum for funding, and budgets can be voted down by the community. The amount of control exercised by local or state boards of education or by the voters in a referendum is in direct proportion to the amount of funds they control. In states where the major portion of education funding comes from state rather than local revenues, state officials maintain closer control over the local budget process than in states where most school funding is locally generated.

Public school educators now face a public demanding test scores at or above the national average, merit review for teachers, cost accountability for expenditures, and confirmation that the educational program is meeting the objectives set by school personnel. The trend toward reductions in funding for education directly affects funding for the school library media center.

States may mandate a minimum amount to be spent for school library media materials. This amount is usually based on a per-pupil allocation calculated by average daily attendance in the individual schools, called "attendance centers." If the amount is not specified, the local education agency or school district may grant a specific amount to be spent per pupil. In other districts, principals may receive a sum for the total program in their building, and they decide how much will be allocated to each teacher or classroom program. In other situations, the library budget is allocated through the supervisor of the library media program.

In situations where a sum is specified by the state or the school superintendent, it is much more difficult for the individual building-level media specialists to influence the amount they receive. When the budget is given to the district library media coordinator for reallocation, the needs of each school may be assessed; school library media specialists should understand the method of budget making and the placement of funds in each category.

The fiscal year

School districts usually match the state government pattern. That is, if the fiscal year is January 1–December 31, all materials must be ordered, received, and paid for no later than December 31, or the expenditures will be charged against the next year. If the fiscal year is July 1–June 30, the books will be closed June 30, and all expenditures not cleared by that date will be charged to the next year's budget.

Business managers often require that all purchase orders be issued in enough time to receive the merchandise, confirm shipment of the appropriate items, and issue payment before the end of the fiscal year. In some cases, no purchase orders are issued within four months of the end of the fiscal year, so that orders will be completed in ample time before closing the books. Library media specialists seldom have large budgets and any loss of funds can be crucial. Items that require longer times for shipment should be ordered early in the budget year, if at all possible, to allow maximum time for receipt. Also, equipment that might require testing before payment should be ordered as early as possible. Moreover, library media specialists should be aware of what happens if a shipment is not received before the books are closed. It may be charged against the next year's budget, in effect costing double. This is because funds were lost from one year and became an unanticipated purchase added to next year, decreasing that budget by that amount. Many of these errors can be avoided if the fiscal officer is aware of the interests of the media specialist.

The need to handle fiscal matters promptly is one of the reasons fiscal officers sometimes wish to limit the media center to one or two book orders each year. Limiting orders seriously affects the media specialist's ability to provide materials for students and teachers when needs arise. Working closely with business managers and clerical staff can help overcome this problem.

The library media specialist should be as supportive of the fiscal officer as possible. Most media specialists present necessary buying information to the purchasing agent by submitting order cards, special order forms, school or district requisitions, or purchase orders. All forms must be completed accurately, from correct name and address of the supplier to correct spelling of author, title, and publisher for books, accurate item numbers for supplies, accurate model numbers for equipment, and accurate quantities desired, unit item costs, and item totals. Any erroneous information on an order may cause an incorrect shipment or incorrect billing, which will result in additional correspondence from the business office for the return or exchange of items. This costs staff time in the accounting office and may lead the business manager to restrict the media specialist's freedom to issue a requisition or purchase order.

As more and more routine ordering is performed electronically, orders may be submitted through terminals or handheld recording devices directly to the supplier. Whatever the method, the school library media specialist should be sure that item numbers, addresses of suppliers, quantities desired, and other information are carefully submitted so that errors are minimized. Orders must also be checked to see that the item supplied meets the written specification.

SOURCE: Adapted from Blanche Woolls, *The School Library Media Manager*, 2nd ed. (Englewood, Colo.: Libraries Unlimited, 1999), 177–182. Used with permission.

How school libraries are funded

by Betty J. Turock and Andrea Pedolsky

School library media specialists may adopt a broad model using a business model of financial planning as strategic planning.

Purposes of financial planning

By creating a financial plan, the library manager will be better able to:

define and quantify the library's overall service goals and objectives in monetary terms;

assess progress in meeting financial goals and objectives;

establish indicators that will identify significant deviations in the library's use of its assets;

provide direction in safeguarding the library's assets;

allocate technical, human, organizational, and financial resources to support service priorities; and

attract potential fund providers.

Think of your financial plan as an action agenda. It is the platform from which you: determine and measure your library's need for funds; raise the necessary funds and allocate them; make certain the funds are used properly; evaluate the impact of new investments and programs on your library's operations; ensure accurate financial reporting; analyze financial results; and set future projections to ensure the efficient and effective use of resources.

Among the reasons for preparing a financial plan, the most important is to cultivate a solid and diversified funding base for your library. Developing a financial plan will show potential fund providers how you are preparing to meet the library's future needs. As a retrospective evaluation tool, the financial plan shows whether the library has been able to stick to its budget and still meet its goals and objectives.

The financial plan is comprised of eight basic segments:

1. An analysis of the library's financial status: What is the library's current financial condition?
2. A situation analysis: What economic, legal, political, social, technological, and organizational factors are impacting on the library and shaping its financial future?
3. A market analysis: Who comprises the library's current and potential customer base? Are the library's current and potential programs, services, and products responsive to their needs? What is the library's competition?
4. Assumptions about the future: What are the library's financial goals and objectives, which will help demarcate the path the library will take for a healthy financial future?
5. Three-year outlook: Budgetary forecasts for three years that will feed into the formulation of annual operating budgets and bring financial challenges into clearer focus.
6. Funding strategies: What alternative sources of funding will pay for the library's growth and development?

7. Evaluation: An evaluation of the financial plan so that you know whether you are on the right track.
8. Executive Summary: A concise version of your financial plan to communicate your library's case for support to fiscal decision makers.

SOURCE: Adapted from Betty J. Turock and Andrea Pedolsky, *Creating a Financial Plan: A How-to-Do-It Manual for Librarians* (New York: Neal-Schuman, 1992), 3–4. Used with permission from Neal-Schuman Publishers, Inc. Copyright 1992 by Betty J. Turock and Andrea Pedolsky.

The budget

by David V. Loertscher

Library media programs are expensive. Salaries, physical plant, and sports probably head the list in the school budget, but a million-dollar investment in a library media center (LMC) is not uncommon. Yet many schools lack the investment needed to support the children and teachers in any meaningful way.

What is the cost in your home of your information connection, including telephone, Internet, and cable? Whatever the figure, we can hook any child up for the same price per month. Do the math and you will be amazed at how much your LMC budget would be for a typical year ($50/month × 500 students × 12 months would be $300,000 per year). In fact, if you added all salaries, physical plant costs for the LMC, utilities, equipment, supplies, and materials together, you would see that it does take a substantial investment. We continually understate our needs.

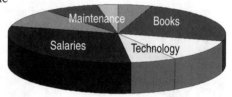

So many administrators have planned to spend once for technology and then coast along with minimal budgets. Like school buses, such will never be the case. There is the initial investment, constant maintenance and replacement of wornout equipment, and upgrading to new models in buses as well as technology. Both involve a constant and very large investment.

Most schools have a number of pots of money from which they fund the LMC. First, they will have salary money for personnel, which may come from regular funds or from grants. Second, there is usually capital outlay money to build infrastructure (buildings, plumbing, wiring, remodeling, etc.). Finally, there will be money for materials for the library. Somewhere there might also be a supply budget for such things as paper clips and computer disks.

Library media specialists may discover quickly that the "official" budget for library materials has been traditionally very small, in fact, impossible to work with. Thus, most library media specialists turn into entrepreneurs. There are usually two games to learn how to play. First, find out about all the various pots of money that exist within the school and learn how to tap them. Second, play the grantsmanship game. Those are the normal sources. There is another: the political arena. Library media specialists have discovered that district, state, and national agendas have to be influenced if any significant investment in children is to be realized.

11

Local funds

First things first. Learn all you can about the local school budget, including how it is created and divided and who makes the decisions. This can vary, from the principal getting the money and dispersing it through some system of benevolent "ask me and I'll see what I can do" to a site council that has the power over the entire school budget. Whoever controls the purse strings will control how much the LMC gets. It is wise to learn how to play the political games well enough to extract what you need. You cannot assume that everyone will have the kids' interest at heart and be very generous. Quite the opposite. When there are hard choices to be made, you can expect to have to fight for top spot, or any spot, for that matter.

For school funds, you can expect to have to prepare a budget complete with justifications. As at home, this document should begin with needs and extend to wants. Start with three categories: equipment, supplies, and materials. Find previous budget documents and discover how they were formatted. Then follow those templates to start with. But as your experience grows, different types of budget documents will need to be created if extensive funding is to be secured.

Many decision makers and decision-making groups are impressed with several procedures. The first is how well you can justify what you are asking for. It helps to know how to present your case in a few words accompanied by a picture (graph or chart). But behind those few words should appear a sense that solid research has been done to back up what you are saying. The second factor is trust. Over time, you will want to develop a reputation that if you are given money, you spend it wisely and there will be a reportable result. Third, it is not usually wise to submit your requests alone. Budget proposals that have the endorsement of many teachers, parents, and key opinion leaders have an infinitely better chance of being funded than just from your say-so. And it is wise to have those endorsing the proposed budget at the meeting where decisions are made. Key success rule: Don't go it alone.

Jealousy often arises among library media specialists who are well funded and those who are less well funded. The author has known many entrepreneurial spirits who are well connected politically and over time have built incredible financial support. Just across the street might be another school with an impoverished library media program. The have-nots are usually quite vocal about their lack of resources and instead of being congratulatory are critical. We would all like to be well funded. Realistically, money and politics are bedfellows. Those that know how and who, have.

Grants

Another major source of funding will be the grants you initiate for the LMC. This requires some expertise in knowing who has money to give, what they are interested in funding, how they wish to be asked, and what strings they will attach to the money if granted. The first rule of thumb is just to keep your eyes open and be ready to respond at a moment's notice. Often you will have less than 24 hours to come up with an idea and a written proposal. Knowing this, you should have numerous ideas already waiting in the wings just needing a quick rewrite or fine-tuning to be ready to submit.

One librarian told the author that he had found great success in being a "bottom feeder." This meant that he found a source of many granting agencies who were giving $300–$500 or $1,000 grants. They usually required a single-page justification. This person wrote many such mini-grant proposals and received over $20,000 in one year.

Grant opportunities abound from local, district, state, and federal sources. While you might be wildly successful at times, you can also expect major disappointments even after sending in applications that have required a great deal of time and energy to prepare. Such is the nature of the game. There are many good "tips and tricks" books and other resources to help you learn how to write grants. Find and use them to your advantage. Read winning proposals to see how they were constructed. And finally, know when to play the politics needed before the grant is even written. That is, you can have the inside track on money and have already gotten the promise of success before you even begin to write the proposal.

SOURCE: Adapted from David V. Loertscher, *Taxonomies of the School Library Media Program*, 2nd ed. (San Jose, Calif.: Hi Willow, 2000), 227–229. Used with permission.

Understanding budgeting procedures

by Ruth Bell

New budgets are usually based on expenditures of past years, present encumbrances, and proposed programs for the next year. Exactly how the budget is expended, and who does it, depends on the type of budgeting permitted in the district or state, and the method of allocating funds within these guidelines. At present, districts use either a centralized disbursement procedure or a decentralized budgeting process.

Centralized disbursement

With the centralized process, funds for district schools and programs are allocated from the central administration office. When this is the budget method, it is the responsibility of the director of media programs to present the program to the superintendent and the immediate administrators to whom the director reports, to assure that adequate funds are allocated to the district center and to each media center.

When budgets are centralized, all buildings are usually treated with a degree of equality. Even if principals do not support the media program, the media specialist will be given a budget, usually on a per-pupil basis. Inequality may still occur if the amounts are allocated on a higher scale for high school students than for elementary or middle schools.

Decentralized budgeting

When budgets are decentralized, each principal is given an amount to be used for all programs in the school. Principals then create a budget for their school, based on the assessment of needs and the priorities that have been set for each school. Allocations are redistributed to different departments via the distribution process established for that school.

With a decentralized budget, media center allocations vary with the amounts the principals receive and, in turn, assign to individual departments. When principals are closely involved in the development of the media program, they are careful to see that a large proportion of the school's budget is given to the media program. The media specialist becomes a major force in this process. While the director of media programs can work with the principals, to explain the purpose of a media program and to keep them aware of the rising costs of materials and equipment, media specialists must demonstrate the worth of their media programs to the students and teachers in the school if they wish to receive a higher proportion of the funds.

When principals are proud of their media programs, and work as media team members along with teachers and media specialists, they are very generous with their support. When teachers and students are heavy users of the center, and units of curriculum demonstrate the integration of the media collection, the necessity of replacing, adding, and expanding will be documented, and the generosity will continue. With the decentralized budget, the media specialist and the media program in each school are rewarded for the quality of program offered.

Relations with business offices

Just as budgets may be centralized or decentralized, the bookkeeping for disbursement of funds may be in the central office, with the director of media programs, or in the individual schools, with the media specialist or the principal's office staff responsible for recordkeeping.

When the budget is disbursed from the central office, it is essential that good interpersonal communications be established with all staff. Requests from business office staff should be promptly honored. It will be their responsibility to pay invoices on time, and they will answer telephone requests to pay overdue invoices. Care should be taken to confirm shipments and to give the needed information if items are missing. Directors who help the business office staff will be rewarded; others may have difficulty getting orders processed, finding out information about remaining funds, or ascertaining the status of current orders.

When the director of media programs is responsible for the media program budget, care must be taken to keep accurate records. Since few media specialists have been trained as accountants or bookkeepers, it is essential that a staff member with these skills be employed or a present staff member be trained. The director of media programs further keeps principals and media specialists informed of the status of the media program budget. Principals and media specialists need to know the amount available in their media accounts, and they will expect timely, regular reports of actual expenditures related to encumbrances and the amount remaining in the various line items. They cannot fully plan their expenditures if they do not have complete information on the status of their encumbrances, shipments, actual billing, and payments. They will also need to know when items are marked out-of-stock or out-of-print, so they can reorder in a timely fashion. Media specialists must also be informed about the discounts for materials and the vendors selected for most purchases. In many school districts, it is possible to give each media specialist a monthly computer printout of the media center accounts.

In some school districts, records of ordering and payments are kept in the individual schools. When this is the pattern, the building level media specialist will be directly responsible for media center expenditures. The director of media programs should be notified if problems arise with vendors, or with the quality of materials or equipment supplied, but the director is less likely to have any direct contact with media center budgets under this system.

The director of media programs is responsible not only for the status of the present budget, but for keeping principals informed of future needs to be budgeted. If a new technology is to be implemented, they must be made aware of the budget implications. If the media center budget is targeted for reduction, the principals will become allies to fight for as small a cut as possible.

Justifying expenditures

The first step in justifying budgets for media programs is to confirm the status of each media center in relation to the district's established standards. If each media center is to offer equal opportunities for students, guidelines describing a core collection of materials, equipment, and services must be developed based on *Information Power* (1998, pp. 100–121), or standards for each state. Using the standards as a guide, the director of media programs then works with each media specialist to help develop a long-range plan for the media center. Individual plans carefully detail costs associated with any new services to be offered.

Goals and objectives have been established for the district, and goals and objectives for each media center have been written. A study is made of the present schools' collections and equipment. Present holdings are analyzed, taking into account not only quantity, but also *quality*, which is defined as relevance, accuracy, duplication necessary, and other points. A complete inventory of materials and equipment available in each building (including quality and quantity) is maintained at the district level, so that inequities can be identified. The equipment inventory contains a record of the date of purchase, an indication of the use, and repair and maintenance information. This helps establish a replacement plan for all equipment in the district, and costs for this plan can be calculated.

Media specialists then determine what they will need to meet the district standards over the time allocated for the long-range plan. District priorities are established by the director of media programs, in conjunction with advisory committees, principals, and other administrators. A consensus should be reached whenever possible, although other directors will support their own programs, and principals will have the best interests of their schools to protect at any time. Principals and directors will be better able to accept lower-priority assignment of their requests if they fully understand the documented needs of higher-priority programs.

Preparing budgets

Budgets are prepared based on the needs assessments, the long-range plan, and the cost of materials and equipment. If, in developing the long-range plan, the materials and equipment needed for implementation of activities related to objectives have been identified and added, it will be simple to present the budget in priority order, with the cost analysis attached for each component.

Another major factor in budget preparation is curricular changes that create gaps in subject areas of media center collections. Directors of programs in curricular areas may need to be reminded that it is as important to notify the district level director of media programs of new assignments as it is to have teachers tell media specialists when they are planning special projects at the building level. Such information is crucial at all levels if the media collections and activities are truly to support and enhance the curriculum.

Budgeting for maintenance, especially for newer technologies such as computers and related equipment, has become a major investment. In some situations, the equipment is more costly to repair than to replace. Maintenance of much of the equipment may be provided by the district center if a technician and additional staff are available. Costs of repair services and maintenance contracts with outside vendors can be compared to the costs of district staff and the need to keep an adequate spare-parts inventory. One advantage of an in-house maintenance service is the ability to have equipment repaired quickly. There is no need to rely on the staff of a commercial firm, who may not view repairs for the school district as a high priority. An in-house repair service usually means that pick-up and delivery of broken and repaired equipment can be made through the media system. Equipment need not be as carefully packed as it might if it were being shipped elsewhere.

Budgeting for replacement involves an estimate of the life of the piece of equipment, based on the amount of use. Records of equipment breakdown also help determine whether to replace or repair. When the need for repair becomes too frequent, and the equipment is judged to be unreliable, replacement is more practical than continued repair.

Replacement also occurs with upgrading equipment. More storage capacity in computers, faster modems, and color cameras for television production all spell replacement and add to budget costs. Students should be allowed to use the best equipment possible, and upgrades may save money over time even if they are more expensive when purchased.

Capital outlay for materials is usually built into the budgets for new buildings or extensive remodeling. Capital outlay permits the purchase of furniture, materials, and new equipment, but usually does not cover maintenance contracts on equipment or computer software beyond one year. Allowing for additional service charges when maintenance agreements expire becomes a major component in planning annual budgets. Maintenance costs may quickly exceed the purchase price of the hardware or software.

Another expenditure to consider for the district media budget is the hiring of outside consultants. When no staff member in a district is available for, or capable of accomplishing, a task, it may be possible to contract for services. This is done for in-service programs, for planning or evaluation, or when the expertise for any phase of the media program is not available in the district. It is sometimes very worthwhile to bring in an expert even when expertise is available within the district; the very fact that a consultant is from outside adds credibility and importance to the training or the recommendations presented.

SOURCE: Adapted from Ruth Bell, "Budget," in *Supervision of District Level Library Media Programs,* by Blanche Woolls (Englewood, Colo.: Libraries Unlimited, 1990), 70–73. Copyright 1990. Used with permission.

Sample budget process

by Ann M. Wasman

The following is a quick "walk through" of a possible budgeting scenario. The specialist is told budget requests are due by *x* date and must be presented according to whatever system the district is using. The specialist develops requests. Clearly it is too early to list every title of every item that will be needed, and how, if any school districts require that information at this time. However, they do want a general idea of what types of items will be purchased. The specialist requests may look like the Capital Outlay: AV Equipment list shown below with an added column for the particular account number used in the district for that type of item.

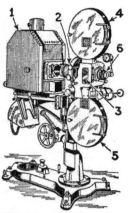

Motion-picture Projector. 1 Lamp House; 2 Shutter; 3 Housing containing Intermittent-Movement Mechanism; 4 Upper, and 5 Lower, Film Magazine; 6 Projection Lens.

Capital outlay

The capital outlay category, regardless of budget system or process, is considered part of the building; it's more permanent than supplies. Capital outlay items require maintenance and repair and are not "consumed" by the educational program. (Obviously, these budget experts have not seen how some teachers and students use the equipment.) Because the capital outlay category is a big portion of every budget, including items such as copy machines, furniture, football seating, security systems, etc., a district may require that each capital outlay request be itemized. In other words, AV equipment—$5,000—must be broken into types of equipment, numbers, and amounts.

Capital Outlay: AV Equipment	
5 audiocassette tape recorders @ $50	$ 250
5 VCRs @ $250	1,250
5 TVs @ $250	1,250
5 overhead projectors @ $275	1,375
1 computer @ $875	875
TOTAL	$5,000

11

Line-item budgeting system

The line-item budgeting system is typically used in most schools. In this system the requester lists line-by-line the item needed, the amount requested, the category number assigned, and, perhaps, an explanation of the item's relation to the program. Some districts include the amounts previously allotted for the category and a rationale for any increase. Some library media specialists add these figures so the administrators can see their past allotments. Line-item budgets typically restrict expenditures to exactly what is approved. Thus a shortage in one area cannot be covered by an overage in another.

Item	Amount Requested*	Explanation/Justification
Supplies	$ 250	Office and related supplies for processing, repairing, and circulating materials and equipment
Books	$2,500	Reference and regular circulating books as requested by students and staff and as identified for curricular projects; includes funds to update 5% of the science collection
Multimedia Materials	$ 500	Materials requiring use of equipment that relates to classroom projects and teacher requests, as well as development of materials for use within the LMC
Computer Software	$ 250	Software programs for the computers within the LMC
Periodicals and Databases	$ 750	Periodicals, pamphlets, and necessary indexes for current information
SUBTOTAL	$4,250	
Repair	$ 500	Maintenance and repair of AV and LMC equipment
Capital outlay: AV Equipment	$5,000	Cassette tape recorders, videocassette recorders, TVs, and overhead projectors to replace equipment that is no longer reliable
GRAND TOTAL	$9,750	

*Figures are "samples" rather than true projections.

SOURCE: Adapted from Ann M. Wasman, *New Steps to Service: Common-Sense Advice for the School Library Media Specialist* (Chicago: American Library Association, 1998), 155–158.

Proposal writing

by Blanche Woolls

Securing funding to provide adequate school media programs is a continuing concern. School library media specialists are looking for ways to alleviate this problem. One method to consider is to locate agencies that have funds for designated projects and obtain a grant to fund the proposed project. Few people today have had experience with the actual proposal-writing process. The need for proposal-writing skills has increased with the decrease in available funds.

Writing grants to secure funding from the federal government is not a new phenomenon. One need only locate the appropriate source of funding. The federal government has been a source of funding for local schools through state departments of education.

In addition to securing funds from government sources, school library media specialists should also learn to prepare grant proposals for local agencies, businesses, and foundations. School library media specialists can become avid and skillful proposal writers.

The process of asking for grants is similar to writing a letter to Santa Claus. People make a list, grant readers check it twice, and the Santa of Funding then decides. When money was plentiful, people could afford to attempt esoteric grant proposals. As the need for funds has intensified, more careful planning and justification is required to get a project funded. That is to say that projects must meet state-designated learning objectives or required curricula, or raise skill levels or test scores that are below a national or state norm.

For some time, "professional" grant writers have been actively seeking funds. Many of these have built up lengthy lists of funded projects. In many school districts special administrative personnel are still designated to apply for government funds for that district, and the project specialists coordinate all proposal writing. Because these "experts" exist, many school library media specialists may consider the proposal-writing exercise futile. They may feel that their efforts will not be competitive with those of people who have been active in the grant-writing arena. However, the bright, new idea with the fresh approach will stand out in a crowd of projects that will use standardized vocabulary and pat formula responses to the request for proposal. School library media specialists are even more necessary in districts where the grant writer position has been eliminated. In others, the veteran grant writer may welcome someone else's fresh idea or willingness to complete the application form.

Even at the present time, there is plenty of money to be given away, but the project defined in the proposal *must be worthwhile*. Also, the project proposed must have a better justification than the others being submitted, and the proposal writer must *believe* in the project and keep in mind the need to transform a clever idea into a well-thought-out plan of action that will accomplish a worthwhile, important objective.

Much may be gained from the process of writing grant proposals. The first is the obvious willingness to exert effort to improve programs and secure funds from sources beyond the local funding agency. In an era of reduction in funding and cuts in all areas of education budgets, the school library media specialist who is willing to try to secure funds rather than bemoan the state of local funding will be perceived as a positive, active, and creative educator by the school administration. This will increase the visibility of the school library media program in a very positive way.

A second outcome may be the actual securing of money from outside sources. The school library media specialist will not be writing proposals for the daily expenditures of the library media center, but for programs beyond what is presently being accomplished. Additional funding will allow a new approach to an old problem and will be rejuvenating to all involved.

A third outcome is that planning a project may help school library media staff rethink the way something is currently being done. Improvements may be started even before the notification concerning the awarding of the grant arrives. Then, even if the project is not funded, some changes will have been implemented.

Fourth, in planning and preparing the grant proposal, a school library media specialist learns to present a proposed program in a logical step-by-step way. School library media specialists who master this logical approach to program planning may transfer the method to preparing their requests for all funding and all programs at the local district level. Budget requests will then be based on established program needs, asking with a purpose, not just asking.

11

Preparing to write the proposal

A series of steps lead to the decision to write and submit a proposal. These include selecting an idea which should be implemented, finding an agency, and securing the request for proposal (RFP) or the guidelines for the submission of a project proposal. In submitting a proposal, the proposal writer must have an idea that is a little different or a different approach to an old problem. It requires developing a clever idea.

Having the clever idea

Perhaps one of the first problems for the proposal writer is "hatching" the clever idea. A number of steps can lead to a clever idea.

1. Read project proposals that have been funded. If the project was funded by national or state government competition, the proposal is public property and should be available in the appropriate government office.
2. Go to conferences and listen to what people are trying or would like to try. Attend sessions where funded research results are being reported. Persons who are conducting or have completed funded projects are usually eager to discuss the project. They may suggest additional activities which should be implemented.
3. Ask teachers what they need that might be an expansion of a current activity or a new and different approach to teaching.
4. Ask other school library media specialists what they think might be the burning issues to be tested. These persons might be willing to join in the project planning.
5. Listen to people talk. Parents who are concerned about educational programs might have constructive suggestions which can be built into a proposal.
6. Read the literature in both education and library and information science. Often a challenging article can point out a need for change in the media center program.

When going through the above steps, record the suggestions or ideas that occur. The potential proposal writer should keep a folder full of ideas provided from any of the above suggestions or from another source.

The other option is to psych out the staff of the funding agency and come up with an idea which will be attractive to them. Often the priorities of the funding agency are a part of the grant proposal; other times they are not.

Responding to the RFP

The most important rule in responding to the RFP is to follow the guidelines. These have been carefully determined by the funding agencies, and most personnel resent receiving more information than is asked for in the guidelines. It is seldom wise to try to point out what should have been required by sending unsolicited information or activities which imply that the proposal writer thinks something is missing from the RFP.

Responding to the guidelines is a little like working a crossword puzzle. One must fit the right information into a designated number of spaces or the pieces will not lead to the next section. Often the guidelines will indicate a minimum or maximum number of pages to respond to each point. Make a note of such restrictions so that they can be followed. Double-spacing or single-spacing, margins, and placement on the page may all be characteristics of the final format. Ignoring these may cause the proposal to be disqualified. It will certainly *not* impress the proposal readers.

Also, note carefully the address for submitting the proposal as well as the deadline for submission. The proposal writer must make sure that the proposal is sent to the proper location. A proposal writer who ships the proposal to an office may find out that a central clearinghouse receives all proposals for the various departments. Sending it to a different address may disqualify the proposal or may cause it to arrive after the deadline. In fact, it may not arrive at all.

Whether one is writing a letter of intent preliminary to writing a full proposal, or a letter to a foundation or corporation, the key elements to be included are the cover page or signature page, the abstract or summary, the project preface material, the body of the proposal, the budget, the staff and facilities, and the evaluation. The only difference between any letter or full proposal is the length of each section. This may vary from one to two sentences in a letter to 10 or more pages in a full proposal.

Within the body of the proposal, the writer must include a narrative description of all proposed activities. The budget will include all costs for each activity and may require a justification for all expenditures if they are detailed in the narrative. The applicant's credentials and the curriculum vitae of staff as well as any compliance documents are a part of the completed proposal. Finally, any further endorsements from the proposing institution or any other partners or supporters in the project are attached.

Proposal writers who have discovered a funding agency, determined that they wish to submit a proposal, secured the approval of their administration, and discussed their idea with the appropriate persons both in their organization and in the funding organization are ready to write the proposal.

Writing proposals is a way of life in many situations. In others, it may be a way to get additional funds, expand a program to meet a specific need, add equipment, add materials, or try a different way to provide materials to help teach students.

Most persons who have one proposal funded are very willing to write another. They have been given an opportunity to improve their school library media center, to test a new method, to offer a new service, to provide more materials for students and teachers.

To write a proposal is to enter a competition, and the process is similar to any other competitive endeavor; sometimes you win, sometimes you lose. Sometimes it may seem better to lose. One gains all the applause for the effort to establish needs, develop objectives and plans of action, and write and submit the proposal. It is an opportunity to meet new colleagues and reestablish communication with old acquaintances. Sometimes you win, and then you have to work to see that the project succeeds.

SOURCE: Adapted from Blanche Woolls, *Grant Proposal Writing: A Handbook for School Library Media Specialists* (New York: Greenwood, 1986), 1–17, 194. Used with permission.

Creating a working campaign to secure funding

by Pattie Allen

While it remains the responsibility of the school district to provide adequate funding for school libraries, politically astute school librarians may choose to seek additional funds from other sources: businesses are one source and writing grants is another.

School–business partnerships

Books . . . online subscriptions . . . computer applications . . . telecommunications . . . reference materials . . . automation . . . computer technology! The list of requirements school media coordinators must address daily lengthens.

Major issues involved are not whether such materials are justified or if public school students should have access to such materials. The time of accountability for all school programs has dawned.

The major issue has become how to fund acquisitions on a yearly basis with continually decreasing school budget allotments. Schools with small student populations, schools in rural areas, and school systems located in poor economic regions are impacted more strongly by this dilemma than their larger school counterparts.

However, one fact remains true: students throughout a state deserve equal access to media services and technology regardless of the location and size of their school environments. As site-based decision making takes root and struggles for funding increase, the responsibility of providing information access for all public school students is passed primarily to the school media coordinator. Public school personnel in diverse curricular areas are attempting to meet mandated competencies with restricted funding empowerment, while also expecting media services to be in place as needed to support their own specific state standards.

How can media coordinators meet these expectations? How can funding be generated at levels which promote successful media programs and materials? One solution is the creation of partnerships between individual school media programs and local businesses. The process is direct and mutually beneficial to both participants.

Both the [business] and the school benefit in that incentives help schools generate funds for special needs, and also increase traffic to the [in this case] restaurants. Furthermore, the corporate business world becomes aware of the goals of the school programs and the level of funding actually available to promote such goals. Additionally, the community becomes actively involved in an effort that strengthens communication among schools, homes, and businesses.

An alliance between school media programs and businesses is limited only by the creative imaginations of those persons involved. In some instances the business may choose to donate money to the media program without any special project activity on the part of the school and community. However, the project activity does tend to link all people involved and build communication bridges among the school, home, and business environments.

The process for developing such a partnership is relatively simple. One key idea to remember is that businesses work on the premise of goals, needs to achieve goals, and outcome accountability.

The first step is the development of goals and objectives for the media program. Media coordinators should assess strengths and weaknesses of the programs constantly and accept responsibility for providing necessary materials to enhance achievement of the goals. These goals, objectives, and strategies should be written for documentation and shared with anyone in positions that may be able to offer support. Local school administrators, school faculties, school system administrative personnel, and parents should be aware of the total media program.

After development of goals and strategies, careful examination of existing programs and available materials should occur. Objective scrutiny can lead to the realization of the most effective materials necessary to bring the goals to fruition.

A major component in the process is the selection of the business approach. Businesses having a vested interest in the particular school make excellent choices for selection. To identify them, media personnel should survey students and the community. Business enterprises that employ parents of the school's students or that are frequented by the school community are strong candidates to consider.

The most difficult aspect of the corporate partnership is the initial contact of the business by the school. The media coordinator [need] never directly approach the company officials. A parent who is employed by the company and who also understands the need of funding of the media program may arrange the project. Parents and community members may be the school's most qualified and effective ambassadors. If such a parent is not available, the alternative course is a direct one—call the business (probably the public affairs office) and request a meeting. The media coordinator should be ready to present written documentation of goals, objectives, and strategies as well as to corroborate the existing needs and the outcomes that will result. These outcomes will not only benefit the school; businesses will profit directly as well, since the student population they are assisting today will become the workforce they will employ tomorrow.

Origination of project details may not be within the local school's control. Some businesses may choose to support the program by making a single financial contribution without requiring any participation on the part of the school and community. Other businesses, however, may appreciate the opportunity to become directly involved with the school. As the project guidelines and activities are outlined, carefully examine the participation expected by the school to ensure that the activities are plausible. Expectations that require more than the school can provide will result in unsuccessful outcomes.

After collaboration on project details, procedures publicizing the event must be detailed thoroughly. As with any campaign, lack of public knowledge can become the major detriment of the campaign. The community cannot support an unknown program. Various methods and media should be used in publicizing the partnership. The business can provide letters to be distributed to parents. The school's art department can design flyers. Announcements can be made over the school's public address system. Promotion of the project can occur during parent–teacher meetings.

At the conclusion of the project all components should be carefully evaluated. What actions were strengths? Which components weakened the program?

11

Public awareness may be perceived as a possible weakness if, in spite of many efforts to publicize, contacts that impact the total and larger community are overlooked. Notices through local newspapers, radio stations, cable television networks, and telephone hotlines might encourage and alert community members who otherwise remain untouched.

Cooperative efforts between media programs and corporations are a concept of the future with infinite benefits to all participants. A collaborative effort that will generate funding sources to assist ailing school media center budgets can occur successfully by following six basic steps:

1. develop media program goals
2. assess strategies to accomplish the goals
3. select an appropriate business
4. cooperatively develop the project
5. publicize
6. evaluate

SOURCE: Adapted from Pattie Allen, "Business–School Partnerships: Future Media Center Funding Sources," *North Carolina Libraries* 53 (Spring 1995): 8–9. Used with permission.

Think money in the bank for your school

by Mary R. Hofmann

In 1992, district officials encouraged our middle schools to write grant proposals for a share of the state's pot of school restructuring funds. Having little or no choice, a task force formed at my school and charged in blindly. None of us believed we had a prayer, but somewhere midway through the process we became true believers in our mandated project. To our utter amazement, our proposal not only brought us a million dollars but was also selected as the example for judging other proposals. Since then I've been involved in writing several other smaller grants (from $25,000 to $90,000— not exactly peanuts) and have so far batted 1000. I've also read and scored other schools' proposals.

I've learned many lessons along the way, not the least of which is that grant writing isn't for the meek. There aren't any quick and easy tricks; every grant is different. On the other hand, some patterns do exist, providing a bit of consistency, and some elements of style have worked more successfully than others. I'm happy to share these tidbits if you promise two things: write only proposals you believe in, and write them only with a group of believers. (One voice is best, but it should represent a team.) Grant readers can tell.

While every RFP (request for proposal) has its own peculiarities, most have fairly standard sections. Typical are:

1. Program abstract or executive summary. This is the whole ball of wax on one page. I know I'll either hook the proposal readers or lose them here, so I usually do this page last, and with care and flair. The abstract must include the problem (in a paragraph or so), the solution (a synopsis of the proposed project), the funding requirements (a paragraph on where the money will go and how the project will continue without it), and whatever the RFP says the funding source needs to know about your school.

2. Statement of need. In a page or two, I try to address the reasons for the proposal; that is, the problems we need to solve with the help of the grant money. In my writing I answer questions such as:

What do we want our students to be able to accomplish? A need isn't, for example, computers. Instead, our kids need to learn to become proficient users of technology and the solution to that need might require additional computers. (Remember, it's all about kids, not about books or equipment or stuff, except insofar as stuff helps kids.)

How do we know students have a need? Here's where we trot out test scores, demographics, information about parent involvement, and any other documented evidence of need, buttressed by lots of research evidence.

How will the grant make a difference? Here's where I wax optimistic, building toward the Goals and Objectives section. But I'm also careful to show my readers we aren't pathetic. Our kids and staff are terrific—they just need a boost!

The statement of need is about people and their needs. *Think who and why.*

3. Goals and objectives. Teachers must write goals and objectives for their classrooms, and this isn't much different. A goal is huge and general (e.g., our kids need to become information literate), while an objective is, well, objective and measurable (e.g., students will learn to use a networked computer to access information on the World Wide Web). The goals and objectives need to tie nicely back to the needs.

This section is about fulfilling the needs: *Think what.*

4. Method/description of plan. Whatever it's called, this section is about implementation. I meticulously, but colorfully, describe what we're going to do, tell how we justify what we're doing with research and expertise, explain exactly how we're going to go about doing it, and show how our actions will address the needs we identified. Here's where either we make the reader a believer or we don't.

This section details the plan: *Think how.*

5. Evaluation. Evaluation should be an integral part of any plan, from a lesson plan to a grant proposal. How can we tell—throughout the project and at the end of it—that we've fulfilled our end of the deal and had the desired impact on the kids? We look for ways of tracking our progress, such as logs, reflections, surveys, as well as students' progress, like benchmarks proficiencies. And we propose a culminating evaluation that the grant source can use as its assessment.

This section is the test: *Think so?*

6. Budget. When filling out the budget forms, I am careful to work with district requirements, making sure we can do what we say we'll do, and that what we do fits what our plan says we'll do. The rubber hits the road in the budget. Grant readers can see right through deceptions. *Think oh, really?*

7. Conclusion/future support documents. Grant sources are specific in what kinds of support materials they require. I give them exactly what they ask for.

Standing out from the crowd

Most RFPs come with gruesomely detailed instructions, which the wise grant writer follows to the letter. Grant readers look at scores of proposals and have rubrics to follow in scoring them. They will literally cut off excess pages, gag at cutesy creativeness, and knock off points for wordiness. The proposals that jump out and make grant readers want to cheer do two things: They follow the instructions and rubrics precisely and the writing makes the project come alive on the page. How do you accomplish this?

I start by making a "frame," or outline, literally copying the headings and pertinent instructions from the RFP onto my computer. I can then fill in holes and delete the fluff. This outline keeps me firmly on task and aligned with the rubric that the grant readers will be using.

Since I want the readers to "see" my vision as clearly as I do (and I do my best to know what kind of readers they will be), it's important that I keep my writing personal and vivid. I want to show them what the grant money will accomplish, so I draw word pictures, rather than list colorless jargon.

If I write a list, I list with flair. I believe visual impact is vital. One way grant readers know we're capable, talented, and able to pull this thing off is by reading a proposal that reflects competence, but not glitz. It should have no errors, should look clean and professional, and should have an occasional graph or chart to add clarity and break the monotony of text.

Last, I always have several people read the proposal, both fellow planners and others who haven't been involved. I make sure they're all people who will have no qualms about criticizing the proposal. Money's at stake here and I don't need a cheering section. I promise them I won't whine or get defensive, and I don't. Invariably, they find problems, and invariably (well, almost invariably), I fix them.

SOURCE: Adapted from Mary R. Hofmann, "Think Money in the Bank for Your School," *The Book Report* 17, no. 1 (May/June 1998): 22–23. *The Book Report* is now published as *Library Media Connection.* Used with permission.

Finding funds to go high-tech

by Dennis LeLoup

Technology has spawned a great interest in grant seeking among school librarians. The first lead in locating money for computers and programs may be as close as the stack of magazines on your desk. Among the widely known journals that publish columns on grants and other opportunities to add technology to the schools are *Electronic Learning* [now *Electronic Learning in Your Classroom*], *Media and Methods*, and *Technology and Learning*.

Entire issues of *Electronic Learning* have been devoted to funding including tips on writing grant proposals. *Technology and Learning* runs a fairly regular column, "Grants, Contests, etc.," which provides information on monetary awards, fellowships for advanced study, special contests, technology programs, and other publications or newsletters devoted to grants. A free publication

for educators, *T.H.E. Journal*, is also a valuable source of information. Among the newsletters that cover news on grants is *Educational Funding and Educational Grants Alert* [now *Education Grants Alert*]. Newsletter subscription rates are often significantly higher than journal prices but most newsletters are published weekly or biweekly. Many contain general information about funding sources and are not just technology related.

State and federal agencies

State governments usually have special programs, grants, and loans. They also know about and can direct you to other funding sources, including local options such as cooperative projects with businesses or other schools.

State education agencies can also direct you to federal sources for funding including competitive or contract grants. They may offer grant writing courses or direct you to one. The Office of Educational Research and Improvement [now the Institute of Education Sciences] can direct you to publications, clearinghouses, new programs, the Educational Resources Information Center, and grant opportunities, loans, or other potential monetary resources.

Investigate foundation center sources

The Foundation Center is a national nonprofit organization established for the purpose of organizing, collecting, analyzing, and disseminating information on foundation and corporate benevolence. Access to this information is offered through two national collections (New York and Washington, D.C.), field offices in San Francisco, Cleveland, and Atlanta, and 200 cooperating libraries across the country. The cooperating libraries contain a core collection of the Center's works. This information can also be accessed online through Dialog Information Services. The Center's publications program features over 50 titles on philanthropic giving and other nonprofit sector concerns.

Some Center titles of potential interest to school library media and technology coordinators include the *National Guide to Funding for Elementary and Secondary Education*, *National Guide to Funding for Libraries and Information Services*, and *Foundation Grants Index*. Each of these indexes includes complete information for each corporation listed: address, areas of giving, assets, total expenditures, figure, amount and number of grants paid for the previous year, types of grants and support offered, application information, person to whom proposals should be addressed, and recent grants awarded, among other information.

The Foundation Center also offers daylong seminars led by fund-raising professionals in various localities. The purpose of the seminars is to assist fund-raisers in writing winning grant proposals. Topics include proposal writing techniques, grant proposal elements, locating the right contributor, and developing relationships with the grantor. Included in the cost is *The Foundation Center's Guide to Proposal Writing*.

Corporate funds

Corporations are frequent supporters of educational programs or activities. Information on corporate giving can be obtained through reading professional journals and perusing the *Foundation Grants Index*. Other sources of information about corporations that have a special interest in educational connections are conference program planners, consultants in state departments of education, and school library media professionals who have been successful in getting corporate funds. Some corporations, particularly the larger ones, maintain education departments and are eager for opportunities to network with schools.

Log on the Internet

The Internet is a source of information on various forums, agencies, or publications. Information on monetary aid or grant information is frequently imbedded with conference notes and other information from professional associations, corporations, and governments, and will not come up with a simple Internet search.

SOURCE: Adapted from Dennis LeLoup, "Finding Funds to Go High-Tech," *The Book Report* 14 (January/February 1996): 19–20. *The Book Report* is now published as *Library Media Connection.* Used with permission.

Grant writing made easy

by Sheryl Abshire

With the scarcity of money and schools reorganizing for efficiency, school boards may be forced to slash more jobs and resources, including badly needed technology funding.

What's a school librarian to do? If you're willing to commit the time and effort, start applying for grants—and do it now. Getting that money for your library is a lot easier than you expect, thanks to Congress's reauthorization of the Elementary and Secondary Education Act (ESEA). ESEA now contains some very good news for school libraries, especially for those in need of tech upgrades. Under the provisions of the new act, individual schools, school districts, and state departments of education are eligible to compete for as much as $1 billion annually through fiscal year 2007.

School media specialists need to take action now to guarantee a piece of this funding pie. The first step is finding out if your school has a technology plan, then checking when it was last updated. Your school's plan will need an overhaul if it's several years old. Be sure to collaborate with your district technology department, since your plan should be compatible with the district's overall vision and tech strategy. The National Center for Technology Planning (http://www.nctp.com) is an excellent resource with many ideas and tips on technology assessment and planning.

Once your tech plan is up to date, it will serve as a guide as you prepare your grant application. Identify the appropriate grants to fund your ideas, and then be prepared to let the real work begin. Remember that you're competing against hundreds of other applicants, so your proposal must stand out. Organizations fund projects that demonstrate they can improve student learning with the requested funds. Following the grant organization's guidelines exactly is the first step to getting those hard-to-find dollars. Your letter of intent—an introduction to your proposal, explaining what you'll accomplish with the grant money—should not exceed one page. Hunting for funds is the perfect opportunity for librarians to reach out and collaborate with colleagues. Look for colleagues who understand your school's educational problems and needs, who can help write the grant proposal, and who will benefit from the funding.

This is not the time to be meek or mild. The grant proposal is an opportunity to sell your ideas, so make a compelling argument for your funding requirements. Your writing should be convincing, assertive, and concise. Discard words such as "may," "might," and "can." Instead, show your potential for success by using phrases like "we will." Always use specific examples and avoid generalities. Never assume that the grant selection committee knows your needs or the reasons why your school would be the best grant recipient. Provide concrete ideas on how the grant will improve learning in your school or district with more or new technologies.

A little known secret is that a phone call can go a long way. Many program officers are happy to clarify details of the grant over the phone. Take that opportunity to get the person's feedback on your ideas, and then get his name so you can address the application to a specific person. When listing your objectives, avoid the common mistake of using too much educational jargon. Don't try to fix all the school's problems at once. Stick to an achievable objective and create a realistic roadmap that uses the grant money to reach that goal. My school district, the Calcasieu Parish Public Schools in Lake Charles, Louisiana, has received over $1 million from the Technology Literacy Challenge Fund over the last three years to purchase new technologies and to provide professional development for teachers and principals. Our grant proposal focused on schools that were economically disadvantaged and had low test scores. The result? With an infusion of technology and more than 80 hours of technology training for our teachers and principals, we've seen growth in student achievement and new learning strategies introduced into classrooms districtwide.

Politeness never hurts. Send the potential grantor a thank-you note for the opportunity to apply and ask when the next round of funding begins. This puts your name in front of the grantor one more time. Another tip: once you receive the grant, send the organization all newspaper clippings, newsletters, announcements of presentations about your project, or any bit of PR. That way, if you're applying for additional money from the same source, you can bet they'll remember you, your school, and more importantly, the success of your project.

11

It's a good idea to get in touch with the tech division of your state department of education to inquire about regulations concerning funding. You can ask to be placed on your state's listserv to keep updated on how these funds will be disbursed. Keep an eye on the U.S. Department of Education's funding forecast page, which will keep you informed about funding opportunities, as well as when state competitions are taking place. The funding forecast for discretionary programs can be found at: http://www.ed.gov/fund/grant/find/edlite-forecast.html.

If your initial application is turned down, just try, try again. A rejection letter is quite common the first time around, so don't get discouraged. Call the organization and ask if the selection committee's comments are available. This can serve as valuable feedback before resubmitting your application. You may have missed the mark the first time, but keep revising and ask your colleagues for help. An outsider may provide more insight, so ask those beyond the education profession for their comments. That input might very well be the essential ingredient to help you get the funding.

How to avoid getting rejected? Apart from not mailing the grant application before its deadline, some grant-giving organizations say the number one reason a grant is not awarded is because the applicant's methods, procedures, and evaluations were not related to its educational goals and objectives. Other important reasons are:

Needs statement is not of sufficient importance or may not produce any increase in achievement;

Not enough evidence to support the need;

The problem is much bigger than the author realizes;

The problem is of local concern and does not affect enough people in the community;

The idea is too ambitious and its goals and objectives are unreachable;

The writing is too vague to the reviewers;

Description is not clear;

Overall project design is sloppy;

Materials posed are not suited to the problem;

Staff does not have adequate experience or training to resolve the problem or there are not enough personnel to implement your program.

Remember that grants aren't the only source of money. Take advantage of your job's access to students and their parents. Many moms or dads are involved in community organizations that are potential funding sources. Talk to students about where their parents work or which organizations they belong to. Write a proposal about the school and its needs and send it to local businesses that might be interested in funding your project. Following up with a phone call might give them that extra nudge to commit as your "partner in success for students." Explore the potential for "in-kind" support if you need matching funds for a larger grant. Many local businesses are willing to help your school in some way, but they've never been asked.

Use the Internet's resources to find the perfect funding match for your library. Visit my district's website (http://www.cpsb.org/scripts/abshire/grants.asp) for links to sites that will help your funding dreams come true.

A comprehensive site that's a must-see is Foundations Online (http://www.foundations.org/grantmakers.html), a directory of hundreds of foundations and grantmakers.

Another great site is Foundation Finder (http://www.fdncenter.org/funders/), a free search tool that provides basic facts on more than 61,000 private and community foundations in the U.S.

The U.S. Department of Education's Office of Educational Technology (http://www.ed.gov/about/offices/list/OS/technology/edgrants.html) offers a great site that lists a variety of grants.

You must register at School Funding Center (http://www.schoolfundingcenter.com), but don't worry, it won't release the information. It's worth it since the site, dedicated to helping educators locate every funding source available in the U.S., provides comprehensive information.

SOURCE: Adapted from Sheryl Abshire, "Grant Writing Made Easy," *School Library Journal* 48, no. 2 (February 2002): 38–39. Courtesy of *School Library Journal.*

A wealth of information on foundations and the grant seeking process

by Janet Camarena

Every day I have the satisfaction of knowing I have helped various worthy causes to continue by guiding people through the grant seeking process. As a reference librarian at The Foundation Center–San Francisco, I regularly help nonprofit organization representatives research foundation grants using both print and electronic resources.

The Foundation Center (http://www.fdncenter.org) is a national non-profit organization that was established by foundations in 1956. The center's mission is to foster public understanding of the foundation field by collecting, organizing, analyzing, and disseminating information on foundations, corporate giving, and related subjects. We accomplish this mission in several ways: we maintain a database that contains information on virtually every active grant making foundation in the United States, we operate five libraries and maintain the Cooperating Collections network, we publish titles in the field of philanthropy and nonprofit management, we conduct research on trends and growth in the foundation  field, we provide information electronically via an extensive website, and we offer various educational programs related to the funding research process.

Understanding foundations and grant seeking processes

More than 50,000 private grant making foundations exist in the U.S. today. By conducting focused research, grant seekers can compile a targeted list of foundations based on a much larger pool of funders. However, before you begin to research, it's important to understand the field of foundations. Let's start with some basic definitions.

The Foundation Center uses the tax and legal definition for the term "private foundation." A private foundation is a nonprofit, nongovernmental organization with a principal fund or endowment of its own, managed by its own trustees or directors, established to maintain or aid charitable activities serving the common good. There are three types of private foundations: independent, corporate, and operating foundations. Independent foundations are grant making organizations whose funds are derived from an individual or family. This category is the largest, and the majority of giving to libraries comes from independent foundations. Corporate foundations are private foundations whose grant funds are derived from the contributions of a profit-making business. A corporate foundation may retain close ties with the donor company, but it is a separate legal entity. Operating foundations are private foundations whose primary purpose is to conduct research, social welfare, or other programs determined by its governing body or establishment charter. An operating foundation may award some grants but the total is relatively small compared to the funds used for the foundation's own programs. The largest operating foundation in the country is the J. Paul Getty Trust in Los Angeles.

11

All private foundations are required by the IRS to pay out 5% of the market value of their assets each year and each foundation also must file a 990-PF form with the IRS. This document is often used by researchers to identify grants given by foundations, since most foundations do not have the staff to produce annual reports or develop websites. This document is available at all Foundation Center libraries and at some Cooperating Collections.

Corporate giving is another source of potential revenue for libraries that are seeking funds, equipment donations, or volunteer assistance. I mentioned above that corporations can establish private foundations, but they also have another option for giving and that is through what is called a "direct corporate giving program." These are grant making programs that are administered within a profit-making company, and their annual grant totals generally directly relate to their current profits. They are not required to file a 990-PF with the IRS, so it is often difficult to find information on these direct corporate giving programs. In-kind gifts (which are non-cash donations) and employee volunteer time are two types of support that have become increasingly attractive to corporate giving programs in recent years. Some corporations have opted to have both a direct corporate giving program and a corporate foundation, so this means you have to carefully read the guidelines for each to determine which is the best prospect for your library.

When researching foundations to identify appropriate prospects, keep in mind that your basic research strategy should be to establish a match between the activities/goals of your library and the funding interests of a foundation. You should aim to establish a partnership to achieve common goals. To assist grant seekers with the research process, The Foundation Center has established a "prospect worksheet" (http://fdncenter.org/funders/wrksheet/) for this type of research. The worksheet helps you develop your search strategy by asking you to provide "vital statistics" about your organization that will shape the search. It outlines the basic research approaches to foundation grant research, which are to use subject, fields of interest, geographic focus, and type of support (by type of support, I mean building/renovation, program development, general operating, etc.) criteria to target appropriate funders.

Resources to use for foundation grant research

This research can be conducted at any of The Foundation Center's libraries or Cooperating Collections, since all of our libraries and affiliates are free and open to the public. The Foundation Center operates five main libraries—in New York, Washington, D.C., San Francisco, Cleveland, and Atlanta. Additionally, our more than 200 Cooperating Collections around the country also house our database and print directories for prospect research. You can find contact information for all of these libraries on the home page of our website at http://www.fdncenter.org. The Dialog database, files 26 and 27, also contains Foundation Center data that you can use to conduct fund-raising research.

The best way to structure a search is to look at descriptions of recently awarded grants that have gone to programs or projects similar to your own in order to build a list of prospective names. Remember to be creative in your search strategy by designing several different searches that represent different aspects of the services your library provides. In addition to searching for foundations that have had a history of giving to libraries, I recommend that in one search you identify funders that are interested in a particular population group that your library is serving, or a particular program interest (such as adult literacy), or a certain type of support (such as for conservation).

We publish the Grant Guides series, and FC Search: The Foundation Center's Database on CD-ROM, both of which contain this data and are available for free use in all Foundation Center libraries and Cooperating Collections. FC Search is the most comprehensive resource in our libraries for researching foundation grants for nonprofit organizations, since it contains profiles of more than 50,000 foundations and 200,000 grant descriptions for recently awarded grants. Many  grant seekers also use the *Chronicle of Philanthropy* (http://philanthropy.com) or file 27 on Dialog to track recently awarded grants.

Once you have a list of prospective foundation names, you can then look up full profiles for these funders in numerous sources. In addition to our own publications, a foundation's own website is often the best place to gather in-depth information. Our website provides a gateway to all the foundations in the country that maintain websites (http://www.fdncenter.org/funders/). If the foundation you are researching does not have a website, you might try our free look-up tool, "Foundation Finder" (http://lnp.fdncenter.org/finder.html) to obtain basic contact information. File 26 on Dialog also provides descriptive profiles of foundations. I've listed even more online grant resources in the following section.

Regardless of the sources you use to gather prospects for your library, you will want to be consistent in noting certain details. Look into the funding history of each of your prospects. Have they been funding projects in your subject area? Look for and read a funder's purpose and activities statement when it is available. This will give you insight into the organization's goals. Review selected grants that a foundation has made to determine an appropriate dollar amount request. Compare several years' worth of grant lists, if possible, to help you determine whether a giving pattern exists that matches your requirements. Approaching more than one potential funding partner is generally a good idea; request an appropriate amount of your overall budget from each, based on your research. Always follow a foundation's guidelines for applying, if available. Pay particular attention to initial approach information, since many foundations prefer that you send a letter of inquiry prior to actually submitting a full proposal.

Here are two things to keep in mind as you proceed with your prospect research:

1. You must do your homework! Being informed always gives you an edge, and this is especially true in the area of funding research. Grant makers look for evidence that you've done this homework before you apply. Grant seeking can be a time-consuming process, but the payoff can be well worth the effort.

2. Keep in mind that support from foundations should be just one part of an overall fund-raising strategy and plan. Other sources might include individual gifts, special events, and government funding.

11

Although by now you may be feeling overwhelmed by the amount of work involved in the grant seeking process, keep in mind the magic that you are making. I have my own favorite metaphor for this process: I like to think of it as a modern-day alchemy. By conducting thorough research to make the right connections, we have the ability to transform paper into gold. Happy prospecting!

A handy list of point-and-click grant resources

Free online resources

Chronicle of Philanthropy (http://philanthropy.com): The site is organized into broad topic areas—Gifts and Grants, Fund Raising, Managing Non-Profit Groups, and Technology—and offers a summary of the contents of the Chronicle's current and previous issues, a listing of award and requests for proposal (RFP) deadlines, job opportunities in the nonprofit sector, a listing of forthcoming conferences and workshops, annotated links to other nonprofit resources on the Internet, and more.

Internet Prospector (http://www.internet-prospector.org): This nonprofit service is located on the University of Wyoming server and is produced by volunteers nationwide who "mine" the Net for research nuggets for nonprofit fund-raisers. You'll find an online newsletter and archives of past issues, a directory of U.S. Secretary of State incorporation records, search engine prospecting and test results, and tips for foundation searches.

Philanthropy News Digest (http://fdncenter.org/pnd/): This is The Foundation Center's own online journal that serves as a weekly news service. It is a compendium in digest form of philanthropy-related articles and features that are culled from print and electronic media outlets nationwide. The Digest features top philanthropy news stories, recent book and web reviews, a searchable archive, and RFP postings.

Philanthropy News Network Online (http://www.pnnonline.org): A daily news service about the nonprofit world.

Fee-based online resources

Chronicle of Philanthropy Guide to Grants (http://philanthropy.com/grants/): The Guide to Grants is an electronic database of all foundation and corporate grants listed in the printed *Chronicle* since 1995.

GrantSelect (http://www.grantselect.com): A subscription database of funding opportunities, including funding from state and federal governments, corporations, foundations, and associations, as well as from Canadian and other non-U.S. organizations.

FD Online (http://www.fconline.fdncenter.org): A subscription database that can be used to generate targeted lists of funding prospects from more than 10,000 of the nation's largest foundations.

SOURCE: Adapted from Janet Camarena, "A Wealth of Information on Foundations and the Grant Seeking Process," *Computers in Libraries* 20, no. 5 (May 2000): 26–31. This article has been printed in part from the May 2000 issue of *Computers in Libraries*, with the permission of Information Today, Inc., 143 Old Marlton Pike, Medford, NJ 08055 (USA), http://www.infotoday.com.

Preparing a proposal budget

Preparing a budget for a project proposal requires much care to make sure you have included all the probable expenses. School library media specialists who have never prepared a budget may use this form (adapted from one prepared by the National Endowment for the Humanities) as a checklist to make sure they have included all possible charges:

Requested Grant Period

Project Director _____ From _____ To _____

Applicant Organization _____

1. Salaries and Wages. Provide the names and titles of principal project personnel. For support staff, include the title of each position and indicate the number of persons who will be employed in that capacity.

Name/title of position	No.	Method of cost computation $ per hr., $ per mo., $ per yr.	Total
_____	_____	_____	$ _____
_____	_____	_____	$ _____
		Subtotal	$ _____

2. Fringe Benefits. If more than one rate is used, list each rate and salary base.

Rate		Salary base	
_____ % of	_____		$ _____
_____ % of	_____		$ _____
		Subtotal	$ _____

3. Consultant Fees. Include payments for professional and technical consultants and honoraria.

Name/title of consultant	No. of days on project	Daily rate of compensation	Total
_____	_____	_____	$ _____
_____	_____	_____	$ _____
		Subtotal	$ _____

4. Travel. For each trip, indicate the number of persons traveling, the total days they will be in travel status, and the total subsistence and transportation costs for that trip. When a project will involve the travel of a number of people to a conference, an institute, etc., these costs may be summarized on one line by indicating the point of origin as "various." All foreign travel must be listed separately.

From/to	No. of persons	Total travel days	Subsistence costs +	Transportation costs =	Total
_____	____	____	$ _____	$ _____	$ _____
_____	____	____	$ _____	$ _____	$ _____
				Subtotal	$ _____

5. Supplies and materials. Include consumable supplies, materials to be used in the project and items of expendable equipment (i.e., equipment items costing less than $5,000 and with an estimated useful life of less than one year).

Item	Basis/Method of cost computation	
_____	_____	$ _____
_____	_____	$ _____
	Subtotal	$ _____

11

6. Services. Include the cost of duplication and printing, long distance telephone, equipment rental, postage, and other services related to project objectives that are not included under other budget categories or in the indirect cost pool. For subcontracts provide an itemization of subcontract costs on this form or on an attachment.

Item	Basis/Method of cost computation	
_____	_____	$ _____
_____	_____	$ _____
	Subtotal	$ _____

7. Other costs. Include participant stipends and room and board, equipment purchases, and other items not previously listed. Please note that "miscellaneous" and "contingency" are not acceptable budget categories. Refer to the budget instructions for the restriction on the purchase of permanent equipment.

Item	Basis/Method of cost computation	
_____	_____	$ _____
_____	_____	$ _____
	Subtotal	$ _____

8. Total direct costs (add subtotals of items 1 through 7) $ _____

9. Indirect costs. (These vary from institution to institution and are sometimes negotiated annually by a school district or public library.)

❏ Current indirect cost rate(s) has/have been negotiated with state or federal agency.
❏ Indirect cost proposal has been submitted to a state or federal agency but not yet negotiated.
❏ Indirect cost proposal will be sent if application is funded.
❏ Applicant chooses to use a rate not to exceed 10% of direct costs, less distorting items, up to a maximum charge of $5,000 per year.

If indirect costs are charged:

Rate	Base		Total
_____ % of	_____		$ _____
_____ % of	_____		$ _____
		Total indirect costs	$ _____

10. Total project costs (direct and indirect) for budget period $ _____

If your budget is multiyear, you would need budget categories and each year's expenditures:

Budget Categories	Year 1	Year 2	Year 3	Total Costs for Entire Grant Period
1. Salaries and Wages	$ _____	$ _____	$ _____	$ _____

Project Funding for Entire Grant Period

Requested from Agency
$ _____

Cost Sharing
    Applicant's contributions $ _____
    Third-party contributions $ _____
    Project income $ _____
    Total cost sharing $ _____

Total Project Funding (Requested from Agency + Cost Sharing) = $ _____

SOURCE: Adapted from the budget form for proposals submitted to the National Endowment for the Humanities.

STAFF DEVELOPMENT

CHAPTER TWELVE

Training needs of school library staff for service delivery to students with disabilities

by Janet Murray

Few library-specific training materials are available on the provision of services for people with disabilities. Few staff development programs on this aspect of service run by libraries have been reported in the literature. If the viewpoint is narrowed to staff development programs for school library staff, evidence of any library-specific training is hard to track down. This suggests that school librarians can provide themselves with staff development by visiting other school libraries that cater for disabled students, or can undertake some action research in their own library that focuses on disabled students. In Australia, some staff development programs on service provision for people with disabilities are available, but provision is still sporadic. None of these programs has been targeted at school librarians.

Research shows that there has been limited coverage of library services for people with disabilities in preprofessional training programs. There appears to be little staff development of any type available for school librarians. Such programs as are offered are rarely reported in the literature. Peggy Heeks and Margaret Kinnell found that in the United Kingdom, a range of staff development activities were available to school librarians, but the identification of those suitable for individual school librarians was inhibited by the lack of confidence by line managers in assessing the individual school librarian's staff development needs. Earlier research by Karlene K. Edwards and Isabel Schon identified professional reading, attendance at conferences and seminars, training provided by school districts, involvement in professional associations, and formal tertiary education courses as being the chief training activities engaged in by school librarians. There appeared to be no evidence of staff development programs being run specifically for school librarians to assist them in providing services to disabled students. Comprehensive literature searches conducted over the last two years have not identified any articles other than those discussed here.

If little is being done for these professionals from the library perspective, what is happening in education circles? Dianne F. Bradley and Frederick J. West investigated the staff development needs of classroom teachers who were teaching disabled students in mainstream schools. Results showed that teachers wanted staff development that covered: how to modify educational programs; working and teaching in a team; the impact of the inclusion of a student with a disability on other students in the class; knowledge of specific disabilities; attitudes to disability; expectations of disabled students included in their classes; and background information about special education, integration, and inclusion. Unless teachers have studied special education in either pre- or post-professional courses, they may have no knowledge of these areas.

The study

I recently completed a study that evaluated the library services provided to disabled students enrolled in mainstream schools. Data about the availability of staff development programs and training needs for school librarians were collected through both a longitudinal survey and case studies. The survey instrument, a self-administered questionnaire, included two questions about staff development. The first asked if any programs related to disabled students had been offered in the school and invited comments about this topic. The second asked about the awareness of school librarians of disability legislation that affected library services. Those who were aware were then asked to identify the source through which they became aware of the legislation. The options included the school principal, library literature, professional networks, educational publications (including professional literature and publications made available through the education system), the media, or training/education. The survey was administered twice; the second survey (Survey 2) was administered 18 months after the first (Survey 1).

Fourteen schools across the two states participated in the study as case study schools. In conducting interviews in case study schools, I asked school librarians about the staff development programs that had been made available to them or their staff. School library staff discussed their personal experience of disability. Special educators were asked what type of staff development programs they had made available to staff in the school and whether library staff were included.

Results

A total of 207 respondents (52%) to Survey 1 reported that staff development programs related to disabled students had been available; 104 respondents (27%) to Survey 2 reported that such programs had been available in the period since Survey 1, a decrease in staff development programs in the 18 months between surveys. Qualitative responses to this question indicated that most of the training was in-house; there were no library-specific programs. Training covering a wide range of disabilities was mentioned; visual impairment, hearing disability, and learning disability were the most frequently mentioned. The programs consisted of special staff meetings, in-services or talks by personnel from external organizations, or staff being sent to external courses; this latter option was available only to special educators. Where school librarians were aware of disability legislation, their main sources of information were evenly distributed across the six sources identified. There was a drop in the percentage of respondents quoting training as a source between 1994 and 1996, from 22% to 15%, which is consistent with the decrease in training available in the same time period. The two surveys showed that 57% of respondents were totally unaware that legislation existed that affected the services offered to disabled students.

Several school library staff members working in case study schools had personal experience of disability. These came from a range of experiences: teaching, community work, or through the involvement of family members in the disability field. Special educators in nearly all case study schools provided training activities of some kind for teaching staff, but these either did not include non-teaching staff, or they were held outside of school hours and non-teaching staff were not willing to attend in their own time. Schools often provided intensive staff development programs when disabled students were first enrolled, but this was not an ongoing activity as it was presumed there was no further need. Often special educators briefed a small group of teachers who taught particular disabled students, but the school librarian was not included in this group.

Discussion

The survey results showed that few opportunities were provided for the library staff to participate in staff development programs related to service provision for disabled students. In 1994, just over half of the schools with disabled students enrolled had offered whole school programs; in 1996, this had dropped to 27%. Although professional library staff would no doubt have been able to attend any programs offered to the teaching staff, it is questionable whether these programs would also have been offered to technical or clerical staff in the school library. It is interesting to note that more staff development programs have been offered in the government schools sector than in the private schools sector. Given that government schools are the largest school sector, this could be due to the availability of training activities run at the regional or state level for school staff.

Although school librarians in the case study schools were able to attend training activities offered to the whole school teaching staff, none had received any library-specific training, nor had they provided it for technical or clerical library staff. In some schools, little or no information was provided about disabled students to the school librarian by special educators, often because the special educators failed to recognize that the school librarian would be likely to deal with most students in the school and therefore should be included in briefing sessions about particular students. The lack of ongoing disability training in some schools did not take into account the needs of newly appointed staff.

12

The training needs of school librarians

The survey results and discussions with librarians in the case study schools and in schools visited during fieldwork in Canada and the UK indicate that staff development programs are needed in several areas, some of which correspond to Bradley and West's findings. School library staff who do not have personal experience of disability would benefit from disability awareness training. Unless they have personal experience of disability, it is quite likely that school library staff may have misconceptions about disability that need to be overcome. Some staff may be well informed, but may need to enhance their communication skills to enable them to deal more effectively with students with particular needs. It is important that all school library staff are given the opportunity, in a relaxed and informal atmosphere, to discuss any fears or apprehensions they might have about dealing with students with particular disabilities.

School librarians need the knowledge about resources and technology to enable them to improve services. They need to be aware of the existence of disability legislation and of guidelines and standards, both national and international, for library service to people with disabilities. Information is needed about available support services and the range of alternative format material published. School librarians should also understand the need to provide quality information about disability and fiction that portrays disability in an understanding and empathetic way.

The greatest need is for school librarians to receive specific information about the disabled students in their school and how to deal with them, how to teach them, and how to meet their needs. School librarians should be included in briefing sessions on particular students and in meetings of students' individual learning support groups when information resourcing is an issue to be discussed. This includes being given the opportunity to work with special educators in modifying materials used in information skills teaching to suit individual students. However, school librarians need to ensure they always attend general staff meetings and other forums where information about disabled students may be disseminated. Training in working with others is not such an issue for school librarians, as they are experienced in this area through their endeavors to integrate information skills teaching into the curriculum and by working alongside other library staff, although some do work in isolation. But as classroom teachers and special educators receive much-needed training, as many of them have worked independently in the past, information flow and cooperation between them and the school librarian should improve.

School librarians would benefit from gaining knowledge about special education, the purpose and processes of integration and inclusion of disabled students into mainstream schools, and particularly the legislation governing this area. Beyond the staff development needs identified by Bradley and West, school librarians need training in the library-specific areas of policy formulation, collection management, and technology requirements. The survey results showed that 5% of respondents had a formal policy on services for disabled students in 1994 (3% in 1996). Few of the case study school libraries had formal policy statements, even those with exemplary school librarians. The lack of policy statements indicates lack of awareness of need. Both survey and case study results showed that the school librarians provided good collections of informational materials about disability and of fiction materials that treat disability in a realistic and sensitive way. However, most school librarians have a limited knowledge of the alternative format materials that are available and of the external libraries or organizations where these can be accessed or borrowed. Although school librarians are experienced users of information technology, there was no evidence of recognition of the role of technology in compensating for disabilities. Although adaptive technology can provide many options, such as access to print for visually impaired students and keyboard use for students with little motor control, it was provided only in a small number of school libraries.

Meeting these staff development needs involves a variety of mechanisms. Caren L. Wesson's suggestion that individuals should take charge of their own staff development is realistic, given the isolation experienced by most school librarians and the frequent lack of understanding of their staff development needs by their line managers. Individuals can pursue professional literature. Several good videos and some training packages on disability and disability awareness could be used effectively by one person or by a small library staff together. Some school districts and school clusters provide staff development programs for school library staff that could address collection management and information technology issues. Conferences and seminars held by professional associations are another avenue, although my experience indicates that specific seminars held at a district or local level will be more successful than running a session at a general conference. Opportunities for staff development are so limited for school librarians, and emphasis on information technology so great, that any topic considered at all peripheral will be ignored where a choice of sessions is offered at a conference.

Clearly all these areas must be reinforced in ongoing staff development activities, but there is an argument for including them in professional education courses. Although there is no room for additional subjects in the already crowded curricula of pre-professional courses, disability awareness training and information about resources and technology can be built into existing subjects. This is, in fact, preferable, so that the information needs of disabled people are seen as a valid and appropriate consideration in all types of library service. An obvious example is in the collection management area where information about alternative format material can be included. Evaluation of fiction that portrays people with disabilities could be an interesting inclusion in any subject that looks at literature, whether adult, children's, or young adult literature. The curricula of most library schools address communication skills, and a session on dealing with disability would be appropriate and probably organized at little extra cost or effort, as voluntary agencies in the disability field will frequently provide trainers free or at a reasonable charge. At the post-professional level, flexibility in offerings could enable school librarians to undertake a subject in a special education course available in their university.

Further research in the area of library services to disabled students is needed. My own study highlighted two particular areas needing further research: an evaluation of the learning outcomes for disabled students undertaking information skills programs; and an assessment of the benefits of electronic information sources for students with disabilities.

Conclusion

Staff development programs on services to disabled students are rarely provided for school librarians or other school library staff. University departments offering courses in librarianship and information management should be encouraged

12

to address library services to people with disabilities in mainstream curricula, so that newly trained professionals would be sensitized to the needs of this client group. The inclusion of alternative format materials in collection management subjects, as suggested above, could be easily achieved. In most countries, such materials are produced and published by major disability agencies. The most obvious example is materials for blind people. Most national libraries, such as the National Library of Australia and the Library of Congress, include alternative format materials in their catalogs and databases.

Encouragement of staff development activities at a personal level and lobbying of professional associations, tertiary institutions, and education authorities to provide more programs in this area seem to be the most viable solutions to the lack of staff development activities for this specialized area. A short course run by any of these groups should include disability awareness training, information about disability legislation, and information about specific services and publications that could be accessed by school librarians.

There are several good training kits available that provide videos and other resources that can be used to raise awareness of disability. If a library deals specifically with clients with a specific disability, staff might pursue training that facilitates their dealings with that particular group. Staff from disability agencies are available to talk to groups about specific disabilities. In a school, there are many visiting professionals, such as physiotherapists, speech therapists, and visiting specialist teachers, who may be available to talk to library staff. Library staff from the larger agencies that provide specialist library services can provide information about alternative format materials, where they can be purchased or borrowed, and criteria for their selection.

As mentioned above, school librarians need to be proactive in both gaining information about students with disabilities enrolled in their school and ensuring that any staff development activities offered in the school are made available to all library staff at professional, paraprofessional, and technical-clerical levels. In addition to this, there are three other options to ensure the library is accessible to any students with disabilities who are enrolled in the school. First, libraries could be audited for physical accessibility, possibly by a staff member from an agency for physical disability or by self-assessment using one of the published lists available. Second, disability awareness training for all staff could be provided. Again, tools are available that could be used by a school librarian to provide this training for the staff, possibly with some assistance from special education staff in the school. It is advisable to seek advice from local disability agencies about suitable training kits. Finally, school librarians can find out which adaptive technology is currently being used by disabled students in the school and ensure that the necessary equipment is available so that it can be also used in the library. This often requires something straightforward such as a power point in a particular position or a particular socket or add-on device for computers and other equipment. These are straightforward, cost-effective steps that can be taken by any school librarian to prepare for the enrollment of any student with a disability in the school.

SOURCE: Adapted from Janet R. Murray, "The Training Needs of School Library Staff for Service Delivery to Disabled Students," *School Libraries Worldwide* 6, no. 2 (July 2000): 21–29. Used with permission.

Professional development for the library media specialist

by Susan Miller

The daily trials of the library media specialist can be draining, if not over-whelming. The media specialist is a little bit of many things and a lot of every-thing. How can this person consistently stay current with the profession? What about the newest technology application, the award-winning titles, the state mandated curriculum changes? Can one keep the spirit, knowledge, skills, attitude, and relevance in the job while trying to be all things to all people? Certainly not without some professional development. There must be times to learn from others who can dispense the knowledge, success stories, or dem-onstrations of new methods of operation. These are opportunities for the li-brary media specialist to evaluate and assess the impact of the job.

Participation in conferences at local, state, and national levels is a neces-sity. Picking up extra coursework only benefits the job and people who make up the library's community. Reading professional journals in the library and educational field is automatic. Learning about implementing the Internet capabilities is a given. Are there other invigorating hints to homespun profes-sional development? There are many different ways to rejuvenate, inspire, and simply put dazzle into the eyes of the drained professional library media specialist. Here are a few suggestions that build on obvious choices for job enrichment with a perspective that helps the media specialist stay on the cutting edge of the profession:

1. Professional organizations. Do more than merely joining and attending the yearly conferences! Present, present, present—share your successes and collaborations, invite other media specialists, administrators, and teachers to participate in joint programs.

Cutting edge: Become active as an officer, local representative, board mem-ber, or volunteer within these organizations. Then every meeting becomes a professional development session as you learn from your fellow professionals, who are the leaders, by discussions and questions. Join an interest group of the parent organization. Meet with this smaller group of professionals (middle school, elementary, high school, private schools, administrators) periodically for lunch. You may have to drive for an hour or two, but network, network, network! Being with library media specialists in the same position or working with the same grade levels, size of school, or number of professionals in the district is therapeutic. Group together and prepare workshops, round tables, and sessions at state conferences. Focus on more than library related organiza-tions. Reading and technology associations are obvious, but administration, curriculum, and general educational groups are important and beneficial to the job.

12

2. Course work. Picking up college credit through advanced studies has always been an option. Scan the regional educational centers in your area for workshops that offer pertinent training, lectures, and hands-on experience for less cost and possible CEUs (if offered in your state). Many companies trying to sell their software/hardware, curriculum coursework, or published materi-als provide free training. Take advantage of the opportunity.

Cutting edge: Offer your talents to local educational centers as a guest lecturer or trainer, or offer your site for classes. Contact the local college education department to investigate what information is provided to prepare teachers to be media center literate upon graduation. Perhaps there is a spot for your input in this department.

3. Professional journals. So much is available in the educational, technology, and library fields, it would take a full-time reader to plow through it. Guess this is where skimming and quick absorption of facts and figures come in handy.

Cutting edge: Publish or perish? Not exactly, although taking the time to express your ideas, philosophy, tricks, and trials only adds to the expertise of the profession. Verbalizing is a learning style, writing is a form of verbalizing; so chatter on.

4. Internet investigations. The array of information on the WWW is awesome and overpowering. Thankfully, in the world of library media, there are truly brilliant, creative, and dedicated professionals out there (in cyberspace) who create, collect, and present attainable conglomerations of school/library related links. Local area schools, regional centers, and universities have home pages with related spots already linked. Use them.

Cutting edge: Someone needs to create these pages—if you have the creativity, time, and talent, by all means, use them. The Web is a forum for many fellow professionals to sparkle! For those of us who admire from afar, do some professional development from the confines of home or cottage. It takes nothing but time to find the sites that fit special needs. Travel into the school, public, or university library pages and find the tremendous number of links to myriad information. Learn to discriminate and maintain this array of knowledge and set up links of information for staff, student, and community users.

SOURCE: Adapted from Susan Miller, "Professional Development for the Library Media Specialist," *The Book Report* 17, no. 5 (March/April 1999): 20–21. Copyright 1999. *The Book Report* is now published as *Library Media Connection.* Used with permission.

The value of staff development

by Mary Alice Anderson

Staff development is one of our newest yet most important roles. By becoming involved in staff development we increase our opportunities to shape the curriculum and be viewed as instructional leaders. *Information Power* challenges media specialists to take "a proactive role in promoting the use of technology by staff, in determining staff development needs, in facilitating staff learning explorations, and by serving as a leader in staff development activities."

A dearth of meaningful staff development opportunities has put a crimp in educators' ability to use technology to help students learn better. Teachers are relying on technology more than ever, but, as an increasing number of studies show, not necessarily more effectively.

Studies show that exemplary technology-using teachers work in an atmosphere of collegial support and prefer to learn from their peers rather than from an outside trainer or someone they perceive as too technical. A media specialist may be the perfect person to teach staff development classes and facilitate peer support groups. The more we reach out to others, the more we increase the odds that our expertise is valued. If you aren't already involved in staff development, here are five compelling reasons why now is the time to start:

Most teachers are inadequately prepared to use technology. With an average of only 12 hours of technology training per year, most teachers have had more training in areas such as diversity, standards, and district initiatives. Some states require technology training, but the requirement is not universal and teachers often oppose it. Studies show only half of today's teachers consider themselves skilled technology users. Beginning teachers are often inadequately prepared to use technology beyond reading e-mail messages or searching the Internet. It can take years for teachers to feel comfortable with technology and too few take advantage of the learning potential technology offers. Too often, teachers simply use technology to do the same old thing, only electronically.

Staff development provides connections between technology, curriculum, and information processes. Technology classes usually emphasize software and hardware. Getting comfortable with a new online grade book is more important for many teachers than learning the secrets of searching the Internet. Media specialists can and should teach technology skills: the Excel class that we teach may provide a forum for discussing curricular issues.

Think about what you do on a daily basis, what you know, and with whom you interact. Librarians are the only teachers who work in all areas of the curriculum, with all of the students and staff. Our daily interactions with curriculum and teachers are occasions for informal staff development and offer insight into staff needs. Sharing your insights with curriculum directors, information systems coordinators, and others can make a difference. Combine organizational, curriculum, technological, and teaching skills to develop and implement extended staff development that reaches the entire learning community.

Staff development has a positive impact on instructional strategies and student learning. Once teachers realize the potential of technology, they often become eager to use it and to try new teaching techniques. Varied instructional strategies have a positive impact on student achievement. Teachers with even a small amount of technology training teach more effectively and have a better understanding of how students learn. Initially, trying new approaches may overwhelm a teacher. As an educational peer, media specialists can provide technical assistance and instructional support, which is another form of staff development. Research has shown that the more time media specialists spend providing in-service training to teachers, the higher the level of academic achievement by students. Researcher Keith Lance's studies have demonstrated that a librarian's proactive, leadership role sets the stage for collaboration and, in turn, leads to higher achievement. A study by the Software Publishers Association has demonstrated that teacher training influences the type of software used, which, in turn, increases students' test scores. Training in software selection and implementation is yet another way in which media specialists can become staff development leaders. These studies validate the need for staff development and suggest avenues for media specialist involvement.

12

Staff development is an opportunity to introduce new resources. We've all heard teachers say, "I wish I'd known about that." A teacher who never uses the media center and its resources might attend a staff development session. For example, a workshop about a new online resource or some new educational software may be an occasion to increase a teacher's awareness of related books and videos. During an informal staff development session, an English teacher got so excited about Inspiration, a software program that encourages critical thinking and writing skills, that she used the program with her students the next day.

Bringing a variety of resources to the learning experience increases the chances of students' success. Staff development sessions can generate a wealth of ideas and provide openings for future partnerships. Like the English teacher mentioned above, it's not uncommon for a teacher to schedule a new student activity immediately following a staff development session.

A staff development role contributes to increased job security. Administrators and teachers want and need tech-savvy media specialists. Administrators at a small rural school were surprised and pleased when they discovered a media specialist might be just the person to help their school overcome the problem of underutilized technology. Consider these remarks by other administrators and board members:

> "We're doing fine with the literature activities; we need someone to help us with the technology."
>
> "We need a media specialist to help with the Internet and searching for online information."
>
> "Are you the person a teacher can turn to if they need help with Excel?"
>
> "How are our teachers doing with their technology skills?"
>
> "She's always right there when I need help with my computer!"
>
> "Please contact our media specialist about the workshops; he's in charge of staff development."
>
> "How would your administrator describe you?"

Curricular involvement and requests for technological assistance provide insight into big-picture needs and a tool to develop further staff development options. Staff development involving technology can also substantially strengthen the image teachers have of media specialists. Be the person teachers can turn to when they need help. Extend that assistance to others working in the school. It will not go unnoticed. Grab those opportunities that exist, seek out others, and be at the forefront. Staff development is our most important role.

SOURCE: Adapted from Mary Alice Anderson, "The Value of Staff Development," *School Library Journal* 48 (November 2002): 34–35. Courtesy of *School Library Journal*.

ISSUES
CHAPTER THIRTEEN

> This sacred Privilege is so essential to free Governments, that the
> Security of Property, and the Freedom of Speech always go together;
> and in those wretched Countries where a Man cannot call his Tongue
> his own, he can scarce call any Thing else his own. Whoever would
> overthrow the Liberty of a Nation, must begin by subduing the Free-
> dom of Speech.
>
> —*Ben Franklin*

Information power

Principle 6. The library media program is founded on a commitment to the right of intellectual freedom.

Goals for the school library media specialist

1. Collaborate with teachers, administrators, parents, and other members of the learning community to create and disseminate policies related to freedom of information that are consistent with the mission, goals, and objectives of the school.

2. Promote the principles of intellectual freedom by providing services and resources that create and sustain an atmosphere of free inquiry and by serving as an active advocate for intellectual freedom within the school and in the larger learning community.

3. Collaborate with teachers, administrators, and other members of the learning community to build and maintain collections that are appropriate to the learning needs of all the students in the school.

4. Model the openness to the ideas and the free and robust debate that are characteristic of a democratic society.

5. Guard against barriers to intellectual freedom, such as age or grade-level restrictions, limitations on access to electronic information, requirements for special permission to use materials and resources, and restricted collections.

6. Collaborate with teachers to use the information literacy standards for student learning to design and integrate learning activities that equip students to locate, evaluate, and use a broad range of ideas responsibly and effectively.

Principle 7. The information policies, procedures, and practices of the library media program reflect legal guidelines and professional ethics.

Goals for the school library media specialist

1. Maintain an in-depth understanding of current legislation and regulations regarding access, copyright, and other legal issues that affect the library media program.

2. Demonstrate a commitment to the principles of the library profession regarding intellectual freedom, confidentiality, the rights of users, and other intellectual property concerns.

3. Collaborate with teachers, administrators, and others to develop and publicize policies and procedures that advocate compliance with copyright and other relevant laws.

4. Model ethical and responsible use of information and information technology by observing all legal guidelines related to access and duplication, by ensuring the confidentiality and security of information for all members of the learning community, and by providing equitable access to information and ideas in accordance with the principles of intellectual freedom and the needs and abilities of learners.

SOURCE: Adapted from "Information Access and Delivery," chapter 5 in *Information Power: Building Partnerships for Learning* (Chicago: American Library Association, 1998), 91–94.

Library bill of rights

The American Library Association affirms that all libraries are forums for information and ideas, and that the following basic policies should guide their services.

I. Books and other library resources should be provided for the interest, information, and enlightenment of all people of the community the library serves. Materials should not be excluded because of the origin, background, or views of those contributing to their creation.

II. Libraries should provide materials and information presenting all points of view on current and historical issues. Materials should not be proscribed or removed because of partisan or doctrinal disapproval.

III. Libraries should challenge censorship in the fulfillment of their responsibility to provide information and enlightenment.

IV. Libraries should cooperate with all persons and groups concerned with resisting abridgment of free expression and free access to ideas.

V. A person's right to use a library should not be denied or abridged because of origin, age, background, or views.

VI. Libraries which make exhibit spaces and meeting rooms available to the public they serve should make such facilities available on an equitable basis, regardless of the beliefs or affiliations of individuals or groups requesting their use.

SOURCE: Adopted June 18, 1948. Amended February 2, 1961, and January 23, 1980. Inclusion of "age" reaffirmed January 23, 1996, by the ALA Council.

Questions and answers on intellectual freedom

Intellectual freedom is the right of every individual to both seek and receive information from all points of view without restriction. It provides for free access to all expressions of ideas through which any and all sides of a question, cause, or movement may be explored.

Why is intellectual freedom important? Intellectual freedom is the basis for our democratic system. We expect our people to be self-governors. But to do so responsibly, our citizenry must be well-informed. Libraries provide the ideas and information, in a variety of formats, to allow people to inform themselves. Intellectual freedom encompasses the freedom to hold, receive, and disseminate ideas.

What is censorship? Censorship is the suppression of ideas and information that certain persons—individuals, groups, or government officials—find objectionable or dangerous. It is no more compli-cated than someone saying, "Don't let anyone read this book, or buy that magazine, or view that film, because I object to it!" Censors try to use the power of the state to impose their views of what is truthful and appropriate, or offensive and objectionable, on everyone else. Censors pressure public institutions, like libraries, to suppress and remove from public access information they judge inappropriate or dangerous, so that no one else has the chance to read or view the material and make up their own minds about it. The censor wants to prejudge materials for everyone.

THE NAZIS BURNED THESE BOOKS

...but free Americans *CAN STILL READ THEM*

U.S. Office of War
Information poster, 1943

How does censorship happen? Censorship occurs when expressive materials, like books, magazines, films and videos, or works of art, are removed or kept from public access. Individuals and pressure groups identify materials to which they object. Sometimes they succeed in pressuring schools not to use them, libraries not to shelve them, book and video stores not to carry them, publishers not to publish them, or art galleries not to display them. Censorship also occurs when materials are restricted to particular audiences, based on their age or other characteristics.

Who attempts censorship? In most instances, a censor is a sincerely concerned individual who believes that censorship can improve society, protect children, and restore what the censor sees as lost moral values. But under the First Amendment to the United States Constitution, each of us has the right to read, view, listen to, and disseminate constitutionally protected ideas, even if a censor finds those ideas offensive.

What is the relationship between censorship and intellectual freedom? In expressing their opinions and concerns, would-be censors are exercising the same rights librarians seek to protect when they confront censorship. In making their criti-cisms known, people disseminate the material to which they object. Their rights to voice opinions and try to persuade others to adopt those opinions are protected only if the rights of persons to express ideas they despise are also protected. The rights of both sides must be protected, or neither will survive.

13

How do censors justify their demands that information be suppressed? Censors might sincerely believe that certain materials are so offensive, or present ideas that are so hateful and destructive to society, that they simply must not see the 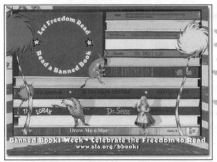 light of day. Others are worried that younger or weaker people will be badly influenced by bad ideas, and will do bad things as a result. Still others believe that there is a very clear distinction between ideas that are right and morally uplifting, and ideas that are wrong and morally corrupting, and wish to ensure that society has the benefit of their perception. They believe that certain individuals, certain institutions, even society itself, will be endangered if particular ideas are disseminated without restriction. What censors often don't consider is that, if they succeed in suppressing the ideas they don't like today, others may use that precedent to suppress the ideas they do like tomorrow.

Aren't there some kinds of expression that really should be censored? The United States Supreme Court has ruled that there are narrow categories of speech that are not protected by the First Amendment: child pornography, defamation, and "fighting words," or speech that incites immediate and imminent lawless action. The government is also allowed to enforce secrecy of some information when it is considered essential to national security, like troop movements in time of war, classified information about defense, etc.

How do you guide children when you can't be with them 24 hours a day? Parents who believe that the current state of society and communications make it difficult to shield their children must nevertheless find a way to cope with what they see as that reality within the context of their own family. Libraries can be extremely helpful, providing information about parenting, open communication between parents and children, how to communicate with caregivers and the parents of your children's friends about your rules, and the opinions of various organizations representing a wide spectrum of points of view about materials for children. If a child borrows something from a library which that child's parent believes is inappropriate, the parents are encouraged to return the item and make use of the expertise of their librarian to locate materials they prefer, among the hundreds of thousands of choices most public libraries make available.

Don't librarians censor everything they choose not to buy for the library? No library can make everything available, and selection decisions must be made. Selection is an inclusive process, where the library affirmatively seeks out materials which will serve its mission of providing a broad diversity of points of view and subject matter. By contrast, censorship is an exclusive process, by which individuals or institutions seek to deny access to or otherwise suppress ideas and information because they find those ideas offensive and do not want others to have access to them. There are many objective reasons unrelated to the ideas expressed in materials that a library might decide not to add those materials to its collection: redundancy, lack of community interest, expense, space, etc. Unless the decision is based on a disapproval of the ideas expressed and desire to keep those ideas away from public access, a decision not to select materials for a library collection is not censorship.

SOURCE: American Library Association, Office of Intellectual Freedom.

Stolen words: Copyright in a nutshell

by Carrie Russell

The phenomenon of "the librarian-caught-in-the-middle-of-copyright-questions" occurs when, say, the school librarian provides copyright advice, then discovers that the teacher or student questions that advice. Librarians report that after the copyright information is given, the student or teacher does one of three things. One, the student or teacher ignores the advice and proceeds to do what he or she wanted to do in the first place. Two, the student or teacher grudgingly accepts the advice and never talks to the librarian again. Three, an argument ensues. (Though statistically insignificant, I do note the very rare instance when the student or teacher accepts the advice and thanks the librarian for broadening his or her understanding of the copyright law.) Copyright is tremendously complex, and your role as a knowledgeable information specialist and occasional copyright adviser is a difficult one. You are asked to provide sound advice on copyright to your users, and you must strive to be consistent and fair. Moreover, while working within the spirit of the copyright law, it's also your job as a librarian to protect your patrons' rights to use and share information, whenever legally possible.

I'd like to suggest five guidelines for librarians dealing with copyright issues. Please note that this advice applies just as well to public librarians, who deal with many of the same issues as their school counterparts.

1. Embrace your role as copyright adviser.

Librarians are the information professionals of American society. As such, we protect the interests of library users and strive for the free flow of information. The term "free flow" does not mean that information should be "free" but, rather, that access to information should be as "barrier-free" as possible. Unfettered access to information is critical to a democratic society and essential to schools and other educational institutions. Librarians are the only professionals charged with preserving this access. Thus, it is natural and correct that librarians should be recognized as the copyright experts of the schools, because of who we are and what we represent. Since copyright is a legal doctrine with tremendous impact on information flow, this is not a role we want handled by others.

2. Stay informed and commit yourself to learning about copyright.

Obviously, digital technology has made copyright law more complicated. Materials in digital formats can be easily replicated and distributed over computer networks. Quite simply, it is now easier to infringe copyright. (However, it is also easier to create new barriers to information, a fact people in the media industries often leave out.) As a result of digital technology, holders of copyrighted materials pushed for, and got, a major revision of the copyright law known as the Digital Millennium Copyright Act (DMCA) of 1998. This law is extremely complex, but it's safe to say that, overall, the tide has shifted to the interests of copyright holders over the interests of those who wish to use copyrighted materials. In effect, the DMCA places tighter controls over access to and use of copyrighted materials. Many of these changes are now

13

being asserted or challenged in court, so in the next few years we can expect even more changes as the courts interpret and apply new statutes.

For their part, librarians should continue to advocate for a balanced approach to copyright, one that recognizes that copyright exemptions are particularly necessary for educators and library users in order to uphold the constitutional purpose of the law—"to advance the progress of science and the useful arts." All of this change requires that librarians be aware and vigilant. Don't wait for someone else to tell you that what once was a lawful use is now an unlawful use. Stay on top of the subject.

3. Remember, users have rights, too. The fact is, teachers and students are right some of the time: copyright law can be infringed under certain circumstances. This sounds ridiculous, but it's true. Copyright law includes numerous exemptions that allow users to make and distribute copies, play videos in the classroom, and use excerpts from copyrighted materials—especially in nonprofit educational institutions. For instance, if a teacher wants to show the film version of *Hamlet* starring Ethan Hawke as part of so-called face-to-face instruction, the school librarian does not need to get special permission to screen the film. Of course, each situation should be evaluated on the facts, but there are occasions when even an entire book can be photocopied! I know school librarians take very seriously their responsibility to protect the school from potential lawsuits. But don't let your aversion to risk weaken the ability of teachers and students to exercise their rights. *Your primary goal should be to find legal ways to give users access to the information they need.*

4. Promote fair use. Every librarian, especially those working with students, teachers, and faculty, should understand and be prepared to apply the concept of "fair use." The Fair Use Doctrine is found in Section 107 of the copyright law. It states that under certain circumstances, users have a legal right to make copies or engage in other activities without permission from the copyright holder. The doctrine originated in judicial decisions in which copyright infringement was excused because the use was deemed beneficial to society or because it caused little or no harm.

Briefly, fair use must be applied on a case-by-case basis considering the following four factors:

- the purpose and character of the use, including whether such use is of a commercial nature or is for nonprofit educational purposes;
- the nature of the copyrighted work;
- the amount and substantiality of the portion used in relation to the copyrighted work as a whole; and
- the effect of the use upon the potential market for or value of the copyrighted work.

While each case must be evaluated based on the facts, the use of copyrighted materials in libraries and schools frequently passes the fair-use test. For example, students can photocopy a chapter from a book or an article from a magazine as a matter of fair use. Of course, this does not mean that *all* uses of copyrighted materials are fair use. In these cases, librarians should request permission from the copyright holder. Think of fair use as your friend. Use the doctrine with teachers and students to explain your reasoning for copyright decisions. Without this important exception, the constitutional purpose of the copyright law—to promote the progress of science and the useful arts— could not be achieved.

5. Consider the source of copyright information. When you read articles and educational guides about copyright, don't forget to critically consider the perspective of the author. A librarian's perspective is to preserve copyright as a balanced law—one that respects both the rights of copyright holders and the rights of the public who need access to copyrighted materials. Librarians also recognize that they must "think" for their public. The public, including teachers and students, may not have a clue about copyright, so we have to help them understand it. Publishers and software vendors, on the other hand, have a very different perspective, which is based, obviously, on a desire to protect their investments. For them, users' rights may be more limited than they would be from my perspective. Writers and other creative types may have yet another perspective. And law professors and practicing attorneys hold views on copyright that differ widely. Always consider the source and critically evaluate the information presented.

Resources

Copyright Essentials for Librarians and Educators by Kenneth Crews (ALA, 2000). Although this book focuses on higher education, much of it applies to the K–12 environment.

"Regents' Guide to Copyright," University of Georgia, http://www.usg.edu/admin/legal/copyright/. Written with higher education in mind, but includes fabulous examples of fair-use situations that commonly occur in any educational setting.

SOURCE: Adapted from Carrie Russell, "Stolen Words," *School Library Journal* 47 (February 2001): 40–43. Courtesy of *School Library Journal.*

Managing copyright in schools

by Carol Simpson

Copyright clearance is difficult for those who seek to follow the law. For those who are unaware of the requirements of copyright, the smallest act of compliance is a tremendous shock to long-standing habits and seemingly reasonable excuses. Compliance can be divided into two phases: things and people. People are easier to manage if things are tracked and clearly identified so the people are constantly reminded. Several suggestions for tracking and marking copyright-protected materials are included in this article. People require education, commitment, and administrative support to follow through on compliance issues. Specific guidelines for bringing staff and administrators into compliance are also included.

Copyright is a quagmire. Like most laws, federal and state, repeated revisions have made simple reading and interpretation difficult. New versions

13

refer the reader to previous revisions that allude to amendments, and on and on. Beyond the laws, there are copyright guidelines that interpret the statutes and give guidance and confusion in equal measure. Taking the guidelines and laws and sorting out the complex exemptions of educational or library fair use requires someone with a particular, and sometimes obsessive, bent.

We spend our lives developing, creating, or using instructional materials and are more worried about disseminating content than restricting it. But we must protect our own creations, and we must teach the legal and ethical precepts of copyright to students and colleagues. These mandates require that we both understand and manage the tangle that is copyright.

Understanding is different from managing

Those of us who follow copyright laws and guidelines have sufficient background to recognize references to sections of current statutes; but conveying the complexities and interrelationships of laws, guidelines, and ultimate practice to those who aren't as obsessive about copyright may require considerable tact and patience. Not only do these folks not care much about copyright, many perceive instruction on the obligations of copyright laws to be counterproductive to their missions. Few people accustomed to working freely with copyrighted materials will welcome someone coming to tell them that their long-held practices are suspect.

Being a conscientious member of the educational team, however, the copyright aware person knows the potential danger ahead for the school that blithely ignores copyright mandates. The educator who knows about copyright, however, is likely a rarity in a K–12 school building. Knowing and understanding the law makes this person a bellwether, and as such she will likely find herself in a position to advise and manage copyright in a building. Managing those who seek management is difficult enough, but attempting to manage those who see no need to be managed makes the job of the copyright manager even more troublesome. As manager of copyright, one must manage both people and things. Since things are more accepting of management than people, let us begin our discussions there.

Managing things

As a practical matter, it is a good policy to have the things under control before concentrating on the people. People will resist and forget, and having the appropriate notices, stickers, and practices worked out in advance can ease the transition into compliance.

Reminder: compliance will address the five rights of the copyright holder—reproduction, adaptation, distribution, public performance, and public display. Some rights will have more effect on certain materials than others.

Print. Knowing the rights on a given piece of printed material is essential to proper management. Books generally have copyright information printed on the back of the title page. If the author grants any rights other than the standard fair use exemptions, they will be listed here.

Magazines usually list copyright information on the masthead page. This page is recognizable by the names of the editors, publishers, etc. Sometimes this page is shared with the table of contents. Copyright control information will be included on this page. Items included will be the organization with which to clear reproduction rights beyond fair use, and any additional rights granted by the copyright owners, such as the ability for a classroom teacher to make sufficient copies of anything in a worksheet magazine for use in that teacher's own class.

Plays are controlled under the print guidelines, but the most common abuse of the copyright of plays is performance of all or part of the play to a public audience. Keeping a record of any performance rights purchased with the scripts (either in the library or the department in which the play resides) will make it clear what activities are allowed under the contract, if any. These rights should clearly delineate if rights to tape and sell or give away copies of performances are also included.

Poetry is also controlled by the print guidelines. Watch the back of the title page for copyright control information. Anthologies, in particular, are tangles of copyright clearances. Adaptations will be the big problem with poetry, as students use the poems as lyrics, greeting card verses, or poster slogans, many of which will not be curricular applications.

Images are also protected under the print and/or multimedia guidelines. Individual images usually have some notice of copyright attached to the print, or listed in the credits section if published in book form. The term *images* includes more than photographs and art prints. Cartoons, greeting card drawings, sketches, and logos are all considered images. Adaptation, distribution, and reproduction will be problematic with this genre. Public display of images on web pages is an up-and-coming problem.

Video. Video will require tracking both incoming and outgoing. The essential fact to retain regarding purchased, prerecorded video is what performance rights were purchased with the tape. Public performance rights are required for noncurricular showings. Being able to quickly locate a tape for an after-school celebration or to amuse a group of children while their parents meet can be a boon to PR. Most tapes purchased with public performance rights will cost considerably more than the bargain tape purchased at the local Kmart. The rights should be specified on an invoice or other paperwork.

Off-air video requires significant tracking. Each tape made in-house should have a prominent notice on the expiration of the rights (which vary from the standard 10/45-day period to life-of-tape rights granted by certain producers to educational users). Since the same teacher cannot request to retape programs after the expiration period, a database or other means of tracking requests is essential. Any off-air tapes brought in from students or teachers should have a certification of eligibility signed before use.

Audio, including music. Audio requirements are similar to video. Stickers can quickly locate audio with public performance rights for noncurricular performances. Using music as background for multimedia productions will likely be the largest demand. A collection of royalty-free music clips is a sound investment for any building or district media center.

Computer software. Unlicensed computer software will provide the biggest challenges. Tracking what software is installed on which machine will require significant record keeping. For software that is checked out, specific copyright notice is required. Stickers to notify borrowers of their copyright obligations are available.

13

Hardware. Many common pieces of AV hardware in a school are capable of being used to violate copyright. Just as unattended copy machines must have copyright notices attached to protect the host library, placing prominent notices on other machines with infringement potential is a good plan. Place stickers on computers, overhead projectors, opaque projectors, video and audio recorders, etc.

Local area network resources. Networked software will also require monitoring. License tracking is available through networking software and third-party products. License restrictions can also be enforced by requiring users to log into the application rather than as an individual. The application login only has rights to run that one application, and the number of logins to that application is limited to the number of licenses.

Internet. While there are few formal guidelines about materials used from the Internet, one can easily interpret fair use item-by-item using the existing guidelines. Include copyright compliance in acceptable use policies and information about copyright in all Internet training. Watch servers and workstation hard drives for Internet pages captured in their entirety. Check websites to see that all images and graphics have permission to post.

Managing people

Books, videos, and CDs seldom complain when someone in the building begins copyright compliance awareness training. Most people, however, will not like the change, and many will be highly vocal in their displeasure. Dealing with the human factor will be the largest problem of copyright compliance.

Students. In days gone by, few worried about student use of copyrighted materials. New multimedia guidelines and the ability of students to publish widely on the Internet have made student use of copyright protected materials a new area of concern.

The new multimedia guidelines require that *all* multimedia presentations using copyrighted materials adhere to a set of recommendations that include opening screens that notify of copyrighted content, and credit pages listing complete copyright ownership information for each item used under fair use. Now for student work to be compliant, teachers and librarians must discuss copyright. The steps that must be taken to comply with the new guidelines must be explained to very young students, possibly as young as second grade. These students must understand that they are "borrowing" materials that belong to other people, and they must acknowledge the use through certain prescribed channels.

Students, especially older students, will have more problems with restriction of copyrighted material for entertainment and reward. Teens may have difficulty separating acceptable curricular use of copyrighted materials from nonfair uses such as extracurricular activities, no matter how worthy the project.

Teachers. Teachers may prove to be the copyright compliance project's toughest case. Few, if any, teachers are educated about copyright during training. For many years the teacher has been able to use, without challenge, whatever materials she/he felt necessary or convenient. Few teachers will welcome someone who suddenly (from the teacher's perspective) starts changing the operating rules of media in the classroom. As the instructional leader of a building, the building administrator needs to take a leadership role in guiding the faculty to a new understanding of their obligations regarding copyright. This guidance can be a simple direction: "We will abide by all laws that affect our work." A better approach is to encourage faculty to move toward copyright compliance. A good example of this behavior is obtaining permission for faculty meeting handouts.

One technique that has worked well is to clear all video with the principal. As the instructional leader, the principal may have no idea of the amount of video used in classrooms. One elementary school, in an attempt to achieve copyright compliance, began requiring principal approval of all classroom video. Video use in the building went down by 75%!

Staff. Staff knowledge of copyright is probably minimal at best. Most of staff involvement with copyrighted material will be in photocopying. With the support of the administration, training the clerical staff on copyright of print material will likely be sufficient to raise awareness of what can and should be copied. Encouraging record keeping is a good way to eliminate "end runs" to staff who may not know that a request for copies has been denied.

Administrators. Getting the attention of the administrator is key to copyright compliance in a school building. Few administration training programs mention copyright law in the school law class, and those that do usually gloss over the specifics. Knowing that the building-level administrator is likely to be named in any copyright infringement action can also get an administrator's attention.

How to juggle professional responsibilities and still keep your friends

As the person charged with copyright compliance, or as the person who knows the risks involved in copyright violations, you will find yourself between a rock and a hard place. Following are some suggestions to get started in a school that is less than enthusiastic about copyright compliance, and which seems bent on shooting the messenger:

1. Suggest to the principal that you track requests in one area for a grading period. A good start is with video use.

2. Prepare a copyright notification slip that will inform teachers and others that a particular use of material (fill in the blank) is likely a copyright infringement. Make the wording helpful and informative, not accusatory. Express concern that you don't want the teacher or the building to get into copyright compliance problems.

3. After getting copyright questionable use notices for a period of time, the reluctant administrator may demand that you stop "bothering" him with the notices. If you are in a position such that you might be considered a contributory or vicarious infringer in the ongoing situations (such as a librarian who must check out a VCR to a teacher when the teacher makes it known that the tape showing is probably a copyright infringement), request—politely— that your administrator put the request to you in writing. Continue to note copyright infringement for your own files. You may need these records to protect yourself should one of the improper uses be litigated.

4. Encourage, request, insist on a copyright policy for your building and district. Board-approved policy gives you a firm footing when trying to raise the standard of copyright compliance.

13

5. Educate, educate, educate. Consult with teachers as they plan units, help students document use of others' materials in their work, help administrators consider copyright implications in noncurricular applications.

Walking the straight and narrow is never easy when one considers the complicated tangle of copyright. As someone with a vested interest in copyright compliance, you are on the right path to inform your colleagues about the potential dangers as well as the ethical responsibilities.

SOURCE: Adapted from Carol Simpson, "Managing Copyright in the Schools," *Knowledge Quest* 28, no. 1 (September/October 1999): 18–22.

Filtered or unfiltered?

by Ann Curry and Ken Haycock

Now that the Web is fully in place in the majority of North American schools and libraries, we wanted to know just how widespread the use of software was. To find out, we surveyed *School Library Journal* subscribers. [*Ed. Note:* This article is based on a survey questionnaire mailed in April 2000 to a randomly selected sample of *SLJ* subscribers: 2,000 school and 1,000 public librarians. A total of 731 surveys (465 school, 266 public) were returned, for a response rate of 24%. It should be noted that this response rate is lower than normal for similar *SLJ* surveys.]

The lay of the land

We discovered that filtering software is widely used across the nation, but despite the flurry of news headlines generated by the issue of Internet pornography, not all communities have chosen to fence the border. In fact, 53% of school libraries filter Internet access. In public libraries, the figure is much smaller: 21%.

Filter alternative

Approximately 96% of both school and public libraries have an Acceptable Use Policy, whether they filter or not. Libraries disseminate these policies to users in a variety of ways—the most common being statements cited on mandatory sign-up sheets in public libraries and information in student handbooks in school libraries. Most school and public libraries (81%) also help with Internet searches by providing links to preselected websites and/or age-specific commercial databases.

When considering filters . . .

1. *Determine whether you can turn it off.* The worst thing, say survey respondents, is not having the authority to temporarily turn off a filter or unblock a particular site—or not having software that's easy to disable when necessary. Some organizations have decided that only the superintendent or the director can decide if particular sites can be unblocked, which, according to angry librarians, can "literally take days." By this time, the teachable moment has certainly passed. Librarians must convince upper management to give them control over filters.

2. *Know what you're buying.* Find out how particular filters work, what they block, and who is compiling the hit list of blocked words or sites. Filters have a major impact on how much information will be in your "collection"—you wouldn't let someone reject a substantial number of your book selections and not inquire about what was rejected and why. Why accept it from a filter?

3. *Be involved.* Impress upon upper management that the librarians—the people working directly with users—must be involved in deciding whether to filter and, if necessary, in choosing the filtering software. This survey revealed that in many cases, inappropriate software had been purchased and installed at great expense before the librarians could be involved—just to solve a political crisis and "protect the district's derriere"! Slow down. Gather facts about vendors and software from those who have already installed systems and from surveys like this one.

The mystery surrounding filters

The survey showed that a significant percentage of staff in all types of libraries understood little about how their filtering software works. Thirty-five percent of school librarians who use keyword filters said that they "didn't know" who—the vendor or the school—selected the restricted keywords. Of those whose filters blocked particular websites, 44% did not know who supplied or controlled the site-blocking list. A larger number (69%) did not know if their filter was based on a web rating system. Public librarians were slightly more knowledgeable: 19% lacked information about their keyword blocking, 27% about site blocking, and 60% about web rating systems. In some cases, the "don't know" response could also indicate uncertainty about which type of blocking their filter employed.

Do filters work?

When evaluating filtering software, two aspects are key: that the product blocks the kind of sites you want blocked and that it won't screen out the rest. Most librarians surveyed are generally satisfied with their product's ability to block objectionable sites, but they are dissatisfied with the product's ability to let through the "good" sites. Overall, 16% of the 264 librarians with filters are "very satisfied" and 40% are "somewhat satisfied" with the ability of their filters to not block out good sites (such as Superbowl XXX or breast cancer information). Twenty-eight percent are "somewhat dissatisfied" and the remainder (15%) are "very dissatisfied." School librarians appear to be more frustrated than public librarians with this aspect of filtering: 47% said that they were "somewhat" or "very dissatisfied" with the ability of their filter to let good sites through, compared with only 27% of public librarians.

When asked if they were satisfied with their decision to install filtering software, most respondents said they were. Just over three-quarters (76%) are either "very satisfied" or "somewhat satisfied." Nearly one-quarter are not.

13

SOURCE: Adapted from Ann Curry and Ken Haycock, "Filtered or Unfiltered?" *School Library Journal* 47, no. 1 (January 1, 2001): 42–47. Courtesy of *School Library Journal.*

Web of deceit

by Walter Minkel

When Christine Pelton, a high school teacher in Piper, Kansas, flunked 28 sophomores who had copied parts of their botany projects off the Internet, she unwittingly exposed her community's—and by extension, the country's—ambivalence about online plagiarism. Pelton's decision to enforce her written policy of failing students who cheat made national headlines in February, after the principal and superintendent flip-flopped on their support of Pelton, eventually siding with the students and their angry parents. The incident highlights a disturbing culture of permissiveness among a cut-and-paste generation of students and parents who lack an understanding about why it's wrong to copy.

More than 98% of America's public schools now have Internet access, thanks to the government's E-rate program, which began providing discounted Net  service for schools and libraries in 1996. Furthermore, a survey by the Pew Internet & American Life Project found that 94% of students between the ages of 12 and 17 with access to the Web use it for research, with 71% citing it as their main source of information for school projects. But the Web has turned out to be a double-edged sword: while providing swift access to sought-after information, it has also made cheating irresistibly easy and more pervasive. A May 2001 Rutgers University survey of 4,471 high school students discovered that more than half had stolen sentences and paragraphs from the Internet, and 74% admitted to cheating on a test. While there's no denying that the Web has emerged as the resource of choice for most students, librarians and teachers must take it upon themselves to confront plagiarism before the epidemic spreads.

Many librarians have already taken decisive steps. They're showing students how to define plagiarism, how to recognize when they're committing it, and how to credit and cite others' works correctly. They're also working with teachers in setting plagiarism policies and checking search engines to determine whether or not an assignment has been copied. However, despite the Internet explosion, says Carol Kuhlthau, a professor of library and information science at Rutgers University, schools have yet to establish nationwide rules to guide educators in dealing with this growing problem.

Sadie Longood, a librarian at Dallas (Ore.) High School, thinks now is a good time to start laying down those guidelines. Longood has conducted research on plagiarism policies in schools across the country and learned that "many schools do not address the issue of academic integrity at all." Longood was surprised to learn that the Oregon School Boards Association didn't have plagiarism policies for local school districts. And when she investigated further, she found that most local district policy handbooks didn't cover other forms of cheating either. Longood took it upon herself to outline the following recommendations for school librarians who are concerned about plagiarism:

Increase student awareness of cheating and plagiarism.

Define and determine the threshold of cheating, plagiarism, and academic
integrity.

Train faculty on how to recognize cheating, how to document suspicions, and how to create assignments that don't lend themselves to cheating.

Disseminate information on cheating and plagiarism to parents and the community.

Support the idea of swift and sure consequences.

Recommend that the school board address academic integrity in its district's policy.

Kuhlthau suggests that librarians begin the school year by defining plagiarism in detail, and explaining to students why it's unethical. "We need to teach students what intellectual property is," she says. "When students think of themselves as authors working with an idea they've constructed, it becomes personal. Once they've created an original idea, we need to ask them, 'Do you want your neighbors using your idea as their idea in their paper?'" Kuhlthau believes teachers and librarians should work as partners: the teacher devises an assignment that requires students to answer questions that an encyclopedia or website can't answer, and the librarian demonstrates how to use available research materials to create and support an original idea.

But even with instruction, some students will still plagiarize. When they do, the extent of the punishment should be determined by individual school districts. That's why it's increasingly important for schools to spell out the consequences of plagiarism in their student handbooks. David Lininger, a library media specialist for the Hickory County (Mo.) Schools, offers his school's student handbook's statement on plagiarism as an example: "Any student who plagiarizes material from any source, print or multimedia, shall receive an F for the project. The student shall also receive disciplinary action deemed appropriate by the principal or assistant principal. Legal action will be pending."

It's so easy to copy from electronic resources, Lininger and other librarians say, that many students don't bother to change even a few words of the copied text they turn in. Others don't bother to change the fonts. Consequently, identifying a plagiarized paper is often amazingly easy. Not surprisingly, the biggest red flag that alerts teachers about plagiarism is when students hand in work they normally wouldn't be capable of doing. [*Ed. Note:* Minkel offers some plagiarism busters, great websites that can help you sniff out cheating and cite electronic sources accurately. Please see the complete article for these sites.]

One of plagiarism's greatest detriments is that students miss out on learning useful research skills. Librarians should do whatever they can to teach kids research skills and do it early.

There are also cases in which the motivation for cheating becomes increasingly complex. Cheating involving students with special needs addresses a different set of motives. According to Janell Brown, a librarian at the Ohio State School for the Blind, "Students know they are not working at a competitive level, and it's an ego problem." To impress other students, they will sometimes plagiarize on a research project or creative writing assignment.

Rather than accepting plagiarism as inevitable, educators need to give students assignments that require traditional sources of research that don't revolve around the Web. Students should be required to list their references. Marcia Jensen, a library media specialist at Davenport (Iowa) West High School, says elementary school teachers should design assignments that discourage copying and pasting, and school librarians should be the key people they collaborate with. As an example, Jensen suggests redesigning a simple, standard assignment—the "animal report" for primary kids. Most teachers assign primary school students animal reports in which students look up information about a particular animal and answer questions like: What does my animal look like? What does my animal eat? Where does my animal live?

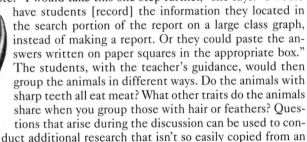

Assignments like this, says Jensen, practically invite students to copy and paste. "I would take this one step further," she says. "I would have students [record] the information they located in the search portion of the report on a large class graph, instead of making a report. Or they could paste the answers written on paper squares in the appropriate box." The students, with the teacher's guidance, would then group the animals in different ways. Do the animals with sharp teeth all eat meat? What other traits do the animals share when you group those with hair or feathers? Questions that arise during the discussion can be used to conduct additional research that isn't so easily copied from an online encyclopedia or a website. The goal of this kind of assignment, Jensen says, "is an opportunity to teach students how to interpret information." Learning how to interpret information requires teachers and librarians who care whether their students know how to think. And knowing how to think is not an easy thing to copy and paste into students' minds.

RHINOCEROS HEAD.

SOURCE: Adapted from Walter Minkel, "Web of Deceit," *School Library Journal* 48, no. 4 (April 1, 2002): 50–53. Courtesy of *School Library Journal.*

Obtaining permission to copy or perform a work

by Rebecca P. Butler

As educators we are concerned with how we can make sure that the media we want to use or copy does not violate copyright law. Since the purpose of this column is to promote social responsibilities, which includes following the law to the best of one's ability, we will look at how to obtain permission from the author or owner of a work—the most ideal way of making sure that the law is being followed.

Obtaining permission

Sometimes the owner of a work will state up front in his or her document that permission is being given to a user for certain rights. One example of this is from a web page created by Brad Templeton: "Permission is granted to freely print, unmodified, up to 100 copies of the most up to date version of this document from www.templetons.com/brad/copymyths.html, or to copy it in off-the-net electronic form." If that is the case, then the would-be user simply follows the copyright owner's specifications. But what happens when the owner has not placed any use agreements, other than a copyright notice, on his or her product? Well, you ask for the rights that you need from the owner or purchase a license to use or copy the work. Remember that the copyright owner has the right to either give, sell, or refuse your request to use his or her work.

Permission requests

It is always best to put requests in writing so that you have a record of the permission criteria should any disagreements occur between you and the copyright owner or clearinghouse. Once you have found the owner of the work, the process of permission is as follows:

> Identify what it is that you want permission to use by author, title, format, and other identifiers.
> Determine what kind of permission you need, such as how, where, and how many times you are going to use this item.

Remember to request permission as early as possible. Just because you do not hear from an owner, you cannot assume that he or she has tacitly agreed. Thus, you may find that you need to follow up on permission requests or contact another source if the organization you contact is not the owner. Also, if your request is refused, starting early gives you time to find a substitute for your original request (see http://fulcrum-books.com/html/permissions.html).

What is a license?

A license gives the user the rights of the work that he or she obtained from the owner or organization representing the owner. For example, the American Society of Composers, Authors, and Publishers (ASCAP), which functions as a clearinghouse representing a large number of those who compose, write, and publish music, gives those who obtain one of their licenses the "right to perform ANY or ALL of the musical works in our repertory." See http://depts .washington.edu/uwcopy/index.php.

Give credit where credit is due

Payment is not necessarily required for permission. The owner or author may want nothing more than to be recognized for his or her work. Thus, always give credit to copyright owners in a reference or citation section at either the beginning or end of the use of the work. You are now on your way to obtaining the permission necessary to use the work.

When you need to obtain permission from the copyright owner to use a copyrighted work whether it is print or nonprint, you need to write a letter requesting permission from the owner. Here's how.

Permission letter

If you are asking for permission, formats may require different criteria. Such criteria will be discussed below as much as is possible. (Criteria need to match the format and type of request.)

Sample general information includes:

- author, title, format
- type of permission you are asking for (how often you will use, number of copies, etc.)
- your name, address, phone and fax number, e-mail
- your signature
- a place for the copyright holder's signature

13

Print material requests should also include:

- volume number
- edition
- ISBN (book) or ISSN (magazine)
- editor, compiler, or translator
- publisher
- place of publication
- copyright date
- page, figure, table, or illustration identifiers
- a copy of what you want to borrow

Other nonprint material requests should also include:

- how borrowed item (multimedia project, online class, etc.) will be used
- distributor
- where you plan to use or market your creation
- expected date of publication or use (if appropriate)
- copyright date
- URL, site manager, name of site (if part or all of a website)
- footage amount (if a video or television program)

You may also add a date by which you would like to hear back from the copyright owners. While they do not need to comply with your request, it may be an incentive to receiving permission information more quickly. In addition, you may wish to ask them to provide you with the correct copyright owner if you have sent your request to the wrong place. It is also important to thank those you are requesting permission from for their time and effort in providing you the use of their copyrighted items. Remember, the more complete the information that you include and request, the quicker the response time may be.

Send the request for permission letter to the copyright owner, clearance center, distributor, or publisher of the works.

Sending and receiving the permission letter

Including an SASE (self-addressed, stamped envelope) may speed up response time. Make sure that the permission is both sent and received either in a letter, fax, or e-mail form. It is imperative that you have a written record of all copyright permissions granted. This way no one can come back at a later date and claim, "I did not say that," or "That's not what I meant."

Many websites have sample permission letters available for your perusal. Start with Association of American Publishers, Campus Copyright Education Program, Standard Permission Request Form at http://www.publishers.org/about/copyrequest.cfm and go from there.

Disclaimer: The information in this article is based on those interpretations of copyright law of most interest and importance to school library media specialists, teachers, and administrators. While a marked emphasis has been placed on accuracy and thoroughness, it is for information only and not to be construed as legal advice. For legal counsel, confer with a copyright lawyer.

SOURCE: Adapted from Rebecca P. Butler, "Social Responsibility: Obtaining Permission to Copy or Perform a Work, Part I," *Knowledge Quest* 30, no. 2 (November/December 2001): 43–44; and "Obtaining Permission to Copy or Perform a Work, Part II," *Knowledge Quest* 30, no. 3 (January/February 2002): 32–33. Used with permission.

School libraries and student achievement: Proof of the power

by Keith Curry Lance

Background

Philosophically, these studies are rooted in the *Information Power* model espoused by the American Association of School Librarians and the findings from six decades of research related to the impact of school library media programs on academic achievement.

The latest edition of the Association's *Information Power: Building Partnerships for Learning* identifies three roles for school library media specialists (LMS). In a learning and teaching role, the LMS advances the instructional goals of the school. As a provider of information access and delivery, the LMS develops collections and services and facilitates their use. And, as a program administrator, the LMS serves as the library media center (LMC) manager as well as a school-wide advocate and trainer for information literacy.

Previous research findings

Over the past half-century there have been about 75 studies on the impact of school library media centers on academic achievement. Each of the study reports summarized herein contains an exhaustive review of this literature to that date. For that reason, only a thumbnail summary of that review is provided here.

Many early studies of this topic demonstrate the value of the mere presence of a professionally trained and credentialed library media specialist. Such correlations, however, beg the question of what the LMS is doing that makes a difference. In more recent studies, the LMS's contributions as a creator of and a collaborator in a learning community have been the focus. These studies indicate that students perform better academically where the LMS

- is part of a planning and teaching team with the classroom teacher,
- teaches information literacy, and
- provides one-to-one tutoring for students in need.

Information access and delivery

One of the most consistent strands of research on this topic is comprised of studies that demonstrate the value of

13

quality collections of books and other materials selected to support the curriculum,

state-of-the-art technology that is integrated into the learning/teaching processes, and

cooperation between school and other types of libraries, especially public libraries.

Program administration

A key role of the library media specialist, but one that has only been the subject of research for a decade, is program administration. In today's schools, the LMS is not only the manager of the LMC, but also an advocate for information literacy with the principal, at faculty meetings, and in standards and curriculum committee meetings. In addition to being an advocate, the LMS is a trainer who provides in-service programs for teachers on resource-based learning, integrating information literacy into the curriculum, and getting the most out of technology, as well as teaching students.

To be a successful advocate for information literacy, research shows, the LMS must

have support staff who free him or her from the LMC to participate in important meetings,
win and keep the support of the principal,
manage networked technology, and
raise funds successfully.

Motivations for further research

Given the substantial body of research already available on the impact of school libraries, it might be asked why yet another study, let alone multiple studies, needed to be done. There were two motivations behind these studies: confirming the findings of the original Colorado Study and expanding on that study in several ways.

Time, place, and educational policies were the key issues related to confirming the original Colorado findings.

Do these results hold up over time?
Are they consistent from one state to another?
And, perhaps most importantly, do the claimed relationships between library media programs and student performance exist when a state's standards-based tests are substituted for a norm-referenced test (i.e., the *Iowa Tests of Basic Skills*, or ITBS)?

The original Colorado Study identified the importance of the library media specialist playing an instructional role in the school, but it did not define what that meant or what it involved doing. Further, while the study's findings implied the value of principal and teacher support, they did not exactly address those issues, and it failed in an attempt to demonstrate the important relationship of information technology—particularly school networks—to the LM program.

In the four most recent studies, all of these motivations for further research were addressed successfully.

Results

While the results of the four studies varied somewhat, on the whole, the findings concerning what aspects of school library media programs are important were remarkably consistent.

In all four states, the level of development of the LM program was a predictor of student performance. In all four states, data on staffing levels correlated with test scores. In Pennsylvania, Colorado, and Oregon, additional data on collections and expenditures were predictive of reading scores. Where LM programs are better staffed, better stocked, and better funded, academic achievement tends to be higher.

Levels of student performance were also related, in all four states, to the extent to which LM staff engaged in particular activities related to the teaching of information literacy and to the exercise of leadership, collaboration, and technology.

In Alaska, Colorado, and Oregon, individual students' visits to the library media center correlated with test scores. Notably, group LMC visits did not demonstrate such a correlation in Alaska or Colorado, but did in Oregon. This last state had mounted a statewide initiative to encourage teacher–librarian cooperation in connection with class visits to LMCs.

Technology. In Alaska, the availability of Internet-capable computers in the LMC was tied to test scores. In Pennsylvania, Colorado, and Oregon, where similar questions were asked about technology, achievement levels increased with the availability of networked computers both in the LMC and elsewhere in the school that provided access to catalogs, licensed databases, and the Internet.

Distinguishing results. Though the four recent studies consistently yielded the foregoing common findings, each study also produced some distinguishing results.

The *Alaska* study was the first to identify the importance of library media specialists as teachers of information literacy. It was also the first to demonstrate the impact on achievement of the library media specialist as an in-service trainer of teachers.

The *Pennsylvania* study was the first to delineate the special activities of library media specialists involved in an integrated, collaborative approach to teaching information literacy.

The second *Colorado* study was the first to distinguish the leadership and collaboration activities of library media specialists and to demonstrate the critical pro-active contribution of leadership activities to setting the stage for collaboration and, in turn, higher achievement levels for students.

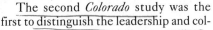

The *Oregon* study demonstrated that the group visits to LMCs, particularly those for information literacy instruction, as well as individual visits can be a predictor of test performance. This study was also the only one of the recent group to indicate the value of time library media specialists spend developing collections and of interlibrary loan activities.

13

Controlling for school and community differences. The distinguishing feature of the research model employed in the original Colorado study as well as its recent successors in Alaska, Pennsylvania, Colorado, and Oregon is controlling for school and community differences. Claims by earlier studies to have established cause-and-effect relationships between characteristics of library media programs and academic achievement did not do this. Consequently, their results were called into question readily. For example, when it was found that higher library media expenditures correlated with higher test scores, it was easy to explain away this relationship by attributing the test scores to higher school expenditures generally. The cause of higher achievement was not spending on the library media program in particular, but rather being a prosperous school that could afford to spend more on everything. To preclude this and similar criticisms and to establish a stronger claim that reported correlations reflect cause-and-effect, these studies encompassed data on schools (i.e., per pupil spending, teacher–pupil ratio, various teacher characteristics) and their communities (i.e., poverty levels, racial/ethnic demography, adult educational attainment). These additional variables address most, if not all, of the stronger arguments that could otherwise be made to discount the consistent findings of this line of research.

In all four states, analyses were conducted to measure the impact on test scores of each library media, school, and community characteristic while controlling for the others. After accounting for the considerable impact on academic achievement of community socioeconomic conditions—from one-third to three-quarters depending on the state and the school level—library media predictors almost always outperformed other school characteristics, such as teacher–pupil ratio and per pupil expenditures.

Implications

Recommended actions by school officials. The practical implications of these research findings are a clear and straightforward call to action.

> School library media programs should be funded sufficiently to employ both professional and support staff and to have both information resources in a variety of formats and the technology necessary to extend the LM program beyond the walls of the library media center.
>
> Library media specialists should be recognized and utilized by principals and teachers as professional colleagues in the teaching and learning enterprise. Where such recognition and the collaboration to which it leads do not exist, the LMS must exercise some leadership in changing the environment.
>
> Technology is an essential part of a successful LM program. Information resources, including licensed databases, should be available throughout the school via networked computers in classrooms, labs, and offices.

Library media specialists who wish to make effective presentations of the findings of these studies may find helpful another publication, David V. Loertscher's *Powering Achievement: School Library Media Programs Make a Difference: The Evidence*. It provides handouts and presentation slides for presentations of varying length and focusing on different issues.

Other research questions. Like all research, these studies raised almost as many questions as they answered. They call for further research, both qualitative and quantitative.

> How can library media specialists be taught the leadership skills they need to succeed? While such training is fairly widely available, there is little extant research identifying best practices in this area.
>
> How should LM specialists, teachers, and students interact to improve academic achievement? While studies such as these establish relationships between test performance and certain types of staff activities—

cooperative teaching, for example—these findings do not offer much in the way of practical advice to LM specialists about how they can successfully engage teachers and students.

How does the availability of and involvement with information technology affect the interactions of LM specialists, teachers, and students? These studies indicate that the presence of technology and LM staff involvement with it are important, but they do not explain how electronic access to information facilitates effective relationships between LM specialists and others.

SOURCE: Adapted from Keith Curry Lance, "Proof of the Power: Recent Research on the Impact of School Library Media Programs on the Academic Achievement of U.S. Public School Students," ERIC Digest, 2001. Used with permission.

Does an unsupervised clerk in the LMC make a difference in academic achievement?

by Keith Curry Lance and David V. Loertscher

In many school districts, the need to economize through budget shortfalls often creates the temptation to staff library media centers with clerical personnel rather than professionals. These unsupervised support staff keep the library open, allow students and teachers to use the collection and technology, and in the elementary schools, might provide a planning break for classroom teachers. But do unsupervised clerks make a difference in academic achievement?

The research from the Lance studies and other research documents indicate clearly what actions by the LMC staff do make a difference:

LMC staff planning and teaching cooperatively with teachers
LMC staff providing professional development to teachers
LMC staff meeting with principal, attending faculty meetings, and serving on standards and curriculum committees
LMC staff managing computer network that provides remote access to LMC resources

When a clerk is unsupervised and is in charge of a library media center, why don't they perform these activities? Simply because *none* of these activities is properly in the job description of the clerk. Rather, their efforts center on the operation of the organization rather than reaching out into a leadership role in the school and its curriculum.

In the various Lance studies, this topic was not addressed in the final reports although present in the data collected. However, in the Alaska study, this comparison was addressed. Consider the difference between students scoring below average in schools having professional library media specialists versus those where only a clerk is present.

13

LMC Staffing Level	Students Scoring *Below* Average	
	Elementary	Secondary
With a full-time LMC specialist	17%	8%
With an unsupervised clerk	41%	49%

The conclusion is that:

Unsupervised LMC clerks do not engage in activities that make a difference. And, as a result, more students score poorly.

Because school libraries require a considerable investment in facilities, budgets for materials, salaries, utilities, computer networks, and the like, staffing the LMC with a clerk promotes a sense of false economy. Saving the cost of a professional negates the LMC's impact.

SOURCE: Adapted from Keith Curry Lance and David V. Loertscher, *Powering Achievement: School Library Media Programs Make a Difference* (San Jose, Calif.: Hi Willow, 2003), 11–12. Used with permission.

Relationship with public libraries

by Blanche Woolls

Schools and public libraries have had a long history of contact, communication, and cooperation. The length of time such cooperation continues and the degree or the depth of the relationship varies from year to year and from location to location. A public library at one time could have close communication with a public school system, and at another time, no contact at all. In a speech in 1876, Charles Francis Adams Jr. (right), a trustee of the Quincy (Mass.) Public Library, noted that, "Yet though the school and library stand on our main street, side by side, there is, so to speak, no bridge leading from one to the other." Adams ended his presentation with

> I want very much indeed to see our really admirable Town Library become a more living element than it now is in our school system. . . . To enable you to do this, the trustees of the library have adopted a new rule, under which each of your schools may be made practically a branch library. The master can himself select and take from the library a number of volumes, and keep them on his desk for circulation among the scholars under his charge. . . . From that time, both schools and library would begin to do their full work together, and the last would become what it ought to be, the natural complement of the first—the People's College.

Differences exist between school library media centers and public libraries in almost every area—facilities, management, clientele, and services. Schools should have their media center located in the center of the building, accessible to all while public libraries should be in the center of the greatest population movement, whether downtown or a branch. Public librarians report to a board of trustees while school librarians report to their principal. The youth librarian at the public library reports to the director, another librarian, while the school library media specialist reports to the principal, an educator.

School library media centers serve the students who are assigned to their attendance center and who are a captive audience, for students are sometimes sent or taken there and left while the teacher takes a contractual preparation period. Public librarians must seek out their clientele.

Another challenge exists when a public library serves a different geographic district than the school and may not be able to serve all the students attending a single school.

Media centers in schools exist to integrate learning resources and references into the curriculum while the public library is, indeed, more of a research library to serve the needs of all the clientele under its jurisdiction. The need to share the topics assigned at the school each year becomes one of the most critical needs for cooperation between schools and public libraries so that materials available can be "protected" from one person's taking everything whether useful or not.

School and public library boards often suggest combining these two entities. Shirley L. Aaron has given us the pros and cons for combining school and public libraries. Her three-phase study concluded that the successful programs had

A separate area set aside in the library exclusively for adult use.

Much community involvement in and commitment to the decision to have this combined library including citizens as well as the two legal boards in the planning process.

In addition,

A single board was established to assume governance.

A formal written agreement was adopted.

A head librarian with the required expertise and commitment to the concept was selected.

A location suitable to both school and public library was chosen.

Professional library personnel and others planned with the architect for both development and construction.

Efforts were made to get people to consider this as an integrated whole rather than separate school and public library programs.

Both boards contributed funds.

Materials for children and adults were shelved in separate areas.

No restrictions were made on materials that children, young adults, or adults could check out or examine in the library.

Emphasis was given to achieving a well-balanced collection to support use by both clienteles.

No restrictions were placed on materials selection.

Many more recommendations are given, with one interesting note: "There was no documented evidence that this organizational pattern was more economical than separate programs."

Lawrence L. Jaffe, in a later study, found that "combined school/public libraries invariably cited their need for additional space." Also he reported as challenges adequate staffing and the need for a formal agreement, and some librarians worried about access by children to the adult collection. While this is a violation of the Library Bill of Rights as it affects access, it often remains a real concern.

In 1995, Patricia T. Bauer conducted a case study to identify factors affecting operations of a combined school/public library program. Her conclusions were that

Proactive planning provides the most practical perspective for planning for a combined library program.

13

> Planning processes which allow for participation by all important stake-holder groups is the best hope for meeting the information needs of both public and school library users.
>
> Intergroup conflict between the separate public and school library programs is affected by factors which the organization can influence.
>
> Programming excellence, the product of a talented and committed library manager, is the key to successful articulation between school and public library programs.
>
> Governance of a cooperative program must involve stakeholders' representatives in true decision-making processes.

This study included the implication that the effectiveness of an organization, when dependent on a single individual, can prove disastrous if no plan exists for dealing with personnel changes. In fact, the library from the Jaffe study cited above did lose its librarian and the combined branch closed. The personnel factor should be considered if the proposal is to merge two successful individual organizations.

School and public libraries need to cooperate at all times, but in the present funding climate, this remains essential. The current trend seems to be to fund projects that combine the efforts of several agencies, thereby increasing the numbers and variety of persons who will benefit. Guidelines for federal and private dollars are predicated upon shared efforts that will get the most bang for the bucks. Agencies should join hands, choose project ideas that will benefit all, and apply for funding as a consortium. School and public libraries are natural friends because they serve the same children.

While joint proposal writing provides a convenient mechanism for joining forces, school library media specialists and public librarians must communicate and cooperate. I suggest that no single library collection can or should attempt to meet all the needs of students in schools. Library service to students is the joint responsibility of school and public libraries with school library media center activities concentrating upon curriculum-oriented programs and the public library offering its wide range of reading and other varied program possibilities. Much has been accomplished if both agencies communicate and cooperate.

SOURCE: Adapted from Blanche Woolls, *The School Library Media Manager,* 2nd ed. (Littleton, Colo.: Libraries Unlimited, 1999), 12–19.

Knowledge Quest author guidelines

Submission of manuscripts

Author responsibility
1. Submit only manuscripts that have not been submitted or accepted elsewhere.
2. Write the article in correct, simple, readable style.
3. Check all statements, names, and references for accuracy.

Submission format
1. Single space the entire manuscript including quoted material, references, and tables.

2. Feature article manuscripts average 2,000–3,000 words in length; column manuscripts average 800–1,000 words in length.
3. Write a 100-word, descriptive abstract built around the key words found in the article.
4. Submit references on separate pages at the end of the article. (Do not use the automatic footnote function.)
5. Number each table consecutively, provide a brief, meaningful title for each, and submit each on a separate page at the end of the paper. Mention each table, by number, in text.
6. Supply camera-ready copy for each illustration. Accompany each with a number and a brief, meaningful caption. Photographs should have captions and, where appropriate, credits. Black-and-white photographs (5" × 7") are preferred.
7. Send one electronic copy (either on diskette or via e-mail) and one paper copy of the article, with the following header on the first page:

Knowledge Quest
Article title

For each author please include the following information in the header:

Name

Author identification: One to two sentences that indicate author's title, affiliation, a recent publication or other relevant information

Address (home and work)

Telephone number (home and work)

E-mail address (home and work)

Can you read Adobe Acrobat documents: Yes/No

Style
a. Choose terms that reflect the philosophy in *Information Power: Building Partnerships for Learning* (Chicago: American Library Association, 1998). The terms *library media specialist, library media program,* and *library media center* should be used. Avoid sexist language.
b. Consult the *Random House Webster's College Dictionary* for spelling and usage.
c. Consult the *Chicago Manual of Style*, 15th ed. (Chicago: University of Chicago Pr., 2003) for endnote and bibliographic style, capitalization, abbreviations, and design of tables. Endnotes should appear in the style described in the *Chicago Manual of Style*, with the list of references arranged in order of their appearance within the manuscript. For example:

1. Grant Wiggins, *Educative Assessment: Designing Assessments to Inform and Improve Student Performance* (San Francisco: Jossey-Bass, 1998).
2. Charlotte Danielson and Thomas L. McGreal, *Teacher Evaluation to Enhance Professional Practice* (Princeton, N.J.: Association for Supervision and Curriculum Development, 2000).
3. Jo Ann Wahrman, "The Impact of Assassinations," *Knowledge Quest* 27, no. 1 (September/October 1998): 33–34.

13

4. American Association of School Librarians, *A Planning Guide for Information Power: Building Partnerships for Learning* (Chicago: American Association of School Librarians, 1999).

Electronic documents cited should also be referenced. Examples for documentation of materials obtained from computer information services and standards adapted from the *Chicago Manual of Style* for citing electronic documents are provided in *Online! A Reference Guide to Using Internet Sources* (New York: Bedford/St. Martin's Pr., 1998), chapter 7: "Using Chicago Style to Cite and Document Sources," which is available online: http://www.bedfordstmartins.com/online/cite7.html.

Use references to document the text, not to amplify it.

Web-based content

Knowledge Quest on the Web, the online companion to the print journal, publishes web-based documents to complement each print issue's editorial content. Each author is strongly encouraged to submit with his/her manuscript a "package" of informative links, resources, and/or sidebar material to further educate the reader on the topic. This web-based content should take advantage of the power of hypertext and links to point readers to material that expands upon and supports the article or column. Manuscripts that include this complementary web-based content will be given priority consideration for publication.

Submission process

One electronic copy (either on diskette or via e-mail) and one paper copy of feature article or column manuscripts, including any complementary web-based content, should be sent to Debbie Abilock, 783 Cereza Drive, Palo Alto, CA 94306-3145; e-mail: kq@abilock.net. All manuscripts will be acknowledged by the editor within one week. The editor has final responsibility for the action taken on the manuscripts. The above process normally is completed within 15 weeks.

Rights of publication

Each author, in granting of publication to *Knowledge Quest*, guarantees that the manuscript has not been published/accepted for publication elsewhere. Upon acceptance of an article, each author is required to submit a signed ALA Author Copyright Agreement. Signed copyright agreements for articles accepted for publication in *Knowledge Quest* should be faxed or mailed to:

Knowledge Quest
Attn: Managing Editor
50 E. Huron St.
Chicago, IL 60611-2795
Fax: 312-664-7459

Copyright

A manuscript published in the journal is subject to copyright by the American Library Association for the American Association of School Librarians. Additional information about copyright policies is available from the ALA Office of Rights and Permissions.

Scheduling publication of manuscripts

Accepted manuscripts will be scheduled for publication on the basis of appropriateness to an issue theme and availability of space. Consideration will be given to scheduling manuscripts while content remains timely.

Copies of issues

Each author whose manuscript has been accepted for publication will receive two copies of the issue in which the article appears.

SOURCE: Adapted from http://www.ala.org/ala/aasl/aaslpubsandjournals/kqweb/aboutkq/authorguide.htm.

Library Media Connection author guidelines

Linworth Publishing, Inc. publishes *Library Media Connection.* Our magazine contains feature articles on library management and operation, columns on specific topics, and reviews of books and other library materials. Most of the content is written by practicing school librarians. We invite you to join in this dialogue.

Submissions

We consider both solicited and unsolicited manuscripts. Letters of inquiry or preliminary outlines are not required.

Manuscript guidelines

In all articles and other submissions, the emphasis should be on the author's actual experiences or personal observations. Manuscripts (usually 1,500–2,500 words) should be submitted on paper, typewritten or computer printout, and double spaced with a PC disk in Microsoft Word 6.0 or 97, or ASCII text. Indicate on the disk your name, date, name of article, and which computer program you have used. You may also submit articles by e-mail to linworth@linpub.org. Photos, illustrations, charts, and diagrams of reproduction quality should be submitted in separate files even if embedded in the text. Please send either the original print artwork or on a disk in .tiff, .jpg, or .EPS format. Insert a reference to the graphic file within the article (Example: Insert graphicone.tiff here). Please do not e-mail artwork.

Manuscripts accepted for publication are edited for length, clarity, and conciseness. Please be sure to include subheads in your article to help readability.

Please provide an author byline for each author of the article. It must be in the following format.

Byline information

In sentence structure, Name, Title, School, City and State (spell out state name). If school has the name of the city in it, put the state name in parentheses following the city name.

13

Byline information in italics only with a period at the end.

Absolutely no social security numbers, phone numbers, or addresses in byline.

Byline may include an e-mail address.

Examples

Jean Ark is a Library Media Specialist at Orange Elementary School in Geneva, New York.

Donald Smith is a Library Media Specialist at King High School in Gnome, Arizona, and can be reached at ds@abc.com.

Terms

Manuscripts are submitted for consideration with the understanding that Linworth, as a condition of acceptance for publication:

requires assignment to the publisher of all rights in the accepted work;

requires that it is your original work and not previously published (if permission for reprinting has been secured from the original publisher, please let us know), does not infringe any copyright or other right (see sample "Request for Permission to Reprint" Form), and does not contain any matter that is libelous or otherwise unlawful; and,

reserves the right to edit accepted works to conform to house style and space limitations.

If your article is chosen for publication, you will be paid an honorarium, acceptance of which indicates your acceptance of these terms of submission. If your article is chosen for publication in Tips or Shoptalk, you will receive a book or other item of your choice from a list of professional materials. All writers receive a personal copy of the issue in which the work appears.

Writing style

Articles should be written in a clear, conversational style. A review of recent issues of the magazine is the best guide to the preferred writing style.

The preferred style manual for questions of capitalization and punctuation is *Words into Type* by R. Gay & Marjorie E. Skillin (Prentice-Hall). Generally, footnotes and endnotes do not appear in our articles. If the footnote is important, include its content in the text. Publication data about books and articles quoted or referred to should appear in parentheses within the text. Please give full title, publisher, and year of publication.

Types of manuscripts

Feature articles. Feature articles vary in length, depending on the topic. An average length is 5–7 pages. Feature articles may deal with theme topics or other subjects of interest to school librarians.

Essays, Opinion Pieces, and Backtalk. Opinions on controversial issues, personal viewpoints, literary puzzles, and humor are sought for use within the magazine.

Tips and Shoptalk. Tips and Shoptalk are regular columns of brief how-to articles or helpful hints that vary in length from a few sentences to several paragraphs. The emphasis should be on what you did to solve a specific problem or how you found a better way to accomplish a task.

Columns. Columns are assigned to writers. If you are interested in becoming a columnist, please submit a resume and a sample of your writing to the editors.

Reviews. Reviews of books and electronic media are assigned to librarians who serve in this capacity. No unsolicited reviews are accepted. If you are interested in becoming a reviewer, contact the editor.

Compensation
If your article is accepted, you will receive an honorarium upon publication. Writers of Tips and Shoptalk receive a book or other item of their choice from a list of professional materials. All writers receive a personal copy of the issue in which their work appears.

For more information
Questions, letters of inquiry, and manuscripts should be directed to Editor, Linworth Publishing, Inc., 480 E. Wilson Bridge Road, Suite L, Worthington, OH 43085. Email: linworth@linpub.org.

SOURCE: Adapted from http://www.linworth.com/writeforus.html#Aguidelines.

School Library Journal author guidelines

The editors of *School Library Journal* welcome original manuscripts to consider for feature articles or columns.

Types of submissions

Features
Manuscripts for feature articles should be 1,500–2,500 words in length on any topic relating to the collaborative and leadership roles the librarian (or library staff) has with educators, as well as articles relating to youth librarianship in school or public libraries. Features should be written in an easily accessible, conversational style that is free of academic or professional jargon.

Although most of our readers are educators, submissions should be written as though intended for a general-interest magazine audience, rather than an academic journal.

We encourage writers to include anecdotes and specific examples of their programs and concepts.

Columns/sections
Up for Discussion: an 1,800-word column on aspects of book selection. The honorarium is $300, paid upon publication.

What Works: an 850-word column that describes, step-by-step, a successful library program that could be easily and inexpensively replicated by a librarian. The honorarium is $175, paid upon publication.

Make Your Point: an 850-word opinion piece on any issue affecting librarians or library service. The honorarium is $175, paid upon publication.

13

Educator's Resource Kit: a 1,500-word column providing library media specialists with the insight, strategies, and resources they need to cultivate their collaborative and leadership roles in the school.

Learning Quarterly: a new quarterly installment of *SLJ* focusing on the most challenging, hot-button issues in education. *Learning Quarterly* offers hands-on strategies and solutions for librarians on how to collaborate with teachers and administrators to meet those challenges, and will include commentary from administrators on how they've met specific challenges by working with school librarians.

Procedures

Editing
SLJ editors reserve the right to edit and revise accepted manuscripts for clarity, accuracy, and length. For style questions, we suggest that you look at *The Chicago Manual of Style* or *The Associated Press Stylebook* and back issues of *SLJ*. Please avoid footnoting and, when citing a book within the text, please put the name of the publisher and year of publication in parentheses immediately following the title. For example, Lois Lowry's *The Giver* (Houghton, 1993).

To submit a manuscript
Send double-spaced submissions via e-mail (Word documents are preferred) or mail. In your cover letter and manuscript, please include your name, address, title, place of employment, daytime and evening telephone numbers, fax number, and e-mail address.

Notification
We will notify you by postcard or e-mail when we have received your manuscript. You can expect a decision regarding publication within two to three months.

Author photographs
If your manuscript is accepted, we will request a color head shot and a brief biography for our contributor's page. Digital photos are preferred.

Where to send manuscripts
Send *What Works* submissions to: Debra Lau Whelan, Senior News and Features Editor, dlau@reedbusiness.com

Send *Up for Discussion* submissions to: Luann Toth, Senior Book Review Editor, ltoth@reedbusiness.com

Send all other submissions to: Rick Margolis, News and Features Editor, rmargolis@reedbusiness.com

School Library Journal
360 Park Avenue South
New York, NY 10010-1710
Telephone: (646) 746-6759
Fax: (646) 746-6689
E-mail: slj@reedbusiness.com

SOURCE: School Library Journal.

DIVERSITY
CHAPTER FOURTEEN

Improving computer-use success for students of diverse backgrounds
by Lori S. Mestre

Our country is becoming more diverse than it has ever been. Many educational institutions have begun to examine their programs to assist students from a variety of ethnic groups in using computer applications. In these efforts they hope that students' educational attainment and achievement will be increased. Effective study and computer skills are indispensable tools for succeeding in school.

Technological preparation in grades K–12 will help prepare students for college and beyond. In the classroom, computers are increasingly being used as tools for composing and submitting work. Finding information through networked computers is one way to create enthusiasm in learning. By altering the way information is presented to students, educators can be an important influence in motivating students to learn.

It is also a way to allow students to access information that is relevant to them. Culturally relevant material has been noted as a major motivational force for Latino students. Using technology in the classroom is a way in which all students can participate. When students are able to be creative, to find information relevant to their needs and interests, and then to shape a project including what they find, they will usually have a more positive outlook on what they are doing. As students gain proficiency in collecting, organizing, analyzing, evaluating, constructing, and publishing knowledge, they become active learners. They also acquire skills and attitudes that will help prepare them for lifelong learning.

Digital divide

In most computer labs, few mentors and role models exist for minority students. In addition, advanced students usually fare better than others in competition for computer time, thus widening the knowledge gap between majority and minority students. Some analysts such as C. Pillar warn that unless disadvantaged students are introduced to the more exciting uses of computers, they may be consigned to a new technological underclass. According to the U.S. General Accounting Office, African Americans and Hispanics will account for more than one-fourth of all entrants to the labor force between 1998 and 2005. The past two decades have witnessed increasing emphasis on information and service industries and decreasing emphasis in manufacturing and agriculture. The ability to use technology is becoming an essential requirement for workplace success.

K. T. Schwalm reports that these groups will need computer literacy skills if they are to compete in the future labor force. Those who do not have prior experience using productivity tools such as spreadsheets, databases, and word processors may spend their available time doing tasks manually, running out of time (and energy) before they get to more intellectually rewarding activities.

The need for special instruction

Differences in learning styles and levels of computer competence can present certain barriers to using the tools. Not all students understand instructions in the same way. Although there is an abundant source of material for using computers to improve the writing process of students, little is available that addresses the concern of nonnative English-speaking students learning to navigate online databases.

Some studies found that students who are secure linguistically and academically have little trouble mastering word processing commands and so can benefit more fully from the capabilities of the electronic medium, especially in the short term. Students who are insecure about their language, their academic abilities, or their writing skill may take less advantage of the potential of the computer medium than will risk takers or those who are confident in their linguistic, academic, and writing skills.

The Internet as a tool for broadening ethnic and cultural interaction

The Internet holds great potential to link classrooms and people to exchange cultural information and address common problems. The Internet provides links to resources that are updated continuously, thus allowing for the creation of a curriculum that is current and exciting. Linking computers also increases social interaction and collaboration. Students who are reluctant to converse with those outside their racial, ethnic, or cultural group may find greater ease in communicating via the Internet as differences based on age, ethnicity, race, gender, and disability are generally not noticeable.

Through Internet communication, students develop critical literacy skills as they discuss problems and potential solutions to those problems with others in class and with others from around the world. Educators can help foster these skills with appropriate lesson plans and guidance using social issues that are real to students. E. Fiske in "The Undergraduate Hispanic Experience" lists the following:

Each student can take on all kinds of roles: world traveler, foreign correspondent, explorer, intelligence analyst, scientist, artist, musician, published author, and respected commentator.

Teachers can include or ask students to find sites that incorporate aspects of different cultures.

Students can explore aspects of culture, politics, history, and geography, including daily newspapers, now that rich Latin American resources have come online. Through e-mail with other schools in Hispanic countries, students can learn what is happening, sometimes even as it happens, and they may undertake action as a result.

While broadening their world view, students should be encouraged to find primary and secondary sources related to their own ethnicity. It is common for minority students to go through school rarely seeing their ethnic group portrayed as achievers.

Creating optimum learning

As the number of minorities continue to rise, it becomes more imperative than ever for educators to understand the cultural, linguistic, and socioeconomic backgrounds as well as the socialization patterns and preferred learning modes of their students so they can provide effective service to them. There are many ways to make learning more conducive for students such as using cooperative learning; active learning techniques; allowing time for response and practice; and matching nonverbal and verbal communication patterns, as much as possible, of both parties. Following are some of the differences that might be present among Latinos, although it is important to keep in mind that these characteristics also may be present in other students.

Cultural differences

Cultural values strongly affect teacher–student relationships and classroom behavior. S. G. Wagman reports that if children are raised in a strict environment and learn not to challenge their parents or teachers, the atmosphere in mainstream classrooms (and libraries) may foster reliance, inhibit independence and the growth of inductive reasoning, and nurture inactivity and submission.

Differences in value systems can have an impact on how individuals learn. Generally speaking, Anglos value independence as the basis of their own identity and their relationship with others, while Latinos build relationships of interdependence, especially within family. V. Zanger found that Anglos also are more independent and expect to do things for themselves through self-reliance and competence, whereas Latinos identify with a group and emphasize cooperation and loyalty.

When a teacher misunderstands culture, a major conflict may arise in the classroom. Students can learn almost any subject matter when they are taught with methods and approaches responsive to their learning style strengths and cultural values.

Nonverbal communication

In his book *Non-Verbal Behavior,* A. Wolfgang states that much of our behavior is at the nonverbal level and its impact on communication can be powerful and easily misunderstood, particularly by students and parents from other cultures who may have learned different cultural rules of when, how, where, and to what degree to express certain behaviors. Librarians need to understand the role of nonverbal behavior in communication and its role in the library in particular.

In body language, for example, some cultures communicate more with the eyes and by touch and nods. To Westerners a nod is a positive signal, but to people from other cultures, a simple nod can be quite complicated. It could mean yes or no, or it can be used to express a lack of comprehension or to assure that the speaker is being listened to, or it may be considered rude.

Nonverbal behaviors can facilitate or hinder the communication process. Thus, how a librarian behaves nonverbally may have more importance than

14

what the librarian says, and one who deliberately displays such nonverbal behaviors as touching, leaning forward, and smiling may elicit a favorable or unfavorable response in the patron.

Kinetic behavior. According to C. J. Nine-Curt, certain behavior (such as moving hands when speaking, lowering head, moving legs, wrinkling the nose, wiggling the nose, squinting eyes, folding arms in front of the chest) can have conflicting meanings across cultures. Nine-Curt found that facial gestures such as smiles also have diverse meanings. Smiles by Latinos may mean "hello," "please," "thank you," "you're welcome," or "may I help you?" They also may be seen when one is embarrassed or confronted with bad news (especially in females).

Eye contact. In the United States it is a sign of respect and attentiveness to look someone in the eyes. However, when Latino children are being reprimanded, they are generally taught to lower their eyes. Anglo children are usually taught to maintain eye contact. Prolonged direct eye contact among Latinos is usually interpreted as being disrespectful and often is reserved for intimacy. Eye contact can also signify, "Excuse me, may I talk to you, show you this, etc.?" without the verbal equivalent. It can replace the verbal clues of being polite.

Personal space. "Invasion" of one's personal space, according to L. Larason and J. S. Robinson, elicits responses ranging from discomfort to anger. Unawareness of cultural differences in personal space can seriously hamper communication between individuals. Nine-Curt also says that the distance at which an Anglo feels comfortable differs from what is preferred by most Latin Americans. Generally, what is personal space for a Latino is intimate space for an Anglo. In face-to-face conversation, to be at arm's length from the person being spoken to tends to be comfortable for the mainstream society, and elbow's length may be representative of the comfort distance for the Latino. Anglos will attempt to back away if their space is invaded, whereas the Latino will try to maintain the space. The result is that Anglos may see Latinos as being too close, too pushy, or too sexy, while Latinos may see Anglos as being aloof, cold, or uninterested.

Group vs. individual. Some cultures are oriented toward managing one thing, one situation, and one person at a time (monochronic behavior) whereas handling many things, many situations, and many people at a time (polychronic behavior) appears to be the mode more comfortable for other groups. Anglos tend to fall into the monochronic group, whereas Latinos tend to display polychronic behaviors. This contrast in Anglo and Latino cultures is evident in the apparent ability of Latinos to talk at the same time and to expect people to be able to do many things at the same time. The Latino may not understand why the Anglo cannot handle more than one person at a time, and the Anglo may be upset at the Latino for not waiting in line.

Suggestions for working with diverse students in a computerized environment

The following includes suggestions based on learning styles, cultural considerations, alternative ways of presenting material, language considerations, searching strategies, and alteration of the classroom environment in order to make learning more conducive to students from diverse backgrounds.

Learning styles/preferences. Hands-on time is important because students tend to learn well by doing and by touching, seeing, and manipulating concrete objects rather than by discussing or reading about them.

Provide a lot of individual instruction initially so that students can become acquainted with the world of computers. Latino students may relate better to a person-centered rather than an object- or idea-centered session.

Latino students also tend to like to work in groups or with others they know. Planning sessions so that there is a type of camaraderie can contribute to the success of students or the goals and objectives of the session.

If possible, the educator should team up with a Latino assistant, not only to assist with the language, but also because this individual can more readily identify with the culture and serve as a role model.

Cultural considerations. Educators must learn to count students' experiences and cultural knowledge as strengths. Thus, making sessions relevant culturally to the students is important, as is using students' examples and possible digressions as learning experiences and opportunities to explore other topics.

Presenting material. Teachers should set students at ease, maintain an involved and supportive posture with the students, and actively determine that they understand the directions.

Both oral and written directions should be provided, if possible, in the student's native language.

Latino students may need to finish a task and process what has been presented before proceeding to the next task. A facilitator should wait until the students have mastered the function before describing how that function or task can be applied.

Latinos seem to be more concerned with doing a job well, regardless of the time required, than they are in finishing rapidly. By having guides printed ahead of time, students can work at a relaxed pace.

In presenting new material, after a short introduction of what will be covered, the educator might provide a brief online demonstration to the whole group and allow participants the majority of the session to complete the desired tasks with a handout.

Once the session begins, the facilitator should allow digressions from the topic at hand. These digressions make a more personal, relaxed atmosphere, providing opportunities to observe concerns, priorities, and views, which will improve later instruction.

Language. Of major importance is the issue of language. It is advisable to assume nothing, not even that students know terms such as Space Bar, Enter, or Click. Assessing students prior to the sessions makes it possible to arrange the sessions to best accommodate beginning, intermediate, and advanced users of technology.

Students from various cultures and languages might assist with library guides by critiquing them and by helping to rewrite them so that the terminology and instructions are clear. Further, by having a written step-by-step guide of what will occur in the session, those who are more experienced can move at a faster pace.

14

It may be necessary to have a few facilitators on hand to move around the group and answer questions.

If possible, it is helpful to use bilingual methods with limited-English-proficient students.

Train yourself for cross-cultural communication by becoming aware of your own expectations and the cultural values of others.

Step back and listen to the way you give instructions. Are you using jargon or slang? When working with students, it is important to choose words and construct sentences carefully so that they communicate precisely what is intended.

Break down the questions and problems into chunks and use basic terminology. By asking several questions (going step-by-step) rather than a general or broad question, the student might be able to explain or illustrate what he or she needs.

To check for comprehension, ask the student to paraphrase (or demonstrate) what was just said.

Searching strategies. Success in searching databases and the Internet and using computer applications usually depends upon how comfortable students feel using computers. When searching databases and the Internet, experienced users experiment with refining a search in order to get only results that are truly relevant. But novices feel intimidated about going beyond what is presented and should be encouraged to take risks.

Classroom environment. The classroom environment and faculty involvement with the students are important. The students prefer teachers who develop a personal and friendly relationship. Some suggestions for personalizing interaction include:

utilize physical contact when expressing approval and acceptance;
stand close to students when talking or relating to them;
provide more guidance and feedback;
show an interest in what they are doing both in and out of class;
learn about the students' cultures, experiences, backgrounds, and educational needs;
integrate cultural readings into the curriculum; and
communicate to each student in the class that he or she is important in the teacher's life.

It is vital that librarians/teachers have a strong commitment to helping students achieve. They need to provide a nurturing environment and have high academic expectations.

Librarians and media specialists have key roles when it comes to assisting students and teachers in learning computer applications and educational technology within a multicultural society. They need to be innovative and demonstrate to their students alternate ways to access information. However, in doing so, they must keep in mind that students do not all learn in the same way, and they will have to vary the way they assist students from diverse cultural backgrounds in acquiring information through technology.

SOURCE: Adapted from Lori S. Mestre, "Improving Computer-Use Success for Students of Diverse Backgrounds," *Knowledge Quest* 28, no. 5 (May/June 2000): 20–28. Used with permission.

LIBRARIANA

CHAPTER FIFTEEN

What practicing school library media specialists say about collection development

by Ramona Kerby

First-year experiences

The first year you are at a school, you have to take a deep breath and live with the collection, because it's a mistake to order before you know your children.

—*Pam Lichty, Owings Mills Elementary School,*
Owings Mills, Maryland

Life for me as a first-year media specialist is often like riding a roller coaster. . . . Last week, I felt I had really accomplished something when I had pulled 40 African American biographies for a teacher and weeded 10 outdated sports biographies, all before 8:00 a.m.

I work on orders at home. To me, looking through book reviews is like hunting for buried treasure. If only a genie would appear and weed those old science filmstrips for me.

—*Kathy Ginsburg, Monocacy Elementary School,*
Frederick, Maryland

As a new media specialist, I was overwhelmed with the feeling that there were so many books in the collections that I would never be able to help anyone find information. It must be truly overwhelming to the new media specialist today to develop a collection. Despite those who prophesy the demise of the printed page, a core collection of carefully selected, reliable materials accessible through a thought-fully arranged collection will still be the nucleus of a sound research process.

—*Floyd Pentlin, Lee's Summit North High School,*
Lee's Summit, Missouri

Importance of cataloging

The library media specialist cannot be expected to have total recall of the maze of information and ideas found in each individual library media center. But if the school catalog is not accurate and current, then the library media specialist must fill the role of guide to the collection.

Bibliographic records are essentially patterned sets of clues leading to items. A book's title is one clue to its content, subject headings provide others, notes add more detail and depth. Students need good bibliographic records if they are to become intelligent users of information.

Such records also help in collection development. Good catalogs:

- prevent duplication, including works issued under more than one title
- identify gaps by subject, author, language, date, and award
- identify strengths
- identify similar materials by author, title, subject, and date
- identify age of collection
- identify presence of added physical formats of works.

—Joanna Fountain, Texas Library Connection,
Texas Education Agency, Austin, Texas

Selection criteria

In any school library media center, the selection criteria are quite naturally tailored to the curriculum that, in our school, teachers develop over the summer. Some themes repeat, but usually with a new spin. For example, in our study of the Southwest several years ago, we included a unit on the Hopi and Navaho. This year, we're focusing on "The Shape of Time" in terms of geology and archaeology. How do archaeologists date artifacts or use tree rings to learn about the climate and culture of the past? After we return with our students from Mesa Verde, we'll examine the concept of time—in music, historical fiction, or fantasy; how different cultures deal with time; the evolution of the measurement of time; and so forth.

As a school for the gifted, we assiduously collect fiction about gifted children. In addition, we tend to select more adult material and material for older students than one might for a heterogeneous K–8 population. Nonetheless, we're careful not to confuse intellectual prowess with social and emotional maturity—particularly in the area of fiction.

Lastly, we see the parents as our partners and choose material to help them understand the nature of gifted students. We have a program called Literary Club in which two trained parents (or a parent and teacher) meet weekly to discuss a book with a small group of students. Our fiction collection includes many titles that we believe to be provocative and discussable, so that we can suggest them to leaders who are selecting books for their group.

—Debbie Abilock, The Nueva School,
Hillsborough, California

I have a selection policy and I tend to focus my purchase on areas of curricular need, then areas of student interest. It's a happy event when those two areas converge! I have to consider so many variations in ability and learning styles—we serve grades 8 through 12, with a great number of students identified as gifted and others with serious learning issues—and I buy audio and video, as well as print.

I also consider purchases with teachers' instructional styles in mind. For instance, some prefer primary sources, some like simulations, while others use fiction around historical or scientific themes.

I consider my web page as a "collection annex" and I extend my collection development in my selection of links from the free web, the invisible web, and the subscriptions services I select.

I tend to look at *VOYA*, *School Library Journal*, *Book Report*, and *Booklist* for reviews. I'm attracted to the new items in vendors' catalogs, and I get excited when I can actually touch these at conference exhibits. I have accounts at local and Internet bookstores to meet unexpected and urgent student needs.

—*Joyce Valenza, Springfield Township High School,*
Philadelphia, Pennsylvania

My selection criteria are readability and curriculum. It also has to have a good visual impact or the students won't bother to pick it up.

—*Jeanne Mayo, Banneker Middle School,*
Burtonsville, Maryland

Selection sources

My favorite tools for selection are *Booklist* and *VOYA*. I also use recommended book lists from other libraries or organizations. Another important source is the student. We encourage our students to submit suggestions of titles they want to read or titles they recommend to their peers. Although we can't always honor their requests, we try to purchase as much as we can from their recommendations.

—*Linda Stevens, Birdville High School,*
Fort Worth, Texas

Weeding

Weeding is an essential component of a good collection development plan. It keeps media collections relevant, accurate, and useful. It also facilitates more effective use of space in the library media center. So despite decreasing budgets and my natural inclination to save everything, I use these guidelines to determine what media materials should be weeded. Materials are considered for withdrawal if they are:

- in poor physical condition
- seldom circulated
- mediocre or poor in quality
- duplicates of titles that are no longer in demand

15

- titles that have been superseded by new or revised editions
- materials with outdated or unattractive covers, formats, or illustrations
- titles that are inaccessible because the book lacks an index or table of contents
- outdated in content, use, or accuracy

Copyright date is important in subjects such as computers, science, and technology. However, in most areas the decision to weed is not based solely on copyright date.

—Lorraine Brunn, Olney Elementary School,
Olney, Maryland

SOURCE: Adapted from Ramona Kerby, "What Practicing School Library Media Specialists Say about Collection Development," *School Library Media Activities Monthly* 18, no. 9 (May 2002): 26–27. Used with permission.

Periodical publishers

This list includes information about the publishers who so generously allowed us to use articles that would help readers better understand how school libraries function, their management, and their role in the education of students. We thank them for sharing their authors and the content of their publications with us.

American Libraries
American Library Association
50 E. Huron Street
Chicago, IL 60611
Telephone: (800) 545-2433, ext. 4216
Fax: (312) 440-0901
E-mail: americanlibraries@ala.org
http://www.ala.org/alonline/
Editor: Leonard Kniffel

Colorado Libraries
Colorado Association of Libraries
c/o Arapahoe Library District
12855 E. Jamison Cir.
Englewood, CO 80112
Telephone: (303) 463-6400
Fax: (303) 798-2485
E-mail: edumas@ci.aurora.co.us, jlee@regis.edu
http://cal-webs.org/publications.html
Editors: Eileen Dumas, Janet Lee

Computers in Libraries
A division of Information Today, Inc.
143 Old Marlton Pike
Medford, NJ 08055-8750
Telephone: (609) 654-6266
Fax: (609) 654-4309
E-mail: custserv@infotoday.com
http://www.infotoday.com/cilmag/default.shtml
Editor: Kathleen L. Dempsey

Impact
Journal of the Career Development Group
7 Ridgmount Street
London WC1E 7AE
England
Telephone: +44 (020) 7255 0500
E-mail: editor@careerdevelopmentgroup.org.uk
http://www.careerdevelopmentgroup.org.uk/impact/index.asp

Knowledge Quest (formerly *School Library Media Quarterly*)
American Association of School Librarians (AASL)
A division of the American Library Association
50 E. Huron Street
Chicago, IL 60611
Telephone: (312) 944-6780, ext. 4386
Fax: (312) 664-7459
Editor: Debbie Abilock
http://www.ala.org/aasl/kqweb/
(Detailed guidelines for authors available at website.)

Library Journal
A division of Reed Business Information
360 Park Avenue South
New York, NY 10010
Telephone: (646) 746-6819
Fax: (646) 746-6734
http://www.libraryjournal.com/
Editor-in-Chief: John N. Berry III

Library Media Connection (formerly *The Book Report*)
Linworth Publishing Co.
480 E. Wilson Bridge Road, Ste. L
Worthington, OH 43085
Telephone: (614) 436-7107
Fax: (614) 436-9490
http://www.linworth.com/lmc.html
Editor: Carol Simpson

North Carolina Libraries
North Carolina Library Association
4646 Mail Service Center
Raleigh, NC 27699-4646
http://www.nclaonline.org/NCL/index.html
Editor: Plummer Alston "Al" Jones, Jr.

Ohio Media Spectrum
Ohio Educational Library Media Association
17 South High Street, Ste. 200
Columbus, OH 43215
Telephone: (614) 221-1900
Fax: (614) 221-1989
E-mail: oelma@mecdc.org
http://www.oelma.org/

School Librarian
School Library Association, England
Unit 2
Lotmead Business Village
Lotmead Farm
Wanborough
Swindon SN4 0UY
England
Telephone: +44 (0) 1793 791787
Fax: +44 (0) 1793 791786
E-mail: info@SLA.org.uk
http://www.sla.org.uk/

School Librarian's Workshop
Library Learning Resources, Inc.
Box 87
Berkeley Heights, NJ 07922
Telephone: (201) 635-1833
Fax: (201) 635-2614
E-mail: editors@school-librarians-workshop.com
http://www.school-librarians-workshop.com/
Editors: Ruth Toor, Hilda K. Weisburg

School Libraries in Canada:
The Journal of the Canadian School Library Association
Canadian Library Association
328 Frank Street
Ottawa, ON
Canada K2P 0X8
Telephone: (613) 232-9625
Fax: (613) 563-9895
E-mail: jbranch@ualberta.ca
http://www.schoollibraries.ca
Editor: Jennifer L. Branch

School Libraries Worldwide
Department of Elementary Education
University of Alberta
551 Education South
Edmonton, AB
Canada T6G 2G5
E-mail: doberg@ualberta.ca
http://www.iasl-slo.org/slw.html
Editor: Dianne Oberg

School Library Journal
A division of Reed Business Information
360 Park Avenue South
New York, NY 10010
Telephone: (646) 746-6759
Fax: (646) 746-6689
E-mail: slj@reedbusiness.com
http://www.schoollibraryjournal.com/
Editor: Evan St. Lifer

School Library Media Activities Monthly
LMS Associates
17 E. Henrietta Street
Baltimore, MD 21230
Telephone: (410) 685-8621
E-mail: Paulam@crinkles.com
http://www.crinkles.com/schoolmedia.html
Editor: Paula Montgomery

School Library Media Research
American Association of School Librarians
A division of the American Library Association
50 E. Huron Street
Chicago, IL 60611
Telephone: (800) 545-2433
E-mail: callison@indiana.edu
http://www.ala.org/aasl/SLMR/
Editor: Daniel Callison

Teacher Librarian (formerly *Emergency Librarian*)
P.O. Box 34069, Department 343
Seattle, WA 98124-1069
or
101-1001 West Broadway, Ste. 343
Vancouver, BC
Canada V6H 4E4
Telephone: (604) 925-0266
Fax: (604) 925-0566
E-mail: editor@teacherlibrarian.com
http://www.teacherlibrarian.com/
Editor: Ken Haycock

Index

BLANCHE WOOLLS is the director of the School of Library and Information Science at San Jose State University. She was an elementary school librarian and a district-level coordinator of school libraries before managing the school library credential program at the University of Pittsburgh. Woolls is the author of several books and articles in publications such as *School Library Journal* and *Knowledge Quest*.

DAVID V. LOERTSCHER is a professor at San Jose State University's School of Library and Information Science where he manages the school library media teacher credential program. He has taught at Purdue University, Oklahoma University, and the University of Arkansas where he was the program director. Loertscher has spoken at library and education conferences around the world, including the International Association of School Librarianship, IFLA, and ALISE.

Both authors are past-presidents of AASL and both have been honored with its Distinguished Service Award.